T0326775

TURKEY UNDER ERDOĞAN

TURKEY UNDER ERDOĞAN

How a Country Turned from Democracy and the West

Dimitar Bechev

YALE UNIVERSITY PRESS
NEW HAVEN AND LONDON

For information about this and other Yale University Press publications, please contact:
U.S. Office: sales.press@yale.edu   yalebooks.com
Europe Office: sales@yaleup.co.uk   yalebooks.co.uk

Set in Adobe Garamond Pro by IDSUK (DataConnection) Ltd
Printed in Great Britain by TJ Books, Padstow, Cornwall

Library of Congress Control Number: 2021950213

ISBN 978-0-300-24788-6

A catalogue record for this book is available from the British Library.

10 9 8 7 6 5 4 3 2 1

CONTENTS

MAPS

PREFACE

This book came about over the course of an intense year and a half, part of it spent in lockdown. I started my work in bucolic North Carolina and completed it in Oxford. This was a comeback of sorts, as it was there, at St Antony's College, that I had first immersed myself in all things Turkish years ago. The volume is the product of more than a decade of researching, writing and thinking about Turkey. This has not been a happy time, in honesty, not least for the country itself which went through countless ordeals, seeing erstwhile hopes for a peaceful and democratic future ruined. Intellectually, however, Turkish politics and society have never ceased to fascinate me. As a scholar and analyst, I have been fortunate to occupy a special niche. Usually, books of this kind are written from one of two vantage points: that of authors native to Turkey who know intimately their country, vast and diverse though it is, and are deeply invested in it, and that of Westerners many of whom, I hasten to add, have a level of knowledge as well as linguistic and cultural expertise I could only aspire to. My positionality, to use a term dear to anthropologists, is in between those two. Originally coming from a nearby country which was once at the heart of the Ottoman state, has a vast Turkish and Muslim population and remains to this day in some ways fixated on its neighbor gives me some insights while at the same time allows for a sufficient degree of critical distance. Or so the theory goes.

The book would have not been possible without the generous help I received from friends and colleagues. There is a long list of people to whom I owe a debt of gratitude. Special thanks go to Ayşe Kadıoğlu, Berk Esen, Suat Kınıklıoğlu, Lisel Hintz, Marc Pierini, Erdi Öztürk, Venelin Ganev, Emre Çalışkan, Kerem Öktem and Soli Özel who all read and commented on parts of the draft. I am also indebted to the two anonymous reviewers at Yale University Press for their feedback and suggestions. Over the years, I have greatly benefited from conversations and exchanges with Galip Dalay, Mehmet Karlı, Karabekir Akkoyunlu, Kemal Kirişci, Gönül Tol, Ömer Taşpınar, Elaine Papoulias, Ioannis Grigoriadis, Aaron Stein, Nigar Göksel, Has Avrat, Michael Werz, Nate Schenkkan, Sinan Ciddi, Lenore Martin, Soner Çağaptay, Henri Barkey, Amberin Zaman, Sinan Ülgen, Nathalie Tocci, Barış Kesgin, James Ker Lindsay, Robert Jenkins, William Armstrong, Sinikukka Saari and Stanislav Secrieru. I could easily fill several more pages with names. Needless to say, all omissions or errors of fact and interpretation are entirely my fault.

Institutional backing made a difference, too. A huge "thank you" to Taiba Batool, who originally encouraged me to embark on such an ambitious journey (my initial plan was rather more modest) as well as to Julian Loose, who saw the project through as commissioning editor at Yale University Press. I should also acknowledge the kind support of the Institute for Human Sciences (IWM) in Vienna, which awarded me a fellowship in 2020/21 allowing me to finish the draft in time. Thanks to the Frontier Europe Program at the Middle East Institute in Washington, DC, which likewise supported my work on Turkish foreign policy, and to the Center for Slavic, Eurasian and East European Studies at the University of North Carolina at Chapel Hill where I was based between 2016 and 2020.

Last but not least, I owe a great debt to my family. My wife Galina and our children, Emanuil, Anthony and Sophia, have been a source of endless inspiration throughout this journey.

Oxford/Vienna
June 2021

ABBREVIATIONS

AKP	Justice and Development Party (Adalet ve Kalkınma Partisi)
ANAP	Motherland Party (Anavatan Partisi)
BDP	Peace and Democracy Party (Barış ve Demokrasi Partisi)
BOTAŞ	Turkish energy company
CHP	Republican People's Party (Cumhuriyet Halk Partisi)
DP	Democratic Party
DSP	Democratic Left Party
DTP	Democratic Society Party (Demokratik Toplum Partisi)
DYP	True Path Party (Doğru Yol Partisi)
EC	European Community
ECtHR	European Court of Human Rights
EEC	European Economic Community
EEZ	exclusive economic zone
EU	European Union
ESI	European Stability Initiative
FDI	foreign direct investment
FETÖ	Fethullahist Terrorist Organization
FSA	Free Syrian Army
GNA	Government of National Accord
HADEP	People's Democracy Party
HDP	Peoples' Democratic Party (Halkların Demokratik Partisi)
IMF	International Monetary Fund
ISIS	Islamic State in Iraq and the Levant
JİTEM	Gendarmerie Intelligence and Counter-Terrorism Organization (Jandarma İstihbarat ve Terörle Mücadele)
KCK	Kurdish Communities Union (Koma Civakên Kurdistan)

ABBREVIATIONS

KRG	Kurdistan Regional Government
LNG	liquefied natural gas
MGK	National Security Council (Millî Güvenlik Kurulu)
MHP	Nationalist Action Party (Milliyetçi Hareket Partisi)
MİT	National Intelligence Organization (Millî İstihbarat Teşkilatı)
OHAL	Governorship of Region in State of Emergency (Olağanüstü Hâl Bölge Valiliği)
PKK	Kurdistan Workers' Party
PYD	Democratic Union Party (Partiya Yekîtiya Demokrat)
SDF	Syrian Democratic Forces
SHP	Social Democratic Populist Party (Sosyaldemokrat Halkçı Parti)
TİKA	Turkish Cooperation and Coordination Agency (Türk İşbirliği ve Koordinasyon İdaresi Başkanlığı)
TPAO	Turkish Petroleum Corporation (Türkiye Petrolleri Anonim Ortaklığı)
TRT	Turkish public broadcaster
TÜSİAD	Turkish Industry and Business Association (Türk Sanayicileri ve İş İnsanları Derneği)
UAE	United Arab Emirates
UN	United Nations
YPG	People's Protection Units (Yekîneyên Parastina Gel)

TIMELINE

1919–22	Turkish War of Independence.
1923	The Republic of Turkey is founded.
1938	Mustafa Kemal Ataturk, the republic's founder, dies in Istanbul.
1946	Turkey transitions to multi-party politics.
1950	The Democratic Party (DP) comes to power after defeating at the polls the Republican People's Party (CHP) established by Ataturk.
1952	Turkey joins the North Atlantic Treaty Organization (NATO).
1960	Prime Minister Adnan Menderes (DP) deposed by a military coup and later sentenced to death.
1963	Association agreement with the European Economic Community (EEC) signed in Ankara.
1971	A military coup removes a cabinet led by Süleyman Demirel (Justice Party) from power.
1974	Turkey intervenes in Cyprus and takes control of the island's north.
1980	A third military coup ousts the government, headed again by Demirel. Chief of the General Staff Kenan Evren runs Turkey for the next three years as the head of the National Security Council (MGK).
1983	Tugut Özal becomes president after the Motherland Party (ANAP) wins the elections following the passage of a new constitution.

1984	Attacks by the Kurdistan Workers' Party (PKK) mark the beginning of an insurgency in southeast Turkey.
1987	Turkey applies for EEC membership.
1989	The Grand National Assembly elects Özal president of the republic.
1991	The first Gulf War.
1993	Turgut Özal dies of a heart attack.
1994	Recep Tayyip Erdoğan elected mayor of the municipality of greater Istanbul after the Islamist Welfare Party (Refah Partisi) triumphs in the local elections.
Jan. 1996	The Turkey–EEC Customs Union comes into force.
Jan. 1996	Tensions between Greece and Turkey in the Aegean Sea nearly lead to a military showdown.
June 1996	Refah's leader Necmettin Erbakan becomes the prime minister.
Feb. 1997	A memorandum issued by the Turkish military leads to Erbakan's resignation in June ("the post-modern coup").
1998	Syria expels PKK leader Abdullah Öcalan after Turkey threatens a military invasion.
1999	In Helsinki, the European Union (EU) leaders recognize Turkey as an accession candidate.
Feb. 1999	Öcalan is captured by Turkish commandos in Kenya.
2001	Turkey hit by a major banking and financial crisis.
Aug. 2001	Former members of Erbakan's Islamist movement establish the Justice and Development Party (AKP).
Nov. 2002	AKP wins the elections and forms a cabinet headed by Abdullah Gül.
March 2003	Turkish parliament defeats a government motion to join the US-led coalition in the second Gulf War. Erdoğan replaces Gül as prime minister.
2004	Turkish Cypriots endorse a United Nations (UN) plan for the island's reunification at a referendum, yet a majority of Greek Cypriots reject it. The Republic of Cyprus joins the EU, leaving the north in limbo.

2005	EU decides to open membership talks with Turkey.
2006	Several of the negotiation chapters are "frozen" because of Turkey's unwillingness to allow Greek Cypriot ships and aircraft into its ports and airports.
2007	AKP re-elected amidst a major domestic political crisis. The new parliament votes Abdullah Gül president.
Oct. 2007	A majority approves changes in the constitution, introducing direct election of the republic's president.
2008	The Ergenekon investigation is launched. The Constitutional Court rules that the AKP violated the principles of secularism but stops short of closing down the party.
2009	Ahmet Davutoğlu is appointed foreign minister. The "zero problems with neighbors" policy comes into the spotlight.
Sept. 2010	At a referendum, a majority of Turkish citizens approve constitutional changes on a range of issues, notably the governance of the judiciary.
Dec. 2010	Protests in Tunisia spark the beginning of the Arab Spring.
June 2011	AKP gains a historic third term in power in the elections but falls short of constitutional majority.
Sept. 2011	Turkey cuts relations with the Assad government in Syria.
March 2013	The Kurdish Peace Initiative ("Solution Process") is unveiled in Diyarbakır.
May–June 2013	Gezi Park protests.
Dec. 2013	A corruption scandal marks the final rift between AKP and the Gülen movement.
Aug. 2014	Erdoğan elected president.
Dec. 2014	In Ankara, Vladimir Putin announces plans for a gas pipeline across the Black Sea ("TurkStream").
June 2015	AKP loses its parliamentary majority at a general election. Violence returns to southeast Turkey, spelling the end of the Kurdish Peace Initiative.
1 Nov. 2015	Repeat elections restore AKP's parliamentary majority.
25 Nov. 2015	Turkish jet shoots down a Russian military plane at the border with Syria.

March 2016	Turkey and the EU conclude high-profile agreement on refugees.
July 2016	Rogue military units stage an abortive coup attempt against President Erdoğan. Emergency rule is introduced.
Aug. 2016	The Turkish military and the Free Syrian Army enter northwest Syria.
April 2017	Changes in the constitution introducing a switch from a parliamentary to a presidential regime are narrowly approved in a referendum.
June 2018	Erdoğan re-elected as an executive president under the new constitutional rules. The AKP comes in short of a majority in the parliamentary elections and forms a governing coalition with the Nationalist Action Party (MHP).
March 2019	AKP loses the mayorships of Istanbul and Ankara in local elections. A re-run in Istanbul confirms the united opposition's win.
Jan. 2020	Turkey openly intervenes in the civil war in Libya.
Feb.–March 2020	Turkish troops in northwest Syria stop a major offensive by the Assad regime.
Sept.–Nov. 2020	Turkey's military intervention helps Azerbaijan recover Armenian-held territory around Nagorno-Karabakh.
Dec. 2020	US imposes sanctions on Turkey over the acquisition of Russian-made missiles.
Dec. 2020	EU sanctions Turkish officials for illegal drilling for oil and gas in the Eastern Mediterranean.
June 2021	Erdoğan meets US President Joe Biden in Brussels to reset ties.
6 Oct. 2021	Turkey joins the Paris climate agreement.
23 Oct. 2021	Erdoğan orders the expulsion of ten Western ambassadors but later reverses his decision.

INTRODUCTION: THE STRONGMAN'S PLAYBOOK

That day in October 2016 Istanbul felt like the fulcrum of worldwide authoritarianism. An A-list of strongmen lined the front row at the cavernous Congress Center in the downtown district of Harbiye. One after the other, Vladimir Putin, President Ilham Aliyev of Azerbaijan and Venezuela's Nicolas Maduro took the stage to share their thoughts about volatile oil prices, global investment and economic development with the audience at the 23rd World Energy Congress. But that was not the real purpose of their gathering. Rather, the cast of international dignitaries had made their way to Turkey to put on display their unbending support to the host, President Recep Tayyip Erdoğan. Having defeated a coup attempt – "a heinous terrorist act" – three months prior, the Turkish leader spared no word of gratitude. "On this occasion, you support our nation, our country and our democracy. Personally, I would like to thank you on behalf of my nation."[1]

His nation indeed. Like no other statesman since the republic's founder Mustafa Kemal Atatürk, Erdoğan had grabbed vast powers in his hands. By 2016, the governing Justice and Development (Adalet ve Kalkınma Partisi, AKP), the bureaucracy, the courts, the media, the business establishment, the army and the police (the last two having recently gone through a sweeping purge) were all beholden to him alone. The Turkish state itself had morphed into a family fief. Those disagreeing with the direction taken by Erdoğan's proclaimed "New Turkey" faced denunciation as terrorists and fifth columnists – if they were lucky. Indeed, many were in for long jail sentences, had lost their jobs or had been forced to flee abroad, whether they had anything to do with the attempted military takeover or not. Selahattin Demirtaş, contender in the most recent elections on behalf of the pro-Kurdish Peoples' Democratic Party (Halkların Demokratik Partisi, HDP), was about to be detained. Having condemned the coup was no excuse for his lack of deference to the chief (or *reis*, as Erdoğan's aficionados liked to call him).

Then there were Turkey's friends such as Vladimir Putin. The Kremlin's master took credit for standing by Erdoğan in the aftermath of the putsch, putting aside quarrels over Syria and the Su-24 ground-attack aircraft downed by the Turkish air force back in November 2015. Putin knew a thing or two about Western-concocted plots to engineer regime change, the Turkish president's partisans murmured. The United States, a presumed ally, meanwhile stood accused of having masterminded the conspiracy to overthrow or even physically eliminate Erdoğan, backstabbing Turkey. Vladimir Putin, naturally, had no objections to this narrative. So long as Ankara ordered top-of-the-range Russian missiles, to the dismay of the rest of NATO, and cooperated with Moscow in Syria, "dear friend" Putin was content. Coming to Istanbul, he oversaw the signature of a multi-billion deal for TurkStream, a gas pipeline under the Black Sea, too. But Erdoğan was happily playing the Russia card himself. The Kremlin green-lighted a Turkish military operation in Syria clipping the wings of US-backed Kurdish militants. Why stick with the West then? The Russians were paying heed to Turkish national interests and delivering on commitments. Who was better: Putin or the unreliable Obama,[2] not to mention the duplicitous Europeans keeping Turkey at arm's length?

What change a decade makes! As I was marveling at Erdoğan and Putin's show from the audience in Istanbul, I could not help but go back to the first time I had a chance to see the Turkish leader speak live. On 28 May 2004, the then Turkish prime minister delivered a speech titled "Why the European Union Needs Turkey" at St John's College, Oxford. Flanked by Kalypso Nicolaidis, a French-Greek professor of European politics, and the late Geoffrey Lewis, the doyen of Turkish studies at Oxford, the swaggering Erdoğan pledged "to make European values Ankara's values." Europe, he argued, was a normative union where Turkey deserved a place, not "a narrowly defined geography." Erdoğan furthermore went over a list of issues bedeviling relations between Brussels and Ankara, from the rights of the Kurdish community to the division of Cyprus.[3] His was a hopeful message: Turkey was doing its best to carry out democratic reforms, confront the ghosts of the country's troubled past, improve human rights and deliver economic growth.

The recipe seemed to work fine. In little more than a year, on 3 October 2005, the European Union (EU) decided to start membership negotiations with

Turkey, a belated reward for the achievements scored by the AKP as well as, it shouldn't be forgotten, its predecessors in office. Nobody believed accession would be an easy ride, given the tough obstacles ahead. Membership in the EU could not be taken for granted either. But it was Turkey's own transformation which counted, when all was said and done. To borrow from Constantine Cavafy's "Ithaka," it was all about "the marvelous journey," not the destination.[4]

WHAT WENT WRONG?

This book grapples with the question of what changed so drastically and so quickly. Why did Turkey succumb to authoritarianism, take to nationalism and turn away from the West?

For many people, there is of course one simple answer: Recep Tayyip Erdoğan. A shrewd operator, he took advantage of electoral democracy to seize ever more authority and eventually install a one-man regime. The mission was completed with the change of the Turkish constitution in 2017 replacing parliamentary with presidential rule. Erdoğan's commitment to democracy and human rights, once lauded in the West, proved skin-deep. This, in turn, points at another, related explanation: Turkey's Western allies were complicit. Put bluntly, Erdoğan duped the EU and the US. A tactical alliance with Brussels legitimated his power grab. Europe's democratic conditionality allowed a demagogue to defeat opponents, notably the military and the diehard secularists in the bureaucracy and the judiciary. Washington accepted at face value the whole spiel about Muslim democracy, blinded by the missionary zeal driving its policy in the Middle East. Once the partnership outlived its usefulness, not least because the EU gave Turkey the cold shoulder, Erdoğan cut the West loose. His detractors, crying foul at the sight of an Islamist lionized in Western capitals, had a point all along.

What the above account overlooks is the long-term structural and institutional forces shaping Turkey's domestic politics and, by extension, foreign policy. As cunning and ruthless an operator as Erdoğan is – and he does have a stellar record in that department – what were the other reasons he was able to climb the greasy pole and retain power for nearly two decades? The AKP's rise would have been unthinkable without taking into account the cleavages rooted in

Turkey's top-down modernization in the twentieth century driven by secularist state elites. Starting from the 1970s, political Islam gained ground among pious Anatolian masses as they gained prominence in public life. The rise of a conservative entrepreneurial class coupled with the rapid pace of urbanization in the 1980s and 1990s not only blurred the social and geographic distinction between the center and periphery but also fomented strife.[5] Culture became an arena of ideological struggle waged over the issue of the place of faith in the public sphere. Turkey's brand of Islamist populism pitted the privileged minority usurping the state vs "the people," the ordinary folk – Turks, Kurds or others – discriminated against because of their adherence to religious values and lifestyles.[6] It was the people, not Erdoğan, who vanquished the so-called tutelage system (*vesayet*) whereby generals and unelected mandarins had the final word over the affairs of the state. It was the people who were building a democracy worthy of its name. It was the Ahmets and the Mehmets who stood up to tanks on that fateful night in July 2016 and paid with their lives. This is what the Erdoğan brand is all about.

Populism, to be sure, is hardly Erdoğan's invention. It had long been the oxygen of Turkish party politics, with the ilk of Süleyman Demirel and Bülent Ecevit, on the right and on the left respectively, excelling in its dark arts. Erdoğan perfected the trade, turning his emotive connection to the masses and his personal story – a poor boy from an underprivileged area of Istanbul rising to the top[7] – into a formidable political instrument. His rule, he would argue, has been the triumph of the "national will" as expressed through the ballot box. Then common men (women, needless to say, figure in supportive roles) rose against the oppressive and self-serving elites and reclaimed what was theirs by right. "It is not that we had Oxford in Şanlıurfa," he chuckled while quoting the *Arabesk*[8] star İbrahim "İbo" Tatlıses at a youth gathering in 2018, "but I preferred not to study there!"[9] On that occasion, Erdoğan was taking credit for a rise in the number of universities, from 75 to 206, on his watch, expanding access to higher education and upward mobility to the previously disenfranchised. This was the New Turkey, with its world-class hospitals, highways, glitzy shopping malls, gargantuan airports and towering housing estates, all for the people. In the first decade under the AKP alone, GDP per capita had more than tripled, from $3,600 to $12,600 (plunging back to $8,000 by 2020, however).[10] At the same time, Erdoğan's populism differs from that of his predecessors. No other Turkish leader has been willing and able to take on the establishment, to change the country to such an extent and remake it in his image. He is in a league of his own.

So far so good. The problem with Erdoğan's version, however, is that "the national will" he claims to represent does not match electoral reality. Not until the first direct presidential elections in 2014 was the AKP able to clear the 50 per cent threshold. Pious voters defected in large enough numbers to deliver opposition victories in Istanbul and Ankara, along with the bulk of the remaining big urban centers in the 2019 municipal elections too. The previous year, the AKP lost its parliamentary majority and now governs in tandem with the Nationalist Action Party (Milliyetçi Hareket Partisi, MHP). In addition, Erdoğan has been the beneficiary of rules and institutions, amplifying his performance at the polls and consequently his power. Formal rules matter, even in an arena as informality-ridden as Turkey's. Back in 2002, the exceptionally high electoral threshold of 10 per cent kept the AKP's rivals on the right out of parliament, and propelled the party to power with roughly a third of the vote. As a result, it monopolized the right-wing and conservative space which had traditionally been where the bulk of the electorate gravitated. Subsequently, the AKP took advantage of constitutional provisions allowing for amending the basic law through referendums. Plebiscites tilted the political system towards majoritarianism, polarizing society and, in effect, delivering to Erdoğan a winner-takes-all bonus. Now, of course, the playing field is skewed in the president's favor because critical institutions, such as the Supreme Electoral Council, are doing his bidding.

Turkey's transformation from an electoral democracy to a competitive authoritarian regime has a lot to do with the high costs of the AKP losing power. Karabekir Akkoyunlu and Kerem Öktem have written about the condition of "existential insecurity."[11] Through the 2000s, the party faced a robust challenge by secularists, the courts and the military, responsible for the closure of its predecessors. It survived a bona fide coup attempt in 2016, likely orchestrated by its former allies from the Gülen movement. Its long tenure has been marred by a sequence of corruption scandals which have set off damaging court cases in the West. From Erdoğan's position, there is arguably no alternative to holding on to power as long as possible through a variety of means, including constitutional engineering and outright repression. This is a predicament shared by all authoritarian and semi-authoritarian systems. Think about the counterfactual: in a country where the rule of law is upheld by independent institutions, moving from government to opposition and back is a less risky affair.

One should not lose sight of the enduring appeal of nationalism either. It is the common thread connecting Erdoğan's New Turkey and the Turkey of old with all its authoritarian baggage.[12] The collapse of the peace talks between the state and the Kurdistan Workers' Party (PKK) in 2015, the renewed conflict in the Kurdish-populated southeast, the AKP's alignment not only with the far-right MHP from 2016 onwards but also with Kemalist factions hostile to the West and to minority rights, and the clash with Greece in the Eastern Mediterranean are all chapters in this story. The rollback of the public use of the Kurdish language, for example, the removal of bilingual signs in the city of Diyarbakır in 2018 and the removal of elected officials carry a distinctive back-to-the-future flavor, too. The image of Turkey as a beleaguered fortress threatened by enemies abroad and their internal abettors has become central to Erdoğan's messaging.

Erdoğan's evolution, from an EU-friendly "Muslim democrat" to a strongman, speaks to the weight of illiberal legacies. In essence, he and his partisans appropriated the cult of the strong, sovereign and indivisible state, adding to it a (Sunni) Islamic tinge.[13] Individual rights and freedoms are secondary to raison d'état, as interpreted by the president and his entourage. Thanks to the AKP's fusion with the state, Erdoğan has become, to quote Soner Çağaptay, "the anti-Atatürk Atatürk."[14] Though even the parallel between the two remains an anathema to secularists and the Republican People's Party (Cumhuriyet Halk Partisi, CHP), it is reflected strongly in official memory politics. Indeed, breaking with tradition, New Turkey's historical narrative shifted the focus from Mustafa Kemal's Westernizing reforms to his role as savior of the state in the face of mortal danger during the War of Independence.[15] Witness, too, the campaign around the centennial of the republic to be marked in 2023, set to be a celebration of Erdoğan's sultan-like ascendancy. Paradoxically, Ataturk has found himself in the AKP's pantheon cheek by jowl with Sultan Abdülhamid II idolized by conservatives for his pan-Islamist worldview but very much the "Other" from the Kemalist perspective.[16] Both statesmen thus feature as Erdoğan's forerunners, along with leaders in the center-right tradition such as Adnan Menderes or Turgut Özal.

At the end of the day, Turkey's illiberal trajectory could be best understood by Turkey's own illiberal features: its polarized society, undemocratic institutional arrangements and exclusionary nationalism. The corollary is that the country's fate is in its own hands. It is to Turkey's voters that Erdoğan owes his career. They will ultimately decide how the story ends too, and whether Erdoğanism as a system of governance outlives its founding father. Do Western leaders share some of the blame about how Turkey has turned out? Probably they do. The EU was essential for triggering democratic reforms in the late 1990s, and early 2000s, but it then left Turkey high and dry, particularly when French President Nicolas Sarkozy made it clear that membership was not on the cards in 2007. With internal checks and balances gradually dismantled, the EU could only restrain Erdoğan and help depolarize domestic politics if membership were actually a credible prospect. Yet here a bit of counterfactual analysis might again come in handy. What would a Turkey inside the EU have looked like? Would it have remained committed to liberal democracy or, on the contrary, backslid like Viktor Orbán's Hungary? We will never know the answer, but that does not invalidate the question.

The regime's deep sociological and historical roots do not imply in the least that Turkey is doomed to authoritarian rule. The country has a history of competitive politics stretching back more than seven decades,[17] advanced level of socio-economic development and links to the West that, other things being equal, favor a return to electoral democracy in the future. Citizens believe their vote counts and still turn up in high numbers at the polls. There is a real opposition which has proven its ability to cooperate, setting aside ideological and identity differences. That contrasts with other authoritarian polities, say Azerbaijan, Russia or Abdelfatah Al-Sisi's Egypt, where multi-party politics and elections are a mere façade. We cannot be certain whether, when and how Turkey will transition back to democracy but equally there is no reason to rule out such an outcome ex ante.

THE LONG GOODBYE

Turkey's democratic decline has opened a chasm between it and Europe and the US. For a long time, the West provided the normative horizon the country aspired to attain. Whether it was Ataturk's reference to "contemporary civilization" in the 1920s and 1930s, the post-war vision of Turkey as "little America" or the EU's accession criteria, Turkish society measured its achievements and failures against Western benchmarks. Of course, the relationship was ridden with ambivalence. After all, was it not the European powers who conspired with non-Muslim minorities to bring down the once mighty Ottoman Empire? The Kemalists, but also the Tanzimat-era reformers, emulated the West partly in order not to fall prey to it. During the Cold War, too, anti-Americanism was rife not only among the Turkish left but also within the Millî Görüş (National Vision) movement, the Islamist strand AKP sprang from. The political and military establishment resented US policy in Cyprus and Western Europeans' reluctance to welcome Turks into their exclusive club. These days, it is common for some analysts on both sides of the Atlantic to wax nostalgic about the halcyon days when Ankara was fully and unreservedly on the Western team. Such a golden era never truly existed, except for the 1950s. Still, all things considered, the love–hate relationship would lean on the side of attraction, with membership in NATO and the bid to join the European Economic Community (EEC) and subsequently the EU as cornerstones of Turkish foreign policy.

This is obviously not the case nowadays. In the words of Galip Dalay, (the current) decision makers in Ankara have given up on "the idea of the indispensability and uniqueness of the West." The Atlantic Alliance and belonging to Europe, Dalay observes, are no longer central to Turkey's geopolitical identity through which it "filters relations with non-Western powers" nor are they the points of reference in domestic affairs.[18] The alliance with America, eroding since the Cold War ended, hangs by a thread. An overwhelming percentage in Turkey looks at the US as the foremost threat to national security. Turkish–EU relations are in bad shape too, even if 60 per cent continue to support membership.[19] Erdoğan pledges that his country's future is in Europe, but both sides know this is a charade. Accession talks have ground to a halt but neither Ankara nor Brussels (or rather, a majority of member states) have an interest in walking out first. In consequence, Turkey turns to the EU and US selectively when there are gains to be made. Witness the Syrian refugee deal struck with Brussels in March 2016[20] or Erdoğan's being able to talk Donald Trump into letting Turkish troops enter northeast Syria in October 2019.

To be fair, the West itself is not blameless. First, many of its leaders likewise approach Turkey with a transactionalist mindset and are happy to wheel and deal with Erdoğan. Second and more fundamentally, however, the West's own ills manifest in the rise of illiberal populism have dented its claim to a moral higher ground. "Instead of us becoming little America, you became a big Turkey," quips political scientist Ersin Kalaycıoğlu.[21] Joking aside, the West is much less coherent and, as a result, influential compared to the heyday of its power in the 1990s and 2000s. It is not accidental that Donald Trump's lone-wolf idea of foreign policy, not to mention his cavalier attitude to constitutional norms and penchant for mixing personal interest and the affairs of the state, struck a chord with Erdoğan and his courtiers. The "liberal international order," which conditioned the AKP's early reforms, seems like something from a bygone era.[22] Turkey feels at home in the brave new world of today.

Rather than a Western periphery, Erdoğan's Turkey imagines itself as the center of its own universe spanning the Middle East, the Balkans and the Southern Caucasus, all the way to sub-Saharan Africa. The shift has also reversed what Malik Mufti calls the "Republican Paradigm." Rooted in the trauma of the Ottoman collapse, it was underpinned by "[a] strong bias in favor of the geopolitical status quo; and a powerful aversion to foreign entanglements" as well as a "conviction that the external world is essentially hostile and threatening; an anxiety about the ability of external enemies to infiltrate the body politic by exploiting internal divisions."[23] Erdoğan's rise and the demise of the Kemalist elites made Turkey outward-looking and self-confident. From a liability, imperial legacy turned into a geopolitical asset. "The New Turkey" of today claims leadership over global Islam and professes a moral obligation to Muslims – the *ummah* – wherever they may be.[24]

Some analysts have labeled this new role conception "Neo-Ottomanism," courtesy of the obsession with the distant past.[25] Reality is, of course, messier. Russia and Iran, two of the empire's fiercest rivals, have been at the forefront of the outreach to neighbors. Ottoman nostalgia cohabits with *Realpolitik* and the pursuit of economic interest. In addition, Erdoğan is not the first to espouse "the Imperial Paradigm," which Mufti defines as the belief in the benefits of trying to reshape the external environment.[26] Indeed, many of Ankara's policies and initiatives date back to the 1980s and 1990s, when Turgut Özal pushed for engagement with the Middle East, the Balkans and post-Soviet Central Asia. With the end of the Cold War, he revived the notion of Turkey as a model, originating from the early republican period, but also as a conduit of Western influence. The same theme reappeared again under Erdoğan, first in the wake of 9/11, when the Bush administration enthused about it, and then before and during the Arab Spring, with Ahmet Davutoğlu in charge of the foreign ministry in Ankara.

Has Turkey lived up to its hegemonic ambitions? Not quite, this book argues. The brutal and devastating war in Syria turned everything upside down. The conflict precipitated a regional contest where other players, notably Russia and Iran, frustrated Ankara's aspirations to mold the Middle East in its own image. The Syrian tragedy, furthermore, deepened Turkey's rift with the West, exacerbated the democratic backslide at home and ultimately caused the militarization of the country's foreign policy. With Erdoğan facing no internal checks on his authority and always eager to whip up nationalist fervor, the appetite for taking risks has grown. Force projection far beyond national borders, as in Libya and the Horn of Africa, has become the norm. The current Turkish elite believes the only way to prosper in an increasingly competitive world is to be able to act decisively and punch hard, leveraging capabilities developed by one's own defense industries. Soft power, though not entirely irrelevant, is the main focus. The lesson Erdoğan learned from Putin's intervention in Syria – military power works – has sunk in.

Where does Turkey fit in the global order? The future, Erdoğan and his entourage believe, belongs not to America and its Western allies but to "the rest." Turkey feels comfortable in G20, enjoys its newly discovered influence in Africa, poses as a leader of Muslims across the globe and has deepened ties with the likes of Russia and China. On 15 January 2021, Erdoğan took a shot of the Covid-19 vaccine developed by the Chinese firm Sinovac Life Sciences. Back in June 2020, the Turkish central bank had activated a swap agreement with the People's Bank of China, allowing local companies to pay for Chinese imports in *yuan*.[27] It was Beijing coming to Turkey's rescue amidst the pandemic, in the same way Moscow had shown solidarity after the 2016 coup attempt. Remarkably, Erdoğan – who is not known for mincing his words – has not called out China for the repression of Uyghurs and other Turkic Muslim groups in Xinjiang (or East Turkestan). But is Turkey likely to team up with the revisionist powers in mounting a frontal challenge to Western dominance in international affairs? Despite Erdoğan's combative tone, the answer is no. Instead, Turkey will juggle between various centers in search of advantage: a power in the middle or perhaps an entrepreneurial vendor in an increasingly crowded geopolitical bazaar. "Turkey does its own thing," Nigar Göksel and Hugh Pope have argued.[28]

Going forward, Turkey will stay in NATO and keep the connection with Europe. Good news for those in the West who have not given up on Turkey as well as for those in Turkey who persist in their belief in liberal democracy. But there is bad news, too, for both of those constituencies. A post-Erdoğan Turkey might not rush back to the West but instead stick to the script set by the current regime. Whether the script itself works or not is another matter.

OVERVIEW OF THE CHAPTERS

The book opens with two chapters looking at Turkey in the late 1980s and the 1990s to tell the story of the domestic transformations leading up to the AKP's emergence. Chapter 1 explores Turgut Özal's reforms and their impact on society, politics and the economy, as well as the rise of the Kurdish issue and political Islam, in sowing the seeds of polarization. Though Erdoğan and his comrades rose to power in 2002 on the promise to provide a clean slate, the 1990s was far more than a "lost decade," as the period came to be portrayed. EU integration, in particular, injected dynamism into the Turkish economy and set the conditions for democratic reform. Coming to office, the AKP could build on the achievements of their predecessors, marred though they were by corruption scandals, a boom-and-bust economy and, ultimately, a financial meltdown in 2001. Similarly, Chapter 2 zooms in on Turkish foreign policy in the era. Though brinkmanship and conflict with neighbors such as Greece, Syria, Armenia and others grabbed the headlines, politicians such as Özal or Foreign Minister İsmail Cem articulated an alternative vision, stressing economic integration, diplomacy and soft power. Taking advantage of the Cold War's end, Turkey sought to assert itself as a regional leader in Eurasia, as well as a torchbearer of Western influence, but had to reckon with a variety of internal and external constraints.

The discussion then moves to the early AKP era. EU-guided and conditioned reforms, Chapter 3 argues, galvanized a broad coalition including Islamists, liberals, democratic Kemalists, Kurdish nationalists and the business elite which generated momentum for democratic change. This coalition saw Erdoğan through a major political crisis in 2007, helping him prevail over the military and the hardline secularist opposition. The AKP also benefited from a benign international environment: a strong global economy prior to the 2008 breakdown and an EU in expansionist mode. However, the unresolved Cyprus issue and the opposition to Turkey's membership from key member states of the EU such as France undercut Brussels as an agent for change. By the end of the decade, Ankara turned its attention away from Europe and to neighboring countries and regions. Chapter 4 explores the "zero problems with neighbors" phase, when Turkey sought to establish itself as a leader in the Middle East, the Balkans and the Caucasus through trade, aid, cultural exports and diplomacy geared towards conflict resolution. The period saw a reassessment of the country's strategic alliances and growing divergence with the US in the wake of the 2003 Iraq invasion.

It is hard to overstate the impact of the Arab Spring, the subject of Chapter 5, on Turkey. Ankara saw changes south of its border as an opportunity to promote its "model" but ended up importing instability. The war in Syria created major headaches for Turkish policy makers, deepened the rift with the West reluctant to intervene, and ultimately took its toll on democratic institutions in the country. The conflict coincided with the backslide towards authoritarianism in Turkey (Chapter 6) with Erdoğan establishing full control over the AKP, reining in the judiciary and crushing the Gezi Park protests in 2013. The effort to resolve the Kurdish issue became his regime's only saving grace but it, too, fell victim in due course to the Turkish government's half-hearted commitment to reaching a settlement coupled with the fallout from the Syrian conflict. The HDP's reluctance to become complicit in the installation of an executive presidency presaged a return to violence in Turkey's southeast. Chapter 7 chronicles the country's transition to a competitive authoritarian regime, accelerated by the failed coup attempt in July 2016. Erdoğan's "New Turkey" installed a neo-patrimonial system of governance which failed to deliver efficient policy making or economic growth, contrary to the promises made. The voters have acted accordingly, defecting from the ruling party and rewarding the united opposition.

The last three chapters take stock of Turkish foreign policy since the mid-2010s. As Chapter 8 argues, Erdoğan has turned to Russia to pressure the US and attain his ambitions in Syria, but he also relies on the US and the Western alliance as a hedge against a resurgent Russia. With the AKP in charge, Turkey sees itself primarily as a Middle Eastern power but it has set sights on far-flung areas in sub-Saharan Africa too. Chapter 9 explores Ankara's stand-off with rival blocs in the region, led by Saudi Arabia and Iran respectively. In contrast to the 2000s and early 2010s, now military power – rather than the attraction

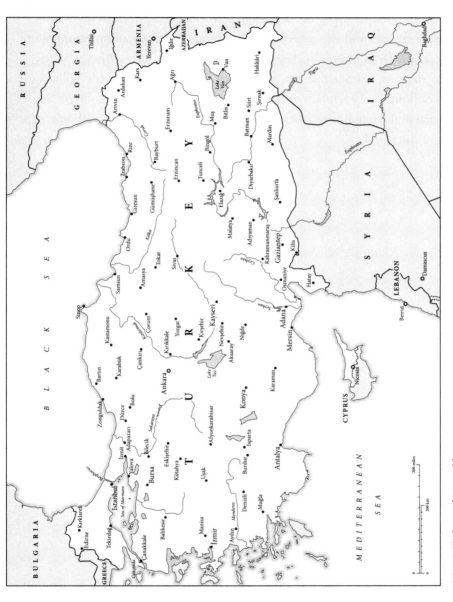

Map 1. Turkey and its neighbors

of its political system, economic prowess or popular culture exports – is at present Turkey's principal asset. The book ends with a chapter on relations with Europe. Despite Erdoğan's polarizing rhetoric, the use of the refugee issue to squeeze the EU and the tensions in the Eastern Mediterranean, economic interdependence still binds Turkey and European countries together as it has done in the past. Europe has lost its leverage over Turkey's domestic politics, but it continues to be relevant to its interests. As Turkey prepares to mark the centennial of the republic in 2023, it is confronted with turbulence at home as well as in the world.

1

THE PAST ISN'T ANOTHER COUNTRY

For all its charms Istanbul has always had a rough edge. Those who lived there through the 1990s could attest to that. The sprawling metropolis was struggling to cope with a dizzying population surge from 3 million to 10 million in a space of a decade. Water shortages and service cut-offs were common, particularly in scorching summers. In areas populated by recent arrivals from far-off corners of Anatolia, locals would line up at neighborhood fountains, hauling plastic containers (*bidon*). Some would venture out on "water hunts" across town. Bathing and doing laundry in the street were a daily sight in poor quarters. The substandard quality of drinking water made matters worse. In 1993, when health officials closed off the Elmalı reservoir due to high levels of ammonium, the crisis spread to upmarket boroughs along the Bosphorus and the Marmara Sea. Sea and air pollution turned a one-time promise by former mayor Bedrettin Dalan to make the waters of the Golden Horn "the same color as [his blue] eyes" into a running joke. Local officials from the Social Democratic Populist Party (Sosyaldemokrat Halkçı Parti, SHP), which controlled major municipalities at the time, were overwhelmed by the colossal challenge confronting them.

Istanbul's plight mirrored the general state of disarray in the country. While the 1980s carried the promise of a new, dynamic and globalized Turkey, the decade that followed is remembered as a time of turbulence and discontent. Stories of political strife, of conspiracies and subversion, of saber-rattling and brinkmanship filled the newspaper front pages. In April 1993, President Turgut Özal suffered a deadly heart attack, halfway into his term. His successor, the veteran politician Süleyman Demirel, would see a succession of weak, fractious coalitions coming in and out of power. In 1994, the economy recorded its worst slump in decades, with GDP contracting by 4.7 per cent. Amidst galloping inflation, the Turkish lira plunged from 15,000 to 38,000 to the US dollar from January to December. The International Monetary Fund (IMF) rushed to the country's rescue. One thousand security personnel lost their lives fighting the separatist Kurdistan Workers' Party (PKK), a war that pinned down 250,000 troops in the restless southeast provinces. The term for mandatory military services was extended from 15 to 18 months. Greece, a sworn adversary, was obstructing Turkey's integration into the EU. It was indeed not a time many Turkish citizens would think of fondly.[1]

The image of the restless 1990s lie at the heart of Recep Tayyip Erdoğan's mythology. From early on, he portrays his rule as a remedy to the "lost decade," much as Vladimir Putin cast himself as Russia's savior from the chaos he inherited. But in fairness Erdoğan grew as a politician in those days, another similarity with Putin, whose career skyrocketed during Boris Yeltsin's presidency. In the local elections of March 1994, a plurality of disgruntled voters cast their lot with the Islamist Welfare Party (Refah Partisi), propelling the ambitious young politician to the mayorship of the Istanbul metropolitan municipality. Refah won across Turkey, including in the capital Ankara. In Istanbul, electoral rules (first-past-the-post/one round) and the edge of less than 12,000 voters over the runner-up from the Motherland Party secured Erdoğan's victory. However, there was no denying that his message resonated with voters. Improving living conditions in neglected areas in the inner city, such as his native Kasımpaşa, and on the edges of urban sprawl became Erdoğan's trademark.[2] It has stayed so till the present, despite the economic hardship of the late 2010s and the AKP's loss of Istanbul in another local election in 2019.

Yet back in 1994 the triumph in Istanbul charted the Welfare Party's inexorable rise at the national level. To the dismay of Turkey's secularist establishment, as well as of many Turks who revered the legacy of Mustafa Kemal Atatürk, Refah won the capital Ankara as well, along with 25 provincial centers. At the next general elections, in December 1995, the party emerged as the largest faction in the Grand National Assembly. Six months later, Professor Necmettin Erbakan, the party leader and the founding father of political Islam in Turkey, took office as prime minister. Secularists sensed a threat to the fundamentals of political order. On 28 February 1997, the General Staff of the Turkish Armed Forces, then a bastion of Kemalism, issued a thinly veiled threat which, in several months, would see Erbakan resigning from office. The

Constitutional Court banned Refah as violating the principles of *laiklik* – the separation of state and religion, inspired by France's *laïcité*, but, really, the subordination of faith to the state. Erdoğan had his mandate curtailed and ended up in prison for four months for inciting religious hatred. The "post-modern coup" of 1997 set off a political struggle, played out through the ballot box and in the courtroom, in national media and in international diplomatic fora, which would shape Turkey's trajectory going forward. The episode burnished the reputation of the AKP – an offshoot of Refah – as champion of the ordinary folk against self-appointed guardians of the state, and a true expression of popular will.

Looking in the rearview mirror, the "lost decade," as the 1990s came to be known, helps in understanding the Turkey of nowadays – its bold aspirations and unfulfilled promises.[3] The war with the PKK, the so-called "deep state" (a cabal of corrupt politicians, mafiosi and security operatives), tensions in the Eastern Mediterranean and the Cyprus issue – all have come back with a vengeance. Though history never repeats itself, it rhymes, as Mark Twain once remarked. Much has changed in the intervening years indeed. The Turkey of nowadays is a much richer and more confident place, run by a new ruling elite under a mark-edly different system of governance. But in some ways Erdoğan's New Turkey has come full circle. Times gone by shine a light on the present.

THE SHADOW OF TURGUT ÖZAL

Özalism defined

In April 1988, Margaret Thatcher became the first British prime minister to pay an official visit to Turkey. As is customary, she opened her dinner speech with a quip: "1987 was obviously a vintage year for elections. We had one in June; yours was in November and the outcome was extremely satisfactory in both cases. In Britain the electorate thoroughly endorsed my Özalite policies." Thatcher went on to commend Prime Minister Turgut Özal for his belief in "enterprise, in initiative, in incentives, in giving people something to go for."[4]

For a long time, Turkey's value lay in its strategic location and the part it played in containing the Soviet Union in Southern Europe and the Middle East (all given due credit in Thatcher's toast). But Özal had accomplished something few could foresee at the time he entered office. Turkey had become a poster boy for the benefits of the free market economy. State-driven industrialization based on import substitution and mapped out in five-year plans, a nod to Soviet doctrines as much as to French *dirigisme*, was out. A new strategy in line with neoliberal precepts charted the way forward (ironically enough, with a former functionary of Turkey's State Planning Organization at the helm). Özal had spearheaded structural reforms such as the slashing of import tariffs and the abolition of quotas, the privatization of state-owned enterprises, the phasing out of subsidies and eventually, in August 1989, the liberalization of the capital account.[5] Links with the EEC had burgeoned after Turkey submitted a membership application (in 1987) and started the process to complete a Customs Union with the bloc.[6] Such policies had helped attract foreign direct investment, boost exports and fuel growth. Turkish GDP expanded by 7 per cent in 1986 and 9.5 per cent in 1987.[7] Nowhere was the change more visible than in foreign trade. Exports went up by an annual 40 per cent, from $2.9 billion in 1980 to $11.7 billion towards the end of 1988. Manufactured goods overtook agriculture in Turkey's outside sales: from 36 per cent in 1980 they reached 80 per cent five years later.[8]

Turgut Özal made an unlikely hero.[9] Following stints at the World Bank and the Turkish private sector, the native of Malatya had served as undersecretary in Süleyman Demirel's cabinet (1979–80) and earned himself a name as a capable technocrat. That was what qualified him for the deputy prime ministerial position in the cabinet installed by General Kenan Evren after the 1980 coup. But the high-ranking position proved to be a launching pad for a partisan career. Once the military junta lifted the ban on political parties in the run-up to the 1983 general elections, Özal's newly established Motherland Party (Anavatan Partisi, ANAP) swept up over 45 per cent of votes and emerged as the largest force in the Grand National Assembly. ANAP seized a good chunk of the conservative, center-right electorate previously aligned with Süleyman Demirel's Justice Party (Adalet Partisi) – of which Özal himself had once been a member. With his former mentor Demirel banned from politics by the military-drafted constitution of 1982, the one-time apprentice was at an advantage. The army-backed Nationalist Democracy Party, which Demirel famously refused to endorse, flopped, and trailed behind in third place. The ballot box transformed a former bureaucrat into a bona fide national leader as well as an agent of change.

The prime minister grew into his new role. His policies did deliver, even if the benefits were far from evenly distributed. From Istanbul's newly inaugurated stock exchange, to the Oyak Renault factory churning out new automobiles in Bursa, to the textile factories in Anatolian towns such as Kayseri and Gaziantep, the economy thrived. Western consumer goods such as cigarettes and electronics became widely available too, unlike in prior decades.

Özal's public displays of religiosity went a long way in bolstering his legitimacy with the grassroots too. Korkut Özal, his brother, had been a prominent member of the Islamist National Salvation Party and even served as minister in the early 1970s. Özal himself had stood, unsuccessfully, as a candidate for parliament on the party's behalf. The Özals had links to the imam of the Naqshbandi *tarikat* (pious order) and the intellectual Mehmet Zahid Kotku, who preached at a mosque in Fatih, a conservative quarter tucked into Istanbul's old city. Religious conservatives hailing from inner Anatolia, like former mayor of Konya Mehmet Keçiceler, wielded influence in ANAP too. The 1980s was a period when Fethullah Gülen's movement took off as well. Özal himself paid respect to the gospel of *laiklik*. For all his attacks against the "status quo lot" (*statükocular*) and his closeness to the *tarikats*, he didn't confront the republic's shibboleths head-on. His chosen role was that of an arbiter, a unifying figure who could bring various strands together.

ANAP, too, subscribed to big-tent politics and welcomed people of various persuasions: liberals, nationalists, Islamic conservatives and even social democrats. That was precisely the formula the AKP was to emulate in the 2000s as it captured the center ground in Turkish politics, distancing itself from the more radical, anti-Western and anti-capitalist policies advocated by its predecessors in the political Islamist tradition. No wonder Özal became posthumously co-opted into the party's narrative.

Polarization

Özal's presidency planted the seeds of polarization between secularists and the religiously devout in Turkey. In the 1980s, the military and bureaucratic establishment could tolerate Islam's higher profile in public affairs. Article 24 of the new constitution passed in 1982 made religious education compulsory in schools, rather than optional as before. Piety would work as a bulwark to a rebound by the left. Mosque construction peaked, in part in response to the needs of Anatolian settlers in the metropolitan centers of the West. The number of students at the so-called *imam hatip* institutions, religious middle schools and lycées whose graduates were now legally allowed to enroll in universities, went up from 200,000 to 300,000 between 1980 and the early 1990s.[10] Islam's rising prominence in public life was, on one level, a natural occurrence in light of the democratizing trend, as it reflected the values of sizeable groups in society. However, many secularists grew worried, seeing Iran's post-1979 trajectory as a forewarning. Those leaning left blamed Islamicization on US foreign policy and its alliance with forces of conservatism in its quest for global dominance. With the demise of the unifying figure of Özal and the subsequent rise of the Islamist Welfare Party, fears and tensions escalated.

The Özal years were a missed opportunity with regard to the Kurdish issue. Coming from the southeast and counting Kurds among his ancestors, Özal was open-minded about Kurdish identity. It was under him, in 1991, that the ban on Kurdish language and the celebration of Nowruz, the new year feast central to the ethnic traditions of not only Kurds but also many Turkic groups, was removed. Departing from the rigid conception of Turkishness, Özal spoke of Turkey as an amalgam of ethnic communities bound in a single nation, drawing a parallel to America's proverbial melting pot. Internal migration, bringing millions of Kurds to metropolitan Turkey over the 1980s and 1990s, literally brought this point home to the majority. ANAP included prominent Kurds assimilated into the Turkish mainstream; the Bitlis-born diplomat and government official Kâmran Inan would even run as the party's presidential candidate in 1993. Nationalist Kurds gravitated towards the left and had their own faction within the SHP in 1989–90, having been represented by other leftist formations prior to the 1980 coup. Last but not least, Özal – who had introduced a state of emergency in Kurdish provinces in 1987 – was prepared to negotiate with the militants, too. His initiative made headway in March 1993 when Abdullah Öcalan declared a ceasefire. Özal also perceived the potential for a win-win engagement with Kurds in the broader region. Jalal Talabani, a Kurdish leader from northern Iraq, was one of the go-betweens with the PKK. The same philosophy of combining carrots and sticks would come into play under Erdoğan in the late 2000s.[11]

Ambiguous legacy

Ziya Öniş, a Turkish scholar, once described Özal as a "neo-liberal populist."[12] That is hardly surprising, as populism – understood as being of the people and carrying an authentic connection with the common folk – was and still is the staple of Turkish politics. Özal practiced the same craft as Demirel and others, all the way to Erdoğan. It was his drive to dismantle some of the welfare state which set him apart. There is a caveat of course. Vast strata of Turkish society, rural migrants to the big cities for instance, never fully relied on the state's social safety net to start with, but rather on family and place-of-origin networks as well as on the informal sector more broadly. They created the target audience for a future populist leader with a pro-market orientation, as Erdoğan demonstrated. Second, the negative effects of reforms were cushioned by various forms of support through the national budget. They tended to benefit insiders, however. ANAP cultivated a business clientele, for example in the export sector which cashed in on subsidies and tax rebates, and its reforms overlooked the rule of law. Oversight of spending of the public sector was deficient too. When ramshackle coalition governments took over in the 1990s that spawned corruption as parties milked the departments of the state under their control. Poor financial discipline fueled inflation, which spiraled out of control by the end of Özal's life. He tended to downplay the challenge in the belief that rapid growth – and increased consumption by the populace – justified and cancelled the negative fallout of higher inflation rates. That, too, formed part of the populist credo, yet Turkey would soon have to pay the price.

The blend between the market, Islamic piety, halfway acceptance of ethnic diversity and time-tested clientelism did the job – as it would a generation later under the AKP. In the November 1987 general elections, ANAP enlarged its parliamentary group from 211 to 292. However, limits were becoming apparent too. The party's vote plunged by more than 8 per cent and it was the 10 per cent electoral threshold that helped it win. But Özal's ultimate destination was the presidency. His election by parliament for a seven-year term compensated for ANAP's bleeding support to competitors on the right, such as Demirel's True Path Party (Doğru Yol Partisi, DYP). A constitutional referendum in September 1987 had lifted the restrictions preventing old-time leaders from taking part in political life,[13] overruling Özal who had campaigned, through surrogates, against such change. Left-wing activism, suppressed by the generals, was back with a vengeance, too. Mayday demonstrations by students and trade unionists at Istanbul's Taksim Square in 1988, in defiance of an official ban, brought back memories of the tumultuous 1970s. Tapping into the leftist electorate and capturing Kurdish voters, the SHP was up in the polls, culminating with sweeping wins in the 1989 local elections. Confronted with a shifting balance of power, Özal, now head of state and nominally above partisan struggles, made robust arguments in favor of an executive presidency modeled on the French example. Critics retorted that the absence of properly functioning checks and balances would beget a Latin American-type of *presidencialismo*. He remained convinced, till his sudden demise in 1993 of a heart attack, that the president should be elected directly through popular vote rather than by the legislature. This debate, too, would make a comeback in the late 2000s, under an altogether different political constellation. Needless to say, Özal would serve as a point of reference.

TIME OF FLUX

Özal loved to pontificate that the twenty-first century would belong to the Turks. But he would hasten to add a proviso: "if we do not make major mistakes." And mistakes Turks did make. The years following his untimely death are remembered, to this day, as a period of trouble. Weak governments, volatile economy, political strife and the threat of military conflict marked the mid-1990s. But, in honesty, that new chapter in the country's political history was a reflection of the political, economic and institutional legacy Özal left behind.

The reshuffling of Turkey's political scene was the most conspicuous outcome from the exit of such a domineering figure. By 1995, the Islamist Welfare Party had displaced ANAP and the DYP as the leading parties in the country. Conservative voters, the largest electoral bloc in the country, defected *en masse* from the traditional center-right to Refah. A variety of factors explained the change of heart.

First, the center-right parties faced the challenge of succession. The departure of popular figures such as Özal and Demirel (elected to the presidency, a non-partisan institution), whose charisma always carried at least as much weight as ideology, cost support. That was not the case of other players. The new crop of leaders, Tansu Çiller (DYP) and Mesut Yılmaz (ANAP), could operate the clientelist networks attached to their party, win votes, scheme and wage political feuds. Yet their electoral legitimacy was slowly eroding, especially when they held office and became entangled in corruption scandals. By contrast, the older generation of charismatic leaders, such as Refah's Erbakan or Bülent Ecevit on the left did better with their party's core constituencies.

Second, after Özal's move to the presidency in 1989, neither ANAP nor the DYP were able to govern on their own, but instead relied on shaky coalitions involving leftists (1991–95) and Islamists. After the December 1995 elections, Yılmaz and Çiller formed a cabinet which unraveled in less than four months. With its collapse, Çiller's DYP ended up as the Islamists' junior partner in 1996–97 until the "post-modern coup" installed Yılmaz, whose selling point to the military was the refusal to collaborate with Refah, again. In the 1999 elections, ANAP and the DYP, relegated to fourth and fifth place, played a secondary role. Taken together, they still formed the largest bloc. Yet their inability to cooperate contributed to the mainstream central right's terminal decline.

Third, established elites, both on the center-right and the center-left, eventually fell prey to Turkey's erratic economic performance. Özal's choice for growth over price stability had produced runaway inflation in the 1990s. Annual rates jumped from 35–40 per cent in the early 1980s to 65 per cent in the early 1990s all the way up to 80 per cent towards the decade's end. Marred by infighting, coalitions proved unable to rein in price increases and meet their own targets. With a short time horizon, cabinets' priority was to cater to demands by various interest groups through public spending, for example, through subsidies to state-owned enterprises. That led to budget deficits, unrestrained borrowing and ultimately inflation, which passed the cost to society at large.[14] By the end of the decade, the public deficit (including the central budget, local authorities, social security, extrabudgetary funds and state-owned enterprises) peaked at 11.7 per cent of GDP.[15]

A crisis of legitimacy

The faltering economy put corruption into the spotlight. In good times, citizens would have greater tolerance of widespread practices such as fixing public tenders, channeling loans to cronies at advantageous terms through state-owned banks, tax evasion and so on. Not so in times of crisis such as in the 1990s. Both Refah and the AK ("white" or "pure/untainted") Party made mileage through claiming higher moral ground, thanks to norms inherent to Islam, over their corrupt incumbents. Ceaseless scandals only reinforced the perception of governance failure and abuse of power by vested interests.

The so-called Susurluk incident stood out as a glaring example. In November 1996, a Mercedes crashed into a truck on the highway between Istanbul and Izmir, near the town of Susurluk. Among those who lost their lives in the accident were police chief Huseyin Kocadağ, the notorious contract killer Abdullah Çatlı linked to the ultranationalist (*ülkücü,* literally "idealist") groups, along with his beauty-queen girlfriend. The luxury car's owner, Sedat Bucak, MP from True Path as well as a scion of a prominent Kurdish family from Şanlıurfa, survived. Whether it resulted from an assassination plot or not, the crash put on display the intimate connections between the state establishment and the criminal underworld. The scandal gave rise to a parliamentary enquiry and brought down the interior minister Mehmet Ağar (another DYP member), former chief of the General Security Directorate (Eminiyet Genel Müdürlüğü) overseeing Turkish police. In both positions, Ağar had been at the forefront in the fight against the PKK.[16] To many, Susurluk stood as proof that there was a state within the state, outside public scrutiny, dealing in political influence and profiting from the violence in the Kurdish areas. The scandal followed in the footsteps of assassinations of prominent figures over the preceding years, such as journalist Uğur Mumcu,[17] whose car was blown up by an explosive device in 1993, and a string of Kurdish politicians. It thus fanned suspicions that "the deep state" (*derin devlet*) – a cabal of bureaucrats, army officers, security officials and bona fide mafiosi – was pulling the strings from behind the scenes.[18] That further delegitimized Turkey's political class and prepared the ground, further down the line, for high-profile investigations like the one concerning the Ergenekon conspiracy in the late 2000s.

In this morass, the military could no longer be counted to step in as independent arbiter capable of restoring balance. The coup on 12 September 1980, the ensuing repressions – especially against the left – and the closure of parties enjoyed a measure of popular legitimacy. A majority could forgo political and individual freedoms in exchange for stability. By contrast, the coup in February 1997, though no blood was spilled, signaled that the army is anything but an impartial referee. The repression and the closure of Refah were bound to be resented not only by Erbakan's constituents, but also by democratic and pro-liberal citizens for whom it was a turn towards the past, and away from the EU. It was as if Turkey came full circle: back to the time before Özal's reforms and the opening to the world.

Media revolution

Scandals happened against the backdrop of an increasingly dynamic media market which, literally, brought the latest controversy, corrupt affair or shocking discovery to everyone's living room. The 1990s saw the advent and growth of private TV networks, ending public broadcaster TRT's monopoly. First, it happened informally: Star 1, self-proclaimed "Turkey's first private TV," did a test broadcast in 1990. A constitutional change in July 1993 and Law 3948, passed the following year, liberalized television and radio, established a new public regulator (RTÜK) and paved the way for private channels such as NTV, Kanal D, ATV and Star TV. Players such as Doğan Group, controlling high-circulation dailies such as *Milliyet* and *Hürriyet*, the Uzan Group and businessman Dinç Bilgin established a foothold in the TV market and amassed power. Doğan also started CNN Türk, a local affiliate of the US 24-hour news channel. Family business empires such as Doğuş moved into the media sector as well – launching NTV. It was then that Fethullah Gülen's supporters grew their cluster of outlets, including the *Zaman* newspaper (established in the 1980s), Samanyolu (Milky Way) TV and the Cihan News Agency.[19] Though private TVs main mission was to turn a profit through commercials and thanks to entertainment and sports content, from football derbies to soap operas which mushroomed in the 2000s, it provided a boost to political journalism. And, despite taboos and limits, that involved coverage of sensitive issues such as the plight of minorities or the state of human rights and the rule of law. At the same time, the military kept a watchful eye. Through the National Security Council, they shaped the 1994 law to ensure Islamist messaging be kept under restrictions.

The Kurdish question

The explosion of the Kurdish issue, or Kurdish problem (*Kürt sorunu*), defined the 1990s and has been haunting Turkey ever since. Established in 1978 and energized by the repressions following the military coup of September 1980, the PKK had unleashed a guerrilla campaign against the Turkish state in the southeast in 1984. Beyond the fight to carve out a Kurdish polity, Abdullah Öcalan (known to his devotees as Serok Apo, that is Headman Apo) and his comrades (*Apocular*) saw their mission as forging a new national identity and overcoming entrenched divisions cutting across an imagined community. In the words of Henri Barkey and Graham Fuller, "PKK [was] the first political-military organization transcending regional and tribal ties capable of appealing to a wide range of Kurds residing in different parts of the country."[20] Indeed, the militants faced off with the quasi-feudal structures in southeast and eastern Turkey. Since the era of Ottoman rule, the central state had been able to buy local support by integrating notables in government and offering them a stake in the power hierarchy. The use of military force to suppress challenges to authority, as during the Sheikh Said rebellion in the mid-1920s and the insurgency in Dersim (Tunceli) in 1937–38, went hand in hand with policies aimed at co-optation. In the latter part of the twentieth century, political parties did the job of bridging the gap between the center and periphery and building loyalty to the state. They provided access to resources and social prestige to Kurdish elites in return for votes, a practice which resurfaced in the 1980s as competitive politics made a comeback under Özal.

Starting from the 1970s, leftists from the region, the milieu from which the PKK founders sprang, projected a radically different vision, one based on ideas of self-determination, class struggle, equality and the empowerment of women. The latter included equality between genders, a revolutionary notion in a conservative corner of Turkey where phenomena such as early marriages or honor killings were common. At the same time, ethnic separatism manifest in the PKK's calls for a state for the Kurds and the redrawing of Middle Eastern borders distanced the organization from the left. Though the program, as spelled out in its foundational manifesto of 1978, was never embraced by a majority of Kurds, it won considerable support. The scorched-earth campaign waged by the military, the gendarmerie and local proxies such as the notorious Village Guards, a force established by Özal in the mid-1980s, bolstered recruitment too. The PKK demonstrated a capacity to survive. Its raids killed hundreds of Turkish soldiers (many of them Kurds themselves), village teachers, bureaucrats as well as civilians suspected of collaboration. It burned schools ("instruments of the state's assimilationist policies"), too.[21] Violence escalated in the 1990s, enmeshed with older tribal and personal feuds haunting the southeast. In 1992 alone, casualties reached 2,000, compared to 4,500 at the start of the conflict eight years earlier. By the close of the decade, the number stood at more than 30,000, including 5,828 Turkish officials, 5,390 civilians and 19,786 PKK fighters. Around 4,000 villages had been evacuated. The estimated cost was $86 billion, the size of Turkey's external debt.[22]

Kurdish militants benefited from external support, chiefly by Syria, which hosted Öcalan and set up training camps in Lebanon's Bekaa valley. In the 1990s, northern Iraq became a base from where the PKK could mount cross-border attacks. In mid-August 1992, a group of 700 militants took over the town of Şırnak, set government buildings on fire and killed eight soldiers. Turkey's efforts to pressure neighbors didn't bear fruit. Syria's President Assad, for instance, committed on several occasions to cut support to Kurds but never delivered, seeing the PKK as a bargaining chip in disputes with Ankara – such as over the volumes of water flowing downstream the Euphrates river. Turkey had better luck with the Iraqi Kurdish leaders, Masoud Barzani and Jalal Talabani. Both built strong connections with President Özal, who even provided them with Turkish passports. Yet the internecine war in Iraqi Kurdistan in 1994–97, where the PKK aligned with Talabani against Barzani, undercut plans to enlist local leaders as allies against the insurgents. In the spring of 1995, Turkish armed forces entered northern Iraq to hunt down Kurdish militants but, as in an earlier operation in 1992, failed to inflict significant damage.

Tansu Çiller's term as prime minister, June 1993–March 1996, marked the worst phase in the conflict. Çiller bought into the notion that a military solution to the insurgency was possible. Özal's peace overtures, culminating with a ceasefire announced by Öcalan in March 1993, in the presence of Talabani, were off. The left-wing SHP, coalition partner of the DYP in 1991–95, kept silent, even though it did not share Çiller's approach. President Demirel similarly took a back seat. As a result, the military and gendarmerie stepped up their operations in the southeast – as well as in northern Iraq. Only Öcalan's expulsion from Syria, after Turkey threatened a ground invasion in October 1998, and his subsequent capture by Turkish commandos in the Kenyan capital of Nairobi, as he was leaving the Greek ambassador's residence, reduced tensions. However, the decapitation strategy did not bring about the defeat of the PKK either. Guerrilla numbers declined to just several thousand but the organization was not wiped out and its command structure, including the lead troika comprising Cemil Bayık, Duran Kalkan and Mustafa Karayılan (in control of the Qandil bases), stayed intact. Suppression proved a dead end.

Escalation in the mid-1990s could not but stir public opinion, as news dispatches reported yet another *Mehmetçik* ("little Mehmet," an affectionate name for a soldier) lost to terrorists. At the funerals of murdered servicemen or police personnel there were calls for revenge. Turkish mainstream opinion labeled the PKK as "baby killers" and agents of the state's foreign enemies, rather than legitimate interlocutors for the authorities. The terror tactics deployed by the organization played a part, no doubt. Yet deeply ingrained prejudices against eastern Anatolia, a backward and clannish land, also had some bearing on popular views. Furthermore, much was said about the PKK's links to drug trafficking, a common phenomenon in Turkey's borderlands irrespective of one's politics or ideology. The militants' links with foreign countries at odds with Turkey – Syria, Greece, Iran or Russia – bred public hostility as well.

Another lasting effect was the exodus from the east and southeast. Fighting razed to the ground more than 2,000 villages. Caught in the crossfire, locals sought a better life in the big cities of the west of Turkey or further afield in Europe. The state's ambitious developmental programs, first and foremost the Southeast Anatolia Project (Güneydoğu Anadolu Projesi, GAP) aiming to build a chain of dams and hydroelectric plants, contributed too. A legacy of the Özal era, GAP advanced in the 1990s, siphoning off as much as 7 per cent of all public investment in Turkey.[23] The 20-odd dams built largely in Kurdish areas displaced villagers. Estimates of the out-migration from eastern and southeastern Anatolia vary but might be above 3 million for the whole period from the early 1980s to the late 1990s.[24]

The war and the state of emergency fueled a political movement focused on Kurdish rights. State institutions and a good part of public opinion saw civil society activists and left-leaning Kurdish politicians from the region as a front of the PKK. The first attempt to set up a parliamentary group took place in June 1990, when seven members from the SHP laid the foundations of the People's Workers Party (HEP) which pushed for schooling and broadcasting in Kurdish. The HEP was banned by the Constitutional Court in 1993, a fate which also befell its successors, the Democracy Party (1993–94) and the

People's Democracy Party (HADEP, 1994–2003). In 1991, Leyla Zana, the first Kurdish woman to be elected to parliament, caused a furore when she addressed the Grand National Assembly in Kurdish, right after taking an oath. Three years later, Zana and four other deputies were sentenced to 15 years of imprisonment on terrorism charges. Others fared worse: activists lost their lives in assassinations attributed to JİTEM, the gendarmerie's unofficial intelligence arm in charge of black ops. The list included politician Vedat Aydın, trade unionist Zübeyir Akkoç, writer Musa Anter and others. JİTEM arrested Aydın on 5 July 1991 and his mutilated body was found two days later. Thousands turned up at his funeral in Diyarbakır. One of them, an 18-year-old named Selahattin Demirtaş, would emerge as a leader of the movement two decades later.[25] Despite restrictions and repression, leftist Kurdish nationalists gathered strength. At the 1999 local elections, HADEP captured the mayorship of Diyarbakır as well as five provincial centers in eastern and southeast Anatolia. Öcalan's captivity gave the party a boost. In the eyes of supporters, it turned him into a martyr and undisputed symbol of the nation and its aspirations. "*Biji Serok Apo*" ("Long Live Serok Apo") Kurdish youths would chant at rallies, for example during the annual festivities for Nowruz.

The conflict of the 1990s raised international awareness of the Kurdish issue. It became strikingly obvious that resolution was a *sine qua non* should Turkey wish to move forward in relations with the EU. After Danielle Mitterrand, France's first lady, visited Diyarbakır in 1989, Western European politicians and opinion makers started paying attention. Leyla Zana gained prominence after she won the 1995 Andrei Sakharov Prize for Freedom of Thought presented by the European Parliament and the European Court of Human Rights (ECtHR, a body under the Council of Europe) ruled in her favor in a highly publicized lawsuit. Lobbying by the Kurdish diaspora, galvanized by the developments in the southeast Turkey, weighed in too. "The road to the EU passes through Diyarbakır," was how Prime Minister Mesut Yılmaz framed it in 1999.[26] This was one of the reasons Öcalan, sentenced to death by hanging in April 1999, remained alive. The Turkish government first delayed the execution pending the case at the ECtHR and then, in August 2002, abolished the death penalty in peacetime as part of EU-mandated reforms. EU support and sympathy turned nationalist Kurds into one of the most pro-European constituencies in Turkish politics.

The other reason for Apo's survival was the change in his positions. From the high-security prison on İmralı island in the Marmara Sea, he renounced the goal of an independent Kurdistan and instead argued for "democratic autonomy." From that point, he transformed from public enemy number 1 to a potential partner for Turkish authorities. His metamorphosis set the scene for future negotiations, as during Özal's tenure. The "Kurdish Opening" of the late 2000s came as a consequence.[27]

In the 1990s, Islamists put forward their own approach to resolving the Kurdish issue, which differed from the one advocated by the military or secular politicians not rooted in the region. As an alternative to ethnonationalism and the denial of minority rights, it stressed the shared bond of Islam that united Turks and Kurds. Refah, drawing votes from devout Kurds in both the east and the big cities of western Turkey, was more open to Kurdish identity than the other major parties. Erbakan's term in government brought a relative slowdown in the anti-PKK campaign. The same rhetoric of recognizing Kurdishness under the all-encompassing framework of Islam became a centerpiece of AKP policy after 2002.

The specter of communal violence

While the Kurdish issue was the major cause of violence during the 1990s, it was far from the only one. Other groups like the Alevis, a heterodox Muslim – mainly Turkish-speaking – community, bore the brunt of prejudice and discrimination by the state, too. Unlike the Kurds (some of whom are also Alevi rather than Sunni), their struggles took place in large cities – in front of TV cameras and journalists' eyes – rather than rural areas under state of emergency, more than a thousand kilometers to the east.

In July 1993, Sunni radicals attacked an Alevi festival in the central Anatolian town of Sivas. They were incensed by the presence of veteran leftist writer Aziz Nesin who had recently been in the spotlight because of his attempt to publish a Turkish translation of Salman Rushdie's *Satanic Verses*, which is considered blasphemous by pious Muslims. The crowd set the Madımak Hotel, where the gathering was taking place, on fire. Thirty-seven were killed, including several prominent intellectuals and two of the attackers. The story repeated itself in March 1995, when masked gunmen opened fire with automatic rifles at cafes in Gazi, a working-class district on the European side of Istanbul inhabited predominantly by Alevis. A community leader (*dede*) fell dead and another 25 were injured. In response, tens of thousands of locals rioted. Clashes with police and gendarmerie forces left another 23 dead. Demonstrations spread to Ankara, too. The crisis highlighted the plight and recognition demands of millions of Alevis.[28] Gazi would again be a subject of attention when a 13-year-old resident, Berkin Elvan, was hit on the head by a tear gas canister during the anti-government protests in the summer of 2013 and later died of the injuries he sustained.

MELTDOWN

Despite domestic instability, by the end of the 1990s Turkey was moving forward. Between 1999 and 2002, Bülent Ecevit's coalition government, bringing together the leftist DSP (Democratic Left Party), the far-right Nationalist Action Party (Milliyetçi Hareket Partisi, MHP)[29] and ANAP, bagged several successes.

First, Öcalan's capture led to the de-escalation of violence in the southeast and a shift of focus to the legal strand of the Kurdish movement. HADEP's electoral success in 1999 set a precedent, even if mainstream parties and the military remained skeptical.

Second, Turkey overcame a major natural disaster. On 17 August 1999, the Marmara region was struck by a devastating earthquake. The tremor killed more than 17,000 in densely populated areas around İzmit, a major industrial hub, and Adapazarı. Hundreds of thousands were left homeless. As a result, Turkish GDP shrank by 9 per cent in 1999. The natural disaster led to an outpouring of solidarity in Turkish society with civic activists, non-governmental organizations (NGOs) and informal groups mobilizing to help the victims. The quake led to an overhaul of construction codes and improvement of public infrastructure, a testament to Turkey's ability to design and carry out robust and effective public policy.

Third, the decade closed with the EU's historic Helsinki Council of December 1999. Turkey normalized relations with Greece and, at last, secured official candidate status. This then triggered a series of crucial political reforms which had buy-in not only from across the political spectrum but also, with certain caveats, on the part of the military establishment (more about this in Chapter 2).

Last but not least, despite structural weaknesses, macroeconomic instability and boom-and-bust cycles, GDP growth in the 1990s averaged at 2.4 per cent, which, though lower than the period 1950–80, indicated gradual expansion.

Yet, ultimately, it was two consecutive crises, in 2000 and especially in 2001, that struck the final chord and thus defined the era. The public sector deficits accumulated through the 1990s combined with the surge short-term borrowing in foreign currency by commercial banks proved a recipe for disaster. By 2000, Turkey's external debt, public plus private, hit 60 per cent of GDP. As a result, foreign investors started divesting from Turkish assets, leading to depreciation of the lira, inflation, a slump in domestic demand, rising unemployment and falling wages – and ultimately a wholesale economic meltdown. In late February 2001, at the peak of the crisis, the value of one US dollar went up from 688,000 to 950,000 liras. By the year's end, public debt reached 74.1 per cent of GDP after the government had to recapitalize struggling banks. In layman's terms, ordinary citizens footed the bill for government profligacy and market players' recklessness. It was the legacy of halfway reform in the 1980s. The liberalization of the capital account had not gone hand in hand with the build-up of a robust financial sector, the provision of well-functioning regulatory oversight and long-term measures for fiscal stability.[30]

The crisis spelled the end of Ecevit's long and distinguished political career. His coalition could claim credit for the reset with the EU, for political reforms, for concluding an agreement with the IMF in late 1999, and ultimately for the overhaul of the financial sector, and implementing fiscal consolidation overseen by Economic Affairs Minister Kemal Derviş.[31] Macroeconomic stabilization was taking hold by the end of Ecevit's tenure, with GDP expanding by 6.4 per cent in 2002. Yet voters were prepared to punish all the mainstream parties that had been rotating in power since the mid-1990s. The beneficiary turned out to be the AKP, which promised to carry forward Europeanization and economic reform while sweeping out the old elite who bore the blame for everything that had turned out badly. The populist message worked and yielded a victory at the November 2002 election, amplified by the 10 per cent threshold which left ANAP and the DYP out of the Grand National Assembly.

There was a new outfit waiting in the wings, however, which pledged to bring Turkey back on track. Enter Recep Tayyip Erdoğan and his comrades.

2

TURKEY IN THE POST-COLD WAR WORLD

When the AKP rose to power, it focused on achieving EU membership as well as on upgrading commercial and diplomatic ties with neighbors. Turkey could be part of the West while opening the door wide to countries around its borders. This vision contrasted with the outlook espoused by the military and sections of the secularist establishment. To them, the end of the Cold War spelled trouble. Instability next to Turkish borders, in the Middle East first and foremost, threatened to spill over into the country, a fear fanned by the PKK insurgency. The United States, once a guarantor of Turkey's security against the Soviets, failed to take its ally's needs into consideration. Europe, for its part, was keeping Ankara at arm's length, with mainstream politicians depicting Turks as a Muslim Other unfit for a Christian-majority club. At the same time, EU members were providing a safe haven for Kurdish separatists.

This tension between the two views on foreign policy was nothing new, for they played out under Özal and the coalition governments that succeeded him, too. In the 1980s and early 1990s, integration with the then European Community (EC) went along with opening to the Middle East, and later the post-communist world. But by the middle of the decade, Turkey took a hawkish turn. In early 1996, a few barren rocks in the Aegean came close to triggering an all-out showdown with Greece, formally an ally of Turkey's within NATO. The Turkish military was regularly venturing into Iraq to fight the PKK and in the autumn of 1998 threatened to invade Syria, too. Turkey stood at odds with Russia over the Chechen War, and in Cyprus, as well as on the issue of NATO expansion.

Despite all that, Turkey did not fail to capitalize on the geopolitical opportunities offered by the end of the Cold War. Erdoğan inherited a positive balance, including EU candidate status, an acknowledgement of Turkey's centrality to NATO and improved ties with former adversaries such as Greece, Syria and Russia. Along with Özal, Foreign Minister İsmail Cem (who served between 1997 and 2002) could be credited as the intellectual father of the "zero problems with neighbors" doctrine.[1] On both Europe and the neighborhood, the AKP followed in the footsteps of previous administrations.

ÖZAL ABROAD

Embracing globalization

Turgut Özal viewed Turkey's external priorities through an economic prism. His reforms aimed, among other things, at improving the country's standing in the international marketplace. The reverse was true too: the global environment favored his domestic agenda. By the mid-1980s, the world economy was rebounding following a recession at the decade's start. Buoyed by the Single Market program, the European Community, Turkey's most significant trading partner, expanded once more. West Germany's GDP grew by an average of 2.9 per cent between 1983 and 1990, reaching 4–5 per cent towards the end of the period. Overall, Western Europe trailed behind the US, with its Reagan boom, not to mention the newly industrialized countries, but it provided steady demand for exports. Domestic transformation dovetailed with accelerating globalization. Özal followed faithfully the script set by the international financial institutions by liberalizing foreign trade through cutting down tariffs, abolishing import quotas and opening Turkey to foreign direct investment (FDI) while carrying out "structural adjustment" at home. In turn, such international bodies boosted the prime minister's legitimacy at home. In 1986, Özal presided over the ministerial meetings of the Organization for Economic Co-operation and Development (OECD), the club of rich nations.[2]

Global geopolitical reshuffles worked in Turkey's favor too. The thaw in East–West relations in the late 1980s ushered in by Gorbachev's "new thinking," the fall of the Berlin Wall and the disintegration of the Soviet Union opened hitherto unthinkable opportunities for Turkish business and diplomacy. The initial response in Turkey to Gorbachev's policies of *perestroika* at home and improving ties with the Western alliance was rather cautious. Yet Özal himself was, again, ahead of his time. In 1984, even before Moscow changed course, he oversaw the conclusion of the first contract for Soviet deliveries of natural gas to Turkey.[3] Four years thereafter, the first shipments traveled through Romania and Bulgaria via the so-called Trans-Balkan pipeline, inaugurating the later boom in Turkey's energy links to the post-1991 Russian Federation.

In retrospect, Turkey's application for EC membership in April 1987 was probably the defining moment of Özal's tenure. In the early 1980s, relations had been downgraded because of the military coup: financial assistance was suspended, and the joint association committee and parliamentary cooperation both put on hold. Turkey's abysmal human rights record and the Kurdish question hindered ties as well.[4] The return to civilian politics in 1983 injected fresh dynamism. The government's decision to allow citizens to make individual complaints before the European Court of Human Rights, a body under the Council of Europe and not the EC, signaled a willingness to conform with multilateral organizations' political conditionality.[5] Özal's liberal economic policies made a positive difference as well. As he himself put it in 1987, "the aim of [. . .] our reforms is to facilitate our integration in the European Community as a full member."[6] While European politicians, not to mention the publics, were hardly thrilled at the prospect of Turkey joining, saying "no" did not present a viable option either. The EC Council and ministers turned down a membership application lodged by Morocco the same year, on the grounds that it was not a European country. No such response was given to the Turks. The reason had less to do with the fact that 3 per cent of Turkish territory is geographically in Europe – a good part of Istanbul plus its Thracian hinterland – and more with the spirit of the 1963 Ankara Agreement which acknowledged Turkey's goal of acceding to the Community. In addition, member states had sound strategic and commercial reasons to ensure that a breakdown of ties did not occur. In effect, if not explicitly, their reaction to Ankara's bid approximated a "maybe." European Commission opinion from December 1989 referred to Turkey as a "natural candidate for full Member State status" but made it clear that no negotiations would ensue before 1993.[7]

That assessment was vindicated. The EC, upgraded into the EU with the Maastricht Treaty of 1992, focused on enlarging towards Central and Eastern Europe. In the next few years, relations with Turkey boiled down to the negotiation of a Customs Union, a goal set in the Ankara Agreement. The Customs Union, signed in 1995, could be read as both a diversion from the goal of membership and a stepping stone towards it. Removing all tariff barriers to trade in industrial goods, it presented EU firms with an unprecedented opportunity to invest in Turkey and export their manufactured products back to the home market. Economic integration deepened, bolstering FDI, growth and development in the country. Özal was initially lukewarm towards the Customs Union but later on, following the European Commission's opinion of December 1989, changed tack. The prime minister even lobbied skeptical business associations which insisted that import duties be abolished only if Turkey obtained membership. Özal's U-turn rested on the assessment that the end of the Cold War could reduce Turkey's value to both Western Europeans and the US.[8] Deepening institutional ties with the EC/EU was as much a consolation prize as an insurance – and potentially a basis for even closer integration. In that sense, the Customs Union was Özal's posthumous achievement. It laid the groundwork for the reforms in the late 1990s and the 2000s, the start of the membership talks in 2005, and even today remains the institutional backbone of EU–Turkish relations

Neighborly quarrels

Progress in relations with Europe hinged on Özal's ability to keep conflict with Greece over sovereignty rights in the Aegean and divided Cyprus under control. Joining the EC in 1981, the Hellenic Republic had obtained a strong lever vis-à-vis its neighbor and formidable rival, shared membership in NATO notwithstanding. Tensions boiled over in March 1987 when Turkey announced it would send an exploration vessel, along with a naval escort, to counter Greece's drilling for offshore oil near the island of Thassos. (Parallels to the recent stand-off with Athens in the disputed waters of the Eastern Mediterranean are hard to miss.)[9] In the event, the crisis was defused by Özal and Greek Prime Minister Andreas Papandreou. The meeting between the two in Davos, in January 1988, yielded a joint communiqué, "hurriedly written in clumsy English" in the words of an academic expert on Greek–Turkish relations, laying out a roadmap to resolving conflict through diplomatic dialogue and closer trade ties.[10] But the "spirit of Davos" proved ephemeral. The future had in store more turbulence and, in less than a decade, Greece and Turkey would come dangerously close to the brink of war.

Turkey's dealings with its other direct neighbor to the west, Bulgaria, were equally problem-ridden. The assimilation campaign waged by the communist authorities against the country's Turkish minority, culminating in an exodus of some 300,000 across the border in the summer of 1989, was nothing short of a humanitarian tragedy. The relief offered to co-ethnics in distress as they poured in fostered a strong sense of solidarity across Turkish society. It also gave a boost to Özal's patriotic credentials. He was never averse to grand-standing and wrapping himself in the flag. International events unleashed pressure from below for more assertive policy, too. The case in point was the furore over Greece's handling of Western Thrace, where an elected member of parliament, Ahmet Sadık, was put on trial in January 1990 for declaring the locals were Turks rather than Muslims. By that time, however, the fall of Bulgaria's long-time ruler Todor Zhivkov and the end of the ban on Turkish/Muslim names, as well as Turkish language and the practice of Islam, led to a speedy normalization of ties with Sofia. In the 1990s, Bulgaria, where the Turks-dominated Movement for Rights and Freedoms emerged as a central political player, became a diplomatic and economic partner for Turkey.[11]

The Turkish model

The improvement in Turkish–Bulgarian relations came as an early example of the opportunities the end of the Cold War offered. The disintegration of the Soviet Union in late 1991 and the emergence of newly independent states in Eastern Europe, the Caucasus and Central Asia, many with Turkic and Muslim majorities, caused unprecedented optimism in Turkey. Freed from the shackles of communism and embracing their cultural roots, Azeris, Turkmens, Uzbeks and Kazakhs would look to their "elder brother" (*ağabey*) for guidance and inspiration.[12] The notion of Turkey as a model of political and economic development of other Muslim-majority countries, which had been around as early as the 1920s,[13] made a fresh appearance.

Özal pioneered such arguments, even when the USSR was still in existence. During a visit to the US in 1991, he reflected on the advantages his country offered: "[e]conomically, we have a free market. A pluralistic democracy. And a secular state. It's a good example for the rest of the Islamic world. Turkey plays this important role. And if you can today see compared to what was 10 years ago, you would easily say Turkey is a Western country. But we have the traditions . . ." He went on:

[Turkey] will be a good example for the Eastern European countries: what they have to follow, what they have to do. And we will also have an important [part to] play in the Soviet Union. There are Turkish-speaking people in the Soviet Union. Quite a big number and increasing very fast, population increase, something like seven to eight million. And I think that they all look to Turkey as a good example. I have visited recently some of them. And I think we have agreed with Mr. Gorbachev, Turkey plays a stabilizing effect.[14]

Another exponent of this view was Özal's rival, Demirel, who succeeded him as president in 1993. "Turkic world from the Adriatic to the Great Wall of China" became the elder statesman's beloved phrase, though apparently it was Henry Kissinger who had coined it first.[15] From the vantage point of the early 1990s, it seemed, including to observers in the West, that Turkey had a golden opportunity to build strong connections with both Europe and the newly forming Eurasia. It was a bridge, no longer a barrier.[16]

Turkey launched a number of initiatives, putting words into action. In June 1992, Özal hosted the inaugural summit of the Black Sea Cooperation Organization, a multilateral platform for littoral states, the Russian Federation included, to advance trade, investment and infrastructure links. The same year saw the beginning of regular summits of Turkic countries' leaders. Özal welcomed the countries in question into the Economic Cooperation Organization, the trade arm he hoped to rejuvenate of the defunct Baghdad Pact. Turkish construction companies made advances in the post-Soviet region, while suitcase traders became a common sight in Istanbul's Aksaray district or Black Sea coastal towns. Through bodies such as the Turkish Cooperation and Coordination Agency (Türk İşbirliği ve Koordinasyon İdaresi Başkanlığı, TİKA), a department reporting to the prime minister set up in 1992, Ankara disbursed development assistance and invested in cultural and education ties with Eurasian countries. Under the AKP, TİKA would emerge as the flagship of Turkish soft power in the Balkans, the Middle East, all the way to sub-Saharan Africa.

A side effect of those initiatives was, among other things, putting the republic's president into the spotlight. Previously, the institution did not play a substantial role in comparison to the foreign ministry or the National Security

Council (Millî Güvenlik Kurulu, MGK), the mechanism through which the military would convey its wishes and priorities. Özal's activism and the informal links he nurtured with fellow leaders introduced change. Post-1993, Demirel, who previously paid little attention to foreign affairs, picked up the torch.[17]

However, the inflated expectations as to Turkey's guiding role had to reckon with reality. First, the leaders of newly independent nations in Central Asia did not trade the Russian big brother for a Turkish one. Instead, they opted for a multi-vector policy geared towards autonomy from external pressure and regime stability. Turkey's friends, such as Azerbaijan's President Abulfaz Elçibey, found themselves outmaneuvered by the likes of Heydar Aliyev, a senior member of the Soviet *nomenklatura* and one-time head of the KGB in the republic. Second, Turkish clout in regional security matters was limited. "*Tek Millet, İki Devlet*" ("one nation, two states") pleased nationalists in both Turkey and Azerbaijan, but its political relevance would prove questionable. In the Nagorno-Karabakh war (1992–94),[18] for instance, Ankara offered military assistance to the Azeris and sealed the border with Armenia to put pressure on Yerevan, but stopped short of intervening directly.[19] It was Russia, greatly enfeebled though it was, that played the arbiter for the next two decades. This was the case all the way to the autumn of 2020, when Turkey finally stepped into the fray and helped Azerbaijan recover control over much of the seven districts around Karabakh previously occupied by the Armenians. Back in the 1990s, however, Moscow had reasons to look at the Turks' overtures in the post-Soviet space with suspicion – and push back if needed – not least because it was fearful of its links to Muslim and Turkic groups inside the Russian Federation, notably the restless Chechens, but also oil-rich Tatarstan and Bashkortostan in the Volga Region.

The Balkans

Turkey's overtures to the Balkans enjoyed greater success. The end of communist rule and the collapse of former Yugoslavia allowed Ankara to improve ties with a host of regional countries. Tensions with Bulgaria gave way to cooperation under a friendship treaty signed in May 1992. In parallel, the two neighbors downscaled military deployments along the common border. Ankara advocated for the membership in NATO of both Romania and Bulgaria. Furthermore, it offered a helping hand – including through defense and military training agreements – to Albania and Macedonia, seen as potential allies against Greece. No wonder that Greek political debates in the 1990s were rife with fears of encirclement by an "Islamic axis." Those were clearly stoked by the war in former Yugoslavia, with Turkey perceived as a kin state of sorts for the Muslim Bosniaks. However, Ankara's preference was to work through NATO, rather than intervene unilaterally. Hikmet Çetin, foreign minister between 1991 and 1994, explicitly framed the conflict as one where universal principles were at stake, rather than a clash between religious communities.[20] Turkey contributed to NATO's interventions in both Bosnia (1995) and Kosovo (1999), as well as the peacekeeping missions that followed. In contrast to the AKP period, in the 1990s, Turkey trod carefully when showcasing its Muslim identity and appealing to the Ottoman past, aware of the costs. Particularly at a time when conservatives in Europe were raising voices against Turkish membership in the EU, which they conceived of as rooted in Christianity.[21]

The Middle East

Despite the fresh opportunities in Eastern Europe and Eurasia, Turkish policy makers throughout the 1990s, both in the military and the Ministry of Foreign Affairs, had to pay close attention to the Middle East. Threats were legion – whether real or perceived. The PKK hosted by Hafiz al-Assad's Syria, the Iran–Iraq war fought next to Turkey's borders, Kurdish refugees from northern Iraq crossing the border, ideological subversion by Tehran. The Turkish establishment adhered to a view of Arab countries and, to a lesser degree, Iran, that was a mixture of fear and condescension.[22]

Özal's perspective differed and he did not shy away from making that known, especially in his years as president. From early on, he pushed for engagement with the Middle East. To him, the region presented a source of commercial and strategic opportunities. Özal also believed Islam to be integral to Turkish identity, an asset rather than a burden, a theme the AKP picked up on in the 2000s. Between 1980 and 1985 alone, exports to the Middle East grew five-fold and reached the same level as those to the EC.[23] Neighboring Iran and Iraq took the lion's share, each about a third of the total. Saudi Arabia came next. The Gulf was seen as an attractive source of investment, particularly after Turkey liberalized its capital account.

The first Gulf War proved a critical test for Turkish policy. Özal was quick to denounce Saddam Hussein's invasion of Kuwait and did his best to bring Turkey into the US-led coalition. The military leadership was far from enthusiastic, however. There was stiff opposition in parliament and society too. It was only on 17 January 1991, the day Operation Desert Storm kicked off, that the Grand National Assembly authorized the use of the İncirlik airbase, near Adana, by the anti-Saddam coalition.[24] But the run-up to the decision, as Özal and Prime Minister Yıldırım Akbulut pushed for a parliamentary resolution, was riddled with tension. On 3 December 1990, General Necip Torumtay became the first chief of staff of the Turkish armed forces to tender his resignation before the end of his term.[25] To placate the generals and public opinion, the president was adamant Turkey would stay out of the actual fighting. Yet, by forcing Torumtay's withdrawal, he had scored a victory over the seemingly all-powerful military, mere years after the 1980 coup. This precedent would stick in the memory and feed the image of Özal as an opponent of the "tutelary regime." Though the AKP ended up opposing the second Gulf War in 2003, in effect siding with the risk-averse generals, they nonetheless paid homage to their predecessor's tough stand on the issue of civilian control of foreign policy.[26]

Operation Desert Storm was a mixed blessing for Turkey. It put on display the country's strategic value to the US, now that the Cold War was over. In the wake of the war, America appeared interested in renewing security ties with Ankara.[27] Unlike the Europeans who were giving Ankara the cold shoulder, the Bush Sr. administration treated its friend and ally with respect. At the same time, the longer-term consequences of the Gulf War were far less benign, at least from the perspective of the Turkish security establishment. In the immediate aftermath, over 500,000 Kurds massed at the border and demanded entry. Saddam's defeat and the imposition of a no-fly zone north of the 36th parallel by America and its allies led to the establishment of de facto autonomy for Iraqi Kurds. The PKK became ensconced in the Qandil mountain and could mount attacks against Turkish security forces across the border. Özal's response was to build ties to local Kurdish leaders in northern Iraq, Masoud Barzani and Jalal Talabani, and try to transform economic dependence into a security partnership. For many Turks, however, going along with the US was wrongheaded. National interest had been sacrificed in the name of the alliance with the Americans. Özal's implicit acceptance of Kurdish autonomy in northern Iraq, or even a federal state, set a dangerous precedent. Turkish politicians, including Demirel, started referring to "a new Sèvres," a flashback to the peace treaty concluded with France and Britain along with the rest of the Allied powers in August 1920, which saw the dismemberment of the Ottoman Empire. The Gulf War would come back to haunt relations with Washington for a long time.

A HAWKISH TURN

Domestic turmoil in the wake of Özal's death inevitably chipped away some of Turkey's foreign policy *élan*. Fears rather than ambitions shaped the country's posture and external behavior. Security-obsessed generals wrestled power away from civilian politicians while unstable coalitions undercut the influence of diplomats. Between July 1994 and June 1997, seven foreign ministers held office. The military and the National Security Council, controlled by the top brass again, asserted themselves as decision makers. Turkey's traditional defensive mentality, "the Republican Paradigm" in Malik Mufti's characterization, was back in play following the Özalian interlude.[28] Suppressing the PKK insurgency and keeping political Islam at bay became top priorities, along with checking attempts by foreign powers to leverage those two movements against Turkey. Deterrence and the selective use of hard power took center stage in foreign policy thinking. To secure its interest, Ankara was prepared to go it alone, acting outside NATO or the alliance with the US.

Going to the brink

The disputes with Greece over the Aegean, the Cyprus issue, and the Kurdish problem preoccupied Turkey's leadership. Their deeply held belief was that Ankara's best bet was not to shy away from flexing its military muscle. The ability to draw red lines or, if need be, take on adversaries one by one, represented the essence of the policy.

In the Middle East, unilateral military action was a continuation of the anti-PKK campaign on the Turkish side of the border. Turkish armed forces entered northern Iraq in the spring of 1995 and then twice in 1997 to chase militants and back Masoud Barzani's Kurdish Democratic Party. The following year Turkey mobilized its forces and threatened to invade Syria, which had harbored the PKK leadership since the early 1980s and also appeared to be teaming up with Greece.[29] To avert a showdown, Hafiz al-Assad agreed to expel Abdullah Öcalan, close the organization's bases, cease providing weapons and logistical support, as well as to cooperate with the Turks into the future. The Adana Protocol (October 1998), officializing the above commitments, came in the wake of similar deals struck in 1987, 1992 and 1993 but never implemented. The agreement granted Turkey the right to chase militants 5 km into Syrian territory should it come under attack. This time, Assad delivered, expelling Öcalan and closing PKK facilities near Damascus.[30] However, the Turks were never fully convinced he stuck to his end of the bargain to the full. Yet with the Kurdish militants gone, Turkey and Syria could proceed with strengthening their political and commercial links, the *leitmotif* of the AKP's neighborhood policy in the 2000s. The Adana Protocol would re-emerge from oblivion in 2019, when Russian President Vladimir Putin suggested it could serve as a basis for establishment of a security zone in Kurdish-populated northeast Syria. Turkey could chase away the PKK-aligned militias holding the area, in other words, but only in cooperation with the regime in Damascus.

Hafiz al-Assad caved in to the pressure, partly out of fear of coming between the Turkish hammer and the Israeli anvil. Turkey had deepened its alliance with Israel, Damascus' principal adversary, signing a military training and cooperation agreement in February 1996. Initially kept secret, it was leaked to the media. Two other agreements followed.[31] Beyond pressuring the Syrians, the turn towards Israel amounted to a rebuke of the Welfare Party by the military. In August 1996, Erbakan, a lifetime advocate for closer ties with the Muslim world[32] and harsh critic of both Israel and the West, paid a visit to Iran and signed a $23 billion gas contract, one of the largest deals involving the Islamic Republic. The reinvigorated alliance with the Israelis as well as the US ensured that the military, and not the Welfare–DYP (Refah–Yol) cabinet, dictated security policy. The push against Damascus and its ally Tehran therefore killed two birds with one stone. It dealt a blow to the PKK and ultimately secured the capture of Öcalan, in a joint operation with the US and Israel, following his failure to obtain asylum in Russia and Greece. It also contributed to the pushback against the Islamists, culminating in the intervention of 28 February 1997 ("post-modern coup") and the downfall of Erbakan.

The Greek–Turkish rivalry

Turkey resorted to similar tactics in the Aegean. In June 1995, the Grand National Assembly adopted a resolution by which any unilateral extension of Greek territorial waters to 12 nautical miles stipulated by the 1982 Law of the Sea convention would constitute a *casus belli*. The two neighbors quarreled about sovereignty of the continental shelf and airspace, as well as about the militarization of Greek islands opposite Turkey's shore. While Athens maintained that all such issues needed to be adjudicated by the International Court of Justice, Turkey insisted on settlement through diplomatic negotiations.[33] The most explosive dispute turned out to be the one over who has a title to islets in the Dodecanese archipelago. On 25 January 1996, Greeks from the nearby island of Kalymnos planted the national flag on Imia/Kardak, an uninhabited rock in the middle of the sea. Two days later, Turkish journalists disembarked and hoisted the red banner with a crescent in front of TV cameras broadcasting live. Greece scrambled its navy, as did Turkey. The Turkish armed forces in Northern Cyprus moved armored units towards the Green Line. A Greek military helicopter crashed on the islet killing its crew. It was only thanks to phone calls by US President Bill Clinton ("it was unthinkable that two great countries with a real dispute over Cyprus would actually go to war over ten acres of rock islets inhabited by only a couple of dozen sheep")[34] and his envoy Richard Holbrooke that the situation was defused.

Yet so long as Greece and Turkey were at each other's throats the Turkish EU bid would go nowhere. Athens wielded its veto in the EU Council and blocked any further upgrade of Europe's relationship with Ankara as well as the disbursement of financial aid.

Greece and Turkey clashed over Cyprus too. In 1997–98, the bone of contention proved to be Nicosia's contract with the Russian Federation for the delivery of S-300 surface-to-air missiles. Turkey responded angrily. The anti-aircraft system would both upset the military balance on the partitioned island and, more importantly, jeopardize Turkish security given the 300-km range of the missiles. In September 1997, Turkey's navy and coastguard started intercepting and searching foreign vessels, including those under the Russian flag, to prevent a delivery. This put a strain on relations between Ankara and Moscow, adding to the list of disagreements – from Turkish forays into the post-Soviet space, to the plans to develop pipelines bringing oil and gas from the Caspian to the regional and global markets through Turkey, to the restrictions on international shipping through the Bosphorus, to the expansion of NATO to Eastern Europe, which Turks endorsed. In the event, the US sided with Turkey. Ultimately, pressure by Ankara and Washington yielded a compromise whereby Greece agreed to deploy the S-300 on Crete, while the Greek Cypriots settled for another Russian-made missile system, TOR-M1, with a shorter range.[35]

While Turkey won a tactical battle, it had also been at a long-term disadvantage in the dispute with Greece. At the December 1997 summit in Luxembourg, the European Council (EU heads of state and government) decided to open membership negotiations with the Republic of Cyprus, in effect the Cypriot Greek leadership. That was a gain for Greece, a lobbyist for Nicosia in Brussels and a setback for Turkey which insisted that membership should be preceded by a just settlement of the Cyprus issue reflective of the interests of Turks in the north.

NEW HORIZONS

The outcome of the 1997 Luxembourg Council was deeply disappointing for the Turkish government which had hoped for a positive signal. Eastern European countries with much shorter democratic records and weaker economies took precedence, Turks believed. In response to the slight, Prime Minister Mesut Yılmaz inveighed that Turkey, let down, could freeze ties with the EU and look elsewhere for allies and friends.[36] He brought up the Turkic republics of Central Asia. This was little more than rhetorical bluster, however. The pipe dreams of Turkic unity had failed to bear fruit. The EU's economic and political traction grew, courtesy of the Customs Union. Ankara persisted with its membership bid as vigorously as ever.

At the same time, Turkey had succeeded in diversifying partnerships. Three-way cooperation with Israel and the US was a case in point. While the Europeans criticized Turkey's human rights record in dealing with the Kurds and tolerated PKK networks operating in their midst, Israel was backing it in the fight against the PKK. It provided weapons and valuable intelligence, assisting in the capture of Abdullah Öcalan in Kenya. The US largely gave Turks a free hand, putting strategic links before concerns about human rights. By contrast, Turkey and the EU were at odds on security matters. Ankara obstructed the EU's effort to forge a common defense policy, fearing this could marginalize its role in European affairs. At the 1999 NATO summit in Washington, DC, Turkey blocked proposals for a European Security and Defense Identity, an EU scheme envisioning the establishment of a rapid reaction force which would draw on the Atlantic Alliance assets in intervening in regional crises such as the Yugoslav wars.[37]

Turkey was also making headway with an unexpected partner, Russia. In December 1997, the same month the Luxembourg Council took place, the Russian state monopolist Gazprom and the Turkish government agreed to build an underwater pipeline through the Black Sea to ship natural gas to the port of Samsun and onwards to Ankara. That was the future Blue Stream, which, after it came online in 2005, turned Turkey into a major customer for Russian gas. In addition, Moscow did not push hard against the effort by Ankara (and Washington) to tap into Caspian gas and oil, which bore fruit with the Baku–Ceyhan pipeline agreed with Azerbaijan and Georgia in 1999 and completed six years later. Energy cooperation built on decisions Özal had made the previous decade.

Cooperation spilled over into the area of security. In early 1999, President Boris Yeltsin and Prime Minister Yevgeny Primakov overruled the Duma, the lower house of parliament, and declined to grant asylum to Abdullah Öcalan whom Syrians had put on a flight to Moscow (Mossad, reportedly, notified the Turks). Returning the favor, the Turkish government chose not to take Russia to task over the second Chechen War. On a visit to Moscow in November 1999, where he met Prime Minister Putin, Yeltsin's freshly anointed successor, Bülent Ecevit (then head of the coalition government) opined that the scorched-earth campaign waged by the Russian military was Moscow's "internal business." Turkey, home to a sizeable North Caucasus diaspora, would not back "terrorism."[38] This stance contrasted with Çiller's vocal pro-Chechen stance during the first war in 1994–96 as well as the calls for Muslim solidarity coming from the Islamists. The Russian–Turkish partnership, rooted in increasingly dense economic links and a shared belief in state sovereignty, was formalized through a declaration signed by foreign ministers Cem and Igor Ivanov in 2001.[39] In other words, the foundations of the Russian–Turkish rapprochement, which flourished under Putin and Erdoğan, had already been laid in the late 1990s.

THE HELSINKI SPIRIT

The period of coalition governments in the 1990s, remembered though it is as a time of turmoil and friction, cleared a major milestone on the way to Europe. The triple coalition of Bülent Ecevit's DSP, the Nationalist Action Party and Yılmaz's ANAP (1999–2002) delivered a breakthrough in relations with the EU. At the European Council in Helsinki on 10–11 December 1999, the fifteen member states of the Union agreed to promote Turkey to an accession candidate. This decision, though of no legal consequence, carried important symbolic significance. Exactly a decade after Özal had failed to extract a political commitment from the then EC, and two years following the 1997 Luxembourg debacle, the European leaders confirmed that Turkey could embark on membership negotiations and follow the same path as the likes of Poland, the Czech Republic or Estonia. "Turkey is a candidate country destined to join the EU," the summit's conclusions read.[40] Mesut Yılmaz, at this point deputy prime minister in charge of EU integration, had reason to be jubilant.

The breakthrough was a function of two factors. First, it recognized the reforms under way in Turkey. Second, the EU was emboldened by the remarkable improvement in Greek–Turkish relations thanks to "earthquake diplomacy." The Greek government provided humanitarian assistance after the devastating quake on 17 August 1999, as did large municipalities and the country chapter of the Red Cross. Turkey was then given a chance to reciprocate in September, when an earthquake of lower intensity shook Athens. Foreign ministers George Papandreou and İsmail Cem seized the positive momentum to kick off dialogue on bilateral issues.[41] Following the Imia/Kardak stand-off, the tensions in Cyprus and the Öcalan affair, Athens judged that a rapprochement could be a better strategy to deal with the Turks. Replacing the combative Theodoros Pangalos in February 1999, Papandreou – son of Prime Minister Andreas Papandreou who along with Özal had overseen another warming of ties in the late 1980s – saw Turkey's integration into the EU and democratiza-tion reforms driven by the prospect of membership as the best options on offer. Overnight, Greece turned from a naysayer to a staunch advocate for the Turkish bid to join Europe.

Expectations for democratic consolidation were not off the mark. Both Ecevit's coalition and the military prioritized EU membership. So did other players too, at odds with the authorities: the nationalist Kurds and, importantly, a faction from Erbakan's Islamists which splintered to form the AKP in August 2001. But this unity could not mask disagreements over how far Turkey could go in meeting the EU's conditions on sensitive issues such as minority rights and reaching a settlement on Cyprus. Ecevit, coming from the left, was prepared to move forward on the Kurdish issue – in contrast to the Nationalist Action Party as well as the generals, who feared ethnic separatism as much as what they styled as reactionary Islam (*irtica*). Yet he stood firm on Cyprus, having been the prime minister in office during the 1974 invasion of the island. In the short term, however, the desire to join the EU delivered changes. The pro-Kurdish HADEP took part and did very well in the 1999 local elections. In October 2001, parliament passed 34 constitutional amendments touching on issues such as gender equality highlighted in the European Commission monitoring reports. A new Civil Code guaranteed women's property rights in case of divorce. Three further packages adopted in 2002 abolished the death penalty in peacetime, allowed broadcasting in languages other than Turkish (addressing a long-standing Kurdish demand), and made possible the retrial of cases the ECtHR had found to be in violation of the European Convention of Human Rights.[42]

Europeanization generated momentum for change, opening the next chapter in the country's political history. In November 2002, a plurality of Turkish voters backed the AKP which, in contrast to its predecessor Refah, espoused the goal of EU membership. Yet Europe was not the only legacy Erdoğan et al. inherited. In the late 1990s, Turkey – "a double-gravity state" in the apt words of Philip Robins – opened to the Middle East and Eurasia while knocking on the EU's door.[43] Throughout the period, Turkish foreign policy remained Janus-faced: directed towards the West and the East simultaneously as well as oscillating between hard power and coercive diplomacy, on the one hand, and economic cooperation and multilateral engagement, on the other.

3
GOLDEN YEARS

"We have reached agreement. Inshallah, we are departing for Luxembourg." Foreign Minister Abdullah Gül emerged cheerful after a sit-down with his long-time comrade, Prime Minister Recep Tayyip Erdoğan.[1] That Monday, 3 October 2005, Gül was to meet his counterparts from the 25 EU member states. Less than a year before, in December 2004, the EU's leaders had given Turkey a conditional go-ahead to start membership negotiations. And now they were about to make good on their promise. The location carried special symbolism. After all, it was in Luxembourg where European leaders told Prime Minister Mesut Yılmaz "not yet" back in 1997. But now Yılmaz was history while Gül and Erdoğan stood for Turkey's future. The political duo with roots in political Islam, former acolytes of Necmettin Erbakan who had passionately championed an Islamic NATO and Common Market, had succeeded where their secular predecessors had failed. The AKP's performance in office, with three years of EU-inspired reforms and steady growth, delivered in spades.

By initiating accession talks, the EU acknowledged that a vast, majority Muslim country, whose territory was largely in Anatolia, had its place in Europe. All Turkey had to do to prove eligible was meet the formal criteria for membership: workable democratic institutions, commitment to the rule of law and human rights, an ability to withstand the competitive pressure of the EU economy as well as to take on board the organization's voluminous legislation. It was one of those nail-biting moments. Austria, where in excess of 75 per cent of the populace opposed Turkey's accession, had argued until the very last moment that the negotiations had to lead to some sort of associate status rather than full membership. But in the final lap, Ursula Plassnik, Vienna's first diplomat, had succumbed to pressure from her colleagues who saw this as a make-or-break moment. The EU had the chance to help Turkey democratize and forge an even stronger bond to a strategically important neighbor. Inshallah, there was an agreement indeed.

In retrospect, much of that optimism turned out to be premature. The thaw in Turkey–EU relations proved short-lived. Soon after their start, negotiations fell victim to the unresolved Cyprus issue, made worse by opposition to Turkish membership from major European states such as France. In the meantime, the AKP lost much of its reformist zeal and concentrated on a more pressing priority: surviving in the quagmire that was Turkey's internal politics and, ultimately, neutralizing, one after the other, its opponents and adversaries. Yet the opening of the early and mid-2000s represented much more than a squandered opportunity. Democratic momentum coupled with rising levels of prosperity transformed society's expectations and reshaped the political scene. Turkey's bid to formally join the EU might have hit a wall but arguably the connection with Europe grew deeper.

MUSLIM DEMOCRATS

How to describe the early AKP: a pro-democracy force or wolves in sheepskin? The answer depends very much on one's perspective.

To their detractors, coming mostly from Turkey's hardline secularist camp, what Erdoğan and his people were after was subverting the established order. Like Erbakan and the whole lineage of parties springing from the Millî Görüş movement,[2] the AKP's goal was to Islamicize political institutions and society. While the AKP talked democracy, human rights and Europe, its true mission boiled down to subverting the constitutional order and trampling over the sacred principles bequeathed by Atatürk some seven or eight decades prior. At no time was this rejection of the notion that a Islamist party should run Turkey starker than in mid-May 2007. Hundreds of thousands massed in Ankara, Istanbul, Çanakkale, Manisa and Izmir to protest against the imminent election of Abdullah Gül as president. "*Türkiye laiktir laik kalacak*" ("Turkey is secular and will remain secular") chanted the demonstrators at the so-called Republican Rallies. Hayrünnisa Gül, the headscarf-wearing wife of the AKP nominee, whom he had married while she was aged 15, did not belong in the Çankaya presidential palace, pure and simple. Among the multitude gathered at Atatürk's mausoleum in Anıtkabir, Ankara, was Deniz Baykal, the leader of the main opposition Republican People's Party (Cumhuriyet Halk Partisi, CHP). Had they not been prevented from doing so by the duties of their office, the sitting president Ahmet Necdet Sezer, a former judge and head of the Turkish Constitutional Court, and Chief of the General Staff Yaşar Büyükanıt would have no doubt attended too.

To their admirers, at home and abroad, the AKP came as a breath of fresh air. Conservative Turks saw Erdoğan and his team as part of their own. "In this country there are White Turks, as well as Black Turks. Your Brother Tayyip is from the Black Turks," Erdoğan exploited the (perceived) chasm between the Turkish establishment and the Anatolian masses who, to his mind, had always been the underdog.[3] To be sure, this brand of populism, of us-vs-them, was hardly a novelty in Turkish public life. Süleyman Demirel, hailing from İslamköy near İsparta in western Anatolia, had resorted to similar tactics in the 1960s and 1970s. But beyond his humble origins and religious piety, Erdoğan took credit for his stint as mayor of Istanbul as well as for his imprisonment following the "post-modern coup" of February 1997, for reciting a poem by nationalist writer and intellectual Ziya Gökalp.

The AKP had deeper roots in the conservative base than center-right stalwarts ANAP or the DYP, which voters linked to the corruption scandals of the 1990s. And the new faces in politics seemed to care more deeply about the common man (and perhaps woman, too): delivering better health care, improving housing and infrastructure, increasing access to education. Indeed, the AKP presided over a period of uninterrupted growth; from 2002 to 2007 GDP expanded at an average rate of 7.2 per cent, compared to 2.4 per cent in the 1990s. Economic Affairs Minister Ali Babacan was winning plaudits. (No wonder he was to tout his record in the late 2010s, amidst an economic slump, when he and Abdullah Gül launched a splinter party eager to chip away from Erdoğan's electorate.)

But, in its early years, the AKP appealed well beyond the core Islamist-conservative bloc of voters. To their secular critics' dismay, the party was welcomed by both the EU and the US. The political reforms Erdoğan, Gül and their associates advanced endeared them to liberal democrats in both Turkey and in the West. The market-friendly policies espoused by Babacan and his colleagues, continuing in the footsteps of Kemal Derviş' program to consolidate the financial sector and anchored to the goal of EU membership, secured them the backing of investors and industrial lobbies such as the Turkish Industry and Business Association (TÜSİAD). The fact that a political party could blend, in an ostensibly seamless fashion, Islam and commitment to democratic norms made pundits and policy makers in Washington, DC, bring back the talk of Turkey as a model for the Muslim world. Turgut Özal's pitch from the early 1990s was *en vogue* once more in the post-9/11 era. Instead of a clash of civilizations there would be an alliance of civilizations, an initiative co-sponsored by Erdoğan and Spain's leftist Prime Minister José Luiz Rodriguez Zapatero. Needless to say, the new Turkey stood as a representative of "the Muslim world," an aspiration which sat badly with Erdoğan-skeptics at the time.

The spirit of the era was captured by a widely read and much-quoted paper by the think-tank European Stability Initiative (ESI). Reflecting on the experience of the central Anatolian city of Kayseri, ESI analysts spoke of a new breed of "Islamic Calvinists."[4] Religion, industriousness and immersion into the global markets produced a class of capitalists and entrepreneurs steeped in tradition and oriented towards Europe at the same time. The Anatolian Tigers, born out of Özal's reforms in the 1980s, were transforming Turkey, no matter what the Sezers, Baykals or the Büyükanıts of this world thought, said or did. The AKP cadre certainly took a liking to this thesis. At the time, they marketed themselves as "Muslim Democrats," an analogy of Christian Democracy in Western Europe.[5] Back in 1997, Erdoğan had drawn a parallel to the US too: "As an individual my point of reference is Islam – just as Christianity is for President Clinton."[6] Yalçın Akdoğan, a popular columnist and advisor to the prime minister in the 2000s, coined the phrase "conservative democracy" (*muhafazakâr demokrasi*).[7] Ironically or not, his newspaper, *Yeni Şafak*, would turn into an anti-Western mouthpiece circulating conspiracy theories implicating America, the financier George Soros or "the interest lobby" in plots against Turkey.

In the 2000s, the AKP proved very successful in selling its narrative in the West: first and foremost, because there was substance to the reforms it carried out; second, because it had the right spokespeople. These included the mild-mannered Abdullah Gül, in charge of the foreign ministry from March 2003 until his move to the presidency. Fluent in English, and with international experience thanks to his employment at the Islamic Development Bank in Jeddah, Saudi Arabia, in the 1980s and 1990s, he was ideally placed to popularize Muslim democracy.[8] Then, the liberal intelligentsia in Turkey, fluent in Western languages, often educated abroad and part of international networks, sided fully with the AKP, especially during the face-off with the military and the Kemalist establishment around 2007–8.[9] They saw the party as the vehicle for Turkey's liberalization, integration into Europe as well as for coming to terms with the country's traumatic past. The influential TÜSİAD offered support, too, on account of the government's pro-EU agenda.[10] The AKP's alliance with Fethullah Gülen's movement, known as Hizmet (Service), also helped a fair bit. Wild conspiracy theories about links to the CIA and other foreign intelligence services aside, the Gülenists' pro-Western sympathies were no secret. The movement's assets and networks in the US, including contacts in media and academia as well as the charter schools, helped the AKP burnish its image. *Today's Zaman*, Hizmet's English-language daily set up in 2007, provided a tribune for liberal and pro-Western Turkish commentators as well as foreign pundits supportive of Ankara's EU aspirations.

So what was the early, pro-EU AKP: a force for good or a Trojan horse bent on taking over the Turkish state and handing it over to Erdoğan? The truth lies somewhere in between.

First of all, it is important to remember that, at least initially, the AKP's claim to speak for the majority of Turkish citizens was doubtful. At the watershed elections in November 2002, the party won by securing 34.42 per cent of the vote. The runner-up CHP garnered 19.39 per cent. There were no other parties which made it through the 10 per cent electoral threshold. That's why the AKP ended up with a comfortable majority in the Grand National Assembly (363 of 550 members in total). Put another way, the wasted votes of those 46 per cent, casting a ballot for parties which did not enter the legislature, decided the outcome. The AKP came much closer to the 50 per cent mark in the 2007 general elections but, ironically enough, lost ten seats. The high electoral threshold, a rule designed to curb democratic participation (i.e. keep the Kurds out of parliament), initially propelled the party forward but then worked to its partial disadvantage. Still, this was an achievement no other Islamist party had even come close to in Turkey's political history.

The AKP's commitment to democracy had to be taken with a grain of salt, too. It did talk the talk of promoting pluralism and empowering groups marginalized by the republican regime – not only religious conservatives but also Kurds,

Alevis and non-Muslim minorities. In his first term as prime minister, Erdoğan oversaw reforms such as the lifting of the prohibition on Kurdish-language education and broadcasting. In September 2005, a week before the EU foreign ministers endorsed the start of membership negotiations with Turkey, three Istanbul universities, Bilgi, Sabancı and Boğaziçi (Bosphorus), hosted an unprecedented conference on the 1915 Armenian Genocide. Though Erdoğan did not agree that the extermination and uprooting of Ottoman Armenians constituted an act of genocide, he welcomed the event. His supporters were even less thrilled: "They stabbed us in the back," murmured Justice Minister Cemil Çiçek.[11] Yet it was the judiciary which fought back and tried hard to stop the conference – postponed several times owing to threats to organizers – from happening. Without the EU prodding, in other words, it was doubtful that the Turkish government, of whatever stripe, would have taken such bold steps. While the early AKP had its fair share of members and fellow travelers[12] subscribing to a pluralist vision of democracy, with time the party, and Erdoğan himself, embraced a majoritarian concept. Democracy boiled down to the will of the nation (*millî irade*) expressed through the ballot box, and not to constitutional checks and balances protecting individual and minority rights. The longer the AKP stayed in office and the more power Erdoğan had in his hands, the stronger the majoritarian rhetoric became.[13]

Constitutional amendments making the president directly elected marked the first step towards the consolidation of power. Passed by the AKP in May 2007, the changes were endorsed by a referendum in October. They came in response to parliament's failure to elect a head of state, owing to the obstructionist tactics of the opposition CHP and President Sezer, who took extreme measures in order to block Gül's candidature. The governing party won a resounding victory at the plebiscite, with 68 per cent of the vote. The change kicked in only in 2014, after Gül finished his seven-year term under the old rules. But since Erdoğan – by then the unrivaled master of the Turkish political system – ran for the presidency, direct elections presaged an eventual shift to an executive presidency. In other words, the 2007 amendments made the emergent majoritarian, semi-presidential model all but a sure thing. From one extreme – the ramshackle coalitions in charge between 1991 and 2002 – Turkey veered to the other.

A large part of the responsibility lay with the opposition CHP. Whether it genuinely believed in democracy or was acting out of opportunism, the AKP was implementing changes responding to the EU democratic conditions. By contrast, under the leadership of Deniz Baykal, the CHP drifted in a nationalist direction. The party militated against the Annan Plan to end the partition of Cyprus, for instance.[14] Rather than challenge the early Erdoğan on his economic and social policies, or promise voters to do a better job in narrowing the gap between Turkey and the EU if elected, the hardline secularists chose to go down the identity politics path. Atatürk's republic, their message went, its unity and secular character were all in peril.

Headscarves in government offices and universities, the Kurdish language, restoring property to Christian minorities – all were anathema to the CHP at the time. Crisis justified radical, if need be anti-democratic, measures. "The party of Atatürk" openly flirted with the idea of military intervention to depose Erdoğan, as it had knocked out Erbakan a decade beforehand. The CHP was elated when, on the night of 27 April 2007, the military released on their website a memorandum containing statements such as: "The problem that emerged in the presidential election process is focused on arguments over secularism" and "Those who are opposed to Great Leader Mustafa Kemal Atatürk's understanding 'How happy is the one who says I am a Turk' are enemies of the Republic of Turkey and will remain so."[15] Disbanded after the September 1980 coup, the CHP had turned into a cheerleader for what Islamists and liberals alike decried as "the tutelage system." Onur Öymen, the party's deputy chair, was emphatic, the "General Staff's position is not different from our position. We put our signature below [the memorandum]."[16]

Importantly, the e-memorandum came on the same day the CHP petitioned the Constitutional Court to invalidate the vote in the Grand National Assembly for electing Gül on procedural grounds. The court's ruling in the so-called 367 Case precipitated early elections, which the AKP won fair and square.[17] Not only that, but its share of the vote shot up by 10 per cent. The story repeated itself the following year, when in March 2008 the main opposition party nodded in agreement as Prosecutor General Abdurrahman Yalçınkaya petitioned the Constitutional Court to close the AKP, on the grounds that it had violated the principles of secularism, and to ban its leaders, Erdoğan included, from politics. There was hardly a better way to give credence to the underdog narrative spawned by the Islamists than the CHP's wholehearted embrace of the military and judiciary's attempts to overturn the outcomes of democratic elections.

In a nutshell, from the perspective of the time, the choice between the backward-looking and at times xenophobic Republican People's Party and the AKP, which put forward a democratic and pro-European agenda was therefore clear-cut. While Baykal and his associates stood for the *ancien régime*, Erdoğan and Gül spoke the language of political liberties, democratic participation and Europeanization. It is no surprise that Western governments and individual observers following Turkey from the outside fell for the AKP narrative. There was simply nothing else on offer.

Even more important is that Turkish voters agreed – first re-electing the AKP on 22 July 2007, thereby resolving the political crisis triggered by Gül's candidacy, and then backing the constitutional referendum on 21 October.[18] By that point, the AKP had nearly doubled its support: from 10.81 million ballots cast in its favor in the 2002 elections to the stunning 19.42 million (a little under 69 per cent) in the plebiscite of 2007.[19] Who could deny they were the true representative of the "demos"? In the aftermath of the polls, the new Grand National Assembly elected Gül president on 24 August 2007.[20]

The popular mandate enabled Erdoğan to overhaul constitution-making. Up to 2007, the basic law had been changed on the basis of cross-party consensus in the Grand National Assembly and typically in response to EU conditions. The 2002 abolition of the death penalty would be the example. The direct election of the president – a change which the dogged opposition of the CHP against Gül's candidacy unwittingly helped – set a new trajectory. Fundamental provisions would be amended with a smaller majority, effectively by the AKP alone in 2007–11, and then ratified through a referendum. That was perfectly legal under the 1982 constitution. Politically, however, unilateral changes and the appeal to "the national will" opened a can of worms. The consequences became apparent in the 2010s.

LET THE GOOD TIMES ROLL

Why did the AKP rise to prominence and keep winning through the 2000s? The answer lies as much within Turkey as in what was going on beyond its borders. The country's new rulers benefited from a benign external environment. Before 2008, the global economy went through a boom. The EU had its best days too, with enlargement and deepening going full steam ahead, with Turkey on the bandwagon – despite opposition to its membership.

In the best three years, between 2004 and 2007, global GDP expanded by 4.2 per cent, with Turkey overshooting that trend by three points. Technocrats such as Economy Minister Ali Babacan and his successor Mehmet Şimşek, who no doubt would have felt comfortable in Özal's cabinets in the 1980s, took full credit. Anchored in a series of standby agreements with the IMF from 1999 onwards, the Turkish economy entered a phase of stability. Policies such as the commitment to fiscal discipline, the observance of the Central Bank's independence (in contrast to Erdoğan's meddling in the 2010s) and privatization of public assets bore fruit. By the end of the AKP's first term, in 2007, interest rates and the fiscal deficit had decreased dramatically. Public debt stood at 50–60 per cent of GDP. Historically low inflation and the appreciating lira drove up households' and businesses' confidence. As a result, spending and consumption shot up, as did imports into Turkey. There were costs, to be sure. As exports lagged behind, the current account deteriorated. To keep the books balanced and move along the growth path, the Turkish economy relied on the influx of foreign finance: purchases of bonds and shares, credits to local banks and receipts from privatization. Investors bought assets in banking (Unicredit, BNP Paribas, Fortisbank, Dexia), telecoms (Türk Telekom was acquired by a Lebanese company linked to the Hariri family in November 2005, the biggest privatization deal in the country's history), energy, retail, manufacturing and real estate. From just $10 billion in 2003, the cumulative size of portfolio investment rose to $100 billion four years later. FDI kept soaring: from overall stock of $103 billion in 2005 to $152 billion two years later. In 2007 an all-time record was set of $22 billion of FDI (roughly the size of the current account deficit). Obviously, cheap liquidity available on the global market prior to the 2008 credit crunch, plus Turkey's declining borrowing costs, played a key role.[21]

The golden era was a time of rapid trade expansion. Global flows rose by 6 per cent in 2007, outpacing world GDP by two percentage points. Turkey, like all other emerging markets, partook in the same trend. Between 2000 and 2008, its exports quadrupled and hit $132 billion. Growth in key economic partners, not only the EU, accounting for about a half of Turkish trade, but also Russia and the Gulf, buoyed by high oil prices, was also good news. But rapidly growing Turkey was bringing in more goods than it was sending out. In 2008, imports were valued at some $201 billion. Beyond the EU and Russia, a source of natural gas and oil, China became a prominent player on the Turkish market. Admission into the World Trade Organization in 2001 slashed tariffs and relaxed other barriers to Chinese exports.

Turkey appeared as a true winner from globalization. The turnaround from the boom-and-bust cycles of the late 1980s and 1990s, and the meltdown in 2000–1, could not have been more complete. Growth drove up the popularity of the AKP. As Yeşim Arat and Şevket Pamuk note, "government was able to provide popular public services such as healthcare, major public works (roads and dams), housing and direct cash payments to the poor."[22] However, as under Özal, the picture was more complex. Structural vulnerabilities such as a high current account deficit, inadequate domestic saving rates, dependence on foreign borrowing, inequalities in income distribution, unemployment and low participation of women in the labor force persisted. They would come back to haunt Turkey in the 2010s.

Economic buoyancy was key to the EU's enlargement, the external driver of reforms within Turkey. The EU's expansion into Central and Eastern Europe, in 2004 and then 2007 when Turkish neighbors Bulgaria and Romania made it in, was accompanied by a surge of growth, cross-border trade and foreign investment going from the West to the East. With automakers and other manufacturers setting up shop in Eastern Europe, following large retailers, banks and telecoms, talk of "the China next door" became common. European integration delivered prosperity to post-communist Europe.[23] But what really underpinned the EU's soft power at the time was the narrative that membership conditionality had transformed former authoritarian countries into thriving democracies. Neither recurrent corruption scandals, nor the gains made by populist and xenophobic parties from Warsaw to Sofia, would dent the story. The pro-European consensus seemed durable as were democratic institutions.

The success of enlargement to Eastern Europe fed into calls for further extension of the EU institutions and market order. Former Yugoslavia, now engulfed by the EU, was the next frontier, but the European Neighborhood Policy, launched in the mid-2000s, also aimed at building a "ring of well-governed countries" in the post-Soviet space and, possibly, the Maghreb.

This put Turkey in an awkward position. On the one hand, it had been waiting on the EU's doorstep longer than anyone else. Having submitted a membership application as far back as 1987 and having been a loyal member of NATO for years, Turkey was being leapfrogged by post-communist European countries with a much shorter record of multi-party politics and market economy and, in several cases, lower levels of wealth.[24] More shocking still, Greek Cyprus made it in, while the Turkish North was left in limbo. This outcome deepened suspicion that what informed EU's choices was religious and cultural bias. Christian Democrats' stiff opposition to Turkish membership, as well as the definition of Europe as rooted in "Judeo-Christian civilization" in the vaunted Treaty Establishing a Constitution for Europe (2004),[25] pointed to the same conclusion. Turkey deserved a privileged partnership but not full membership, a view which resonated with voters in key countries in the EU.

Yet, on the other hand, was enlargement truly a plot to exclude Turkey? Not according to the European Commission, which clearly supported the understanding that the same rules as in Central and Eastern Europe applied in its case too. As far as Brussels was concerned, the fulfilment of the democratic and institutional criteria spelled out by the 1993 European Council in Copenhagen opened the path to accession. The "new member states" had set a precedent and trodden a trail to membership that Turkey could follow too. The view that the EU perspective was essential to keep cooperation with Ankara, as well as domestic reforms, on track was shared by a number of member states, from the UK to Italy and from Greece to Poland. In short, rather than shutting the door, the Eastern Europeans' entry into the EU had left it ajar. In December 2002, the EU's leaders announced, again in Copenhagen, that in two years' time Turkey could start membership talks, provided the European Commission issued a positive assessment of the progress of reforms.[26]

AN AGE OF REFORMS

With the EU and Turkey drifting apart in the 2010s, it is easy to forget the profound impact Europe had on domestic politics and institutions during the AKP's first term. To open membership negotiations, a goal governments in Ankara had chased since the 1990s, Brussels required a country to have met in sufficient measure the so-called political criteria: functional democracy, the rule of law, human rights and the rights of the minorities. In 2001–2, the Ecevit cabinet passed through the legislature two harmonization packages, followed by another six under Gül and Erdoğan's premierships in 2003–4. Some 218 provisions in 53 laws were changed.[27] In 2004, lawmakers amended the constitution too: removing the reference to the death sentence, abolishing State Security courts and enshrining the precedence of international legal obligations over domestic law, all requirements put forward by the EU. Pressure from Brussels helped curb the AKP's conservative excesses too: in September 2004, the AKP withdrew proposed amendments to the Penal Code aimed at criminalizing adultery, which were deemed discriminatory against women.[28]

The two areas which mattered most were civil–military relations and the Kurdish issue. In both cases, the AKP had to perform a delicate balancing act, albeit of a different kind. Driving the army out of domestic politics was beneficial for the party, which had been deposed from power in its earlier reincarnation and had been threatened by the military establishment ever since. Civilian control was also a key part of EU conditions. But a decisive push against the armed forces could backfire and cost the AKP dearly. Accommodating the Kurds proved even riskier. Though a resolution of the issue would remove a hurdle on the way to the EU, and possibly win votes, it also risked alienating nationalist constituencies. The general elections in 2007 returned the Nationalist Action Party (MHP) to parliament after it doubled its support, no doubt as a result of the backlash against the pro-minority policies carried out by the government.

Though treading cautiously, the AKP made their move less than one year into their term in government. In October 2004, the Grand National Assembly voted to change the rules regarding the National Security Council (MGK), the transmission belt through which the military would dictate decisions and policies to the cabinet. The MGK would no longer be run by a general recommended as secretary-general by the chief of staff but by a civilian handpicked by the prime minister. Military appointees were removed from regulatory bodies such as the Radio and Television Supreme Council (Radyo ve Televizyon Üst Kurulu, RTÜK) and the Council on Higher Education (Yükseköğretim Kurulu, YÖK). Military courts could no longer try civilians, except over crimes co-committed with military personnel.[29]

As important as they were, these decisions did not spur a huge amount of controversy. They were justified by the goal of opening EU negotiations. The pro-European consensus, which also applied to many among the top brass and the Kemalist opponents of Erdoğan, provided sufficient cover. Importantly, Chief of the General Staff Hilmi Özkok (2002–6) was not in favor of army intervention in day-to-day decision making, too. Often that provoked the ire of his hardline colleagues, such as Yaşar Büyükanıt, who succeeded him in 2006 and made his mark with the e-memorandum of April 2007.[30] Lastly, there were other AKP policies causing greater concern, to do with culture and identity rather than institutional nitty-gritty: such as lifting the restrictions on headscarves in public institutions[31] or enabling graduates of *imam hatip* schools to enrol in universities. As culture wars raged on, the AKP gained ground, slowly but steadily, against the military.

Though the military and the AKP government were deeply at odds, they took care to avoid a head-on collision. The response to the army's e-memorandum showed that, apart from the hardcore secularists, the public had diminished appetite for generals taking the reins. The evolution from the 1997 "post-modern coup" was visible. Erdoğan and his side refrained from taking bold steps as well. The legislative reforms, such as the change of the MGK, had been adopted with support from the opposition. The military's cooperation was essential in making progress on the Kurdish issue. It was not until the Ergenekon trials – kicking off in mid-2008 and culminating with the arrest of General İlker Başbuğ, chief of the general staff from 2008 to 2010 – that the AKP "won" its political battle with the military.

Resolving the Kurdish issue proved a much more complicated and demanding task than making sure the military kept to their barracks. It required an intricate balancing act on the part of the government. The AKP had to respond to at least some of the Kurds' demands in order to meet EU conditions and woo support in the southeast provinces, where it tapped into a large pool of conservative votes. Erdoğan adopted a concilliatory tone, stressed religious bonds between Turks and Kurds and even spoke of the wrongs committed by the state. On 30 November 2002, the AKP's cabinet presided over the lifting of emergency rule in the southeast and the abolition of the supergovernor's office (Olağanüstü Hâl Bölge Valiliği, OHAL) that had overseen it since 1987.[33] That decision paid off. In the 2004 local elections as well as in the general polls

Table 1 Turkish political reforms, 2001–4

Date	Type	Major Changes
3 October 2001	1st Constitutional Package	34 amendments to the 1982 constitution
November 2001	New Civil Code	Gender equality in marriage
February/March 2001	2nd Constitutional Package	Constitutional amendments
2 August 2002	3rd Constitutional Package	Abolished death penalty, revised anti-terror law, allowed broadcasting in languages other than Turkish
3 December 2002	4th Constitutional Package	Operationalized previous reforma, revised Penal Code for torture
4 December 2002	5th Constitutional Package	Retail of all cases decided in State Security courts
May 2003	6th Constitutional Package	Adopted Protocol 6 of the ECHR, converted all death sentences to life imprisonment, repealed Article 8 of April Anti-Terror Law
July 2003	7th Constitutional Package	Revised the National Security Council
7 May 2004	8th Constitutional Package	Ten amendments of the constitution, freedom of press, priority to supranational treaties over domestic law, abolished State Security courts
24 June 2004	9th Constitutional Package	Changed Article 46 of the Penal Code, revised the Higher Education Board and Censure Board
25–26 September 2004	New Turkish Penal Code	Revised laws on violence against women and children, changed the penalties for various offences and redefined offences.

Source: Meltem Müftüler-Baç, "Turkey's Political Reforms."[32]

three years later, the AKP did very well against Kurdish nationalist candidates in the east and southeast. At the same time, concessions could not go so far as to alienate nationalist Turks and boost the numbers for the CHP and especially the MHP. Any bold move would also raise the risk of a pushback by the military and the Kemalist establishment, too. The army felt resentment for having its hands tied by the AKP and the EU and not being able to clamp down on separatism. The PKK was a key part of the equation as well. In pushing reforms, the government expected to extract counter-concessions by the militants, such as ceasefires like the one in August 2005, which would score points for the AKP. Whether the PKK was ready to go along with this depended on the level of trust in the government's sincerity and/or capacity to deliver. To complicate matters even further, the guerrilla organization's decision making remained notoriously opaque, with the military command in the Qandil mountain in Iraq on one side and Öcalan, the movement's undisputed leader, imprisoned by the Turkish state on the other.[34]

The multiplicity of players and interests explains why, in the 2000s, political reforms benefiting Kurds and the efforts at conflict resolution remained piecemeal. Thus, in June 2004, the public broadcaster TRT aired a program in Kurdish for the first time. Commercial TV stations followed suit in 2006 and, three years later, TRT launched a channel in the minority language. Yet what this amounted to was a display of goodwill rather than a legal breakthrough. The so-called Third Harmonization Package with the EU *acquis*, passed by parliament in August 2002, months before the AKP came to power, had amended Article 14 in the law on radio and television (Law 3954) to allow transmissions in "local languages."[35] Though restrictions on foreign languages in education were similarly removed in 2002, Kurdish (meaning the Kurmanji dialect spoken in Turkey) remained outside state schools until 2012, when it was permitted as an elective subject.

In theory at least, Kurdish activists would have benefited from changes whose primary goal was to help the AKP. With the Third Harmonization Package (January 2003), the Grand National Assembly amended the law, raising the bar for closure of political parties. From then on, the Constitutional Court required a three-fifths majority to rule that a certain party's existence broke the basic law. Thanks to this change, the AKP avoided a ban in 2008 by a single vote. The Democratic Society Party (Demokratik Toplum Partisi,

DTP), the latest in the line of Kurdish political groupings, was less fortunate. In December 2009, the Constitutional Court closed down the party, with the blanket argument that it threatened the state's unity because of its organic link to the PKK. It also expelled from parliament the DTP leader Ahmet Türk, along with Aysel Tuğluk, a prominent member of the same party.[36] The ban did not make a huge amount of difference, however. Kurds had already registered their next political platform, the Peace and Democracy Party (Barış ve Demokrasi Partisi, BDP) the previous year.

The tussle over the DTP happened against the backdrop of efforts to bring peace to the Kurdish-populated provinces. In June 2004, the PKK resumed its war against the Turkish government, ending five years of respite since Öcalan had declared a unilateral ceasefire in the summer of 1999. This time, as Gareth Jenkins notes, the strategy was not to achieve victory but rather to bring the authorities to the negotiating table.[37] The PKK formally dropped the call for an independent state, focusing instead on "democratic autonomy," a concept borrowed by the US activist Murray Bookchin whom Öcalan read in prison. Kurdish empowerment would be achieved through the decentralization of power in both Turkey and its Middle Eastern neighbors.

The AKP responded overall positively. Secret negotiations started in Oslo in 2008, though exploratory contacts dated back to 2005. The first face-to-face meeting took place in Brussels on 1 November 2007. It involved Emre Taner, undersecretary at MİT (the National Intelligence Organization, Millî İstihbarat Teşkilatı) and a native of Diyarbakır who had earned a reputation as a leading authority on the Kurdish issue within the state apparatus.[38] The PKK side was led by Mustafa Karasu, a Qandil-based commander and one of the organization's original founders. In the early stages, the DTP, along with Jalal Talabani, provided a channel to Qandil, too, while Turkish security officials were in touch with Öcalan.[39] The negotiations took place in secrecy. It was only in 2011 that the public became aware of them, thanks to recordings leaked to the media, most likely by the Gülenists.

But there was mismatch. Kurds put forward wide-ranging demands: a constitutional recognition of Kurdish (as well as other minority) identities, education in mother tongue, devolution and even autonomy. The fate of Öcalan was an item on the list as well. Nationalist Kurds demanded that he be moved from high-security prison to house arrest. That was too much for the average Turk to stomach. The AKP was cognizant of Turkish mainstream opinion, which was deeply hostile to anything smacking of federalization. Any concession would legitimize separatism, setting Turkey on a slippery slope. With a combative CHP and, after 2007, the MHP breathing down its neck, the best the government could offer was incrementalism.

Through the mid- and late 2000s, Erdoğan followed a two-pronged approach. He was no doubt engaging in good faith with the PKK in the Oslo talks, which remained open-ended and did not seem to touch on the most sensitive aspects of a settlement. Foreign governments, including Norway (the mediator), the US and the UK, along with the EU, rendered support. The harassment of pro-Kurdish parties was attributable to the conservative judiciary, arguably beyond the AKP's control. Erdoğan's rhetoric was conciliatory. At the same time, the government displayed resolve to wield repression to keep the PKK and its extensions at bay. The 2006 amendments to the Law on Fighting Terrorism from 1991 imposed restrictions on free expression, putting journalists and editors, and even publishers and printers, at risk of criminal prosecution for publication of material "disseminating propaganda by terrorist organizations." The Supreme Court ruled that the provisions of the law's Article 7 could be applied to 15–18-year-olds, that is Kurdish youth taking part in the annual demonstrations on Nowruz. If someone carried symbols linked to a terrorist group (implying PKK), they would be treated as a member of the organization.[40]

AKP policy was driven also by the tug of war with the military. Pointing at the uptick in PKK attacks, Chief of the General Staff Yaşar Büyükanıt was arguing that an operation in Iraq was a must. More than 100,000 troops were massed in the three provinces at the border, declared – apparently without consulting the government – a security zone. To put pressure on Erdoğan as he was fighting for re-election in the summer of 2007, the military insisted on parliamentary authorization. However, both sides sought to keep their differences within bounds. After the elections, the AKP, with a reduced majority and with the MHP back in parliament, yielded to the military's demands. An assault against the PKK was launched in February 2008 (Operation Sun, *Güneş Harekâtı*), the first such move since the US invasion.

The PKK played a complex game as well. In June 2004, it called off its 1999 ceasefire and resumed regular incursions into northern Iraq, the threat

Büyükanıt was pointing to. In the month preceding the launch of the secret talks with MİT, PKK attacks killed 40 Turkish servicemen. In a tactical switch, the organization fielded larger units of 200 fighters, instead of the normal squads numbering 6–8. At the time, analysts interpreted the PKK offensive as indicative of a rift between conciliation-minded Öcalan and the central command in Qandil, dominated by Murat Karayılan. In hindsight, it could have been a coordinated strategy.[41]

The relationship between Erdoğan and the Kurds, though they shared a common adversary in the state establishment, remained ambivalent. Both sides saw the benefit of working together, yet neither could trust the other fully, not least because they jockeyed for power at the local level. The so-called Kurdish Opening (*Kürt açılımı*) in 2009 was to shed light on the contradictory dynamics at play. As one seasoned Turkey watcher observed, for all its interest in resolving the conflict with the PKK, the AKP "never seemed to envision a 'Kurdish opening' that went beyond 'cultural rights.' "[42]

THE EU IMPASSE

The eviction of the military from politics and the constitutional and legislative changes to empower minorities would probably not have taken place without the EU. Though they responded to deeply felt needs within Turkish society and, most importantly, fitted the AKP's self-interest, the external anchor provided the necessary means and incentives for Erdoğan to move on and gain legitimacy. Conversely, when the pull of the EU faltered, democratic reforms lost momentum and ultimately ground to a halt. That became obvious in the case of the Kurdish issue, where the peace process engineered by the PKK and AKP, but opposed from the outset by all other Turkish parties, collapsed in the mid-2010s.

Why did negotiations between Turkey and the EU end in an impasse a handful of years after they started? There is blame on both sides.

The EU entered into negotiations without a shared vision of what the endgame should look like. It was a triumph of the belief in diplomatic process over substance. Member states remained divided on the issue of whether membership or some unspecified privileged partnership should be the end of the road. There were disagreements within governments too. In the first cabinet of Angela Merkel (2005–10), for instance, a grand coalition between Christian Democrats and Social Democrats, the former were skeptical of Turkish membership while the latter welcomed it. The same rift persisted in Merkel's second cabinet (2010–13), a partnership with the Free Democrats. In France, President Jacques Chirac thought Turkey's accession would be "desirable," though the road to it would be "long and difficult" in his estimate. But then came Nicolas Sarkozy with his blunt "Turkey is not European" in 2007. To him, the majority Muslim country was a better fit for the Union for the Mediterranean that he co-championed with Egypt's Hosni Mubarak. Sarkozy was certainly not alone. His views were popular in Austria, where both the mainstream and the far-right Freedom Party (FPÖ) firmly opposed Ankara's accession. Swedish Foreign Minister Carl Bildt held a different perspective: "the accession of Turkey would give the EU a decisive role for stability in the eastern part of the Mediterranean and the Black Sea, which is clearly in the strategic interest of Europe." But the most ardent supporter was British Prime Minister Tony Blair. Coming to Ankara in January 2007, shortly after the partial suspension of EU–Turkey talks, he argued: "Turkish accession [. . .] is not just important for Turkey itself but it is of fundamental importance to the future of Europe."[43]

Those disagreements left their imprint on the negotiating framework, a mandate issued to the European Commission by the member states. To accommodate the naysayers, it indulged in diplomatic hair-splitting: "The shared objective of the negotiations is accession. These negotiations are an open-ended process, the outcome of which cannot be guaranteed beforehand." In other words, something other than membership remained in the cards as well: "if Turkey is not in a position to assume in full all the obligations of membership it must be ensured that Turkey is fully anchored in the European structures through the strongest possible bond."[44] At the time, that formula was acceptable for the Turkish government as it delivered the goods. The AKP secured negotiations with the EU and a shot at membership, cementing their position domestically. Besides, the paragraph opened with the proviso that the talks were based on Article 49 of the EU Treaty, that is the stipulation that any European state respecting the values of the EU could become a member. Procedurally, the framework contained a catch. In terms of symbolism however, Turkey obtained institutional recognition as a bona fide European country.

But even at the start of the negotiations it was clear that they were headed for a deadlock. Cyprus proved to be the spoiler. At a referendum on 24 April 2004, the Greek Cypriots rejected, by a majority of 75.83 per cent, the Annan Plan for reunification. By contrast, close to two-thirds in the Turkish-held north voted in favor. Despite the island's lingering division, the Republic of Cyprus (in effect the Greek south) became a member of the EU on 1 May 2004. Thus, Nicosia obtained veto power in Brussels institutions to use as leverage vis-à-vis Turkey. Turkey, in turn, refused – and still does till this day – to recognize the Greek Cypriot-led government as representative of the whole island or indeed the Republic of Cyprus as established in 1960.[45] Ankara had closed its ports and airports to traffic coming from southern Cyprus ("Greek Administration of Southern Cyprus").[46] It also raised objections to EU–NATO cooperation, following Cyprus's accession. In a tit for tat, Nicosia blocked Turkey's inclusion into the European Defense Agency, a flagship of the EU's security and defense policy.[47]

The crunch came with the Additional Protocol to Turkey's Association Agreement with the EU. The legal instrument in question extended the 1995 Customs Union to *all* new member states, Cyprus included. But Turkey dragged its feet until June 2005, when its Permanent Representative in Brussels Oğuz Demiralp signed the protocol, to make sure its actions did not imply a recognition of the Republic of Cyprus. The Turkish authorities finally conceded in the interest of opening membership talks in October 2005. However, Ankara subsequently refused to implement the deal and open the Turkish ports and airports to traffic from the south of Cyprus. That triggered a unanimous decision, taken by all 25 member states in December 2006, to make Turkey's compliance with the additional protocol an opening benchmark for eight chapters in the negotiations.[48] From that point onwards, the talks went downhill, as did EU–Turkey relations more broadly. In December 2009, Greek Cypriots blocked six more dossiers, including Justice and Fundamental Rights and Energy, demanding that Turkey normalize relations with its neighboring state first. From a catalyst of conflict resolution, European integration turned out to be a complicating factor in the protracted dispute.

In fairness, Cyprus represented only the tip of the iceberg, however inappropriate the metaphor may seem in connection to the Eastern Mediterranean. Erdoğan's reluctance to give ground, notably by implementing the additional protocol, had to do with the domestic battles he was waging against his nationalist and hard secularist opponents. With the Kurdish question reignited, the polarization over the headscarf issue and the showdown concerning the 2007 election of Gül as president, yielding on the Cyprus issue, a shibboleth for a large number of Turks, could be an act of political suicide.

More importantly, Erdoğan had few reasons to expect that the EU would reward any courageous step. Sure enough, the eight chapters from December 2006 would have been unfrozen. But the Greek Cypriots, led by President Tassos Papadopoulos who bore responsibility for killing the Annan Plan in 2004, would be emboldened to put forward even more far-reaching demands. What is more, the EU's heavyweights were changing the rules of the game. In May 2007, Nicolas Sarkozy, Europe's leading Turkey-skeptic, entered the Elysée Palace as France's new head of state. Several weeks into his presidency, he single-handedly blocked four chapters, arguing that putting items such as Economic and Monetary Union, Agriculture or Regional Policy on the table prejudged the question of Turkish accession. That changed the entire logic of the talks. At the outset, member states agreed to an open-ended process which could lead to either full membership or an alternative arrangement. By then Sarkozy essentially ruled out accession.

The timing of France's snub could not have been worse. The AKP was amidst its campaign ahead of the pivotal parliamentary elections in July 2007. Europe was no longer the ally it had been earlier in the party's tenure. Turkish policy makers could not fail to appreciate that Sarkozy's views resonated with those of voters, in France as well as in other key countries. In 2005, a majority of both French and Dutch citizens rejected the (Treaty Establishing a) Constitution for Europe, in no small part driven by fears of expansion and by opposition to Turkey's membership in particular. That same year, France introduced a constitutional amendment obliging the president, Jacques Chirac, to call a referendum on the accession of future members of the EU. Chirac aimed at placating public opinion. If Turkey's accession were to be put to a vote, the answer would certainly be a resounding "non." To add insult to injury, the wording of Article 88.5 exempted Croatia, another country negotiating with the EU, from a plebiscite. Sarkozy's constitutional revision of July 2008 introduced a majority of three-fifths in each of parliament's two chambers as an alternative to referendum.[49] But with accession negotiations stalling, this otherwise positive move failed to make a profound difference.

Germany, Turkey's largest trading partner and home to a 2.7 million-strong Turkish diaspora, commanded a special place. On the one hand, German politicians, commentators, experts and civil society leaders (some, like the Green Party's Cem Özdemir, of Turkish heritage) paid disproportionate attention to Turkish politics. On the other, exclusionary rhetoric prevailed, from the opposition to membership by the CDU (Christian Democratic Union) and Merkel to bestsellers such as *Germany Abolishes Itself: How We're Putting our Country in Jeopardy* (2010) penned by Thilo Sarrazin, a social democrat. Sarrazin warned about the impending influx of migrants from Turkey and the Middle East leading parallel lives and eroding German society. Such views contrasted with the sociological reality of many Turks' and Kurds' integration, especially in comparison to other communities of emigrant descent in Western Europe. Yet in Turkey they shaped negative perceptions of Germany as awash with xenophobia and unabashed racism. In the minds of the AKP's conservative supporters, such anti-Muslim talk matched up with Europe's failure to weigh in on their side on issues close to their heart, such as the headscarf ban.[50] Another incident that made an impression on them was a lecture given by the German-born Pope Benedict XVI (Joseph Ratzinger) at the University of Regensburg in 2006. He quoted Manuel II Palaiologos, one of the last Byzantine emperors before the Ottoman conquest: "Show me just what Muhammad brought that was new and there you will find things only evil and inhuman, such as his command to spread by the sword the faith he preached."[51] To Pope Benedict, Europe was the heir to Christendom of old. It had to stay that way. The Turkish government's handling of relations left a lot to be desired too. On a visit to Cologne in February 2008, Erdoğan not only told a crowd of 20,000 Turks it was good to learn German but also described assimilation as "a crime against humanity." His words were heaven-sent for Turkophobes in Germany and beyond.

In the mid-2000s, Erdoğan was fond of saying that should the EU slam the door, Turkey would adopt Ankara Criteria to replace the Copenhagen Criteria. He meant that the country would democratize and achieve prosperity, with or without Europe. It turned out that the EU was a necessary condition, not an extra. The gradual weakening of Europe's pull towards the end of the 2000s sapped the AKP's reformist energy. The party's second term in 2007–11 was marked by a sustained effort to consolidate power. The inward turn came hand in hand with greater attention to neighbors in the Middle East, the Balkans and post-Soviet Eurasia. Shunned by Brussels, or rather by Paris and Berlin, Turkey reimagined itself as a regional hub as well as a player in its own right, rather than a supplicant forever stuck at the gates of the EU. The next chapter tells this story.

4
"ZERO PROBLEMS WITH NEIGHBORS"

Turkey is a European country, an Asian country, a Middle Eastern country, Balkan country, Caucasian country, neighbor to Africa, Black Sea country, Caspian Sea, all these.[1]

Ahmet Davutoğlu

Is Turkey looking West or East? Few other questions have been discussed at such length and with as much passion. It was part and parcel of the culture wars raging through the 1990s and 2000s. Secularists suspected religious conservatives of plotting to tether the republic to the Muslim world, a site of backwardness and strife in their eyes, as they were hollowing out Atatürk's legacy at home. The sight of Prime Minister Necmettin Erbakan in Tehran in 1996 sent chills down the spine of many Turks who feared the Islamic Republic set an example for what the future might look like. Conservatives, in turn, lamented Turkey's estrangement from the Middle East, denying its own Ottoman past and rich cultural heritage. Arriving on the scene in 2002, the AKP offered the perfect solution: Turkey did not really have to choose. It could seek membership of the EU while simultaneously doing business and nurturing political ties with Arab, Persian and Kurdish neighbors. Its imperial history was a unique asset, not a burden. "Turkey enjoys multiple regional identities," contended Ahmet Davutoğlu; "[t]he unique combination of our history and geography brings with it a sense of responsibility. To contribute actively towards conflict resolution and international peace and security."[2] The former academic, along with his paeans to the Ottoman golden era in the sixteenth century, came into the spotlight in 2009. Then he landed the job of foreign minister, having previously advised Erdoğan on international affairs. Davutoğlu came to be associated with a policy with a catchy label he had coined: "zero problems with neighbors" (*komşularla sıfır sorun politikası*).

Here was a confident, newly prosperous and politically vibrant Turkey. Conscious of its historical responsibility, it was ready to make a splash: colliding with Israel, an old-time ally, over Gaza, taking advantage of its temporary seat on the United Nations (UN) Security Council to broker a deal on the Iranian nuclear program, promoting trade and investment across the Middle East and North Africa, challenging the US but also joining forces with it on issues of common interest, vying with the EU as a power broker in Bosnia and Herzegovina, signing off on multi-billion-dollar energy projects with Russia. Davutoğlu, along with the AKP leadership at large, felt their time had come. While Europe and America were smarting from the aftershocks of the 2008 global financial crisis, the Turkish economy grew by over 8 per cent in 2010, hitting 11 per cent the year after. Booming trade and investment, popular culture exports, the Erdoğan brand winning over the proverbial Arab street all contributed to Turkey's soft power.[3]

To be sure, Turkey's outreach to its "near abroad" was nothing new. The AKP built on the inheritance of the late 1990s and early 2000s: the "earthquake diplomacy" with Greece and the opening towards Russia under the Joint Action Plan for Cooperation in Eurasia. It called for "multidimensional partnership" like that foreign ministers İsmail Cem and Igor Ivanov signed up to in New York in 2001, better links with Syria after the 1998 crisis and the deepening of the commercial relationship with Iran. The vision, originally articulated by Turgut Özal, was bearing fruit. What the AKP did, however, was to repackage this legacy in a new geopolitical narrative. The latter portrayed Turkey as an independent power driven by a historical mission, a *droit de regard* over neighbors. By the end of the 2000s, the country had embarked on a quest to assert its leadership in the Middle East and beyond.

MENDING FENCES

The Turkish policy of engagement had economic underpinnings. The flag followed trade. Between 1999 and 2008, trade with the Middle East expanded 9.3 times, from $4.25 billion to $39.33 billion. With Iran alone it grew nearly thirteen-fold, from $792 million to $10,228 billion. With Russia, twelve-fold from $2,962 to $37,847 billon. By comparison, volumes with the EU jumped "only" 3.6 times ($37,949 billion to $138,197 billion).[4] The share of EU trade declined to just 37 per cent of Turkey's imports and 48 per cent of exports in 2008. It had stood at around 55 per cent at the start of the decade. In the same year, 2008, the United Arab Emirates (UAE) came third among Turkey's export markets, behind Germany and the UK but ahead of Italy and France.[5] Iraq made it into the Top 10 too. Unlike the EU, Russia, China and the US, with all of whom Turkey ran a trade deficit, its exports to the Middle East[6] and the Balkans outpaced imports. If there was room for expansion, on the back of closer political ties, it was in such regional markets of the EU where competition was stiffer. Trade came hand in hand with investment. Central Bank calculations showed that Turkish FDI in neighboring countries shot up from $890 million in 2001 to $5,318 billion in 2009.[7]

As a result of its economic upswing, Turkey became a more attractive destination for business, leisure, employment and education. Kemal Kirişci, a political scientist, noted a rise in visits from neighboring countries, "from 168,000 in 1980 to close to 10.9 million in 2010, constituting an increase from 15 percent to 38 percent of overall entries into Turkey."[8] The bustling streets, bazaars and historic sites of Istanbul, the beach hotels in the Aegean and the Mediterranean coastal resorts, the shopping malls on the outskirts of border towns such as Gaziantep drew a steady flow of visitors from across a vast area spanning from Russia to Syria and from Bosnia and Herzegovina to Iran.

Though eventually the turn to the neighborhood emerged as an alternative to EU membership, Turkish policies borrowed heavily from Europe. Ankara launched a network of bilateral free trade agreements with neighbors in the Middle East and the Western Balkans. It also lifted visa requirements for a host of countries: including Syria (2007), Jordan (2009) and Lebanon (2010). Officials talked up the birth of the "Shamgen Quartet," a local response to Europe's Schengen from which both Turkey and its peers were separated by a visa wall.[9] Another innovation was the High-Level Cooperation Councils – a joint session of ministers of the Turkish government with their opposite number from a neighborhood country, from Greece to Iraq and from the Shamgen Four to Russia and Ukraine.

In addition to economic profit, the neighborhood policy pursued security as an objective. After the PKK resumed hostilities against the state in 2004, Ankara sought to co-opt regional actors in the fight against the militant organization. One of its main achievements in the 2000s was the rapprochement with the

Kurdistan Regional Government (KRG) in northern Iraq. In parallel, Turkey forged ties with central authorities in Baghdad, with Prime Minister Nouri al-Maliki declaring the PKK a terrorist organization in August 2007. Maliki followed the example of Iranian President Mohammad Khatami, who had signed such a deal with Erdoğan in July 2004. The implosion of Iraq, a consequence of the US invasion in 2003, posed a challenge to Turkey. It gave boost to Iran, a competitor, and to Kurdish separatism. But ultimately Turkey did its best to take advantage of the reshaping of regional order that followed the war.

A PIVOTAL COUNTRY

Security and economic interests aside, the AKP added its own ideological twist. What set Erdoğan, Davutoğlu and the rest apart from their predecessors in office was the rhetoric they espoused. In their view, the Ottoman past and shared religious identity bound (Sunni) Muslims across the Middle East, North Africa and the Balkans in a community of common destiny. Erdoğan's "balcony speech," delivered from AKP headquarters in Ankara the night he won a second re-election in June 2011, illustrates the thinking which went behind the policy:

> Believe me, Sarajevo won today as much as Istanbul, Beirut won as much as Izmir, Damascus won as much as Ankara, Ramallah, Nablus, Jenin, the West Bank, Jerusalem won as much as Diyarbakır.[10]

Beyond rallying the AKP base, his words advanced the understanding that the Ottoman legacy gave Turkey a unique advantage on the international stage. İbrahim Kalın, chief advisor to Erdoğan, put it eloquently: "Turkey's soft power is different from that of other countries," he wrote. "In the larger Euro-Asian landmass, the common denominator for Turks, Kurds, Bosnians, Albanians, Circassians, Abkhazians, Arabs, Azeris, Kazakhs, Kyrgyz, Uzbeks, Turkmens and other ethnic groups, as well as Armenian, Greek, Jewish and Assyrian communities is the Ottoman experience they have shared and built together." Kalın characterized the past ("historical depth") as key to "Turkey's new geopolitical imagination and the new possibilities in the global political system"[11] More than simply an expression of national interest, foreign policy was grounded in identity. That was why, Kalın opined, social groups and individuals had a role to play in fostering links with neighbors, along with government officials and diplomats.[12]

Nowhere was Turkey's ambition as far-reaching as in the Middle East, a region the AKP felt naturally attached to. In the words of Philip Robins, one of the most perceptive observers of Turkish foreign policy, it "project[ed] itself as a 'central' country in a new international subsystem broadly occupying space in the eastern Mediterranean."[13] The promotion of cross-border integration aimed at enhancing Turkey's status as a "pivotal state" (*merkez ülke*) and regional leader. Davutoğlu himself spoke of the country's calling to be an "order-setter" (*düzen kurucu*) in the Middle East and North Africa. Its cause (*dava*) was a "Grand Restoration" (*Büyük restorasyon*).[14] The borders with Iraq and Syria, in particular, a product of the post-1918 map making by the colonial powers, had to be blurred and ultimately rendered obsolete – just as the EU had done in Europe – by way of trade, investment and people-to-people contacts. Arab-majority countries to the south were no longer a source of threat or even Turkey's "Other," as they had been for generations of secularists, but a pathway to influence and prestige in global politics.

FRACTIOUS ALLIES

Turkey's ambitions put it at odds with the United States. Back in the early 1990s, when Özal was calling the shots, Ankara's regional activism extended Western influence. But two decades down the line, Turkey turned into a headache. The Bush administration faced a country increasingly likely to work with US adversaries in the Middle East and Eurasia. What had happened?

Divergence between the US and Turkey was far from preordained in the AKP's early days. The party took power at the height of the US-led war on terror. The Bush administration hailed the moderate Islamist party friendly to the West winning power in Ankara. In contrast to Erbakan's cosying up to "rogue states" such as Iran or Libya in 1996–7, this time around the US felt it could count on a partner. By late 2002, Turkey had deployed 1,300 troops in Afghanistan and ISAF (the International Security Assistance Force), NATO's mission on the ground, was under the command of Major General Hilmi Zorlu, a Turk. It also came into the crosshairs of jihadi terrorism. On 15 November

2003, trucks laden with explosives drove into two synagogues in Istanbul. Five days later, suicide bombers struck the British consulate and the local headquarters of HSBC, an international bank. The attacks, linked to al-Qaeda, left in their wake 57 killed and 300 wounded.

It was against the backdrop of 9/11 and the war on terror that Americans took on board the idea of Turkey as a model, a notion Özal had proposed a decade prior. "[The Bush administration] has much invested in the success of Turkey's new government," reported the *Financial Times*, quoting sources from Washington, DC, "which it is holding up to other countries around the Muslim world as a model of Islamic administration in a secular democracy."[15] President Bush himself was on the same wavelength. As he put to the audience at Galatasaray University during a NATO summit in Istanbul on 29 June 2004: "Your country, with 150 years of democratic and social reform, stands as a model to others, and as Europe's bridge to the wider world."[16]

Such rhetoric notwithstanding, at the policy level, the relationship between Ankara and Washington proved difficult. The Bush administration hoped to enlist Turkey as an ally in the invasion of Iraq. As in 1991, the American air force could carry out sorties and airstrikes from İncirlik and even stage a land invasion from Turkey. The AKP leadership was, by and large, sympathetic and even prepared to go counter to public opinion. For Gül, the prime minister at the time, and Erdoğan, George W. Bush's resolve to overturn the regime in Iraq presented an opportunity to strengthen ties with America and, potentially, register a win against the military, which opposed intervention and was not thrilled about Turkey being showcased as a model Muslim nation either. On 1 March 2003, following a five-hour debate, the Grand National Assembly voted down the government bill which would have allowed 62,000 US troops to be stationed in Turkey.[17] Seventy-two MPs from the AKP sided with the opposition, while nineteen abstained. "The AK Government is now badly shaken, AK leader Erdoğan and P.M. Gül humiliated, and US–Turkish relations under severe strain," cabled US ambassador Robert Pearson.[18]

Later on, Erdoğan would claim credit for the rebellion to woo anti-American public opinion in both Turkey and the Middle East.[19] Yet, back in those days, he found himself in a comfortable position. While formally Erdoğan was the party leader, he did not hold a parliamentary seat, and therefore was not eligible to take over as prime minister, until he actually won a byelection on 9 March 2003. The ban on his participation in politics dating back to 1998 worked in his favor. But at the time, the rebellion within the AKP ranks led by the speaker Bülent Arınç (who used a procedural trick to declare the motion defeated) and Prime Minister Gül came across as a rebuke to Erdoğan who was working for a "yes" behind the scenes. He was "humiliated" in the words of Ambassador Pearson.[20] Ex-president Süleyman Demirel described the motion in parliament as a matter of incompetence: "Ninety per cent of the public was against the war. They [the government of Turkey] should have told you that they simply could not open a northern front, but would support you in other ways. Then they wouldn't have had to push the (failed) March 1 motion in Parliament."[21]

The invasion itself, shattering the Iraqi state and empowering Kurds, strained ties further. Hilmi Özkok, chief of the Turkish general staff, spoke of "the greatest crisis of confidence" between the two militaries. His comment referred to an incident on 4 July 2003 when US troops detained Turkish commandos in Sulaymaniyah, Iraqi Kurdistan, and brought them to Baghdad handcuffed and hooded for questioning. The bone of contention was the status of Turkish military personnel in the area. The US wanted them under its command, while the Kurdish leaders Masoud Barzani and Jalal Talabani would rather have Turks leave. Turkey, both the government and the public at large, feared the US was oblivious to the threat posed by the PKK and complained about discrimination against Turkmens in northern Iraq. For the Turks, America's policy, from the failure to ensure the cohesion of Iraq to the pressure against Iran, created regional turbulence which brought damage to national interest. Ironically, it drove up the Islamic Republic's stock. The mood of the time was captured by the Turkish expert Soner Çağaptay in a 2007 testimony before the US Congress:

> It is ironic that every time the U.S. State Department says the right things on how we are together with Turks in fighting the PKK and we will deliver security, promising the right things, that same day the Iranians bomb PKK camps. So this is how you read the news in the Turkish press: front page, big headlines, "Iranians Have Bombed PKK Camps" – 12th page, one column, "The U.S. Has Said They'll Support against the PKK." In this regard Iranians walk the walk and they make it look as if the Americans are only talking the talk. And that's a huge problem.[22]

Çağaptay had a point. A Pew survey from 2006 showed that only 12 per cent of Turks viewed the US positively.[23] The bitter memories from the first Gulf War and especially its aftermath, and the near universal rejection of the Bush administration's interventionism by Turkish citizens of all stripes, from the Islamist conservatives to the dyed-in-the-wool secularists to the liberal left, shaped such views.

Still, in the mid-2000s, it was not Erdoğan but rather his domestic rivals who stood as America's most fervent critics. In April 2005, for instance, President Ahmet Necdet Sezer went to Damascus to meet President Bashar al-Assad. At the time, the American ambassador in Ankara, Eric Edelman, was calling on the Turks to side with the West's demand for a Syrian withdrawal from Lebanon.[24] Yet Sezer ignored US opposition. Anti-Americanism thrived among the military and the nationalist (*ulusalcı*) left. In March 2002, while Bülent Ecevit was still in power, the National Security Council's secretary-general, Tuncer Kılınç, argued that Turkey had to seek alliances with Russia and Iran.[25] He was speaking at a symposium hosted by the Turkish War Academies, with former presidents Kenan Evren and Süleyman Demirel in the audience. "The EU will not take us as a member," Kılınç contended. Such views resonated with the top brass too.[26] Five years later, at a gathering of the Atatürkist Thought Association (Atatürkçü Düşünce Derneği), popular with retired officers like himself, the ex-general called for Turkey to leave NATO too.[27] By then he had become one of the faces of Turkish Eurasianism. Originally developed by interwar Russian émigrés and popularized in the 1990s by Alexander Dugin, the doctrine posited that Russia and fellow nations in Eurasia constituted a unique civilization whose mission was to stand up to the "mondialist" Gospel spread by the West. Dugin's ideas entered Turkey thanks to the Workers' Party led by Doğu Perinçek, an ex-Maoist[28] who had become a stalwart of uncompromising secularism.[29] Though Perinçek and Erdoğan were bitter opponents in the 2000s, they later on ended up in the same camp.

While the AKP government had no strong feelings for Russia, it looked with skepticism at the Bush administration's moves in the Black Sea challenging the Kremlin. With the expansion of NATO to Bulgaria and Romania, a decision Ankara favored, the alliance faced demands to embrace other countries run by pro-Western governments, such as Ukraine and Georgia, both of whom had experienced a "color revolution" in 2003 and 2004/5 respectively. The Turkish government, on the other hand, was against upgrading NATO's role in Black Sea maritime security and for strict adherence to the 1936 Montreux Convention limiting access by warships from states outside the littoral. It sought to eschew quarrels with Russia as well as to uphold the Russian–Turkish condominium in the Black Sea. To that end, Ankara invested in regional initiatives such as BLACKSEAFOR designed to keep the US at an arm's length.[30] Turkey's nightmare scenario involved a head-on conflict with the Russians, provoked by the Bush administration, where it would be left to fend for itself.[31]

There was therefore a healthy dose of *Realpolitik* underlying Ankara's choice to distance itself from the US and tilt toward Russia and Iran. Challenging the West though they were, neither of those states posed a vital threat to Turkey. The Iranian nuclear program, which came into the spotlight in 2002, did not change the calculus. As an American foreign policy expert noted, "there are few reasons why Iran would attack Turkey given their levels of cooperation. Turkey would most likely only be at risk if there were an American and Israeli confrontation with Iran."[32] Similarly, Moscow was rapidly becoming an economic partner, with energy trade booming after the launch of the Blue Stream pipeline in 2005, as well as a political interlocutor. Putin's Russia was no longer an existential threat, unlike the Soviet Union at the height of the Cold War.

TURKEY IN THE MIDDLE EAST

The Middle East became the main arena where Turkey enacted its new foreign policy aimed at securing its position as a regional leader.

Israel–Palestine

Initially, despite its Islamist roots, the AKP adhered to the conventional Western policy vis-à-vis Israel. Turkey enjoyed a positive reputation: the only Muslim-majority state to recognize the state of Israel in 1949[33] as well as a security partner thanks to an agreement signed in 1996. Erdoğan harnessed the momentum, paying a visit in May 2005 and laying a wreath at the Yad Vashem Holocaust memorial in Jerusalem. And in November 2007, President Shimon Peres addressed the Grand National Assembly in Ankara. So did

Mahmoud Abbas, the head of the Palestinian Authority, adding to Turkey's credentials as an honest broker. In the Turkish capital, Peres and Abbas signed an agreement for a Turkish-funded industrial plant in Gaza. At that point, Erdoğan could boast links to all parties in the conflict: not just Israel and Fatah but also with the latter's bitter rival Hamas.

The AKP's links to Hamas, an offshoot of the Muslim Brotherhood, steered Turkish policy in a new direction. The visit by the Palestinian organization's leader Khaled Mashal in February 2006 caused an uproar both in Israel and the US which, like European countries, had blacklisted the Islamist movement as a terrorist organization. But Erdoğan stuck to his guns, retorting that Hamas had won fair and square the Palestinian legislative elections the previous month. He had compelling arguments for the Israelis too. Turkey could act as go-between with Hamas. Thus, the Turkish government mediated in talks for the release of Gilad Shalit, an Israeli soldier captured by Palestinian militants in July 2006.[34] President Peres thanked Erdoğan personally upon Shalit's release in late 2011, forgetting for a time the strained relations with Ankara.[35]

Erdoğan sought to leverage Turkey's friendship with Damascus in relations with Israel. In the mid-2000s, Ankara mediated in secret Syrian–Israeli talks which touted the prospect of a (partial) withdrawal from the Golan Heights, occupied by Israel since 1967, in exchange for the conclusion of a formal peace treaty. If successful, the deal would measure up to the Camp David Accords between Israel and Egypt midwifed by the Carter administration. The indirect talks became public in May 2008, after delegations from both countries visited Istanbul.[36] Both Israel and the Syrian regime welcomed Turkey's effort. Bashar al-Assad was keen to break the international isolation imposed on Damascus in the wake of the Lebanese Prime Minister Rafik Hariri's assassination (in 2005), attributed to Syrian agents. Turks had a piece of the action all along. In September 2008, when French President Nicolas Sarkozy paid a landmark visit, Erdoğan turned up in Damascus too, as did his ally, Hamad bin Khalifa al-Thani, the Emir of Qatar. Turkey acted as Syria's advocate before the West as well as an economic partner, capitalizing on a free trade agreement from 2007. In April 2009, the two militaries trained together – a development few could see coming a decade beforehand.[37]

On 22 December 2008, Prime Minister Ehud Olmert came to Ankara in hope of concluding a deal on the Golan Heights. Even though Syrian Foreign

Minister Wallid Muallem failed to show up for direct negotiations, reports suggest the two sides came close to the finish line.[38] Five days later, the Israeli army attacked Gaza (Operation "Cast Lead"), giving the Turks no advance warning according to Turkish officials.[39] What followed was Erdoğan's show-down with President Shimon Peres at the Economic Forum in Davos in January 2009. "Nobody can even speak to a tribe leader so loudly and in front of the international community, and not to the leader of the Republic of Turkey," said he as he stormed out of the stage, becoming at this instant the Arab world's hero. The return of Likud's Benjamin Netanyahu as prime minister in the spring of 2009 sealed the fate of the "peace process," making Ankara's mediation irrelevant. The *Mavi Marmara* crisis of May 2010, when Israeli commandos took over a Turkish ship[40] bound for blockaded Gaza and killed nine of the activists on board, dealt the final blow to the Turkey–Israel partnership. Erdoğan accused Israel of "state terrorism," suspended military cooperation and eventu-ally expelled the Israeli ambassador in September 2010.[41]

After Davos and *Mavi Marmara*, Erdoğan basked in the glory of being the proverbial Arab street's newly discovered hero. Arabs' admiration for "the Conqueror of Davos" was coupled with disdain for their own leaders colluding with the Israelis. To made matters worse, Israel entered Turkish domestic strug-gles. As part of their advocacy of ecumenism, the Gülen movement had also argued for good relations with Israel. The post-2013 purge of the *cemaat* and then the failed coup in 2016 gave license to government-allied media to double down on anti-Semitism. That overshadowed the re-establishment of full diplo-matic ties in 2015, for which the Obama administration lobbied hard.[42] In less than a decade, Turkey turned from a friend of Israel to a fierce critic, if not adversary.

Iraq

Post-invasion Iraq proved more fertile ground for Turkey. Immediately after the 2003 invasion, the situation across the border raised concern. The Turkish government and the military watched warily the Iraqi state implosion, the outburst of sectarian conflict but, above all, the rise of Kurdish nationalism. The KRG's newly gained autonomous status played on Ankara's fears of a Kurdish state turning into an irredentist hotbed, with the PKK already stationed in the Qandil mountains. Iraqi Kurds, moreover, set their sights on the city of Kirkuk as a future capital, leading local Turkmens to solicit help from Turkey. As in 1991, the US invasion disrupted Iraqi oil transit through Turkey and raised the specter of a refugee influx. The Shiʿa community's ascent in post-Saddam politics, coupled with Iran's sway over the country, caused concern as well.

On the positive side, Saddam's removal put an end to sanctions and embargos, and helped reintegrate Iraq into the regional and global economy. Reconstruction kicked in, with Turkey being one of the main beneficiaries. The US military absorbed Turkish goods and services on a large scale. One estimate suggested that 40 per cent of exports from the industrial hub of Gaziantep went to the Americans.[43] Thanks to the US occupation, Iraq became Turkey's most important export market in the 2010s, with the KRG taking the lion's share. Turkish contractors profited from the reconstruction of northern Iraq, building new airport terminals in Erbil and Sulaymaniyah, a university and shopping malls. The vast majority of foreign businesses in the Kurdistan region in Iraq KRG came from Turkey. And in the 2010s, the Kurdish region started to export oil to world markets via Turkish territory.[44]

Ankara identified the KRG as an ally against the PKK. While the Turkish military distrusted Masoud Barzani, accusing both him and his rival Jalal Talabani of being in cahoots with the PKK, the AKP followed a more nuanced approach, reminiscent of Turgut Özal's outreach to elites in northern Iraq in the 1990s. The partnership worked. Barzani and Talabani endorsed the Turkish army's cross-border operation against the PKK in early 2008. At the same time, Erdoğan's policy of strengthening economic and political ties with the KRG dovetailed with the secret negotiations with the PKK, which in time culminated in the "Kurdish opening" of 2009.[45]

Ankara's ambitions in Iraq grew over time. In the 2010 elections, it backed the Iraq National Movement (known as al-Iraqiya) led by Ayad Allawi, a former prime minister and a Shiʿi, which drew support from Sunnis. But, though al-Iraqiya won the highest number of seats, the prime minister's office went to Allawi's rival Nouri al-Maliki. Kurdish parties emerged as kingmakers, delivering al-Maliki the prize in return for a promise to extend the KRG over disputed regions. Turkey suffered a double setback. Al-Maliki, backed by Iran, pushed against Turkish allies, such as Vice-President Tariq al-Hashimi, who sought refuge in Ankara in 2012. And Iraqi Kurds were handed an opportunity to expand territorial control, including over Turkmen-populated territory. Turkey was having a hard time in turning its economic footprint and local networks into proper political clout, a lesson it was to re-learn in Syria with the Arab Awakening.

Iran

In the 2000s, Turkey developed closer ties with Iran, much to the chagrin of the Bush administration in the US. Following in the footsteps of the $23 billion deal for the delivery of Iranian natural gas sealed by Erbakan in 1996, Erdoğan oversaw a contract allowing the Turkish Petroleum Corporation (TPAO) to explore fields in the South Pars region.[46] Another deal he concluded, in February 2007, secured Tehran's acquiescence for the potential shipment of Turkmen gas to Europe through its territory. It gave a boost to the government's ambitions to establish Turkey as a transit corridor. At the same time, supplies of Iranian gas were frequently disrupted by commercial disputes. The Turks fought their corner too. Erdoğan used his first visit to the Islamic Republic in July 2004 to bargain prices down, leveraging the imminent launch of the Blue Stream pipeline.[47]

The fight against Kurdish separatism also brought Ankara and Tehran closer. Having aided the PKK in the past, Tehran was confronted by its offshoot, the Free Life Party of Kurdistan (PJAK), operating from the Qandil mountain in northern Iraq.[48] In return, Turkey promised to expunge Mujahedin-e Khalq, a group fighting the Islamic Republic, from its territory. The Turkish and the Iranian militaries conducted joint operations against Qandil. Yet, much like its ally Syria, Iran never fully discontinued ties with the PKK. Turkish officials suspected Tehran of holding the Kurdish card up their sleeve in order to use it to put pressure on Ankara in the future. The arrest and then release of Murat Karayılan, the PKK's executive leader, by the Iranians (August–September 2011), followed by a truce between PJAK and Tehran, raised eyebrows.[49]

Iran and Turkey went on vying for influence in Iraq and, less overtly, in Syria. Off the record, Turkish policy makers and diplomats sold their neighborhood strategy to the skeptical West as a means to wean the regime in

Damascus from Iran.[50] Turkey hedged its bets too. At NATO's Lisbon Summit in 2010, it agreed to join the US-proposed initiative for a missile shield, a move directed against Iran and Russia. Two years later, an early warning radar was installed at the Kürecik base near Malatya, once used as a surveillance outpost to monitor the Soviet airspace. The system is owned and operated by the US army. While Turkey championed, along with Brazil, a compromise on Iranian nuclear file in May 2010 and later facilitated the so-called P5+1 talks, it invested in an insurance policy against Tehran.[51]

The Iranian regime had good reason to be apprehensive about the spread of Turkey's cultural influence. Visiting Istanbul and the coastal resorts was an eye-opener for educated, middle-class Iranians craving greater freedom at home. Turkish TV series had the same effect on those who couldn't afford the trip. Turkey stood as an example for what Iran could have been under a more open political system and with friendlier relations with the West. (The same, of course, applied as much to Arabs as Iranians.) One of those Iranians was Neda Agha-Soltan. Shot by the Basij, the paramilitary force under the Revolutionary Guard, she came to symbolize the anti-government protests in the summer of 2009 over the disputed presidential elections ("the Green Movement"). Neda had met her boyfriend, Caspian Makan, during a holiday in Turkey. Their plans to be in Istanbul again at the end of June were cut short by that fateful sniper shot. Neda had told Caspian she was dreaming of finding employment in Turkey.[52] But official Turkey was at odds with the country that inspired Iranian youth. Erdoğan recognized Mahmoud Ahmedinejad's re-election, signaling that Ankara was not in favor of regime change.

Throughout the 2000s, the US watched with concern Turkey's engagement with Iran and Syria, as well as Hamas. As early as 2003, Congressman Robert Wexler, co-chair of the Friendship Group with Turkey, went on record: "I can say that we were shocked by Turkey's dialogue with Syria and Iran. We wondered if Turkey was changing axis."[53] Still, there were other voices in the Pentagon, in the State Department and the think-tank circuit which stressed Turkey's lasting importance for US policy in the region. Barack Obama's charm offensive during a well-publicized two-day visit to Turkey in April 2009, part of a tour of Europe and the Middle East following his inauguration, left an impression too. In a speech delivered at the Grand National Assembly Obama evoked his late father's Muslim heritage and called for finding common ground between the West and the world of Islam (of which Turkey was the chosen representative).[54] The US president's discourse hit all the right notes as far as the AKP was concerned. Yet the visit failed to turn the clock back. The *Mavi Marmara* incident substantiated the narrative of Turkey's changing axis to "rogue states" such as Iran.

The Europeans' reaction was more nuanced. Opposing the intervention in Iraq, France and Germany favored negotiations with Iran over its nuclear program, like Turkey and unlike the firebrands in the Bush administration. Together with France and Germany, Turks contributed to the United Nations Interim Force in Lebanon's peacekeeping mission in Lebanon after the 2006 war between Israel and Hezbollah. The decision to send 1,000 Turkish blue helmets could be credited directly to Erdoğan, who faced criticism by President Sezer at the time ("it is not Turkey's responsibility to protect others' national interest").[55] On one level, Ankara's turn to the Middle East testified to the failure to EU integration. On another, Turkey and the Europeans could cooperate on security in the Middle East, a notion which went down well in Paris, London and Berlin.

THE TURKISH–RUSSIAN ENTENTE

Another big story about Turkey in the 2000s, even if overshadowed by relations with the EU and the Middle East, was the rapprochement with Russia. Though foundations were laid in the late 1990s, links thrived under the AKP. The main driver was trade. In 2005, the Blue Stream pipeline came online, turning Turkey into the second-largest customer of Russian natural gas after Germany in the years to follow. Thanks to hydrocarbons, Russia established itself as the top importer on the Turkish market. Blue Stream was a three-way partnership between Gazprom, Turkey's BOTAŞ and the Italian supermajor ENI. The official launch of Blue Stream in the Black Sea town of Samsun (17 November 2005) saw Erdoğan side by side with Russian President Vladimir Putin and Italian Prime Minister Silvio Berlusconi. The new pipeline constituted a major coup for Moscow. It spoke to Russia's reinvention from a shadow of the once almighty Soviet Union, ridden by endless crises and diminished by the West, to an energy superpower expanding its presence on lucrative foreign markets. "[Blue Stream's] launch is yet another step towards creating a single energy system in Europe," Putin remarked, underscoring Turkey's prospects of becoming an "energy bridge between East and West."[56] The Russian leader touted extending Blue Stream westwards to the Balkans and Italy, another major customer, or towards the south, with Israel as an end point.[57] ENI, as well as Berlusconi, basked in the glory of having seen through a challenging engineering project, with pipes laid at a depth of some 2.2 km over a 396-km stretch. Italy, an advocate for Turkey's EU aspirations, was claiming a stake in the dynamic economy on Europe's edge.

At the time, Turkey was discussing with the European Commission and leading oil and gas firms such as Austria's OMV the Nabucco pipeline, designed to pump gas from Azerbaijan and possibly other suppliers such as Iraq, Iran and Turkmenistan. Ankara was in a position to choose between extending Blue Stream (Putin's option) and the EU and US-favored alternative, the Southern Gas Corridor. In either case, Turkey would become a transit country, cashing in on the economic and geopolitical dividends. Among other things, the partnership with Russia allowed BOTAŞ not to meet its commitment to take the entire volume of gas contracted as part of the Blue Stream agreement, a thorny subject which delayed the launch of the pipeline. Russians accommodated Turkey in other ways too. They opened doors even more widely to construction companies which had been gaining foothold in the Russian Federation and across the former Soviet Union since the 1990s. In 2011, Gazprom solicited Ankara's permission to use the Turkish exclusive economic zone (EEZ) in the Black Sea for South Stream, the pipeline Russia proposed in the mid-2000s as an export route to Europe.

Natural gas diplomacy showed that the Russian–Turkish partnership had its roots in geopolitics. Blue Stream, and later South Stream, were conceived by the Russian government and Gazprom as a means to bypass Ukraine, which was leaning towards the West after the Orange Revolution of 2004–5. Both Putin's Russia and Turkey had objections to US unilateralism. In his oft-cited speech at the 2007 Munich Security conference, Putin berated the Bush administration for its doctrine of regime change through intervention, weaving the war in Iraq and the color revolutions in Georgia and Ukraine into a single storyline. By that point, Erdoğan and decision makers in Ankara more broadly had grown critical of US policy in the post-Soviet space. Ankara vetoed giving NATO a more prominent role in Black Sea naval security, though it formally supported the Pact's enlargement to former parts of the USSR. There was an

EU dimension too. Both Russia and Turkey shared a similar plight. Immersed in the European economy yet kept out of the EU's institutions and often cast as "the Other." They joined together in "an axis of the excluded," as Fiona Hill and Ömer Taşpınar argued in a provocative paper.[58]

Russia and Turkey had mostly laid to rest former misgivings they held about each other. It was the West, not Moscow, which Ankara viewed as patrons of the PKK. Having won in Chechnya, Putin's regime did not see Turkey as stirring trouble among the Muslims in North Caucasus, Tatarstan and so on. In short, both recognized one another as status quo players with (partially) overlapping interests. On top of this, Putin earned the appreciation of some quarters of Turkish society, with Şenkal Atasagun, director of the National Intelligence Organization, thought to be an early admirer.[59] "A Kemalist in the Kremlin," enthused the daily *Hürriyet* when the Russian leader came on a state visit, one without a precedent.[60]

Burgeoning ties between Moscow and Ankara drew the attention of experts, diplomats and academics, but broader audiences took note only during the 2008 war in Georgia. Erdoğan faced a predicament. Georgia had been a friend and partner since independence, one of the only two immediate neighbors Turkey actually got along with in the 1990s, together with Bulgaria. It also hosted a section of the Baku–Tbilisi–Ceyhan (BTC) pipeline, transiting Azeri oil to a terminal on the Turkish Mediterranean coast, as well as the Baku–Tbilisi–Erzurum (BTE) gas pipeline.[61] Both of those pipelines were a product of Turkey's cooperation with the US, with the Clinton and Bush administrations putting an effort to connect producer countries in the Caspian and Central Asia to Western markets. But provoking Russia into a head-on military collision which could easily spin out of control was not Ankara's preference either. In the event, Erdoğan chose to accommodate Moscow. The government delayed the entry through the Bosphorus into the Black Sea of two American medical vessels, USNS *Comfort* and USNS *Mercy*. The decision caused consternation. It was the first time, nearly two years before the *Mavi Marmara* incident, that talk about Turkey changing axis gained momentum in Washington, DC. In September 2008, Vice-President Dick Cheney made a point of not visiting Turkey during a regional tour in the aftermath of the Russian invasion of Georgia.[62] Erdoğan tried to burnish his reputation as peacemaker. The day after French President Nicolas Sarkozy, representing the

EU, and Dmitry Medvedev signed a peace plan (12 August), he turned up in Moscow and unveiled a "Caucasus Cooperation and Stability Platform," an initiative to stabilize the region. Though it did not yield any palpable results, the platform aimed to show that Turkey was still relevant in the South Caucasus. In reality, Turkey had recognized Russia's primacy in the security affairs of the area.

THE ILL-FATED ARMENIAN OPENING

That did not imply that Turkey lacked ambition. In September 2008, Abdullah Gül and Foreign Minister Ali Babacan landed in Yerevan, where Turkey was playing a qualifier game for the football World Cup. Though Armenian fans booed the Turkish national anthem, "football diplomacy" presented an opportunity for negotiating a way out of the political impasse between the two countries. The common border had been blocked in 1993, as a punishment for Armenian occupation of Nagorno-Karabakh (see Chapter 2). But now the "zero problems" impulse in Turkish foreign policy, boosted by the informal trade and even labor migration from the Republic of Armenia into Istanbul, set the scene for engagement. Normalization was in tune with the lifting of the taboo over the *Meds Yeghern* ("the Great Crime," as Armenians refer to the massacres and deportations) since a ground-breaking academic conference in 2005. Even though the AKP objected to labeling the extermination and expulsion of Armenians during the First World War as genocide, democratization and the expansion of the freedom of speech allowed critically minded intellectuals and commentators to use the term as they pleased – as well as to mark 24 April, the Armenian Genocide Day. And the 2007 assassination of Hrant Dink, a prominent Turkish Armenian publisher and advocate for reconciliation, had rallied civil society behind the peace initiative. Started by Gül, the "Armenian Opening" culminated on 10 October 2009 with Ahmet Davutoğlu and Eduard Nalbandyan signing a set of accords in Zurich to lift the border blockade and establish diplomatic relations. Their American, Russian and French opposite numbers, Hillary Clinton, Sergey Lavrov and Bernard Kouchner, co-chairing the Organization for Security and Co-operation in Europe Minsk Group on Karabakh, attended as external guarantors. Though the Russians were present, objectively the breakthrough would diminish their influence. Normalization with Turkey diminished Yerevan's dependence on Moscow; it was a way to show the country was not "a vassal of Russia."[63]

Yet hope proved short-lived and the initiative crashed, sobering proof of the constraints Turkey's regional activism had to confront. There were spoilers Gül and Davutoğlu had to reckon with: the opposition, Azerbaijan, and Erdoğan. The Republican People's Party (CHP) campaigned against the Armenian Opening from the very outset. Deniz Baykal, the leader, remarked that he would rather have the football game played in Baku. The Nationalist Action Party (MHP) was true to form, too. Devlet Bahçeli lashed out against US President Barack Obama after he made a reference to the *Meds Yeghern* (though not "genocide") during his 2009 visit to Turkey. But while the AKP could bypass its political adversaries, as it did on other occasions, Azerbaijan – on paper "the little brother" – put a spanner in the works. Erdoğan asserted that there would be no ratification of the Zurich Accords unless Armenians withdrew from the seven districts adjacent to Karabakh they had occupied in the early 1990s. The position had been coordinated with President Ilham Aliyev of Azerbaijan, months before the signature of the agreement. Erdoğan, who was not thrilled with the Armenian Opening to start with, dug in. President Serzh Sargsyan, a native of the disputed region, "suspended" the ratification too in April 2010.[64] An opportunity had been squandered. A decade later, in the autumn of 2020, a changed Turkey – run by a coalition of the AKP and MHP – was to intervene militarily in Nagorno-Karabakh, along with Azerbaijan, to inflict a bitter defeat on Armenia. Hard power substituted the "zero problems with neighbors" diplomacy of the earlier era.

Where Turkey succeeded was in consolidating the three-way partnership with Azerbaijan and Georgia. Coming of age with the BTC (opened in May 2005) and BTE pipeline (December 2006), it also spilled over into other areas such as road infrastructure and even defense. The so-called Southern Gas Corridor linking the Caspian and the EU never ceased to animate debate in Turkey. Here, Turkish interests aligned with those of the US. Diversification of energy supplies and economic integration, moreover, were compatible with the EU's agenda in the region, as spelled out in the European Neighborhood Policy. Arguably, cooperation with the Georgians and Azeris helped Ankara to level the playing field vis-à-vis Russia. For pro-Western Georgia, as well as for Azerbaijan, links to Turkey were a necessary hedge against the Russians too. Yet the fact of the matter was that Moscow had much stronger clout than Ankara in South Caucasus affairs. Even with a military which underperformed in the 2008 war, it showed a willingness and ability to fight and prevail in regional conflicts. In dealing with Georgia, Russia also demonstrated the ability to deploy tactics such as trade embargos, political pressure and information warfare. (The same arsenal would be unleashed against Turkey, for a brief period in 2015–16, with Moscow emerging victorious.) Russia held sway over both Armenia and Azerbaijan owing to the Nagorno-Karabakh conflict. Compared to other post-Soviet regions, such as Central Asia which had attracted Turkish interest in the 1990s, the Southern Caucasus remained on the radar. But with the Middle East going up in flames post-2011, it slipped down the list of external priorities.

BACK TO THE BALKANS

Erdoğan's balcony address of June 2011 made a special mention of Sarajevo. This was not unexpected; the Balkans had come into the spotlight of Turkish neighborhood policy. In October 2009, Foreign Minister Davutoğlu delivered in the Bosnian capital what appeared at the time to be a programmatic address. In it he heaped praise on the area's Ottoman legacy. "During the Ottoman state," Davutoğlu observed, "the Balkan region became the center of world politics in the sixteenth century. This was the Golden Age of the Balkans."[65] Once the imperial order had unraveled in the nineteenth and early twentieth century, the region had become a periphery contested by bickering great powers. Now Turkey was bringing the Balkans back into the spotlight, just like it was doing in the Middle East and the Caucasus, remedying past injustices. Needless to say, his words caused an uproar. Imperial nostalgia was nothing short of a red rag for nationalists. A Serbian academic by the name of Darko Tanasković, a professor of Oriental Studies at Belgrade University, wrote a book decrying Neo-Ottomanism as a vehicle for Turkey's drive for regional dominance.[66] A lively discussion ensued. *Strategic Depth*, Davutoğlu's treatise, was translated in local languages, starting with Greek in 2010.

Contrary to common belief, Turkey was not *returning* to Southeast Europe. It had been active since the 1990s, thanks to NATO's intervention in Yugoslavia and the links Ankara had developed with a number of the countries in the region. The EU's expansion helped trading ties with Romania and Bulgaria, which became members in 2007. The same was true of Greece, which bene-fited from the rapprochement in the wake of the 1999 "earthquake diplo-macy." By the late 2000s, the three countries accounted for more than two-thirds of Turkey's turnover with the region. Investment was flowing both ways. In 2006, the National Bank of Greece (NBG) acquired a 46 per cent stake in Finansbank, a large Turkish lender, rising to 80 per cent the following year.[67] Just as the EU–Turkey Customs Union facilitated commercial ties, NATO provided a platform for security cooperation. Turkish armed forces collaborated with Balkan militaries, with Romania and Bulgaria joining the alliance in 2004 and Albania and Croatia five years later. Human links were strong. Diasporas from Balkan countries acted as a bridge – from Bulgarian Turks who had found refuge in Turkey during the 1989 exodus and often held dual citizenship to people from Sandžak (a region shared by Serbia and Montenegro), to Macedonian and Kosovar Albanians immigrating in the 1950s. Since Özal's days, TİKA had delivered development assistance, while the Directorate of Religious Affairs (Diyanet) engaged in training imams and funding local Islamic communities – in part to counter the influence of the Gulf.[68] As elsewhere, the AKP inherited a network of connections which posi-tioned Turkey in the midst of Balkan politics and economic life.

What the "zero-problems" phase in Turkish foreign policy brought, apart from historic nostalgia, was an ambition to troubleshoot regional problems. Bosnia and Herzegovina drew Davutoğlu's attention. Years of efforts by the EU and US at resolving the institutional deadlock and producing a more coherent structure in a complex polity established under the 1995 Dayton Peace Accords had failed. Turkey stepped in as mediator. Davutoğlu initiated a series of meet-ings with the foreign ministers of Serbia and Bosnia, Vuk Jeremić and Sven Alkalaj. Those yielded some result. For instance, in March 2010, the Serbian parliament condemned the 1995 Srebrenica massacre, the worst atrocity on European soil since the Second World War. After much delay, Serbia and Bosnia and Herzegovina exchanged ambassadors. Davutoğlu claimed credit for both developments. But positive steps aside, three-way diplomacy failed to bring about any breakthrough on the Bosnian internal set-up. Turkish endeavors did not involve a crucial player: Republika Srpska, the Serb-majority entity. In addition, in the 2010 elections for a collective presidency, it bet on

Haris Silajdžić, a Muslim Bosniak politicians, who called for the abolition of Republika Srpska as a "genocidal creation." Silajdžić lost to Bakir Izetbegović, the son of late President Alija Izetbegović, who had led Bosnia during the war. Turkish activism provided an excuse for Republika Srpska's leader Milorad Dodik to deepen his links with Russia, which comfortably slipped into its habitual role as patron of Orthodox Slavs in the Balkans.[69]

If there was one achievement that stood out in Turkey's overtures in the Balkans, it would be forging ties with Serbia. The two had been on opposite sides during the wars of the 1990s, when ordinary Turks sympathized with Bosniaks and Kosovar Albanians while governments endorsed NATO interventions. But, in October 2009, President Gül made his way to Belgrade, the first Turkish leader to do so since 1986 when Yugoslavia was still around. His opposite number, Boris Tadić, who had already been to Ankara in 2007, reciprocated. In April 2010, Gül hosted a summit with Serbia and Bosnia and Herzegovina (represented by Haris Silajdžić, the then chairman of the collective presidency). Serbia saw Turkey as a promising economic interlocutor. The two governments signed a free trade agreement in June 2009. Thanks to this, as well as the size of its economy, Serbia became Turkey's leading trading partner in former Yugoslavia. And as their neighbors, Serbs developed a taste for Turkish cultural imports: the *Magnificent Century* (*Muhteşem Yüzyıl*), a TV series about Süleyman the Magnificent, became an instant hit the moment it was first aired in February 2012 (half a year before it arrived in Bosnia).[70] Incidentally, it was Süleyman who led the conquest of Belgrade for the Ottomans back in 1521.

In the Balkans, Turkey offered no alternative to EU membership. Rather, local countries seized the economic and diplomatic opportunities from engaging with a large and fast-growing neighbor as an add-on to relations with the West. While Davutoğlu's historical nostalgia shaped Turkish policy, the response from the region rested on pragmatism. And even if Turkey presented itself as a rising power and a peer of the EU and the US, a claim it carried over into the 2010s, it lagged behind in terms of resources and appeal. Lastly, substance differed from rhetoric. On critical issues, such as the Kosovo dispute, NATO enlargement and even the EU expansion into the Balkans, Turkey stayed on the same page as the West, in contrast to Russia which chose the role of a spoiler.[71]

Ahmet Davutoğlu remained in charge at the Ministry of Foreign Affairs for a little over five years. When he moved on to become Erdoğan's successor as prime minister, in August 2014, his vision for a regional order already lay in tatters. The Arab Spring and the war in Syria changed the rules of the game. Engagement with neighbors through diplomacy, trade, investment and culture gave way to an interventionist policy focused exclusively on the Middle East and North Africa, a subject examined in the next chapter.

5

A RUDE AWAKENING

Erdoğan's victory lap. That's how international media portrayed the Turkish prime minister's visit to Egypt, Tunisia and Libya in September 2011. The Middle East and North Africa were living through once-in-a-generation changes. Popular uprisings had swept away autocratic leaders who had been around for decades; first Tunisia's Zine El Abidine Ben Ali and then the octogenarian Hosni Mubarak in Egypt. The Libyan dictator Muammar Qaddafi was cornered by rebels in his hometown of Sirte. In Yemen and Syria, Ali Abdullah Saleh and Bashar al-Assad appeared to be hanging by a thread. Erdoğan, by contrast, was basking in glory, with history on his side. "The Turkish state is in its core a state of freedoms and secularism," he told Western journalists ahead of his trip. "The world is changing to a system where the will of the people will rule. Why should the Europeans and Americans be the only ones that live with dignity? Aren't Egyptians [. . .] also entitled to a life of dignity?"[1] Having gotten rid of its own *ancien régime*, Turkey charted a path to the future for the downtrodden masses in the Middle East and North Africa. The Ben Alis, the Mubaraks and the Assads were a relic of the past; the future belonged to parties and leaders willing to emulate Erdoğan's success in marrying "formal democracy, free market capitalism and (toned down) conservative Islam."[2]

Yet, in less than three years, it was all over. The Arab Spring's promise proved stillborn and, as a result, Turkey's star lost its sparkle. In Egypt, the military overthrew the Muslim Brotherhood, ideologically aligned with the AKP. In order to survive, the Syrian regime triggered a devastating civil war which sucked in all regional powers, including next-door Turkey. Ankara faced a perfect storm: a refugee influx on a scale unseen since the 1920s, the rise of the self-styled Islamic State in Iraq and the Levant (ISIS), and an affiliate of the

Kurdistan Workers' Party (PKK) seizing large chunks of northeast Syria. Syria put under strain Turkey's alliance with the US and exacerbated authoritarian backsliding in its domestic politics. The quest for security took precedence over the export of democracy. The vaunted Turkish model meanwhile suffered a car crash.[3] What follows is the story of the rise and fall of Turkey's bid to remake its neighborhood in its own image.

THE ARAB SPRING

In the 2000s, Turkey's engagement with the Middle East and North Africa proceeded at two levels. The Turkish leadership, notably Prime Minister Erdoğan, built strong ties with incumbent elites in the region. The Erdoğans famously vacationed with Bashar and Asma al-Assad in Bodrum in August 2008, at the peak of the Turkish-mediated talks between Syria and Israel. In November 2010, Erdoğan was awarded the Al-Qaddafi Human Rights prize, a recognition of thriving business and political ties between Ankara and Tripoli. The prime minister had landed at the Libyan capital's airport where a new terminal was to be built by a Turkish contractor, TAV. The award came weeks before a Tunisian street vendor, Mohamed Bouazizi, set himself on fire, the event which eventually triggered what came to be known as the Arab Spring. Societies in the region demanded the end of the current regimes, which were blamed for economic decay, endemic corruption and ruthless repression.[4] And Turkey was seen as an alternative to the depressing status quo, not as an ally of autocratic rulers. On top of all this, the AKP had ideological and organizational connections to the Muslim Brotherhood (al-Ikhwān al-Muslimūn), the transnational Sunni movement that presented a viable alternative to the ossified secular nationalist regimes.

When crowds took to the streets in Tunis, Cairo, Benghazi and in major Syrian cities, the Turkish leadership was presented with a stark choice between the resurgent masses, calling for justice, accountability and better life chances, and the status quo. Foreign Minister Ahmet Davutoğlu described the dilemma the following way: "[w]e either could maintain ties to these oppressive rulers, or we could support the popular uprisings to secure basic democratic rights."[5] Previously, Ankara had opted for the former, in order to safeguard national interest. For instance, it had declined to give its blessing to the so-called Green

Movement in 2009, treating the protests against stolen presidential elections as Iran's internal matter. To Davutoğlu, however, ignoring the popular upheaval shaking up the Arab world was the wrong call. Turkey had to be, as he put it, "on the right side of history" and even act as the revolution's standard-bearer. Others in the government, notably Erdoğan, were hedging their bets. Yet events in the region over the first half of 2011 developed at breakneck speed, pulling Turkey along with them.

Tunisia

Turkey's response to the outpour of discontent in Tunisia triggered by Bouazizi's self-immolation was telling. The foreign ministry stayed quiet throughout the protests starting in mid-December 2010. The first statement came only on 14 January 2011 when Ben Ali, abandoned by the army, tendered his resignation and sought refuge in Saudi Arabia. It used generic language, expressing concerns about "the incidents" in the North African country, and contrasted with the stronger language the US State Department deployed days earlier. Ankara was in a wait-and-see mode, all the way until the end of January when it hailed democratic change.[6] Rachid Ghannouchi's subsequent return from exile and the success of his Ikhwan-inspired party, Ennahda, in the Constituent Assembly elections (23 October 2011) deepened relations. Visiting Tunis in March 2012, President Abdullah Gül extolled the Jasmine Revolution which, in his view, demonstrated that Islam and democracy were compatible, contrary to "Orientalist misconceptions." Ghannouchi in turn complimented Turkey and the AKP for setting an example.[7] In short, without taking risks or indeed doing much, Turkey scored a foreign policy coup.

Egypt

The notion of Turkey as a beacon of change took off with the overthrow of Hosni Mubarak in February 2011. Unlike small and peripherally located Tunisia, Egypt's size, history and cultural sway placed it right at the heart of the Arab world – irrespective of its loss of political status compared to the heyday of Nasserism in the 1950s and 1960s. Erdoğan took personal interest in the events unfolding in Cairo. A week into the protests, 1 February 2011, he called on Mubarak to step down, well ahead of US President Obama, who issued a similar demand on 5 February. Erdoğan's decision came as no surprise, in that the stakes for Turkey were not high. Egypt was neither a major economic partner nor a diplomatic ally. There was no love lost between Mubarak and the AKP either, with bitter memories going back to the Erbakan era in the mid-1990s. Regime change would likely benefit the Muslim Brotherhood who had done very well in the semi-free election of 2005, when it garnered one-fifth of parliamentary seats. The ensuing rollback by the regime had not sapped the Ikhwan's strength at the grassroot level. Though the movement was largely absent from Tahrir Square such estimates proved correct. Following Mubarak's downfall, the Brotherhood-backed Freedom and Justice Party (FJP) triumphed in the parliamentary elections and in June 2012 Mohamed Morsi became Egypt's new president.

The ecstatic welcome Erdoğan was treated to in Cairo in September 2011 during his Arab Spring tour, and Turkey's soaring popularity, vindicated his initial bet. Not only did the emergent Turkish–Egyptian alliance strengthen Ankara's hand, it also held out the promise of business dividends. During a visit in November 2012, Erdoğan signed 27 agreements and extended a $2 billion loan to the Egyptians. To be sure, Morsi, whose tenure lasted little over a year, in no way looked upon Turkey as a bigger brother. The FJP rebuffed Turkish advice on the future constitution, while Erdoğan's remark about the value of secularism elicited angry responses. Still, Egypt's new rulers remained ideological fellow travelers as well as partners on foreign policy.

In Turkey, pro-AKP intellectuals and commentators hailed Egypt's political transformation. Taha Özhan, director of the think-tank SETA, spoke of the end of the "Camp David" order in the Middle East upheld by secular autocrats in collusion with powerful Western states. Turkey and Muslim Brotherhood-governed Egypt put forward an alternative vision resonating with the region's societies and deeply rooted in local culture. The overthrow of the Muslim Brotherhood in July 2013 laid waste to such aspirations. However, the Turkish government did its best to exploit Egypt's counter-revolution domestically.[8] The Gezi protests (see Chapter 6) were likened to the military coup deposing Morsi. The four-finger Rabia sign, referencing the brutal crackdown on the sit-in of 14 August and the killing of more than 1,500 Ikhwan members in Cairo, became standard at AKP rallies and in Erdoğan's repertoire.[9] Muslim Brotherhood cadres found refuge in Turkey, with their media setting up shop in Istanbul.[10]

Libya

The next domino, Libya, presented a much tougher challenge. Over decades, Turkey had accumulated a portfolio of construction and energy contracts, with investments estimated at about $60 billion. In 2011, some 30,000 Turkish citizens worked in the oil-rich North African country. Ankara facilitated Qaddafi's international rehabilitation, in the wake of his decision in December 2003 to dismantle Libya's nuclear weapons program.

As the crisis in Libya, pitting Qaddafi against a collection of rebel militias, escalated in February–March 2011, Turkey opposed the military intervention championed by France and Britain. "Libyan people are against it," Erdoğan and Davutoğlu retorted to London and Paris. The prime minister spoke against the EU sanctions imposed on the regime at the behest of French President Nicolas Sarkozy, and denounced Western pressure as a ploy to lay its hands on Libyan oil, "a crusade," as well as "another Afghanistan and a second Iraq."[11] At the same time, Turkey kept channels opened to the anti-Qaddafi camp and sent humanitarian aid to rebel-held areas. As late as 27 March 2011, Erdoğan insisted on acting as a go-between the Benghazi-based National Transition Council (NTC) and Qaddafi.[12] Turkey had made sure to evacuate about 25,000 of its nationals (along with those of other NATO countries) from Libya as well.

With time, Turkey's opposition to intervention softened. Qaddafi stubbornly refused to order a ceasefire. In a TV interview, Erdoğan vented his frustration: "I have contacted [Qaddafi] six or seven times. I sent our special representatives, but we always faced stalling tactics. They tell us they want a ceasefire, we tell them to take a step, but the next day you find out that some places were bombed."[13] Anti-Turkish protests in Benghazi had a bearing on Ankara's views as well. The UN Security Council Resolution 1973 (17 March 2011) authorizing the use of force provided the needed cover for a diplomatic U-turn. The balance of power tilted towards the opposition, owing to the air campaign spearheaded by France and Britain with the US "leading from behind," ostensibly to enforce a no-fly zone. Turkey's partner Qatar, bankrolling Qaddafi's opponents, joined the strikes too, as the Arab League sided with Western powers. Ultimately, Ankara sided with the British–French intervention but extracted a political concession: that it should be placed under the auspices of NATO. Thus, the

Turkish government could gain greater say on the operation and, presumably, post-conflict Libya.[14] Following an overnight parliamentary vote, Turkey deployed its navy to enforce the sea blockade under the Unified Protector operation. Air operations were managed from NATO's Air Command Headquarters for Southern Europe located in Izmir. Yet Turkey was not at the forefront of the campaign, nor did Erdoğan tone down his anti-Western rhetoric. Erdoğan offered Qaddafi asylum in June 2011. Only after the latter rebuffed the offer did Ankara recognize the NTC as Libya's legitimate representative.

Turkish vacillation was anything but exceptional. The Obama administration, intent on downscaling American involvement in the Middle East, was in two minds about the merits of intervening in Libya. In consequence, the US let Britain, France and its Arab allies such as Qatar, Jordan and the UAE do the fighting. In a widely read 2016 interview for *The Atlantic* magazine, Obama furthermore characterized the war as "the worst mistake" of his presidency. The former president bemoaned the absence of a plan for the post-Qaddafi era, repeating errors from Iraq.[15] Russia's response was likewise incoherent. President Dmitry Medvedev did instruct Moscow's ambassador at the UN to abstain during the vote of Resolution 1973, enabling intervention, but then Prime Minister Putin denounced "the crusade" waged by the West. Russia levelled criticism against NATO for going well beyond the limits of enforcing a no-fly zone over Libya.[16] China and non-permanent members of the UN Security Council such as Germany, Brazil and India abstained as well.

Remarkably, Turkey used the turnaround to its advantage. Erdoğan's visit to Tripoli on 16 September 2011, a day after Nicolas Sarkozy and David Cameron, signaled Turkey's support for the NTC. In the following years, Ankara backed the Justice and Construction Party, which was aligned with the Muslim Brotherhood. The party came second in the legislative elections in July 2012 and was part of the government until early 2014. Turkey stayed involved in Libyan politics as the country descended into factionalism and conflict. In October 2014, Erdoğan appointed Emrullah İşler, an Arabic-speaking theologian who had served as deputy prime minister, as special envoy to the North African country. In the new civil war that broke out, Turkey backed the so-called Government of National Accord (GNA) in Tripoli, established as a result of UN-led negotiations in December 2015. Turkish involvement was set to increase, leading the way to military intervention in 2019.[17]

A RUDE AWAKENING

THE TURKISH MODEL, AGAIN

Tunisia, Egypt and Libya bolstered Turkey's normative claims.[18] The idea of Turkey as a model for its neighbors, propagated by Turgut Özal in the 1990s and then by the Bush administration following 9/11, was back in fashion. But this time around the Turkish government was comfortable with the notion that its destiny was linked with that of the Middle East, an idea that secularist elites had frowned upon a decade earlier. The "Turkish model" turned into a default talking point for both the authorities and Turkey-watchers in the West.

That was far from unproblematic. There were people in the AKP uncomfortable with the patronizing overtones the claim to being a model entailed. President Abdullah Gül preferred to speak of Turkey as "a source of inspiration" (*ilham kaynağı*) for neighbors.[19] His caution was warranted. On the whole, Arab societies did look up to Turkey, whose stock further surged thanks to the stand-off with Israel. A 2009 survey conducted in Egypt, Jordan, the Palestinian territories, Lebanon, Saudi Arabia, Syria and Iraq, for instance, found out it came second after Saudi Arabia in popularity. It was ranked first in the Palestinian Territories and Syria (after Syria itself).[20] Yet, as the Egypt example suggested, elites, including Islamists, were not keen on a big brother. Second, various groups in Arab countries cherry picked Turkey's experience. Secularists valued the *laicism* principles, while conservatives went for Erdoğan and the AKP. And for some, the tutelage system defining "old Turkey," with generals and bureaucrats overseeing civilian politicians but not directly running the state, presented a more realistic path forward to a more open system.

Even if Turkey chose to spread its gospel, it did not have the means and the resources needed to rise to the challenge at hand. The public broadcaster TRT set up a channel in 2010 but it could not compete with networks with regional coverage, such as Qatar's Al Jazeera. Out of 135 diplomats working on Arab countries in the early 2010s, only 6 spoke Arabic.[21] The AKP's party-to-party networks could fill in the gap, but only up to a point. Of course, this was about to change in the 2010s, thanks the arrival of millions of Arabic speakers, mainly from Syria. Human connections, a result of war and displacement, brought Turkish society and the Middle East into much more intimate contact than arguably at any point in the history of the republic so far.

THE SYRIAN CONUNDRUM

When demonstrations against Bashar al-Assad's regime spread from the southern town of Deraa to the capital Damascus and other big urban centers in March 2011, it looked as though Syria would repeat the example of Tunisia and Egypt. That expectation proved wrong. Assad's decision to suppress the peaceful protest with brute force fueled a civil war cum proxy battle drawing in virtually all Middle Eastern powers. Turkey was drawn into the maelstrom – and is to this day deeply involved in its neighbor's affairs.

Syria has always been special for Turkey. The two share a 910-km border, which, to boot, is of a relatively recent making given the Turkish annexation of the Hatay province in 1938 from the then French mandate territory. The border cuts through communities: Kurds, Arabs and Turkmens. In the 2000s, it turned from a bulwark to a conduit of goods, people and ideas, thanks to Turkey's open-door policy. Indeed, as Christopher Philips notes, Syria became the "poster child" of the "zero-problems" approach.[22] Having been on the brink of war in 1998, Ankara and Damascus developed economic and political ties, with a free trade deal (in 2007) and an agreement to lift the requirement for visas (in 2009). On any given day, the bustling metropole of Gaziantep would welcome a steady stream of shoppers and business people from nearby Aleppo, Syria's largest city and commercial hub. Between 2006 and 2010, Syrian exports to Turkey shot up from $187 million to $662 million, while Turkey's exports to Syria tripled to $1.85 billion.[23] The two militaries held a joint exercise in April 2009.[24] As late as February 2011, Erdoğan was in Syria to lay the first stone for the so-called Friendship Dam on the Orontes river (known in Turkish as Asɪ), a project he had proposed back in 2004.[25]

The rift with Assad

Close ties with Syria made the Turkish government tread cautiously, as protests intensified leading to a violent crackdown. In the spring and early summer of 2011, Ankara felt it could talk Bashar al-Assad into reforms to defuse tensions. Foreign Minister Davutoğlu and Hakan Fidan, the undersecretary of the MİT and Erdoğan's confidante, made frequent trips to Damascus. Hasan Turkmani, a former defense minister and senior member of the Ba'ath Party, visited Ankara too. Erdoğan and his associates were hopeful they could leverage personal links to Assad. They were not alone in that belief; Saudi Arabia and Qatar engaged with the regime too, concerned about stability.[26]

What Turks and others failed to appreciate was how high the stakes were for Assad, as well as how far the regime was prepared to go in order to ensure its own survival. In war-ravaged towns and villages his loyalists would spray on walls the slogan, "Assad or we burn the country," meaning it literally.[27] Assad clearly disregarded the messages coming from Ankara. The wholesale military onslaught against Hama, where a Muslim Brotherhood-led uprising in 1982 had led to the massacre of more than 20,000, marked a turning point. In July 2011, the Syrian Arab Army and Alawite militiamen laid siege to the city and murdered another 2,200. Turkey saw the timing of the onslaught, continuing into the holy month of Ramadan, as a direct affront. "It's impossible to remain silent in the face of events visible to everyone," President Abdullah Gül said. "I urge the Syrian administration to stop violence against people and to carry out reforms [. . .]. We cannot remain silent and accept a bloody atmosphere."[28] Unlike Saudi Arabia, Bahrain and Kuwait, Turkey was still in a talking mode. Ahmet Davutoğlu held one last parlay, over a full six hours, with Assad on 9 August. It bore no fruit. The regime paid no heed to demands to withdraw its forces from cities.

Ankara responded by suspending trade and eventually, on 21 September 2011, diplomatic relations. Yet it did not join the call by the US and Germany, France and Britain for the Syrian president to step down. Turkey imposed financial sanctions and asset freezes only at the end of November. That was the end. On 13 November, mobs attacked the Turkish embassy in Damascus as well as the consulates in Aleppo and Latakia, burning the country's flag and removing portraits of Atatürk. Turkey upped the ante: "Every bullet fired, every bombed mosque has eliminated the legitimacy of the Syrian leadership and has widened the gap between us."[29] In effect, the Turkish government took on board the demand for regime change.

The sharp turnaround was far from uncontroversial in Turkey itself. The opposition CHP argued that Erdoğan and Davutoğlu's decision to burn bridges was counterproductive. A delegation led by Faruk Loğoğlu, the party's deputy head, visited Damascus for several days in early September 2011 (and kept coming back in the years to follow).[30] Others, while in agreement with the government's decision to cut ties with the regime in principle, were unnerved by alleged its collusion with radical Islamists. Fears peaked when the opposition daily *Cumhuriyet* published evidence in May 2015 of MİT-commissioned trucks delivering weapons and ammunition to northern Syria, a scandal that had been brewing for more than a year.[31] Needless to say, Turkey's adversaries also circulated stories of collusion. In December 2015, the Russian Ministry of Defense released satellite images purportedly showing the involvement by Erdoğan and members of his family in oil trade with ISIS.

Turkey's strategy

From November 2011, Turkey banked on the assumption that Assad's days were numbered (MİT reportedly assessed he could be gone in about six months). Its main goal therefore was to secure its dominant role in a post-regime Syria by molding the political opposition and the nascent Free Syrian Army (FSA). The common border gave Ankara a natural advantage. The FSA, formed by defectors from Assad's forces, reportedly enjoyed a safe haven in Hatay already in July 2011, that is, prior to Turks' break-up with the regime. The fall of eastern Aleppo to the opposition (in July 2012) further strengthened Turkey's advantage, with people, arms, ammunition and materiel filtering through the frontier and the countryside surrounding the city.[32] In mid-July 2012, the FSA seized the Bab al-Hawa crossing between the Turkish town of İskenderun (Alexandretta) and Idlib province. Syrian fighters became a visible presence in towns and refugee camps on Turkey's side of the border. In addition, the Turkish government reportedly set up a coordination center at the İncirlik airbase, in partnership with Saudi Arabia and Qatar and with support from the US.[33]

Turkey sought leadership over the Syrian opposition. Together with Qatar, it threw its weight behind the Istanbul-based Syrian National Council (SNC) in which the Muslim Brotherhood cohabited with liberal figures such as the academic Burhan Ghalioun. While Doha bankrolled the SNC, Turkey had the advantage of being able to access the rebel-controlled enclaves in northern Syria. The Turkish alliance with Qatar and the Muslim Brotherhood sat at odds with Saudi Arabia. To counter the Ikhwan's influence, which it traditionally sought to suppress throughout the Middle East, Riyadh favored the inclusion of secularists and representatives of ethnic and religious minorities. That resulted in the formation of the Syrian National Coalition (National Coalition for Syrian Revolutionary and Opposition Forces) in November 2012, which subsumed the SNC and gained recognition by the West and Arab countries rooting for Assad's removal. Headed by Moaz al-Khatib, the former imam at the Ummayad mosque in Damascus, the National Coalition was under Turkish influence to a lesser degree than the SNC.[34]

Both Saudi Arabia and the Syrian National Coalition's leaders were amenable to negotiating with the regime a transition formula based on power-sharing under UN auspices. As the analyst Hassan Hassan observed in 2013:

> Riyadh today backs Washington's line and has declared an openness to negotiations, although it insists that Iran cannot be part of the process. This openness stands in contrast to Qatar, which (along with Turkey) maintains a desire to see regime change at any cost and which has shown little support for political initiatives, such as the Geneva II initiative backed by US Secretary of State John Kerry and Russian Foreign Minister Sergey Lavrov, or concern with the rise of more radical jihadist forces.[35]

Disagreements came to a head in May 2013 when Saudi pressure for expanding the National Coalition by 43 members led to a public quarrel. Meanwhile, the FSA accused the Muslim Brotherhood of trying to take over from local councils and coordination committees in rebel-held areas of Syria, as well as establishing and funding their own militias outside the common command structure.[36] In January 2014, infighting led to the SNC splitting from the National Coalition, in a disagreement over participation in the UN's Geneva II conference on Syria.

Turkey faced pushback from Iran too. Having welcomed the Arab Spring, describing it as "Islamic Awakening," the Islamic Republic poured out money, arms, training, advice and people to shore up Assad. Its allies from Hezbollah stepped into the fray and recaptured territory such as the town al-Qusayr at the border with Lebanon, an operation masterminded by Qasem Soleimani, commander of the Quds Force within the Iranian Revolutionary Guard. Without entering into head-on collision with the Turks, Tehran denied their objectives. For his part, Erdoğan made sure to keep open channels to the Iranians. In June 2014, Rouhani became the first Iranian president to visit

Turkey for nearly two decades. And, in contrast to Saudi Arabia and its Gulf allies, Turkey welcomed the nuclear deal, or "Joint Comprehensive Plan of Action" (JCPOA), signed by Iran and the so-called P5+1 (the US, Russia, France, UK and China – the UN Security Council's permanent members, along with Germany).[37]

Relations with the West

Turkey expected that US and its Western allies would eventually intervene militarily, establishing a no-fly zone on the model of northern Iraq after 1991 and Libya in 2011.[38] Deprived of airpower, the Assad regime would be denied its advantage against the rebels who would be able to consolidate their gains south of the Turkish–Syrian border. Washington was no doubt receptive to such plans. Hillary Clinton, for instance, welcomed the idea, both as state secretary until February 2013 and during her presidential campaign in 2015–16. Yet the Obama administration, fearful of mission creep and an open-ended presence in Syria, remained reluctant. Foreign policy expert Ömer Taşpınar wryly noted that tables had turned. In Iraq, in 2003, Turkey was asking of the US with no small dose of consternation "What comes next after the regime falls?" A decade later, it was the US asking the same question to its Turkish interlocutors.[39]

Enforcing a no-fly zone in Syria seemed a challenging task. Syrian air defenses, partly modernized thanks to the import of Russian-made S-300 surface-to-air missiles as well as shorter-range systems, were in a better shape than Libya's. At least that was what Western experts believed at a time, rationalizing their governments' inaction.[40] In 2010, Moscow had signed a contract with Assad to deliver long-range S-300 surface-to-air missiles too. Damascus showed resolve to fight back against Turkey: its air force downed reconnaissance jets in June 2012 and in November 2013; the Syrian Arab Army reportedly took aim at three Turkish F-16s flying over the province of Hatay (in Turkish airspace).[41] In October 2012, mortar fire killed five Turkish soldiers in the border town of Akçakale too. Assad signaled that an intervention would carry a cost, a message that reverberated with a Turkish society wary of deeper entanglement.

Still, the regime's action brought Turkey closer to its Western allies. In December 2012, NATO approved the deployment of Patriot missiles by the

US, Germany and the Netherlands at the İncirlik base. The Turkish government welcomed the move. Another win was the UK and France's success in easing the EU arms embargo with respect to moderate opposition, that is, the various factions comprising the FSA, in May 2013.[42]

The honeymoon ended with Obama's refusal to launch strikes in response to the use of chemical weapons by the regime against the Damascus suburb of Ghouta on 21 August 2013, which killed hundreds of civilians. The failure to enforce a red line, set by Obama himself, and the last-minute deal with Vladimir Putin under which Assad committed to surrender its chemical weapons arsenal, came as a wake-up call to Turkey. It proved wrong expectations that the US would be taking a muscular approach after the presidential elections in November 2012, an argument the Turkish government made to the Syrian opposition. John Kerry, who succeeded Hillary Clinton at the State Department, placed his faith in negotiations with Assad's international backers. The US still favored the toppling of the regime, with Obama authorizing in late 2012 a CIA-operated program ("Timber Sycamore") to supply weapons to vetted militias. Yet Assad's removal was not a top priority for an administration looking for a way out of the Middle East. Having brought Erdoğan and the US together initially, Syria opened a chasm between them – which would grow even bigger in the years to follow with the rise of ISIS and Kurdish militias.

RADICALIZATION

From late 2012 onwards, Turkey came face to face with the inexorable rise of radical Islamist militias. Rather than uniting all armed opponents of the regime under a single command, the FSA remained little more than a loose structure of disparate, locally rooted groups. A number of those did not recognize the authority of the Supreme Military Council. The prime strength of the insurgency, its connection to communities and networks on the ground, proved its main weakness as well.[43] Factions competed among themselves, vying for external patronage.[44] Weapons and money poured in from state and private sources in Qatar, Saudi Arabia, Kuwait and Bahrain. The insurgency took a sectarian turn, with the Alawi-dominated regime and Iran branded as enemies of the Sunnis. That was a symbolic coup for Assad, who, from the very outset, portrayed the conflict as a struggle against Islamist radicals and terrorists aided from abroad. Of course, the regime itself saw no problem in fueling sectarianism by soliciting help from Hezbollah and Iran.

Erdoğan paid homage to sectarianism too, instrumentalizing it domestically. On several occasions he singled out Turkish Alevis, a community loosely related to the Alawis (or Nusayris) of Syria, which is known for its left-wing politics, as partisans of Assad, a fellow Alawi. He never missed a chance to castigate criticism by CHP and its leader Kemal Kılıçdaroğlu (an Alevi) of government policy towards the Syrian war, again deploying the Sunni vs Alevi narrative.[45]

The vicious circle empowered al-Nusra Front (Jabhat al-Nusra), an outgrowth of Sunni insurgency in Iraq from the mid-2000s, which spread into northern Syria. Renowned for discipline and prowess on the battlefield, Nusra gained strength at the FSA's expense, turfing out factions such as Liwa al-Tawhid associated with the Muslim Brotherhood and Qatar. It attracted recruits from other groups as well as from the wider region, Western Europe and the post-Soviet space. Nusra came into the spotlight when it pledged allegiance to al-Qaeda.

Even if Nusra's focus was on Syria, the embrace of global jihad inevitably pitched it against the US. In December 2012, the Obama administration blacklisted the force, which by that point numbered some 10,000 fighters. The Turkish government was far from happy. In the words of Nuh Yılmaz, of the SETA think-tank and subsequently MİT, "Ankara was antagonized by Washington's decision to add the most effective rebel fighting force [. . .] to its list of international terror organizations. Turkish officials saw this as weakening the opposition and reinforcing the narrative of the Assad regime." Nusra cooperated with the FSA against the regime and fought Kurdish militias east of the Euphrates, a reason enough for Ankara to tolerate it and even back it, for example by allowing it access to Turkish territory during offensives against Syrian Kurds. That is why, back in 2013, Yılmaz observed that "further tensions between Ankara and Washington may lie ahead over the Syrian endgame."[46] His prediction was spot on.

After the "red line" crisis in August–September 2013, Turkey, as well as Gulf countries, aligned more openly with Salafist militias outside the FSA, capable of inflicting greater damage on the regime on the battlefield. They cast their lot with the Islamic Front, a coalition of powerful Salafist militias such as

Ahrar al-Sham and Jayish al-Islam, which in December 2013 overran the FSA headquarters at Turkey's border in the Idlib governorate. Ahrar al-Sham became Ankara's partner of choice, as well as a counterweight to the jihadis even though it fought side by side with Jabhat al-Nusra at times. Yet the strategy did not deliver. By 2014, the Syrian war had entered a stalemate. Neither side, Assad and his allies Iran and Hezbollah or the rebel forces backed by Turkey and other Sunni powers, was in a position to achieve a decisive victory.

Jihadis gathered strength as a consequence. While Turkey's partners in Syria could contain and coexist with Nusra, the growth of ISIS upended the balance of power. Similar to Nusra, it was an offshoot from al-Qaeda in Iraq, the organization's initial base, but it soon parted ways with al-Qaeda Central and proclaimed a worldwide caliphate headed by its leader Abu Bakr al Baghdadi.[47] The capture of Mosul in June 2014 made ISIS, renamed "Islamic State" shortly thereafter, the dominant jihadi faction. It took hold of a vast cache of US-supplied arms as well as of hard currency stocked in the vaults of the city branch of the Iraqi national bank. ISIS controlled a vast territory stretching from the outskirts of Baghdad all the way to the Homs governorate in Syria, including the oil-rich province of Deir ez-Zor in the country's east. The savvy use of social media (including gruesome videos of mass shootings and beheadings) quickly earned it global recognition and boosted recruitment.

ISIS was bad news for Turkey. Its radical ideology and brutal ways reconfirmed Assad's narrative. Though it put pressure on the regime, ISIS also fought the FSA and the Salafist militias aligned with Ankara too. More than that, in Mosul, its forces kidnapped some 49 staff from the Turkish consulate, including Consul General Öztürk Yılmaz.[48] It also transpired that the jihadis had built a network of cells on Turkish soil, recruiting fighters and facilitating the transfer of money and weapons as well as illicit export of oil. ISIS put those networks into action with a series of deadly attacks in Turkey in 2015–16, culminating with the bombing of a peace rally at Ankara's railway station on 10 October 2015 that killed 109 and injured more than 500.[49] Lastly, the radical group took on the AKP and Erdoğan, decried in its propaganda as apostates.

Yet the Turkish government did not view ISIS as an existential threat. *Daesh* was more of a symptom than the root cause of Syria's tragedy, the main culprit being Assad and his brutal scorched-earth tactics.[50] Ankara dragged its feet when the Obama administration assembled an anti-ISIS coalition in the wake of Mosul. As Operation Inherent Resolve[51] unfolded and allies started launching air strikes against the jihadists in Iraq and Syria, Turkey was reluctant to allow access to the Incirlik airbase. It used the pretext that its diplomats were still held hostage. But in reality it was bargaining for broadening the operation's scope. In Erdoğan's own words: "We will fight against ISIS with the same conviction as before, but we have certain conditions. One: there needs to be a no-fly zone. Two: there needs to be a buffer zone [inside Syria]. Three: we have to train [opposition fighters]. Four: the Syrian regime has to be targeted."[52] Yes, the US could forge a common cause with Turkey, but it had to be on Turkey's terms.

KURDS RISING

The Turkish government's calculus reflected the growing clout of Syrian Kurds. In July 2012, the regime largely withdrew from border areas in northeast Syria in order to mass its forces on other fronts. The gap was filled by the Democratic Union Party (Partiya Yekîtiya Demokrat, PYD) which subscribed to the PKK leader Abdullah Öcalan's program for Kurdish empowerment through the reorganization of Middle Eastern states along federal lines.[53] Embroiled in a struggle with the PKK since the 1980s, Ankara viewed the PYD's rise as a challenge. In July 2013, Kurds declared the autonomy of Rojava (a derivation of Rojavayê Kurdistanê, Western Kurdistan). The entity united three areas ("cantons") along the Syrian–Turkish border: Jazira in the far east, Kobani and Afrin in the northwest, tucked between Aleppo and Idlib. Worse still, the PYD engaged in ad hoc cooperation with the Assad regime, happy to open another front against the opposition.[54] In the city of Qamishlo/Qamishli (Jazira), a small contingent of the Syrian Arab Army remained in place. In addition, Kurds declined to join the Syrian National Coalition, which it saw as beholden to Arab nationalism and/or to the Muslim Brotherhood.

From Turkey's perspective, Jabhat al-Nusra and subsequently ISIS were a check on the PYD. In November 2012, for instance, Nusra together with factions of the FSA attacked from Turkish territory the People's Protection Units (YPG), the PYD's militia, at the town of Ras al-Ayn (or Serêkanyê in

Kurmanji). By early 2014, ISIS-controlled enclaves wedged between the three Kurdish-run cantons and was pushing against the YPG.

The Turkish authorities took direct action to make the YPG's life difficult. They closed border crossings between Nusaybin and Qamishlo, Ceylanpınar and Serêkanyê/Ras al-Ayn/Sêrekanyê, Mürşitpınar and Kobani/Ain al-Arab. The FSA meanwhile blocked Afrin while the Kurdistan Regional Government, another Ankara ally, sealed off the border with northern Iraq in July 2012. In the words of Nursel Aydoğan, an MP from Turkey's pro-Kurdish Peace and Democracy Party (BDP): "Barzani probably wants to delay the development of the [Kurdish] entity in Rojava and will ask for the help of Erdoğan for this [. . .] All this shows that Barzani does not see the developments in line with [his] interests and is trying to delay or maybe stop Kurdish gains [in Rojava]. Syrian Kurds are not on the same page with Barzani. Öcalan's line dominates 80'90 percent [of the Syrian Kurds]."[55]

At the same time, Turkey engaged with Syrian Kurds. In July 2012, it welcomed an agreement brokered in Idlib, establishing the Kurdish National Council (KNC), a power-sharing arrangement between the PYD and pro-Barzani groups in northeast Syria.[56] However, the deal faltered as the PYD/YPG purged its competitors from Rojava. Then, the Kurdish peace process initiated by the Turkish government and Abdullah Öcalan in March 2013 led to a new opening. In July 2013, the PYD leader Salih Muslim visited Istanbul, traveling again to Ankara in October 2014 to meet Prime Minister Ahmet Davutoğlu.[57] Turks pleaded with Muslims to join the FSA in the fight against Assad.

The YPG's stand-off with ISIS at Kobani in the autumn of 2014 was an inflection point. It ramped up Kurdish nationalism on both sides of the border, with scores of volunteers from Turkey rushing to fight in what they portrayed as Kurdistan's own Stalingrad. The episode deepened Kurds' distrust of Ankara, as the Turkish armed forces stood idly by, watching ISIS closing in on the border town and flying the caliphate's black flag. Protests across Turkey on 6–8 October 2014 led to 42 deaths. The Turkish government allowed the KRG's *peshmerga* to transfer heavy weaponry as well as FSA reinforcements through the border only at the very end of October, four weeks into the battle.

Most crucially, Kobani sealed an alliance between Syrian Kurds and the US which unleashed its air power against ISIS. The Obama administration reached out to the YPG as the best prepared local force capable of fighting the caliphate. Though the American authorities listed the PKK as a terrorist organization, it treated the PYD/YPG as a separate entity. Formerly the region's underdogs, the Kurds seized the opportunity and put in an effort to win sympathy in the West. Their heroic resistance at Kobani won hearts and minds, as images of the YPG's female fighters captivated audiences across the globe.[58] With Kurdish nationalism on the march, Ankara felt at a disadvantage. The Obama administration's decision to befriend the PYD pulled the rug from under Turkey-allied militias covered by the Pentagon's Train and Equip program adopted in September 2014. The Kurds' top objective was to expand and secure Rojava rather than depose Assad. "You cannot solve this situation in Kobani alone," Erdoğan reasoned in mid-October 2014; "there are many Kobanis in Syria. If there is Kobani today, there is Aleppo, Hasakah and Mosul tomorrow."[59]

Turkish concerns grew in early 2015 as the YPG had recovered from ISIS the entirety of the Kobani canton and was poised to advance to the west of the Euphrates river, with air support from the US and its allies. The nightmare scenario entailed a land bridge to Afrin which would place the Turkish–Syrian border under Kurdish control. In mid-June 2015, the YPG captured Tal Abyad and connected the Kobani and Jazira cantons.[60] In response, on 6 July, Turkey's National Security Council issued a statement setting the Euphrates as a "red line," the crossing of which could trigger Turkish military intervention against the YPG as well as ISIS, portrayed as two sides of the same coin. Prime Minister Ahmet Davutoğlu argued that the decision aimed at preventing a *fait accompli* and, possibly, setting up a buffer zone in the northern Aleppo governorate, west of the Euphrates. Tensions rose as an ISIS bomb killed 32 left-wing activists in the town of Suruç, opposite Kobani, on 20 July 2015. Two days later, two police officers were shot in Ceylanpınar, next to Serêkanyê/Ras al-Ayn. A PKK faction claimed credit, though it transpired later that the incident had been an intra-police score settling. In effect, Syria brought an end to the Kurdish peace process in Turkey itself (see more in Chapter 7).

SYRIA HITS HOME

The Kurdish issue showed how Syria turned from being a foreign policy issue to a domestic one for Turkey. Indeed, the war transformed Turkish politics and society. There is no better example than the millions of Syrians who poured into Turkey through the early 2010s.

Refugees started crossing the border during the early days, taking advantage of the visa-free regime. In September 2011, there were 7,500 spread across six camps. The number rose to over 400,000 in mid-2013,[61] and to a whopping 3.5 million by the end of the decade. Wealthy, middle-class Syrians settled in Istanbul. Those of lesser means headed to the camps close to the border. As the great majority of the arrivals were Sunni, conservative grassroots communities aligned with the AKP, as well as pious charitable organizations, displayed a strong sense of solidarity. But liberal Turks, too, sympathized with the humanitarian plight of the Syrians. The Turkish state stepped in, providing housing and health care services and enrolling refugee children into schools. At the same time, Turkey denied Syrians refugee status and political asylum under international law. The formal reservation Ankara had made to the 1951 UN Refugee Convention narrowed down its geographic scope to Europe only, excluding arrivals from the Middle East. Instead, the Turkish authorities treated Syrians as temporary visitors who, one day, were bound to head back to their native land.

But though they lacked legal status in their new country, the refugees established a visible presence, for example joining the grey sector. Over time, this gave rise to resentment on the part of local people, especially with the economic difficulties of the late 2010s. Public hostility to Syrians, reminiscent of the treatment of Anatolian labor migrants in Western Europe back in the day, became common. A report by the International Crisis Group found that instances of intercommunal violence against Syrian refugees grew three-fold in the latter half of 2017 compared to 2016. In Istanbul, Ankara and Izmir – marred by stark inequalities – a surge in ethnic rivalry pitted the Arab newcomers against Turks and Kurds.[62] By 2020, two-thirds of Turkish citizens held the belief that refugees would damage public services, with another 82 per cent convinced that Syrians shared no cultural bonds with the locals.[63] An overwhelming majority favored their segregation in camps or resettlement in Syria. This anti-refugee backlash explains in part the gains the Turkish opposition made against the governing AKP in the 2019 municipal elections.

Tensions were nothing new when it came to the border region. The Hatay province, where Alawis – the heterodox sect to which the Assad family belong – comprise a substantial segment of the population, was a case in point. "They walk around with their long beards looking like al-Qaeda," locals in Hatay said to a Western researcher. "I've heard they have told some Turkish Alawis, 'After Bashar, you're next!'"[64]

The government sought to stem the influx from Syria early on. In March 2015, it closed all crossings, with only authorized trade allowed in and out. In 2018, the Mass Housing Administration (Toplum Konut İdaresi, TOKİ) completed a 564-km border fence through the provinces of Hatay, Kilis, Gaziantep, Şanlıurfa, Mardin and Şırnak. Needless to say, the EU welcomed Ankara's move to put an end to the open-door policy as European countries had to deal with asylum seekers arriving from Turkey. In that sense, it prefigured the deal negotiated by Prime Minister Davutoğlu and Europe's leaders in March 2016. On the losing side were Syrian civilians stranded in opposition-held areas and vulnerable to attacks by pro-Assad forces.

Historically, Turkey approached the Middle East in three ways: through containment, through engagement, and through expansion. The military preferred the first option. Özal and, in the years before the Arab Spring, the AKP, opted for engagement through diplomacy, trade, investment and cultural exports, as well as leading through example. Both of those strategies delivered, though not in full. The war in Syria, by contrast, showed the limits of direct involvement in other countries' affairs. Instead of changing the Middle East and North Africa in its own image, Turkey became exposed to political turbulence coming out of the region. The Kurdish issue, ISIS and the refugees being prime examples.

That is why Turkey's objective in Syria changed after 2015. From deposing Assad, Ankara shifted to containing the PYD/YPG as it gained ground across the border. Russia's intervention in the war, discussed in Chapter 8, completed the turnaround. In the process, Turkish–American relations sustained serious damage and were showing no serious signs of recovery since.

Another outcome is Turkey's shift towards a more muscular foreign policy, reliant on the projection of hard power. In hindsight, the setbacks in Syria and elsewhere in the Middle East did not lead to retrenchment. Quite the opposite, they actually prompted Erdoğan to double down by launching successive foreign interventions, starting from Syria and moving to Libya in 2019 and eventually to the Southern Caucasus. But that became possible only after he had strengthened his grip on power at home, the subject of the book's next two chapters.

6
ERDOĞAN WINS

"Democracy is not just the ballot box." President Abdullah Gül's words spoke directly to some Turks' anxieties after AKP won a record third term at the June 2011 general elections. From an underdog, Erdoğan's outfit had morphed, thanks to its loyal voter base, to "the natural party of government," to borrow from Britain's political vocabulary. To its charismatic leader, the AKP epitomized the very spirit of democracy. His critics begged to disagree. Coming first in elections was no excuse for dismantling constitutional checks and balances. The culture wars of the 1990s and 2000s, fought over the meaning of secularism and the place of Islam in public life, had yielded to another debate: what constituted healthy democratic rule? Putting the military back into the barracks was a goal on which a majority of citizens, with the exception of a radical Kemalist fringe, converged. Yet the bone of contention became the executive branch's overreach, with the courts, the civil service and the media bearing the brunt. Erdoğan's detractors feared that, instead of moving forward to an "advanced democracy" (*ileri demokrasi*), Turkey was relapsing into an authoritarianism of a new breed.

Gül's message implied that Turkey had still not passed the point of no return. The trouble was that few seemed to care. By the summer of 2013, when he raised his voice, the president was being sidelined. His own tribe, the AKP, appeared all but completely under Erdoğan's sway. CHP supporters spoke disparagingly of "the Çankaya notary," rubber-stamping decisions crafted in the prime minister's office. Liberals, once sympathetic to the gentlemanly Gül and his vision of the AKP as a big-tent movement, were demoralized. The demonstrations on and around Istanbul's Taksim Square, which occasioned Gül's remarks in the summer of 2013, were crushed with tear gas and police batons. The Western pundits drawing facile analogies to the Arab Spring were off the mark. The urbanites resisting Erdoğan suffered a defeat. The government suppressed the protests with the heaviest of hands. Yet the AKP paid no price in the local and presidential polls that followed in 2014. In a little more than a year, Gül – a co-founder of the AKP and once Erdoğan's peer – drifted away from center-stage. The consensual style of politics he embodied had long outlived its relevance in a country fragmented into irreconcilably opposed factions.

The story of the AKP's second and third terms (2007–15) boils down to how a Machiavellian leader grabbed power, dismantling institutional constraints that checked his unbridled ambition. Erdoğan did not miraculously turn from an exemplary democrat to a Putin lookalike overnight in the summer of 2013. He evolved over years. What the Gezi Park episode did was to hammer home the fact that, following a period of consolidation, Turkish democracy was eroding. There were no constraints to limit the country's leader. The death of the EU accession process made Western criticism ring hollow. Opposition parties remained split along a variety of fault lines. Erdoğan tightened his grip on all levers of power after the divorce with the Gülen movement. Most importantly, the plurality of AKP's conservative voters remained staunchly loyal to the chief. The people's will was the ultimate arbiter. "There is nowhere more beautiful than the ballot box for criticism," Erdoğan had declared in 2007.[1]

"NOT ENOUGH BUT YES"

If one is to pinpoint a date when Turkey started backsliding, 30 July 2008 is probably the best candidate. On this sweaty summer day, the Constitutional Court decided a case brought forward by the Chief Public Prosecutor Abdurrahman Yalçınkaya on whether the AKP, along with scores of its functionaries, were in violation of the *laicist* principles of the basic law.[2] He was reacting to constitutional amendments passed in February, backed by a majority of 75 per cent in the Grand National Assembly comprised of the AKP and MHP, allowing women to wear a head covering (*türban*) in public institutions. With a closure case on its hands, the AKP was under threat of sharing the fate of its predecessors, Refah and Fazilet, abolished in the 1990s. Having voided legislation allowing headscarved women to attend university,[3] the Constitutional Court appeared bent on rolling back Islamists' political influence. Erdoğan's career seemed to be at stake as well. The judgment itself proved to be a draw, however. The constitutional justices did establish that the AKP was undermining secularism yet stopped short of imposing a ban. With six in favor and five against, including the court's president, Haşim Kılıç, the court failed to reach the required qualified majority of seven.[4] Erdoğan survived but it was a close call.

What would have happened if the AKP had been closed down? In all likelihood, Turkey would have gone through yet another turbulent patch, but there was a good chance that a revamped AKP could triumph in the next elections, possibly under a new figurehead leader, still beholden to the widely popular Erdoğan.[5] (In December 2009, the Turkish Constitutional Court closed the pro-Kurdish Democratic Society Party [DTP] for inciting separatism, but it re-emerged under a new name.)[6] In addition, a number of AKP deputies would have kept their seats as independents in the Grand National Assembly, as happened with Necmettin Erbakan's Refah party after January 1998. A closure would not have been the end of the road for the AKP, though it would most certainly have poisoned Turkish politics.

Whatever contingency plans Erdoğan drew up at the time, his main takeaway from the closure case was that the judiciary needed to be tamed. Voters, not unelected magistrates and bureaucratic mandarins out of touch with the common folk, had the right to decide on the nation's destiny. He framed the proposals to expand the government's role in judicial appointments as part and parcel of Turkey's reform effort aimed at narrowing the gap with Western democracies. The AKP was waging yet another battle against the "tutelage system" (*vesayet*). "Yes to freedom. Yes to rule of law. No to the law of the rulers. The tutelage of the coup regime is over."[7] It was the same populist strategy Erdoğan deployed during the political crisis in 2007: pitting "the people" against the elites (that is, the Kemalist establishment, the CHP, the judges and the senior civil servants, sections of the media). Erdoğan stood for the masses, the "true" Turkish nation squaring off with the usurpers. In making this argument, the prime minister fell back on Atatürk's dictum, written on the wall inside the Grand National Assembly, "Sovereignty belongs unconditionally to the people" (*Egemenlik kayıtsız şartsız milletindir*). Kemalism turned against the Kemalists.

In contrast to earlier legislative and constitutional reforms such as the curtailment of the military's role in public affairs or the lifting of the headscarf ban, taking on the judiciary raised delicate issues. The balance between the executive and the judicial branch touched on the very fundament of democracy. Certainly parts of the judiciary were a bastion of retrograde nationalism and a militant form of secularism. In March 2007, a court in Istanbul blocked access to internet streaming and video sharing site YouTube on the grounds that it insulted Mustafa Kemal Atatürk.[8] Intellectuals such as the Nobel Prize winner Orhan Pamuk had been tried for insulting Turkishness under the infamous Article 301 of the Penal Code. Turkey did need to reform not only its judiciary, but also its criminal law and procedure.[9] At the same time, the magistrates' constitutional role was to ensure the accountability of the other two branches, starting with the executive, not just to enforce the state's official ideology. Their mandate was to protect individual and collective rights against the government's fiat, irrespective of who controlled government – Islamists or their *laicist* adversaries. Thus, the principle of judicial independence stood as a litmus test for the health of democracy.

The AKP embarked on a wholesale reorganization of the judiciary. In May 2010, the Grand National Assembly took the first step by endorsing amendments to expand the Constitutional Court from 11 to 17 members, with the legislature appointing 3 and the president another 14. The Supreme Council of Judges and Prosecutors (Hâkimler ve Savcılar Yüksek Kurulu, HSYK), in charge of the appointment, promotion and oversight of magistrates, would more than triple in numbers, from 7 to 22, with lower court judges eligible to serve in the body. But rather than democratizing the HSYK, the reform empowered the minister of justice, who drew up the list of nominees. Those two critical changes were conjoined with a raft of widely popular amendments: allowing MPs from banned parties to serve their full term in parliament, giving citizens the right to petition the Constitutional Court directly, introducing the figure of an ombudsperson/civic advocate, permitting civil servants to enlist in trade unions and lifting immunity for military chiefs – making it possible to prosecute the leaders of the 1980s coup, including General Kenan Evren who had served as president between 1980 and 1989.[10] These were all positive steps, without a doubt, contributing to the democratization of Turkish political life. But the skeptics had a valid question all the same. Was the intent to revise the constitution bequeathed by the early 1980s military junta, approved by 93 per cent at a referendum in November 1982 and amended a number of times since? Or was it, rather, to sugarcoat the judicial amendments to sell them to voters?

What mattered, too, was process. The governing party rammed the constitutional amendments through parliament. Unlike the February 2008 revisions of the constitution to do with the headscarf issue, only MPs from the AKP voted them in. The objections of the CHP, as well as the MHP and the pro-Kurdish BDP, were disregarded. Erdoğan used the cross-party opposition to the bill to push the argument that a "coalition of the evil" (*şer ittifakı*) stood against him and the people.

> The CHP opposes the constitutional amendments. The MHP does as well. So does the BDP. Some media institutions are opposed to these amendments. The gangs, which hope to benefit from darkness, oppose them. The elite, who rely on the status quo, oppose a "yes" vote, as does the terrorist organization [PKK]. What could be more evident?[11]

In ideal circumstances, constitutional change would entail broad consensus. Yet Erdoğan chose to maximize the fault lines in polarized Turkish society which, as the social scientist Ersin Kalaycıoğlu observed at the time, was in the throes of a *Kulturkampf* waged between Muslim conservatives and secularists.[12] Overhauling the constitution through plebiscite, rather than a parliamentary process involving the obligatory give and take, exacerbated the us-vs-them divide ripping apart the body politic.[13]

Still, Erdoğan, ever the skillful tactician, assembled a societal coalition, much as in previous contests. The amendments pleased the AKP's conservative core as it strengthened their chosen representatives against the old regime. Equally, the changes appealed to fellow travelers of leftist and liberal persuasion who had come to view the AKP as a transformative agent thanks to its stance on Europe, individual liberties, minority rights and the struggle with the Kemalist establishment. Thus, the prime minister drove a wedge into the secular bloc, shaping the battlefield. The overhaul of the constitution, drafted in the aftermath of the 1980 coup, was a belated reckoning with the military junta. "*Yetmez ama evet*" (It's not enough but yes) became a common adage. Those liberal/leftist votes did make a difference, as during the constitutional referendum of 2007. The Gülenists mobilized too: "even dead people should be pulled from the grave to cast a vote," in the movement leader's colorful phrase.[14] The AKP would never again be able to win any contest – including the presidential elections and the plebiscite of 2017 on the switch to an executive presidential system – by such a wide margin.

Kurdish nationalists, who had also been the target of state repression like the Islamists and therefore backed reform, could also have been part of the "yes" camp, but in the event they boycotted the referendum. The failure of the so-called Kurdish Opening in 2009 informed the BDP's skepticism of the government's agenda, even though the party could not be in the same boat with the CHP and MHP, which steadfastly embraced Turkish nationalism. The Kurds' response, through the boycott, was simply *yetmez* (not enough).

The referendum held on 12 September 2010, the 30th anniversary of the 1980 coup, proved a master stroke for Erdoğan. He garnered some 21.7 million votes, close to 58 per cent of the total. That was well beyond the AKP's share in the 2009 local elections (15 million) as well as the constitutional referendum (19 million) and the parliamentary elections (16 million votes) in 2007. The triumph at the ballot box gave a boost to the governing party, set it on course to win a third term in June 2011 and hinted at the possibility of passing further amendments to the 1983 constitution down the road. The question remained of how big the AKP's win would be and whether Erdoğan would secure a mandate for enacting a presidential system, an old Özal idea he zealously promoted. The CHP and MHP, of course, pledged to do their utmost to deny him the prize.

To the dismay of the opposition, major Western countries such as the United States and Germany, as well as the EU, stood by Erdoğan once more, just as they had during the 2007 crisis.[15] The European Commission welcomed the referendum's outcome as "an important step towards Europe."[16] The West gave legitimacy to Erdoğan's narrative that the constitutional changes were beneficial to democratization. Was the EU, along with the Obama administration, short-sighted? Perhaps, yes. They failed to see that the unilateral changes to the constitution and Erdoğan's combative populism set Turkey on a dangerous trajectory away from democratic rule. The same virulent rhetoric castigating the Turkish people's enemies could soon be redirected against Europe and the United States, which is exactly what happened later in the 2010s.

Yet it would be wrong to fault the West as the decision was endorsed by an overwhelming majority of Turkish citizens, taking cues from their own leaders rather than Brussels or Washington. In addition, the EU could not be expected to side with the "No" camp either. The CHP under its new leader Kemal Kılıçdaroğlu, who had replaced Deniz Baykal, made a compelling case that the amendments led straight to court packing. However, the main opposition party was still struggling to rebrand itself as a moderately pro-Western, social democratic party. Its past opposition to EU-inspired reforms, including on the Kurdish issue, undermined its case. The CHP's de facto alliance with Devlet Bahçeli's far-right MHP certainly did not help its credentials either.

This raises another point. The MHP flipped in late 2016 by entering into a pact with Erdoğan which paved the way for a presidential system. Indeed, their alliance introduced more significant changes, eclipsing the reconfiguration of the judiciary seven years earlier (see Chapter 7). In other words, in the grand scheme of things, the far right played a more consequential role in Turkey's democratic decline than either the CHP or the partisans of "Not enough but yes."

Lastly, even with the 2010 changes, the AKP's dominance over the courts remained partial. In several politically charged cases, such as on the redevelopment of Gezi Park, magistrates stood up to the government.[17] The Constitutional Court's relationship with Erdoğan remains strained to this day. As the legal scholar Bertil Emrah Oder remarks, the court is still a "space for contestation."[18] Remarkably, the vast majority of the individual petitions to the court, an innovation introduced with the 2010 referendum, have resulted in judgments against the government.[19]

In short, the "told you so" school of thought, calling out Erdoğan's liberal enablers as well as the West, should be taken with a grain of salt.

THE ERGENEKON AFFAIR

Why did the AKP's assurances that it was still a fighting democracy's battle look persuasive in 2010? The Ergenekon investigation, in the years preceding the constitutional referendum, holds a substantial part of the answer.

Ergenekon was the name of a clandestine network of rogue security operatives and ultranationalists (*ülkücüler*) staunchly opposed to the government's (perceived) pro-Western and minorities-friendly policies. Its existence came to light with the discovery of a cache of military-issued hand grenades in Istanbul's borough of Ümraniye in June 2007. In January 2008, prosecutors and police arrested Veli Küçük, a retired general with links to the notorious gendarmerie intelligence service (JİTEM), the lawyer Kemal Kerinçsiz, responsible for the criminal cases brought against liberal writers such as Orhan Pamuk and Elif Şafak as well as against Hrant Dink, the editor of the Armenian weekly *Agos* assassinated in downtown Istanbul in January 2007, and Doğu Perinçek, the leader of the left-wing/nationalist (*ulusalcı*) and xenophobic Workers' Party (Işçi Partisi).[20] Over 2008 and 2009, up to 500 retired military officers, academics, journalists and a few figures from the underworld were taken into custody. In the meantime, police seized more weapons and explosives.[21]

Prosecutors alleged that Ergenekon had hatched plans to kill Erdoğan, the Kurdish mayor of Diyarbakır Osman Baydemir, a well-known BDP politician, and the Ecumenical Patriarch Bartholomew in order to wreak havoc, prod the military to step in and ultimately drive the AKP out of power. The clandestine network was also charged with the murders of a judge at the Council of State (Turkey's high administrative court) in 2006 and of three Protestant converts in the city of Malatya in April 2007. Shocking events in the mid-1990s, such as the assassination of journalist Uğur Mumcu, the attacks against the Alevi-populated Istanbul quarter of Gazi as well as the Susurluk scandal,[22] left a trail leading to Ergenekon too, according to prosecutors.

The investigation and the high-profile arrests polarized opinions. To the AKP grassroots, Ergenekon offered a chance to out and hold to account a cabal uniting high-ranking military officers, security service operatives, bureaucrats and organized crime bosses ("the deep state").[23] In short, all of the pillars of old regime persecuting the left since the 1970s and, in more recent times, taking on political Islamists. Erdoğan took full advantage. Conveniently, Ergenekon broke right at the time when the AKP was fighting for survival at the Constitutional Court in the summer of 2008. Now the tables had turned. The prime minister boldly declared he was the prosecutor in the Ergenekon case.[24] That was in response to CHP leader Deniz Baykal's assertion that he was counsel for the defendants. Baykal decried the investigations and the arrests as nothing less than "a civilian coup." Hardcore secularists and ultranationalists painted Ergenekon as a witch-hunt driven by the CIA with the ultimate goal of perpetuating American hegemony in the Middle East. Their mouthpiece *Aydınlık* (a magazine and later newspaper), edited by Perinçek, slammed "Islamofascists" for using their influence in police and the judiciary to destroy their adversaries. The target of their anger was the Gülen network, which was thought to have infiltrated law enforcement. They pointed to Zekeriya Öz, the prosecutor in charge of the Ergenekon investigation whose links to the Hizmet movement were an open secret. *Zaman*, Turkey's most read daily affiliated with Gülen, which covered the case in minute detail, stood accused as well.

Initially, the government's narrative held sway. Few doubted Küçük's hands were tainted with blood, the traumas of the dirty war in the southeast still vivid in the minds of many. The killings of public figures in 2006–7 gave credence to the claim that a clandestine cell in the bosom of the Turkish state was poised to unleash terror against perceived enemies of the nation. Turkey's liberal intelligentsia, the likes of journalist Yasemin Çongar, the literary critic Murat Belge, the historian Halil Berktay and the writer Ahmet Altan who editorialized on the pages of the daily *Taraf*, demanded justice. Cleaning the Augean stables of the Turkish state was a precondition for building a democracy worthy of the name.[25]

Yet, as new cases were added to the Ergenekon investigation in 2010–11, cracks became more conspicuous. In February 2011, police raided the offices of Odatv, a secularist and left/nationalist (*ulusalcı*) news portal. Its staff writers and columnists faced charges of belonging to Ergenekon. In March, journalist Ahmet Şık was detained and charged. His sin was the discovery of *The Imam's Army* (*İmamın Ordusu*), a book investigating Gülen's influence in society and the state apparatus, on Odatv's hard drives. A colleague of Şık's, Nedim Şener, ran afoul of the prosecutors because of a book alleging that intelligence officers had been implicated in Hrant Dink's assassination. Şener and Şık's case was watched with alarm outside Turkey and triggered criticism from professional bodies such as the PEN Club and Reporters without Borders.[26] Their fate showed that Ergenekon had spiraled out of control and no one was safe.

Ergenekon's most significant impact was the *coup de grâce* delivered to the military. It is true that the failure of the e-memorandum of April 2007 had already spelled the end of the generals' role as arbiter of civilian politics. But the TV images of senior officers in handcuffs was like nothing Turkish citizens had seen before. The Sledgehammer (*Balyoz*) case, initiated in 2010, was a spin-off of Ergenekon, triggered by journalist investigations by liberal *Taraf* relying on leaked documents from the armed forces. Top generals had allegedly plotted to topple the AKP in 2003 by planting bombs in two Istanbul mosques and downing a Greek fighter jet over the Aegean in order to provoke a military takeover. As a result, the commanders of the navy, the air force as well as the Turkish First Army at the time – generals Özden Örnek, İbrahim Fırtına and Çetin Doğan – were charged and sentenced to life imprisonment in September 2012.[27] Others, like the former secretary of the National Security Council Şükrü Sarıışık, received long terms. In 2013, General İlker Başbuğ, former chief of the general staff, was handed down a life sentence too in connection to the 2007 e-memorandum rather than Balyoz.[28]

Putting generals behind bars completed Erdoğan's bid to rein in the military. In July 2011, all top brass, including Chief of the General Staff Işık Koşaner, who had not even completed a year on the job, tendered their collective resignations in protest at the detaining of 250 of their colleagues. That provided an opportunity for the government to appoint officers they deemed loyal – first and foremost Necdet Özel, who succeeded Koşaner.[29] From Özel onwards, Erdoğan could count on support from the military command. This was also the moment that Gülenists, later implicated in the 2016 coup attempt, started rising through the ranks. At the same time, the sweeping purge presented an inconvenience for the government. İlker Başbuğ, for instance, had partnered with the AKP – for example on the so-called Kurdish Opening in 2009.[30] He was believed to have weighed in during the Constitutional Court's deliberations in the 2008 AKP case.[31] Similar to his predecessor, Hilmi Özkok, Başbuğ believed in a *modus vivendi* with Erdoğan. Was the prime minister now throwing the general under the bus? Or rather, were the prosecutors acting alone, without taking into account the AKP's calculations?

In any case, the polarizing effects of the Ergenekon trials and the constitutional overhaul carried political costs for the government. The CHP made gains in the 2009 local elections, helped as well by the economic crisis affecting Turkey. The pro-Kurdish DTP was also in the judiciary's crosshairs thanks to the so-called KCK affair, which had denied the AKP a breakthrough in southeastern cities such as Diyarbakır. In the June 2011 parliamentary elections the AKP did better but the CHP, benefiting from the change of leader, expanded its vote by more than 5 per cent and, reportedly, even managed to transfer

electorate to the MHP to help it clear the 10 per cent threshold. In consequence, the AKP lost seats in the Grand National Assembly, even though it
gained an unprecedented third term and came within a hair's breadth of
winning 50 per cent, its best result ever in general elections.[32] The governing
party was just three MPs short of the 330-strong majority needed to deliver on
Erdoğan's promise of a new constitution.

Ultimately, the Ergenekon and Balyoz trials went nowhere. After Erdoğan
clashed openly with the Gülen movement in December 2013, the Constitutional
Court invalidated most sentences passed in the preceding years. The general,
evidence against whom was highly problematic at best and likely forged,[33]
could walk free. Doğu Perinçek became an ally of the AKP – as did eventually
the CHP's ex-leader Deniz Baykal (who was not targeted by Ergenekon).
The anti-Western rhetoric deployed by the anti-Erdoğan opposition, the
conspiracy theories accusing the US and Europe of schemes to dismember
Turkey, became mainstream. Pro-government outlets such as the *Yeni Şafak*
(New Dawn) daily, owned by the Albayrak Group, spread them far and wide.
The purges of the late 2000s, which served the AKP well at the time, formed
part of the poisonous legacy of Gülen's *cemaat* whose judges and prosecutors
bore responsibility.

In hindsight, Ergenkon and Balyoz produced one winner: Tayyip Erdoğan.
That was far from clear at the time, since Gülenists played such a prominent
role.[34] But as we shall see, their partnership with AKP, and accordingly grasp
on power, proved ephemeral.

BUILDING THE *HAVUZ* MEDIA

From the get-go, Erdoğan knew all too well that his survival in power hinged
on media. This conviction grew stronger as the struggle with the Kemalist
establishment escalated towards the end of the AKP's first term. He needed a
friendly press and the backing of influential columnists, opinion makers and
TV channels. So long as the EU accession process was alive, there was no
shortage of positive stories; mainstream media owned by large business
conglomerates were cautiously supportive of the government. Gülen's *Zaman*,
on the same wavelength as the AKP, even more so. But with time Erdoğan
focused on cultivating his own loyalist media – in his mind, a *sine qua non* in

Turkey's cut-throat politics. In 2007, Çalık, a business group with interests in textiles and energy, assumed ownership of *Sabah*, a leading daily, as well as of the ATV channel. The deal was financed by the state-owned Vakıfbank and Halkbank. Ahmet Çalık never hid his links with Erdoğan whose son-in-law, Berat Albayrak, worked as Çalık Holding's CEO between 2007 and 2013. At the same time, with Ergenekon and constitutional reforms, the government started to face growing criticism from mainstream media.

Unfortunately for Turkey, Erdoğan's instinct was to use the state in order to fight back. In September 2009, the tax authorities slapped a record fine to the tune of $2.53 billion on Doğan Yayın, a major conglomerate whose portfolio included high-circulation dailies such as *Hürriyet* (along with its popular English version *Hürriyet Daily News*) and *Milliyet*, the left-liberal *Radikal*, *Fanatik* specializing in sports, as well as TV outlets such as CNN Türk, part of the global franchise, and Kanal D. The sum was twice the amount of unpaid taxes by the group and came on top of another $500 million penalty levied earlier in the year. What was at play was a personal rivalry between Erdoğan and Aydın Doğan, a street-smart tycoon who had risen to prominence in the 1980s. There was bad blood with *Hürriyet* over its coverage of corruption scandals[35] but going after Doğan came as a warning to business elites in general. The publisher figured prominently in the Turkish Industry and Business Association (TÜSİAD) and had links to other prominent family groups. TÜSİAD came under pressure by Erdoğan to support the "yes" vote in the 2010 referendum.[36]

The tax case proved to be an inflection point. In 2011, Doğan sold *Milliyet* to Demirören, a pro-government group. Sedat Ergin, an outspoken critic of Erdoğan, lost his job as editor-in-chief. Doğan's media retained their critical edge for some years but avoided direct confrontation with the authorities. CNN Türk attracted ridicule during the 2013 Gezi protests for airing a documentary about penguins in an apparent attempt to divert attention away from the events unfolding in central Istanbul.[37] Other parts of the former media empire limped on but ultimately closed up shop. Having terminated its print edition in 2014, *Radikal* folded two years later and its former editor moved to Britain. *Hürriyet* and *Hürriyet Daily News* moved to Demirören in 2018 as did CNN Türk.[38] By that time, terms like "*yandaş medya*" (crony media) or "*havuz medyası*" (literally "pool media") had gained currency.[39]

The shutdown of Gülenist media by the government marked the next step. Outlets like *Zaman* and its English-language subsidiary, *Today's Zaman*, offered staunch support to the AKP by providing platforms to both conservatives and liberal, pro-EU commentators. But when Erdoğan and the Hizmet movement finally parted ways in 2013, they turned into a threat. Authorities put pressure on *Zaman* and ultimately forced its closure in March 2016. The internet archive of both *Zaman* and its English version was wiped out. The Gülenist TV channel Samanyolu (Milky Way) went off air after the coup attempt in July 2016. The purge also targeted Ahmet Altan, who had resigned as editor of *Taraf* in 2012. In 2018, he was handed down a life sentence for being part of "the Fethullahist Terrorist Organization" (FETÖ) and therefore implicated in the coup plot.

Cumhuriyet (Republic), one of the most resolute critics of Gülen, fared not much better. The former mouthpiece of the early republic was never on Erdoğan's side. But the publication of a story about MİT transfers of arms to Syria (see Chapter 5) infuriated the government. In November 2015, *Cumhuriyet*'s editor-in-chief Can Dündar was arrested and later sentenced to five years and ten months in prison for terrorism. He sought refuge in Germany after the Constitutional Court overruled the judgment, only to face another trial – *in absentia* – which resulted in a 27-year sentence in December 2020.

In the 1990s and 2000s, Turkey witnessed gains in respect to media freedom. Sadly, the trend was reversed in the 2010s. From its position of 101 in the Reporters without Borders' press freedom index in 2007, Turkey plummeted to number 157 in 2019. Opposition discourse has been confined to a few printed outlets (e.g. the Kemalist *Sözcü* or *Cumhuriyet*) as well as online portals – such as left-liberal-leaning Bianet, T24 – catering to niche audiences. The proliferation of social media, and greater access to internet, has not provided a remedy – due to the prominence of fake news and disinformation finding fertile ground in the ever polarized Turkish society.[40]

KURDISH OPENINGS

Though the AKP's reformist phase was all but over by the early 2010s, the party still had one redeeming grace: the Kurdish issue as well as minority rights more broadly. The Kurdish openings of 2009 and 2013–15 proved the point.

They were the outcome of negotiations with the PKK that had been taking place outside Turkey since 2007. Pacifying the southeast through a deal with Kurdish nationalists was a goal that suited Erdoğan. Virtually all locals, irrespective of their political leanings, favored greater linguistic and cultural rights for Kurds and the recognition of Kurdish identity. Doing away with the Turkish state's traditional strategy of repression and containment promised to stabilize the region, possibly win votes for the AKP that was anyhow doing well with pious Kurds, as well as strengthen Ankara's foreign policy.

The question was how much the Turkish government was prepared to concede without risking a nationalist backlash. Erdoğan trod carefully, focusing on language and culture rather than accommodating demands to grant Kurds constitutional status. On 1 January 2009, the public broadcaster TRT launched a 24-hour channel in Kurmanji as well as in the Sorani dialect spoken in northern Iraq. The prime minister himself uttered a few words in Kurmanji at the ceremony. The state TV channel was intended to replace the pro-PKK Roj TV, which broadcast from Europe via satellite. But as TRT 6 went on air, the Turkish air force bombed militants in northern Iraq while the general staff hinted that it could launch a ground incursion similar to the so-called Operation Sun a year before. A wave of arrests in 2009 kicked off a mass trial against the so-called Kurdish Communities Union (Koma Civakên Kurdistanê, KCK), an umbrella organization bringing together the PKK and Kurdish parties from Turkey and across the region that subscribed to Öcalan's doctrine of "democratic autonomy".[41]

The government policies appeared to be working. The PKK announced a ceasefire in April 2009. At the end of July, Interior Minister Beşir Atalay unveiled in parliament a new "democratic initiative." PKK fighters would be amnestied and allowed back from northern Iraq. Some restrictions on the use of Kurdish in public institutions (e.g. in prisons during family visits and in sermons delivered in select mosques) were lifted too.

The peace initiative was met with enthusiasm by civil society. TESEV, a pro-EU liberal think-tank, launched proposals for far-reaching reforms – for example, the introduction of Kurdish at schools, initially as an elective subject; a sweeping amnesty and the disbanding of the Village Guards; lowering the electoral threshold from 10 per cent to 5 per cent.[42] The West likewise applauded the initiative. During his high-profile visit to Turkey in April 2009,

President Barack Obama took extra care to dispel fears that the US sympathized with Kurdish separatism. He paid tribute to the government's "Armenian Opening," a parallel process launched by Ankara, by commending the efforts to normalize ties with Yerevan. The EU's regular report praised the creation of "a positive atmosphere around a possible solution to the Kurdish issue." Even though there were formidable hurdles going forward, Brussels noted the emergence of "a vibrant domestic debate [. . .] on this subject, involving public and political authorities."[43]

Yet the 2009 opening turned out to be stillborn. The PKK overplayed its hand – or perhaps the deals it cut with the AKP were flawed from the start. In October, a party of 8 guerrillas and 26 exiles crossed from northern Iraq through the Habur gate. The heroes' welcome they received and the victory parades through the southeast, all televised, fired up Turkish public opinion and offered a prime opportunity to the opposition CHP and MHP parties to score points. The military ramped up its rhetoric while the Constitutional Court imposed a ban on the DTP as well as on its leader, Ahmet Türk. As 1,400 municipal officials from the party were arrested for belonging to the KCK, the PKK renewed its attacks in December 2009. The Kurdish initiative never truly took off.[44]

Still, there was a silver lining. Behind-the-scenes efforts carried on at full steam. In September 2011, leaked recordings showed that Hakan Fidan, director of the MİT was holding secret talks with a team led by Mustafa Karasu, a member of the PKK's top command, in Oslo, Norway.[45] There were definite signs of progress. In August 2010, the Kurdish militants declared a ceasefire, supposed to hold till the general elections in June 2011. In November 2011, Erdoğan created shockwaves when he apologized for the massacres perpetrated by the state in the Alevi Kurd-populated area of Dersim (Tunceli) in 1937–38 (incidentally, a period when the CHP ruled Turkey in a one-party system).[46] While the Turkish state was fighting the PKK, the prospect of peace was still out there.[47]

These efforts bore fruit. During the Nowruz celebrations in March 2013, Abdullah Öcalan issued a letter calling for a new truce, which was read aloud at a rally in Diyarbakır. "We have reached the point where weapons should go silent and ideas speak," Öcalan reflected,[48] while speaking of the brotherhood of Kurds and Turks. The letter came after months of negotiation between him and the authorities, as Erdoğan admitted in late 2012.[49] The PKK announced a ceasefire and committed to pull back to its bases in northern Iraq. A lasting settlement appeared to be within reach, Turkey's own version of the Good Friday Agreement in Northern Ireland.

The new initiative, dubbed the solution process (*çözüm süreci*) or peace process (*barış süreci*), spoke to the fact that the AKP and the Kurdish movement needed one another. The PKK, entrenched in the Qandil mountain, and the Turkish army and gendarmerie had long been locked in a stalemate. Neither side could prevail over the other. In addition, Erdoğan was contemplating a partnership with the BDP. The Kurdish party had done very well in the June 2011 elections, outperforming the AKP in the southeast provinces. Erdoğan could enlist BDP's votes to get to the coveted 330 MPs needed to rewrite the constitution, and fulfil his promise to the voters as well as his long-term goal. Resolving the Kurdish issue, a wound that had festered for decades, would secure his place in Turkey's history and extend his power and influence across the Middle East. For their part, both Öcalan and Selahattin Demirtaş, the BDP's co-chair, insisted on all-out decentralization of the state, rather than limited cultural rights. Such bold demands would be a non-starter for the CHP, even if Kemal Kılıçdaroğlu shared an Alevi Kurdish ancestry, not to mention the far-right MHP for whom peace with the PKK constituted an anathema.

To their credit, Kurdish activists never fully bought Erdoğan's claim that he stood for historic reconciliation and democratic deepening. That was understandable. Skepticism about the Turkish state's good will, no matter who happened to be in charge, Islamists or secularists, was pervasive.[50] Radical voices warned that Öcalan, an idol for nationalist Kurds though he was, had no right to speak on behalf of the entire community. To others, the image of two great men, Tayyip and Apo, in command of their respective tribes smacked of patriarchy.[51] On the positive side, the BDP and its extension, the HDP, made up for that, deciding in 2014 to be led by a male and female co-chair.

As a consequence, Kurdish activists hedged their bets. That is why BDP supporters – but not party cadres! – joined the Gezi protests in the summer of 2013, alongside Erdoğan's opponents from across the political spectrum. The demands for accountability and democracy resonated with them. However,

Kurds' presence was understated and the southeast stayed calm. So long as the peace process ploughed on, the BDP's door to the AKP remained open.

PEOPLE POWER

In its first two terms, the AKP governed in an informal coalition with liberal and pro-Western civil society. The Gezi Park protests spelled the death knell of this alliance, well past its expiry date, once and for all.

When a handful of environmentalists pitched their tents in the green patch next to Taksim Square, few expected their protest against the park's redevelopment into an Ottoman-themed shopping mall would blow up into a political crisis of humongous proportions. What started as a very Turkish version of the Occupy Movement turned into a fight about the very definition of democracy. When police raided the encampment on 29 May 2013, a much larger crowd massed on Taksim Square with protests spreading to Ankara, Izmir and even in the Anatolian heartland. Estimates suggested that some 2 million took part at the peak in June. But unlike the Republic Rallies of 2007, the multitude was more diverse. Environmental activists and middle-class professionals, ultranationalists and Kurds, hippies and old-school trade unionists, the CHP base and LGBT+ rights' campaigners, fans of all three major Istanbul football clubs and a group styling itself "anti-capitalist Muslims" shared the square.[52] They did not foment a coup, as Erdoğan alleged, but simply demanded that the authorities listen to their voice. Protestors wanted to preserve Gezi Park, a rare calm spot in an urban sprawl. They also objected to other vanity projects, such as the planned third bridge over the Bosphorus named after Sultan Selim the Grim (1512–20) and a canal connecting the Black Sea and the Sea of Marmara. Erdoğan's encyclicals about private life, such as a call he made for women to give birth to (at least) three children, alienated liberals formerly leaning towards the AKP, too. At the end of the day, the protest was about the citizens' rights against the wishes of a strongman who claimed legitimacy by appealing to his unique link to "the people."

Early in the protest, the AKP's leadership sought to bring the temperature down. On 4 June, Deputy Prime Minister Bülent Arınç, part of the party's founding triumvirate, apologized to the protestors injured by the police. President Gül struck a conciliatory note as well. "We got the message," he told journalists.[53] Both he and Arınç were probing for a way out of the crisis: such as delegating the decision on Gezi to the courts.

Erdoğan would have none of that, however. Returning to town on 7 June after a tour of North Africa, he blamed the demonstrators for being stooges of the "interest rate lobby" (even if he met with some representatives of the protest later on). Four days later, riot police charged in. By 15 June, they had cleared the square with the help of armored vehicles, pepper gas and water cannons. In parallel, Erdoğan staged a mass rally under the slogan "Respect for National Will" (*Milli İrade Saygı*) in Istanbul's Kazlıçeşme neighborhood on the banks of the Marmara Sea. True to style, he castigated Gezi as "nothing more than the minority's attempt to dominate the majority. [. . .] We could not have allowed this and we will not allow it." They stood for the arrogant old elites. ("According to them we are uneducated, ignorant, the lower class, who has to be content with what is being given, needy.")[54] Erdoğan dubbed protestors marauders (*çapulcular*), spawning a whole new genre of jokes. But his message did energize the grassroots. "One state, one nation, one fatherland, one flag" read one of the slogans at the rally. "One leader" would not have been entirely inappropriate.

Gezi provided a foretaste of what was to come in Turkey. The main take-away was that Erdoğan would tolerate no opposition to his rule. The days of the AKP as a broad-based movement were over, the break with liberal fellow travelers a done deal. Erdoğan fell back on his habitual strategy of drawing fault lines, this time between the ordinary folk and the entitled middle-class urban types who had seen their personal fortunes rise on the AKP's watch. Besides, protests lacked staying power and organizational backbone to turn into a long-term political challenge. "Those guys have nine-to-five jobs," scoffed a pro-government observer at the time.[55]

The crackdown also signaled that Turkey had drifted away from the West. Had the government truly cared about the EU's reaction, it would have followed Gül and Arınç's line. Alas, no. Erdoğan had long given up on Europe, whose influence over Turkey's domestic scene had plummeted with the impasse in the membership talks. Nationalism was the political currency of the day. Gezi highlighted Erdoğan's skill in manipulating Turkish society's deep-seated suspicions towards the outside world. In his telling, the protests boiled down to the machinations of unnamed foreign powers conspiring to thwart Turkey's inexorable rise to greatness. The West was no longer an ally but a hostile force. Never mind the Obama administration's overtures to Ankara or French President François Hollande's decision to lift his predecessor's veto on several key chapters in the EU membership talks. The theme of Turkey facing off with the West would come back with vengeance in the aftermath of the abortive 2016 coup.

THE CLASH WITH THE GÜLENISTS

Gezi marked Erdoğan's divorce from Turkey's liberals, an alignment forged in the AKP's first term and which reached its zenith during the showdown with the Kemalist establishment. But in retrospect what came to shape the country's trajectory going forward was the split within the Islamist movement. As 2013 was drawing to an end, the collision between Erdoğan and Fethullah Gülen's Hizmet movement, simmering for years under the surface, came into the open. The aftershocks are felt to this day, with "FETÖ" put side by side with the PKK ("the terror organization") as the sworn enemies of the Turkish state.

At the outset, the AKP and Gülen's *cemaat* were natural partners. They both shared the belief that Islam should occupy a central place in the public sphere and state institutions and saw the Kemalist establishment as the adversary. Gülenists had capable cadres, recruited from among youth schooled in their private tuition centers (*dershaneler*) and communal homes providing affordable lodging for students from poor backgrounds.[56] The movement's media and business arms backed the AKP government, providing a platform to both conservative and left/liberal critics of the old regime. Spreading far beyond Turkey's borders into the former Soviet Union, the Balkans and sub-Saharan Africa – as well as in the West, the *cemaat* proved a first-rate foreign policy asset as well. In the 2000s, Gülen's schools – noted for the quality of instruction – and trading companies were at the forefront of the Turkish policy of economic and soft power outreach in far-flung corners of the world.

Yet the partnership was far from harmonious. To start with, the Hizmet movement's method of spreading its influence – through reshaping culture and society from the bottom up ("seizing the arteries of the system," as Gülen put it in a video)[57] – contrasted with Erdoğan and the AKP's preference for seizing and centralizing power at the top. The Gülenists' mantras about ecumenism, interfaith dialogue and the like, which gave the movement mileage in the West, sat at odds with the Millî Görüş tradition of fusing Islam and Turkish nationalism. These, to be sure, were not insurmountable differences, so long as both parties shared a common enemy in the Kemalist establishment. But once the enemy was vanquished, the cracks became even more visible. The Gülenists' trademark was the infiltration of its members into the bureaucracy, the police and the judiciary, a process which gathered momentum with the AKP government and which sparked a huge amount of controversy with the Ergenekon and Balyoz investigations. Who were those networks, later called "parallel structures" (*paralel yapı*), accountable to – Erdoğan or the Hizmet movement hierarchy, headed by Gülen himself in his compound in Pennsylvania? .

The question became salient as years went by. The *Mavi Marmara* crisis between Turkey and Israel witnessed the first sparks, as the *cemaat* disapproved of turning against the Israelis and their Western backers – as did others too, to be sure. Then, in February 2012, the prosecutor Sadrettin Sarıkaya summoned Hakan Fidan, the head of the MİT, for questioning over leaked recordings from the negotiations with the PKK in Oslo.[58] This was a direct attack against Erdoğan; it was on his behalf that Fidan – a confidante who also stood by his side during the 2016 coup attempt – engaged with the talks. The wiretaps also put on display the existence of rogue elements within the security apparatus intent on undercutting the government. Gezi also played a role. On 6 June 2013, Gülen blamed the authorities for the brutal suppression of the protests. "Is the shopping center that was to be built there worth a single drop of blood?" he asked in an interview for *Zaman*.[59] In the following months, his media accused Erdoğan of trampling on dissent in ways the anti-democratic former elite had done in the past. Islamism was taking a Kemalist turn. The schism was now public.

The movement's main leverage, however, was access to incriminating information and its sway over law enforcement. As the journalist Aslı Aydıntaşbaş wrote in 2016, "[I]n time, the Gülenists became AKP's version of the 'deep state.'"[60] On 17 December 2013, the Istanbul Security Directorate detained 52 individuals – including officials, a construction tycoon, the general manager of Halkbank, an Iranian go-between by the name of Reza Zarrab and no less than three sons of cabinet ministers – over a scheme to bypass the UN sanctions on Iran and launder the proceeds. Indictments followed. Worse still, leaked tapes appeared, one after the other. A wiretap, released on the internet in February 2014, appeared to show Erdoğan himself discussing the illegal trade with his son Bilal.[61] Erdoğan struck back with allegations of an international conspiracy against Turkey, denouncing the recordings as a stitch-up and calling Gülenists – for the first time – terrorists. The AKP circled the wagons. President Gül and Ali Babacan, who stood in opposition to Erdoğan, spoke of a "mini-coup."[62]

It is difficult to tell what turned the behind-the-scenes rift between the AKP and Gülenists into a bare-knuckle political fight. Possibly, the intention was to harm Erdoğan ahead of the municipal and presidential elections in 2014 with a corruption scandal whose credibility was confirmed in subsequent criminal cases in the United States against Zarrab and Halkbank's deputy manager Mehmet Hakan Atilla. If that was truly the case, the strategy did not work. The AKP did not hemorrhage support to the extent that Erdoğan's bid to be elected as president would be jeopardized.[63] On the contrary, the scandal provided a pretext to settle scores with the Hizmet movement. Having reshuffled his cabinet to remove compromised ministers, Erdoğan took aim at police and prosecutors. Five thousand officers and close to a hundred prosecutors, including those working the Ergenekon case, were reassigned. New legislation widened the MİT's powers. Investigations into illegal wiretapping ensued. A number of Ergenekon and Balyoz defendants had their sentences overturned and were set free. Erdoğan pushed back – and strongly. Gülenists, once a rising faction within the state, were in retreat.

Following the democratic gains in the 2000s, Turkey was clearly backsliding as the AKP entrenched itself in power. That was to a large degree a function of Erdoğan's ambition. Even before he won a third mandate in June 2011, his preferred direction of travel was towards a presidential regime backed by a thinnest of majorities possible and drawing strength from demonizing opponents and, increasingly, the outside world as enemies of the Turkish nation. Not only did he implement the populist playbook, in many respects he authored it. Tilting the playing field was Erdoğan's way of surviving and prospering in politics, the costs of stepping down piling up as the 2013–14 corruption scandal demonstrated. However, there is a word to be said about the systemic factors which enabled his rise. Those include an illiberal opposition which rooted for the outright suppression of the AKP, branded as an irreconcilable foe rather than a competitor, and which failed to propose alternatives on critical issues such as the effort to resolve the Kurdish question. As we shall see, the authoritarian legacies shaping the state were also at play. Once Erdoğan abandoned EU-oriented reforms and minority rights for Turkish nationalism, with a conservative religious tinge, he found many allies and fellow travelers – notably among former enemies.

7
THE NEW TURKEY

On 29 October 2014, Turkey marked the Republic Day. Ninety-one years after the abolition of the Ottoman state by Mustafa Kemal and its replacement with a republican regime, Erdoğan's aficionados were hailing the birth of a new Turkey. A freshly completed presidential palace in Beştepe, on the edges of Ankara, stood as its symbol. Drawing inspiration from Seljuk and Ottoman-period architecture, the august building, spread over an area of 200,000 square meters, boasted some 1,150 rooms, a "National Mosque" as well as a library holding on deposit some 5 million volumes, the largest in the country.[1] The compound came to be known as "the Saray," a flashback to the times of sultans and their courtiers. As far as the authorities were concerned, it was a *külliye*, an Ottoman administrative edifice built around a place of worship.

Whatever you chose to call it, Erdoğan's new home conveyed an unmistakable message. The new Turkish president, elected by a popular vote two months beforehand, was not going to be like any of his predecessors, bar Atatürk. Erdoğan was gearing up to what US historian Arthur Schlesinger once called an imperial presidency. Rather than a residence, Beştepe was meant to be the fulcrum of state power. The *külliye*, the presidency announced, would house staff from across government departments. Whereas previous presidents, including Abdullah Gül, played to the constitutional notion of the head of state as an independent arbiter, removed from the hustle and bustle of everyday politics, Erdoğan saw his new job as means to amass even more power than he already had. And he made sure he saw his plans through. Incidentally, one of the first foreign dignitaries to pay a visit to Beştepe was Russia's President Vladimir Putin.[2]

The Saray was more than a reflection of Erdoğan's boundless ambition. It made a statement about Turkey's identity. The presidential compound was erected on land deemed sacred by Turkish secularists – a plot carved out from the Atatürk Forest Farm which Mustafa Kemal founded in the mid-1920s and donated to the state at the end of his life. But this was not about erasing the Kemalist legacy but rather appropriating and refashioning it in ways fit for the new era. Rather than radical Westernizer who clamped down on Islam and tradition, Atatürk was to be celebrated as a strong-willed leader who saved the state during a life-and-death ordeal and restored Turkey's prestige and power. Erdoğan, the "anti-Atatürk Atatürk,"[3] was in the same line of business. For 2023, the republic's centennial, he listed a raft of bold objectives: making Turkey one of the world's top ten economies, enrolling all citizens into a health care insurance scheme, building three nuclear power plants and so on. "Reaching the level of contemporary civilization" pitched as the Turkish government paid tribute to Mustafa Kemal.[4]

What set "New Turkey"[5] apart from the Turkey of old was the political system Erdoğan forged in his image. His tenure as president saw the emergence of a hybrid regime where multi-party competition cohabited with one-man rule.[6] Completed in 2018, the transition to a presidential system prompted Freedom House to downgrade Turkey to "not free." Democratic erosion had reached its final point as Turkey sank by 31 points in the international watchdog's rankings, with the second-worst performance after Burundi.[7] Scholars noted that the Turkish case defied theory, in the sense that a relatively well-off, middle-income polity had relapsed into authoritarianism.[8] But Turkish citizens were in for an even more striking realization. Unlike other autocratic or semi-democratic regimes in regions such as East Asia, Turkey's presidential system has failed to deliver on its promise to produce high levels of growth and prosperity. There has been no shortage of cases worldwide where constituents trade their freedoms for stability and well-being. With their economy in turmoil, in no small part as a result of mismanagement, the people of Turkey seem to have gotten the worst of both worlds.

INFORMAL RULES

Erdoğan's presidential regime did not start with the 2017 constitutional overhaul but from the moment he assumed office on 28 August 2014. Having completed two and a half terms as prime minister in a country once defined by its volatile politics, he struck a domineering figure. "Love him or loathe him, he is one of Turkey's most successful politicians," commented a BBC correspondent in Turkey during the inauguration.[9] Moving to a new office was not about conforming with the requirements of the position. On the contrary, it was about Erdoğan reshaping the institution to suit the personality of its occupant. In fact, the day before the inauguration, the AKP held an extraordinary party congress at which Erdoğan reiterated that Turkey needed a new constitution. That is why the CHP, including its leader Kemal Kılıçdaroğlu, boycotted the oath-taking ceremony in parliament, with MPs walking out right before the opening.

Formally, Erdoğan paid heed to the constitutional stipulation that the head of state should hold no party affiliation. The AKP congress elected a new leader, Foreign Minister Ahmet Davutoğlu who became the new prime minister. Constitutionally, Davutoğlu was supposed to take charge of the executive and drive the legislative agenda, reliant on the AKP's parliamentary majority. Davutoğlu would select ministers as well as top government officials and pick candidates for the party lists in the general elections slated for the summer of 2015. In practice, however, Erdoğan's departure to the presidency made no difference as he retained control over the AKP, as he had intended to from the start. Davutoğlu was handpicked as a successor precisely because he did not appear to pose a threat. The former university professor had never been an electoral politician; he owed his career personally to Erdoğan. It was a safe bet that Davutoğlu would remain loyal and not attempt to take the reins. In consequence, Erdoğan's unbridled influence over the AKP guaranteed him the final say on key decisions. In the run-up to the vote in June 2015, for instance, he vetted the electoral lists, overruling Davutoğlu who – defying expectations – did try to fight his corner. Breaking with precedent and shedding all pretense of impartiality, President Erdoğan entered the electoral campaign and held rallies, as he had done before as head of the AKP.

Erdoğan acted as a de facto executive president – for example, in chairing a meeting of Turkey's cabinet in January 2015,[10] taking advantage of a rarely used constitutional provision. To be fair, his behavior was not unique. Before Erdoğan, there had been ambitious, larger-than-life figures such as Turgut Özal or Süleyman Demirel, who wished to call the shots from Çankaya Mansion, the seat of the president.[11] Yet no one had stretched the 1982 constitution to its limits like Erdoğan, not even Özal whose Motherland Party (ANAP) controlled the government in 1989–91 while he was in the presidency. Erdoğan argued that, having been directly elected, he enjoyed popular legitimacy and represented the national will to a greater degree than his predecessors.

The ultimate proof that a de facto presidential – or at least, semi-presidential – regime had set in came with the downfall of Davutoğlu in May 2016. By that point, the tensions between him and Erdoğan were out in the open. They disagreed on how to handle senior AKP cadres implicated in corruption, on negotiations with the PKK, on political appointments at various levels and on who ought to represent Turkey internationally. A long list detailing points of conflict between the prime minister and the president, some purely personal and some driven by the institutional logic of semi-presidentialism, were published in a blog in April 2016. Known as the Pelican File, a reference to popular writer John Grisham, the leak came from Erdoğan loyalists backed by his son-in-law Berat Albayrak.[12] It precipitated Davutoğlu's resignation, reportedly tendered on 3 May, and his replacement as prime minister and AKP leader by Binali Yıldırım became official on 22 May 2016. "The palace coup" (*saray darbesi*), as commentators called it, testified that, for all intents and purposes, Turkey functioned as a presidential republic.

Davutoğlu's ouster was the endpoint in the AKP's transformation into a party fully beholden to Erdoğan. It had already shed its liberal fellow travelers who were instrumental to its success in the 2000s. The aftermath of the Gezi protests of 2013 saw off party co-founder Abdullah Gül.[13] Next in line was Bülent Arınç, the third co-founder, who had served as parliament speaker in the crucial years between 2002 and 2007 and as deputy prime minister under Davutoğlu. Arınç resigned in August 2015 over the failure of the Kurdish peace process. Ali Babacan, one of the architects of Turkish economic policy in the boom years in the 2000s, left at that point too.[14] Deputy Prime Minister Yalçın Akdoğan, Erdoğan's former confidante, stepped down together with Davutoğlu in May 2016, followed by Interior Minister Efkan Âlâ in August 2016. At the end of the 2010s, former AKP grandees would provide cadres for splinter parties such as Gelecek Partisi (Future Party) set up by Davutoğlu and Gül and Babacan's Deva (Democracy and Progress Party, Demokrasi ve Atılım Partisi).

What supplanted AKP 1.0 is a circle held together by nepotism and loyalty to Erdoğan, a fatherly figure of sorts, rather than ideology or common roots. The network includes relatives such as Berat Albayrak[15] and the president's brother-in-law Ziya İlgen; supporters from within the army, police and security services such as the National Intelligence Organization's chief Hakan Fidan and Defense Minister Hulusi Akar, both of whom played crucial role in the July 2016 coup attempt; political lieutenants like Süleyman Soylu, a hawkish interior minister, and Binali Yıldırım;[16] and technocrats such as Vice-President Fuat Oktay whose career skyrocketed after the coup attempt in July 2016 or Fahrettin Altun, a sociologist who serves as presidential spokesman and director of communications.[17] Often at odds with each other, these figures and groups have their interests and life prospects solidly tethered to Erdoğan's. First, the dynamic between the different lobbies in power, a much discussed subject, has been the staple of "Saraylogy," Turkey's own version of Kremlinology. Second, the opaque, personalist regime thrives thanks to an alliance with crony business profiting from state-promoted multi-billion projects such as Istanbul's new airport, the third bridge over the Bosphorus or the redevelopment of Taksim Square.[18] Family ties, power and money all go hand in hand. Thus Tayyip Erdoğan and his wife Emine were witnesses at the 2019 wedding between the daughter of Yıldırım Demirören, head of the eponymous holding company, and the son of the founder of Kalyon, another palace-connected group. And, of course, Demirören and Çalık threw their weight in the 2010s behind the pro-Saray media. Turkish public life has never been a stranger to informality, to put it in very generous terms, yet under Erdoğan's watch, and thanks to the unprecedented amount of power he wields, clientelism became the norm, reaching new heights.[19]

SKEWING THE PLAYING FIELD

Even if informal authority and control gave Erdoğan most of what he wanted, he pushed on for an overhaul of constitutional rules to make his ascendancy official. The twin parliamentary elections in June and November 2015 helped him move several steps closer to his objective.[20]

Erdoğan's strategy to get to 330 MPs, the number needed for passing constitutional amendments to be put on referendum, zoomed in on the pro-Kurdish Peace and Democracy Party (BDP). That was rational as the CHP and MHP were adamantly against Erdoğan's plan to take the presidency, and had even launched a joint bid to frustrate it by fielding Professor Ekmeleddin İhsanoglu, a conservative theologian, as a rival candidate in 2014. By contrast, the Solution Process unveiled by PKK leader Abdullah Öcalan in March 2013 provided a basis for cooperation between Kurds and the AKP. However, the BDP's decision to run in the June 2015 elections as a party, rather than following its usual route of putting forward independent candidates in the southeast, ran counter to the Saray's plan, as it threatened to siphon votes away from the governing party. The BDP had a sound reason to act in such way. Its candidate in the 2014 presidential polls, Selahattin Demirtaş (formally representing the Peoples' Democratic Party, Halkların Demokratik Partisi or HDP, a sister formation), had done exceptionally well, garnering 9.76 per cent of the vote, close to the 10 per cent threshold in general elections. The BDP/HDP could expect to expand beyond their Kurdish nationalist core by winning over conservatives in the southeast as well as liberal and left-leaning Turks in the western metropoles disenchanted with both the AKP and CHP.

That is exactly what happened. On 7 June 2015, the HDP secured 13.1 per cent of the vote, comfortably passing the threshold and more than doubling its result in terms of seats from 2011. Demirtaş's gamble to run party lists, rather than independents, had paid off, and handsomely. Resurgent Kurdish national sentiments, buoyed by the successful defense of Kobani against ISIS ("the Kurds' Stalingrad"), the Solution Process legitimating the HDP among Kurdish traditionalists, the remaining momentum from the Gezi protests and Demirtaş's charisma appealing to young Turkish voters all helped the party maximize its result.[21] On the flipside, Erdoğan's negotiations with the PKK and the rise of the HDP also drove up support for the MHP, which won an extra 3.3 per cent compared to the 2011 elections, when it barely made it into the Grand National Assembly.

Gains by the HDP and MHP hurt the AKP. For the first time since 2002, the governing party lost its parliamentary majority. Its share of the vote shrank from a little under 50 per cent to 40.9 per cent, translating into a decrease from 311 to 258 MPs. Still the largest parliamentary force, the AKP needed to form a coalition in order to stay afloat. Even more embarrassing, the result of the June 2015 elections exposed the vacuity of Erdoğan's line about the national will. The ballot box demonstrated that Turkish society was diverse and that compromise, rather than us-vs-them, was the best way forward.

In theory, the AKP could enter into coalition with all three other parties, the CHP, the HDP and the MHP. Each had its pros and cons.

A grand coalition with the CHP[22] would most certainly reduce chronic polarization and put the country on a more stable footing. Surveys showed close to two-thirds favored such an arrangement, with economic growth slowing down to about 3 per cent of GDP over the previous years and concerns about inflation and unemployment on the rise. Being out of power for long years, some CHP cadres favored entering into an agreement – with all the benefits flowing from a return to power. Yet Erdoğan's demand for constitutional revision towards a presidential system, a central point in the AKP election manifesto, was a formidable obstacle. Predictably, coalition talks between Davutoğlu and Kılıçdaroğlu crashed. To the CHP, whose electoral ceiling was in the region of 30 per cent, a turn to presidentialism appeared as nothing less than an invitation to sign their own death warrant. The insistence on Deniz Baykal, the secularists' discredited former leader, becoming the Grand National Assembly's speaker was not conducive to reaching a compromise either.

The other option on the table was partnering with the MHP, ideologically compatible and hungry for power after being in the wilderness over many years. Yet Devlet Bahçeli, the party leader, was adamantly against constitutional change and also demanded an investigation into corruption allegations related to Erdoğan and his family, stemming from the recordings leaked in December 2013. In hindsight, his stance was rooted in tactical calculations rather than genuine principles. Bahçeli was likely led by his belief that the AKP was bleeding support and a repeat of the elections, the fallback option, would see the MHP gain even more strength with conservative voters flocking to its banner.[23]

A coalition with the HDP, whether formal or informal, proved a non-starter as well. Surging Turkish nationalism, tensions in the southeast provinces and Selahattin Demirtaş's uncompromising "No" to constitutional changes left little basis for a grand bargain with the AKP. "We won't make you an [executive] president," Demirtaş famously declared at a meeting of the HDP caucus on 17 March 2015.[24] The only one within the AKP who went on trying to bring the Kurds onboard was Davutoğlu. Meeting the HDP's co-chairs Demirtaş and Figen Yuksekdağ in July, the prime minister insisted his sole purpose was to revive the Kurdish peace process. However, he was giving the coalition one last shot.[25]

In the end, Erdoğan prevailed, forcing a new election – the option he favored. He reckoned the AKP could do better in snap polls because the June vote did not reflect its true strength.[26] To get to a new vote, Erdoğan applied a two-pronged strategy. One, double down on demands for a presidential republic in order to undermine Davutoğlu's attempt to negotiate a coalition cabinet with the CHP. Two, not hand to either the CHP or the MHP a mandate to try to form a coalition, after the AKP's failure to do so.[27] Instead, he left the constitutionally prescribed term of 45 days from the date of the elections to expire, which triggered new polls on 1 November. De facto presidentialism was on full display.

The elections turned out to be a triumph for the AKP, which captured close to half of the vote and regained its parliamentary majority. The HDP, but also the MHP, saw their influence dwindle. The ultranationalists lost about a third of their voters: down from 7.5 million to 5.7 million. The HDP's group of MPs decreased from 80 to 59 as a result of a 14 per cent vote swing in the southeast amidst renewed hostilities between the PKK and the state. Though the AKP was 17 seats short of the coveted 330, there was an opening towards the MHP. Bahçeli's losses chipped away his leverage while Erdoğan's clampdown on Kurdish nationalism narrowed the distance between the MHP and AKP. A coalition on the right between Islamists and ultranationalists foreshadowed Bahçeli's subsequent about-face on the issue of an executive presidency.

The AKP's bounce-back at the polls resulted from the skewed playing field combined with voters' fears. It is true that Erdoğan's decision to step back and leave Davutoğlu, a less divisive figure, to direct the campaign made a difference. Yet, this time around, the AKP mobilized state resources on an unprecedented scale to gain advantage over the opposition. Media played a crucial role. One survey calculated that the public broadcaster TRT allocated the AKP a disproportionate amount of hours compared to the CHP and MHP.[28] The outbreak of hostilities in the Kurdish-populated provinces enabled Erdoğan to wear the mantle of Turkey's defender against subversion, whipping up nationalism and driving up the AKP vote. Conservative Kurds flocked back to the governing party, frightened by violence – waged by PKK, the security forces as well as by ISIS – but no doubt prodded by the state too. The November 2015 polls showed Erdoğan as a brilliant tactician who, once again, overcame an adverse situation, turning it in his favor. But the price the country as a whole paid was steep. The election resulted in Turkey's "exit from democracy"[29] and the metamorphosis of the government into a hybrid regime with an all-powerful president at the top.

HOPES SHATTERED

Erdoğan's turn against the Kurdish movement, his espousal of conventional state nationalism and the resulting alignment with MHP had been long in the making. Cracks in the Solution Process showed as early as the summer of 2014, when Selahattin Demirtaş ran for president. The AKP, but also possibly Abdullah Öcalan, the main interlocutor in the talks, would have preferred a more low-key candidate. Later, during his 2018 trial, Demirtaş maintained that he received a letter from the imprisoned PKK leader, conveyed by Hakan Fidan and Deputy Prime Minister Beşir Atalay, urging him to coordinate with the governing party. According to Cengiz Çandar, an authority on Kurdish politics, the letter possibly asked Demirtaş to withdraw from the presidential race – in the interest of the talks.[30] However, his strong showing and subsequent decision to have the HDP run as a party in the June 2015 elections demonstrated the will to act of his own accord.

Still, the HDP had a partner in the government.[31] While Erdoğan saw it as a threat to his political ambitions, Davutoğlu, invested in the Solution Process, believed the party helped to demilitarize Kurdish nationalism and channel it into the political mainstream. For such an appealing prize, the AKP could tolerate a degree of electoral competition in the southeast. The AKP and HDP could work together because, after all, no other force apart from the Islamists, and certainly not the CHP or MHP, had shown any readiness to accommodate the cultural and linguistic demands of the Kurds. Or so the theory went.

The HDP assumed a central part in the negotiations with the PKK as they gathered speed in late 2014, thanks to the Turkish government finally letting reinforcements reach the town of Kobani, besieged by ISIS. Party representatives acted as go-betweens to the PKK high command in northern Iraq.

Though top operatives such as Cemil Bayık, Duran Kalkan and Murat Karayılan recognized "Serok Apo's" symbolic leadership, their support for the Kurdish Opening was subject to conditions. It was for the politicians to work out the modalities for the militants' disarmament, the concessions and guarantees the Turkish state would offer in return and, most importantly, the sequencing. Each side, the government and the PKK, wanted the other to move first. Ankara insisted on disarmament first, Qandil on political commitment. Brokering a deal was no easy feat even if there was political will.

Difficulties aside, in early 2015, Turkey appeared to be on a cusp of a breakthrough. On 28 February, the HDP leadership and Deputy Prime Minister Yalçın Akdoğan issued the so-called Dolmabahçe Declaration, a roadmap for a settlement of the Kurdish issue. Party representatives Pervin Buldan, İdris Balüken and Sırrı Süreyya Önder, who had been in contact with Öcalan, backed further constitutional changes geared towards democratization.[32] Speaking in front of the TV cameras, Önder made public a call by the imprisoned leader for a new PKK congress to decide on laying down arms and a monitoring committee to oversee the process. It looked as though Kurdish militants and the government had arrived at a deal, even if Qandil's endorsement was in question. Prime Minister Davutoğlu hailed Dolmabahçe as a landmark event.[33] The prospect of a settlement was looming on the horizon as never before – or since.[34]

There was one crucial piece missing, however: Erdoğan. Initially, he, like Davutoğlu, welcomed Öcalan's appeal for disarmament, adding that words had to be followed by actions.[35] But several weeks later the president changed tack. Despite reports to the contrary, Erdoğan claimed to have been kept out of the loop about the Dolmabahçe resolutions and the road towards their implementation. He called on both the HDP and PKK to commit to laying down arms. What changed Erdoğan's tone was, in all likelihood, the HDP's rise in the polls along with their response to his ambitions.[36] Demirtaş's flat-out refusal to play along regarding the constitution ("we won't make you an executive president") on 17 March 2015, not long after the Dolmabahçe meeting, signaled that the ultimate deal, if there was going to be one, would not be on Erdoğan's terms.[37]

From that point on, it was downhill all the way. The AKP parliamentary group took a hard line, no doubt under instructions from the presidential palace. In early April, it voted a new draconian law on internal security, backed by the MHP's MPs. Days later, an altercation between the PKK and the military took place at Ağrı, eastern Turkey.[38] In the meantime, Erdoğan's moves putting negotiations at risk spawned dissent within the AKP's ranks. Deputy Minister Bülent Arınç, one of the party's founders, took the unprecedented step of criticizing the president, in mild terms to be sure. Doubtless Davutoğlu was on the same wavelength as his colleagues. The AKP's pre-election manifesto, released on 21 April, spoke of the continuation of the peace talks after the parliamentary polls.[39] Yet Erdoğan's bellicose rhetoric, hardening with PYD/YPG gains in Syria in June 2015, sent a clear signal that a settlement was becoming elusive. Through the National Security Council (MGK), Erdoğan threatened the PKK affiliate with war should they push across the Euphrates. By that point, the Dolmabahçe Declaration was a fading memory.

Developments on the ground in the southeast made the worst-case scenario come true. On 5 June, two days prior to general elections, an HDP rally in Diyarbakır was bombed. Then on 20 July, a bomb killed 33 and injured 104 leftist activists gathered in Suruç, a border settlement opposite Kobani in northeast Syria. The PKK saw the suicide attacks, attributed to ISIS cells inside Turkey, as a government provocation. Two days after Suruç, on 22 July, two police officers were shot in nearby Ceylanpınar, another district of Şanlıurfa. In response, the Turkish air force bombed PKK targets in northern Iraq. The 2013 truce was over; the Kurdish militants and the Turkish state were once more on war footing. By the end of 2015, some 550 would have lost their lives: Kurdish militants, soldiers, gendarmes and police officers and 150 civilians.[40]

Violence spilled far beyond the Kurdish-populated regions. On 10 October 2015, two bombs wreaked havoc in front of Ankara's railway station, where HDP supporters were arriving for the "Labor, Peace and Democracy" rally. The bloodiest act of terror in modern Turkish history left 109 dead and more than 500 injured in its wake. Shockingly, the ISIS cell behind it turned out to be connected to the June–July attacks at Diyarbakır and Suruç. Şeyh Abdurrahman Alagöz, the suicide bomber at Suruç, was the brother of Yunus Emre Alagöz, who blew himself up in Ankara. The third brother, Yusuf Alagöz, turned out to have been close to Orhan Gönder, the Diyarbakır assailant. All three were revealed to be members of an ISIS cell known as Dokumacılar (*Weavers*) based in the southeastern town of Adıyaman, majority Kurdish but fiercely conservative.[41] Along with Bingöl and Batman, Adıyaman had sent hundreds of recruits to ISIS and other radical militias in Syria. Three thousand Turkish Kurds had lost their lives fighting on the opposite side, in the ranks of the YPG/PYD.[42] Now the war was being waged in Turkey too.

Such attacks destroyed whatever little trust remained between Kurdish activists and the government. Violence spurred a war of narratives, too. Nationalist Kurds asserted that ISIS, the enemy they were fighting in Syria, colluded with the Turkish state.[43] In their telling, the security services had turned a blind eye to jihadi militants, having previously granted them safe haven on Turkish soil. The government, in turn, cast ISIS and the PKK – as well as its alleged extension HDP – as two sides of the same coin, a twin threat to the integrity of the state. It pledged to fight terror relentlessly, whether at home or across the border in Iraq and Syria. Airstrikes against the PKK in northern Iraq on 24–25 July 2015 were codenamed Operation Martyr Yalçın (*Şehit Yalçın Operasyonu*), after a soldier killed in an ISIS attack against an outpost on the Turkish–Syrian border. The Turkish state bundled Kurdish nationalists and Islamist militants, bitter enemies in Syria and Iraq, into a single threat, with the intent of rallying public opinion behind the flag. This was a preview of what was to come during the incursion into northern Syria in August 2016.

In fairness, both sides, the state with Erdoğan on top and the PKK, shared responsibility for torpedoing the peace process. For the president, winning back a majority in parliament was a paramount priority. The rekindled conflict helped the AKP recoup its losses at the re-run of the elections in November 2015. Even if ISIS, rather than Erdoğan, was the ultimate spoiler, the state's clampdown on the jihadis on its soil was a case of too little too late. Years of tolerating radicals on account of their fight against Bashar al-Assad in Syria backfired. The attacks through 2015 showed that ISIS cells operated with ease across Turkey, with the authorities turning a blind eye or, as the HDP but others too suspected, colluding. Demirtaş spoke of "forces embedded in government institutions."[44] Last, and more importantly, the AKP's conversion to the state's nationalist outlook, a departure from the early 2000s, ran counter to the Kurdish movement's demands for autonomy or even a federalization, anathema to Turkish nationalists of all stripes.[45]

Yet the PKK was not without fault either. The retaliatory attacks in July 2015 fanned conflict. Even if the Qandil leadership pursued pragmatic aims

– to bring the authorities back to the negotiation table – they miscalculated.[46] The Turkish state pushed back hard. The best the PKK could hope for was a stalemate. But the escalating violence played into Erdoğan's hands. He had a story to tell: his government was in the business of defeating terrorism, not of denying Kurdish cultural and linguistic rights to which the AKP, it was claimed, remained as committed as ever.

Bringing the fight to the large urban areas was the PKK's worst mistake. The command failed to restrain younger militants, known as the Patriotic Revolutionary Youth Movement (YDG-H).[47] In late August, they started digging trenches and putting up barricades in Kurdish nationalist strongholds such as Şırnak, Silopi, İdil and Cizre, as well as in Sur, Diyabakır's old city, and declared autonomy. Though later disowning their actions, the PKK went with the flow. The KCK, co-presided over by Cemil Bayık, declared there was "no option for the people of Kurdistan but self-governance."[48] But gun-toting teenagers and 20-somethings were a poor match for the Turkish army and police. Police-imposed curfews and mop-up operations cleared the militants by mid-March 2016. The military's use of tanks and artillery in late November resulted in massive property damage in townships such as Cizre, Silopi, Sur and Nusaybin (adjacent to Qamishlo, the main Kurdish center in northeast Syria), tens of killed and wounded, and about 300,000 displaced. On top of that, violence in densely populated urban areas compelled conservative Kurds to defect from the HDP back to the fold of the AKP in the elections on 1 November 2015.

Advocates for peace found themselves between the hammer of the Turkish state and the anvil of the ill-fated insurgency. On 28 November 2015, prominent human rights lawyer Tahir Elçi was killed in the crossfire in Sur. His death epitomized the radicals' triumph. The HDP knew that all too well as it suffered from the blowback. Scores of its mayors and public officials (technically members of the BDP) were removed from office and replaced by government appointees (an episode which repeated itself after the local elections in 2019). Signs in Kurdish were removed from public buildings.[49] The party's branches came under close scrutiny by the state. True, Prime Minister Davutoğlu kept up the semblance of dialogue. Two HDP members, Müslüm Doğan and Ali Haydar Konca, joined the caretaker government tasked with organizing the November 2015 elections, the latter as EU affairs minister and chief negotiator. But a month into their tenure both tendered their resignations in

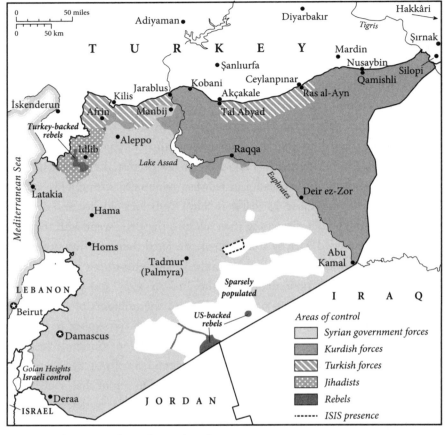

Map 2. Southeastern Turkey and Syria (2021)

response to the security operations in the southeast. After the AKP regained its parliamentary majority, it dropped all pretense that there was an ongoing policy to resolve the Kurdish issue, and reverted to the fight against terror.

With Demirtaş at the helm, the HDP had invested much in rebranding itself from a proponent of Kurdish rights to a broad platform uniting leftists, all ethnic minorities, environmentalists and gender equality activists, and so on. In the Kurdish regions, it had also courted conservative figures and groups, such as the Kurdistan Islamic Initiative for Rights, Justice and Freedom (Azadi), which was at odds with the PKK. But now pro-government media painted the HDP as a proxy for a terrorist organization.[50] That increased the cost for other opposition parties, the CHP first and foremost, for cooperating with Demirtaş. In July 2016, the pro-Kurdish party was quick to condemn the coup attempt. But it was not invited to the million-strong rally at Yenikapı in Istanbul on 10 August 2016, unlike the CHP and MHP. The vaunted spirit of national unity excluded more than a tenth of Turkey's citizens who had cast a ballot for the HDP.

Demirtaş himself paid a hefty personal price for his quarrel with Erdoğan dating back to his presidential run in 2014. The HDP co-leader was detained in November 2016, as part of the post-coup purges, put on trial and sentenced to four years in prison for spreading terrorist propaganda. The same fate befell two of the participants in the Dolmabahçe meeting – Sırrı Süreya Önder and İdris Balüken, the latter sentenced to 16 years in prison in 2018. Civic activists, who may or may not have sympathized with the HDP, bore the brunt too. Criminal charges for links to the PKK were brought against the signatories of the Academics for Peace petition in January 2016 that had demanded an end to the hostilities in the southeast. The case became emblematic of the growing levels of repression and the tightening of authoritarian rule.

With violence back in the southeast and the HDP proscribed, the Kurdish issue, the problem plaguing the Turkish body politic for decades, has been left to fester for another generation. The party proved resilient, though under constant threat of closure, and showed its strength by tipping the balance in Istanbul and other large urban centers won by the unified opposition in 2019.[51] Yet the effect on society of the rekindled conflict, coupled with the Turkish campaign against Kurdish militias in Syria, has been equally harmful. While previously a vast majority supported the government's peace initiative, now the populace has swung to anti-Kurdish nationalism. The extreme nationalist discourse of the 1990s came back with vengeance, especially with terror attacks by PKK factions in big cities like Ankara and Istanbul.

THE 15 JULY COUP ATTEMPT AND ITS FALLOUT

Erdoğan's move to the presidency, the war with the PKK and the repeated election in 2015 pushed Turkey down the path of authoritarianism. But it was the abortive military coup on 15–16 July which proved the ultimate inflection point. A true life-and-death moment, it enabled Erdoğan to complete the journey he had embarked upon in the late 2000s, pass the constitutional changes he had long desired and achieve a quasi-monarchical status. The very moment on the evening of 15 July 2016 when tanks blocked the two bridges across the Bosphorus and jets took off from the Akıncı (now known as Mürted) airbase near Ankara, it was painfully clear that there could be no happy ending. Over the course of twelve tense hours, Turkey teetered on the edge of a civil war – broadcast live on TV, to boot. The sacrifice of hundreds of citizens, Erdoğan's decisive actions and sheer luck precluded such an outcome. Yet the aftermath of the putsch proved nearly as devastating. In the name of protecting democracy, the Turkish government carried out a sweeping purge which literally shattered thousands upon thousands of human lives. Democratic freedoms and the rule of law sustained even greater damage. In a sense, Turkey is still dealing with the consequences of the coup.

Who was behind the attempt at a military takeover? The government promptly pointed in the direction of Fethullah Gülen and his acolytes, or the Fethullahist Terrorist Organization (FETÖ). Virtually on the day after, conspiracy theories proliferated, spread in good part by the Gülenists themselves, that it was a false-flag operation to justify Erdoğan's quest for absolute power. Regrettably, such outlandish claims have gotten some traction in the West. A third explanation, advanced by the CHP, claims that the MİT got wind of the plot but took no action in order to settle scores with the Gülenists once and for all. Oppositionists pointed to writings in the *Türkiye* newspaper in March–April 2016, speculating about a forthcoming coup.[52]

What we know for sure is that the coup did not fit the historic pattern. Unlike the military interventions of 1971 and 1980, or the so-called "postmodern coup" in 1997, it did not involve the top command but primarily the middle ranks.[53] In that sense, it bore some similarities to the 1960 removal from power of Adnan Menderes, lionized by the AKP, along with the unsuccessful coup attempts of 1962 and 1963.[54] A great number of the officers involved in the 15 July event had gained promotion owing to the purges related to Balyoz and the so-called "military espionage case" from 2011 (*Askerî casusluk davası*). As the political scientist Yaprak Gürsoy puts it: "[A]mong the 46 names that were promoted from colonel to brigadier admiral in the navy between 2010 and 2015, 23 of them were implicated in the putsch. [. . .] A similar situation also occurred in the air force. An overview of the 2012 promotions, for instance, shows that only two of the nine colonels who were promoted to brigadier general were not later implicated in the 15 July attempt."[55] That finding indirectly corroborates the claim of Gülenist infiltration, assuming that the appointments benefited affiliates of the movement which was known to be influential in the police and the judiciary.[56] At the same time, up to a third of the 8,651 soldiers involved in the putsch were military academy cadets and conscripts. They were likely following orders, unaware of the operation's true objectives.[57]

What is also clear is that Ergenekon, Balyoz and so on had broken hierarchies and fueled factionalism. An army within the army had emerged in consequence, as the columnist Kadri Gürsel put it.[58] Even if Gülenists led the way in fomenting the coup, they probably acted in coordination with other lobbies and groups – such as diehard Kemalists as well as opportunists jumping on the bandwagon in the hope of career advancement. The plotters named themselves "Peace at Home Council" (Yurtta Sulh Konseyi), a reference to Atatürk. The analyst Metin Gürcan, who has a military background and insight into the Turkish security sectors, has likened the coup as depicted by that theory to a train where a number of different carriages are attached to the engine pulling the whole thing.[59] A polarizing figure like Erdoğan had made a large number of enemies over his political life and united rival clans in the military. Most importantly, the coup leaders would have calculated that the odds of success were strong enough to take so risky a step as trying to overthrow a legitimately elected government. In any case, despite investigations and court proceedings, the inside story of the coup remains shrouded in mystery. The definitive account of the lead-up to the night of 15 July, a highly controversial subject in Turkey and abroad, is yet to see the light of day.

The story of how the coup happened – and why it failed – is much easier to tell.[60] At about 9 p.m. on 15 July, the mutineers made their move, arresting Chief of the General Staff Hulusi Akar and taking him to the Akıncı base. Tanks then secured the two bridges over the Bosphorus, while aircraft flying low struck at special police headquarters in Ankara as well as the MİT building. Yet the commando team dispatched to capture, and possibly kill, Erdoğan failed. The president left the seaside resort of Marmaris for Istanbul shortly after midnight, having spoken to the commander of the First Army. Erdoğan promptly made live call to the CNN Türk TV channel, using iPhone's Facetime function. This proved a gamechanger. AKP supporters rallied en masse to the Bosphorus bridges and at Istanbul's Atatürk airport. All the mosques, acting on the orders of the Diyanet, spread the appeal far and wide. The rogue troops' seizure of TRT and CNN Türk came too late. Clashes between pro-coup forces spilled over into the early hours of 16 July, with military jets striking the parliamentary building in Ankara where legislators had convened for an emergency session. But by the break of dawn, the momentum was clearly on the government's side. In the early morning, the soldiers occupying the Bosphorus bridges surrendered. Less than two hours later, General Akar was set free too. Prime Minister Binali Yıldırım declared the coup attempt was defeated in the afternoon, as the four parliamentary parties signed a joint declaration condemning it. The overnight stand-off had left a deadly trail, with 249 killed and 2,196 wounded, the vast majority of whom were civilians.[61] By a long stretch, this was the bloodiest military intervention in Turkey's modern history.

Though the coup plotters met stiff resistance, they had a chance of success. Had they moved at 4 a.m., as originally planned, they could have prevailed. The failure to neutralize Erdoğan coupled with the support he drew from the loyal military units, the police, MİT and the Diyanet, not to mention the mobilization of AKP's grassroots, won the day. Military interventions were a thing of the past; Turkey had moved on since the mid-1990s. Still, the near encounter with death impacted profoundly on Erdoğan. He accelerated his bid to formalize his already tight grip on power, bent on nipping threats – real or imaginary – in the bud. The coup's defeat averted further bloodshed, or even an all-out civil war which would have torn Turkey apart. The aftermath of Erdoğan's victory, however, proved equally grim.

One immediate consequence was the removal of all remaining constraints on the executive. The government declared a state of emergency on 20 July 2016. Originally, it covered a period of three months but was subsequently extended seven times until July 2018.[62] For two years, the cabinet – and later the president – could legislate by decree, bypassing the Grand National Assembly. During that period, Turkey held a constitutional referendum (16 April 2017) and general and presidential elections (24 June 2018). The state of emergency gave the incumbent a huge advantage over any competitors, an example of skewing the playing field *par excellence*. No wonder its introduction spurred criticism from the very outset from the CHP and HDP. Their chances of thwarting Erdoğan were slim, however, particularly after the MHP crossed the line into the government's camp.

The coup's defeat emboldened the Turkish government to unleash unprecedented purges. By the summer of 2017, the authorities had dismissed 145,000 civil servants, 7,600 military personnel and 5,000 academics. Typically, those individuals found themselves in limbo. The stigma of being linked to the coup made finding a job in the private sector nigh on impossible. Many had their passports taken, which prevented them from emigrating. The post-coup weeks and months also saw mass arrests: 50,510 people were taken into custody, including 8,815 police officers, 169 generals and admirals and 7,098 senior military officers.[63] The air force bore the brunt of the purges. It accounted for nearly a quarter of those removed, while representing 8 per cent of the military's overall personnel. More than 70,000 individuals faced criminal charges.

Over time, the crackdown expanded and took on a life of its own. From September 2016 onwards, Kurdish activists became its target, as the Turkish army entered Syria to take on ISIS, but even more importantly the PYD/YPG – which was labeled an extension of the outlawed PKK much like HDP – was also targeted. That was to be expected. The original decree framed FETÖ and the PYD as two branches of the same terrorist network. The removal of HDP mayors and Demirtaş's imprisonment earned applause from Turkish nationalists who had previously castigated Erdoğan for going soft on the Kurds, and even called him a traitor. Liberals and secularists came next. On 18 October 2017, Osman Kavala, a businessman and philanthropist, was arrested and accused by pro-government media of being linked to Gülen. The indictment charged him with seeking to overthrow the government during the 2013 Gezi protests in collusion with the billionaire George Soros, the protagonist of many a conspiracy theory. Kavala's case[64] was conjoined with that of Can Dündar, the former editor of *Cumhuriyet* (see Chapter 6). Other, less prominent, cases could be explained by overzealous magistrates and police officials trying to score points with their superiors, or atone for their past links to Gülen. But the directive to go after the likes of Kavala, Dündar or the Academics for Peace surely came from the very top. The judiciary became an instrument of repression.

Media took a big hit too. An executive decree from 27 July 2016 closed 3 news agencies, 16 TV channels, 23 radio channels, 45 newspapers, 15 magazines and 29 publishing houses, mostly associated with the Gülenists.[65] Tens of journalists were arrested and charged with links to terrorism.[66] Next came (pro-)Kurdish media. Under an executive decree from October, the authorities closed 15 news outlets (news agencies, newspapers, magazines).[67] *Cumhuriyet*, the flagship of the Kemalist regime during the early republic, was in trouble too. Murat Sabuncu, the daily's editor, and the investigative journalist Ahmet Şık, a fierce critic of the Gülen movement, were detained as well.[68]

But rather than simply justifying repressions, the abortive coup also provided a means for the AKP to mobilize its grassroots. Furthermore, it helped forge an emotionally charged myth of national unity in the face of peril. Like no event before or since, the coup shaped the identity of Erdoğan's New Turkey, rivalling other foundational narratives such as Ottoman nostalgia or the claim to leadership of global Islam. The memory of 15 July became institutionalized in a matter of weeks. In each of the country's 957 districts (*ilçeler*), authorities named public spaces "Democracy." The (first) bridge over the Bosphorus where ordinary folk stood up to mutineers became known as 15 July Martyrs (*15 Temmuz Şehitler Köprüsü*). The government was fully aware that they had a golden opportunity. Mehmet Uçum, a presidential advisor, contended that Turkey was on the cusp of radical transformation. "Just as much as 1789 influenced France and just as the Bolshevik revolution influenced Russia," in his words.[69] Erdoğan likened the resistance to the coup to the War of Independence, latching on to the time-tested theme of Turkey being under threat by internal and external enemies – and saved by a strong-willed leader. The *reis* (captain or chief), as known to his partisans, also drew a parallel between his miraculous escape from Marmaris to Dalaman airport after midnight on 16 July to Prophet Muhammad's *hijra* from Mecca to Medina. Government-controlled channels – public institutions, media, the education system – spread the official mythology around the coup far and wide.

Whipping up nationalism was the perfect political ploy suited to the moment. The AKP sought to woo CHP and MHP voters and broaden Erdoğan's base. In line with the much touted Yenikapı spirit (*Yenikapı ruhu*). As a result, the coup was framed as a Gülenist conspiracy, from start to finish. The state-sanctioned story omitted the possible implication of hardcore Kemalists within the army ranks working together with officers connected to Gülen. The latter had always been a *bête noire* for the secularists. Now Erdoğan, true to his populist instincts, seized on an opportunity to build support from across political fault lines. What also helped was the invasion in northwest Syria targeted against both ISIS and the PKK's affiliate, the PYD, starting on 26 August 2016 (see Chapter 8). It rallied Turks behind the flag amidst the post-coup patriotic surge.

The coup unleashed a wave of anti-Western sentiment. Yet again, the US appeared the prime suspect to undermine Turkish sovereignty and unity, a theme once exploited by Erdoğan's detractors from the hard secularist camp. İbrahim Karagül, editor-in-chief of the pro-government daily *Yeni Şafak*, accused the US government and military of masterminding the plot – or even taking direct part in the putsch on the night of 15–16 July. The AKP faithful pointed to the American forces stationed in the İncirlik airbase. The claim was repeated by high-placed dignitaries such as Süleyman Soylu, who took over the interior ministry at the end of August 2016. Proponents included the Eurasianists and their mouthpiece *Aydınlık*.[70] One-time AKP detractors like Doğu Perinçek, imprisoned as a result of the Ergenekon trial, wholeheartedly embraced Erdoğan. To conspiracy theorists, Fethullah Gülen's residence in the US provided the ultimate proof that Washington was behind the attempt to topple Erdoğan.[71] On 23 July, a week after the events, the Turkish government submitted an official extradition request to the US authorities. The popular perception in Turkey, stoked by the media, has been that the American judiciary's failure to hand over the exiled cleric betrayed the government's culpability. Rather than a matter of the rule of law, the case was purely political – and the Yankees were complicit. Gülen was and always had been Washington's pawn. Added to the American military's de facto alliance with the Syrian Kurds, the link to the so-called FETÖ cast the US as the arch-enemy of the Turkish nation.

The nationalist upheaval was captured in the phrase *yerli ve millî* (local and national). The Turkish nation would invest in its own strengths and capacities and turn its back on foreigners. It took various forms: from boosting home-grown defense industries in order to reduce dependence on the US and other NATO allies[72] to manufacturing automobiles to meet growing local demand.[73] Erdoğan was on a mission to make Turkey self-sufficient, a return of sorts to the *étatisme* of the interwar republic, and capable of projecting power externally to curb threats. Of course, the rhetoric was divorced from reality in that the Turkish economy remained deeply integrated into the EU economy, while the alliance with the US morphed into a transactional partnership but did not expire. But the catchphrase served as a perfect device to rally the populace behind the Turkish flag and draw a line between friend and foe. "You are not *yerli ve millî*," Erdoğan had told HDP deputies in September 2015.[74]

TURKEY UNDER ERDOĞAN

IMPERIAL PRESIDENCY

Post-coup popular mobilization laid the groundwork for the long-pursued constitutional change. The draft with 21 changes to the basic law was ready in November 2016. That was the moment where the MHP jumped ship, making official its coupling with AKP as 2017 began. "A U-turn to make stunt driver proud," mused *The Economist*, noting that the leader Devlet Bahçeli had been one of Erdoğan's "most vicious critics" as recently as October 2016.[75] By tying his political fortunes to Erdoğan, Bahçeli became in effect his junior partner in government, but his leverage has grown over time. Since the 2018 elections, the MHP has held the key to the Saray's control over the majority in parliament. Its imprint on foreign policy has been strong, as demonstrated by the escalation between Athens and Ankara in the Eastern Mediterranean over oil and gas deposits and the intervention in Nagorno-Karabakh in the autumn of 2020.[76] At that moment, Bahçeli even presented Erdoğan with "an ultimatum" to close down the HDP, a testament to his newly acquired strength.

The amendments to the Turkish constitution recast the balance within government, creating an all-powerful presidency. They abolished the office of the prime minister and rescinded the right of the Grand National Assembly, expanded from 550 to 600 members, to endorse members of the cabinet. The president could now dissolve parliament with the sole caveat that he or she, too, should step down and go to the polls. That caused no headache for Erdoğan since holding legislative and presidential elections together would, in theory at least, maximize the AKP vote. The president – head of the state as well as of the executive – could furthermore legislate through executive decrees, to be overturned only if parliament passes laws on the same subject. The amendments allowed the president to be a member of a political party[77] and established a limit of two five-year terms. Erdoğan's first stint under the old system (2014–18) did not count. He controlled the judiciary too because the constitutional changes reduced the size of the Council of Judges and Prosecutors to 13, with 6 appointed by the presidency and the rest by (the AKP-dominated) Grand National Assembly.[78]

Pro-government commentators likened the changes to the US constitution, which likewise features a strong president. The difference, of course, is the absence of checks and balances – a strong judiciary, Congress, the federal system, not to mention a robust civil society and media. Erdoğan and his partisans justified the change on the grounds of the effectiveness of the new governance arrangements. In their telling, presidentialism would help speed up administration, fight terrorist groups posing threat to the state and ensure robust economic growth. Needless to say, the new system elicited a different reaction from the opposition. The CHP drew parallels to the Middle East. "Syria's constitution translated." A majority within the public was skeptical too. A full 58 per cent disproved of the introduction of the presidential system, according to the pollster Gezici.[79]

On paper, the system contains safeguards. The president could be impeached, parliament can replace executive decrees, while the Constitutional Court can review them for conformity with the constitution and lower courts for whether they are in line with existing legislation. Yet the high threshold of two-thirds of all MPs makes impeachment highly unlikely. With the AKP holding a majority, or even a large plurality of the seats, as has been the case since 2018, the odds of the Grand National Assembly overturning a presidential decree are not great either. Lastly, as the Turkish jurist Serap Yazıcı notes with regard to constitutional review, "the Constitutional Court's tendency towards excessive self-restraint, especially after the unsuccessful coup attempt of 15 July 2016, does not give rise to optimism."[80] Amendments reduced the number of justices from 17 to 15, of whom 12 are appointed by the president. Ditto for the lower courts falling under the Board of Judges and Prosecutors' purview. To cut a long story short, the changes established the supremacy of the executive – personified by President Erdoğan – over other branches of government. This is a hallmark of competitive authoritarianism, as defined by scholars like Steven Levitsky and Lucan Way. Indeed, Turkey meets 9 of the 11 criteria outlined by Levitsky and Way.[81]

The constitutional referendum on 16 April 2017 exposed, once again, the deep divisions in Turkish society. With 48.8 per cent voting against, the amendments were passed by a thin margin. In practice, Erdoğan won by a share of the electorate comparable to the result of the presidential elections in 2014. The referendum was, to put it differently, little more than a plebiscite on the president's personality and a test of allegiance. It was not a choice about the optimal governance model resulting from deliberation and backed by broad consensus. The AKP had an inherent advantage, as suggested by scandals triggered by unstamped ballots.[82] Strikingly, the constitutional referendum was the first electoral contest not recognized by the losing side. That had not been the case of the plebiscites of 2007 and 2010, for all the social and political polarization that surrounded them.

CHALLENGING ERDOĞAN

The outcome of the 2017 constitutional referendum contained a silver lining. The "No" side made inroads into Erdoğan's electoral territory – for example in conservative quarters of Istanbul. If the opposition acted in unison – a tall order certainly – they could consolidate such gains in the future. Two years later, at the local elections of 2019, parties challenging the Saray proved that they could move in such a direction.

Realignments in the party scene were clearly a contributing factor. Bahçeli caused a rift within the MHP, which he had led since the death of the party founder, Alparslan Türkeş, in 1997. Dissidents formed the İYİ Parti (Good Party) presided over by Meral Akşener, who had mounted an unsuccessful leadership challenge at the MHP congress in May 2016. During the constitutional referendum, Erdoğan could reasonably expect that the nationalists would bring in a solid voting bloc, given that the AKP–MHP coalition exceeded 60 per cent in the last general elections (November 2015). That did not happen. Akşener, coalescing with the CHP in the "No" campaign, chipped away votes. The plebiscite also facilitated indirect cooperation with the HDP, an unthinkable feat given the ideological differences. The pro-Kurdish party already coordinated with Kılıçdaroğlu's CHP in parliament in obstructing the amendments. Thus, the CHP provided a bridge between seemingly irreconcilable factions which found themselves in the same boat thanks to Erdoğan's polarizing tactics.

Over the next electoral cycles, the opposition demonstrated the capacity to learn and compete successfully against the AKP, even with the odds stacked against it.[83] In both the parliamentary polls of June 2018 and the local elections in March 2019, the CHP and Akşener's İYİ Parti formalized the so-called Nation Alliance (Millet Ittifakı). They were joined by the Felicity Party, the late Necmettin Erbakan's outfit from which AKP had split, and the small center-right Democratic Party (successor to Demirel and Çiller's True Path), both appealing to disgruntled conservatives. Economic stagnation, with average GDP growth rates plunging to 3.2 per cent after 2013, tainted the AKP's reputation for competent steward-ship.[84] In addition, the CHP tailored its message to reach out to the pious base. Muharrem İnce, the party's presidential nominee in 2018, emulated Erdoğan's folkish demeanor and even made references to Islam.[85] The candidate for the mayorship of Istanbul, Ekrem İmamoğlu, aired a similar message in the spring of 2019. İmamoğlu famously set aside time during his campaign to attend Friday prayers. He ran a positive campaign, avoiding frontal attacks on Erdoğan and focusing instead on what he called "radical love." "Everything will be very nice" (*Herşey çok güzel olacak*) became İmamoğlu's slogan.[86]

The strategy paid off, in part. Sure enough, the opposition failed to force a run-off in the presidential elections of June 2018. Though the three major parties – the CHP, IYI and HDP (formally outside the Nation Alliance) – put forward candidates to sweep up the maximum number of votes with a view to uniting behind İnce in the second round, Erdoğan won outright in the first round. He retained roughly the same percentage which had seen him through the 2014 election (when the MHP did not back him) and the constitutional referendum (52.6 per cent vs 51.7 per cent). However, the AKP lost close to 7 per cent in the parliamentary elections, taking place simultaneously with the presidential vote. With no majority in the Grand National Assembly, the AKP became dependent on the MHP. The prospect of the opposition capturing the legislature in the future and being able to exert collective pressure on the Saray was within the realms of possibility.

The gains the opposition made in the local elections in March 2019 were even more impressive. İmamoğlu won Istanbul against Binali Yıldırım by just 13,729 votes or 0.17 per cent. Then, after the Supreme Electoral Council voided the results under pressure from Erdoğan and scheduled a re-run on 23 June, the CHP representative scored an even more impressive victory, with a lead of nearly 10 per cent, or 800,000 votes.[87] Meanwhile, Mansur Yavaş defeated Mehmet Özhaseki for mayor in Ankara, ending the AKP's dominance in the capital, which dated back to Refah's win in 1994.[88] Out of the five largest cities in Turkey, the AKP held on only in Bursa, with a small margin. The economic downturn demobilizing Erdoğan's electorate coupled with the oppo-sition's improved ability to pull together shaped the outcome. The elections showed that, for all the changes resulting from the switch to presidentialism,

Turkish politics had not lost all of its competitive character. The appearance of two new splinter parties from the AKP, Ahmet Davutoğlu's Gelecek Partisi (Future Party) and the Deva Partisi of Ali Babacan, linked to Abdullah Gül, shows that the marketplace is open for entrants who place their bets on the decline of Erdoğan's popularity.

Despite setbacks and the public's disenchantment with the presidential regime, New Turkey seems to be muddling through. AKP and MHP control over the central state looks unassailable. Starting in August 2019, it replaced elected HDP mayors in southeastern cities with government appointees (*kayyumlar*). Then, on 17 March 2021, prosecutors petitioned the Constitutional Court to close the pro-Kurdish party, a move straight out of the "Old Turkey" manual. Attacks against Kurds, leftists and LGBT+ people suggest that Erdoğan is seeking to reignite the culture wars of old in order to drive a wedge into the opposition bloc. Nationalist rhetoric has intensified as Turkish foreign policy has become even more assertive and trigger-happy.[89] There is no indication that the regime is softening in any way. Meanwhile, the state is building two more presidential palaces: in Ahlat on the banks of Lake Van in eastern Turkey and a summer residence near the coastal town of Marmaris.

The question is whether the new system is sustainable over the longer term. Lackluster economic performance, with a recession in the fourth quarter of 2018 followed by the damage wrought by Covid-19 in 2020–21,[90] does not bode well for the regime's ability to appeal beyond the core of AKP supporters. Corruption scandals and leaks, such as the revelations of high-level abuse of power and cronyism made by crime boss Sedat Peker in May–June 2021, which carry the flavor of the anxiety-ridden 1990s, chip away support too. Ditto for the opposition campaign highlighting the squandering of foreign currency reserves by the government at a time when ordinary citizens are dealing with economic hardship and the pandemic.[91] Restoring and maintaining legitimacy is therefore essential. Erdoğan's hints at future constitutional revisions, possibly as a means to divert public attention, and overtures to the EU indicate that the challenges are appreciated. However, they have not come hand in hand with domestic liberalization. Quite the contrary. To ensure stability as well as his survival on the top, Erdoğan has to ramp up repression, as is common to strongmen who are losing electoral legitimacy. Unfortunately, Turkey might be headed for authoritarian consolidation.[92]

8
"OUR SO-CALLED STRATEGIC PARTNER"

Joe Biden was doing the best job he could in Ankara on 25 August 2016. "[T]he American people [stood] in awe of the courage of your people," he assured Erdoğan, reflecting on the failed coup and the threat Turkey faced from ISIS. "And what we saw is the sensitivity that the Turkish people feel about their national security."[1] Biden was right on the money but, sadly, his assurances fell on deaf ears. To start with, Erdoğan's people sincerely believed that the US was behind the putsch, pulling the strings, eager to get rid of a strong-willed leader who would dare oppose their designs in the Middle East. Their conviction was to grow even stronger with time. On top of this, Turks of various political stripes held a grudge against the Obama administration for aligning with Kurdish militants in Syria. In early August, the YPG had seized from Daesh the town of Manbij, west of the Euphrates, crossing a red line drawn by Ankara. The Americans had failed to forestall this development, the Saray believed, letting Kurds have their way. To atone for its past mistakes, the US had to "see Turkey in a new light," or else it was all over, warned Gülnur Aybet, an academic who would go on to become Erdoğan's advisor.[2]

Needless to say, the Obama administration did not share Ankara's analysis. But that did not matter as much because Erdoğan was on the offensive. The day before Biden flew in, the Turkish military and the Free Syrian Army (FSA) launched Operation Euphrates Shield (*Fırat Kalkanı*) in Syria. After years of fighting in Syria through proxies, Turkey stepped directly into the fray to clear ISIS and stop the YPG from marching into northern Aleppo. A strategic chunk of Syrian territory came under Turkish control, giving Ankara a stake in running the war-torn neighbor and boosting its political leverage. Going it alone got the job done.

But Turkey's incursion into Syria was not a purely unilateral move; it received the blessing of one Vladimir Vladimirovich Putin. Euphrates Shield inaugurated a Russian–Turkish diplomatic and security partnership. Having failed to secure regime change in Syria, Turkey moved closer to America's competitors. Yet this did not amount to a "change of axis," as some Western pundits feared. Rather, Turkish policy attempted to juggle between Russia and the West, as well as, it should not be forgotten, China, in pursuit of influence and power. "Turkey uses Russia to balance the US and uses the US to balance Russia," as international relations scholar Evren Balta aptly describes the quest for strategic autonomy.[3] The following chapter explains how we got there.

PUTIN'S SYRIAN GAMBIT

The story starts not in Ankara's Beştepe quarter, but in the Kremlin. It is impossible to exaggerate the significance of Russia's military intervention into Syria in September 2015. Through limited application of coercive force, Moscow changed the course of the conflict and practically saved Assad's regime from unraveling. Ankara proved impotent in fighting back, as its proxies on the ground came under severe pressure and Syrian Kurds, aligned not only with the US but also indirectly with the Russians, made fresh territorial gains. Erdoğan had few choices but to make a U-turn, approaching Putin with an olive branch in hope of recovering at least some influence lost.

In the early days of the war, Moscow and Ankara could agree to disagree and keep Syria separate from other state-to-state business. More than that, Turkey went out of its way to accommodate Russia on matters close to Putin's heart. When "little green men" seized administrative buildings and military infrastructure in Crimea in late February 2014, Turkish diplomacy did not make a big fuss. Ankara formally denounced the annexation of the peninsula the following month, made a show of presenting exiled Tatar leader Mustafa Dzhemilev (Kırımoğlu) with a state order, yet parted ways with the rest of NATO by refusing to join economic sanctions against Russia. In December 2014, during the peak of Russia's international isolation, Putin came to the Turkish capital, only the second international visitor to Erdoğan's Saray after Pope Francis. There, the Russian president first floated the proposal for TurkStream, a gas pipeline over the Black Sea, replacing South Stream that the EU had effectively killed in response to Crimea. But then the Russian intervention into Syria changed Turkey's calculus. Not only did it extend crucial help to Ankara's adversaries, it also dashed hopes that military pressure could force Assad to make political concessions. Turkey's hitherto strategy suffered a defeat.

Why did Putin decide on intervening directly in Syria, having previously limited Russia's role to the provision of material assistance to the regime as well as diplomatic cover at the UN? Sure enough, the Kremlin made no secret of its opposition to the Arab Spring which it saw as a Western-instigated effort sowing chaos in its wake and threatening regime stability in Russia itself. Yet sending the troops far from home, into a region where Moscow had not been present militarily since the 1970s, upped the ante. What mattered was timing. In March 2015, the Army of Conquest, an Islamist alliance of Jabhat al-Nusra and Turkey-backed Ahrar al-Sham, took over the city of Idlib. The fall of a provincial capital could precipitate the downfall of the embattled regime – or at least break the impasse. Russia's intervention in late September, a light-touch affair initially, involving 32 combat aircraft as well as special forces,[4] in coordination with Iran, which fielded its proxy forces along with the Islamic Revolutionary Guard,[5] turned the tide. By the end of the year, core areas held by the rebels, such as the suburbs of Damascus or eastern Aleppo, came under the onslaught of the Russian air force operating out of Hmeimim near Latakia. ISIS and Jabhat al-Nusra were the ostensible targets but in reality any opponent of the regime was fair game as far as the Russian Ministry of Defense was concerned. Civilians were not spared either. The message was surrender or face starvation and death. In less than three years, most opposition enclaves "reconciled" with the regime, encouraged by Russian negotiators.

Success on the battlefield paid off. By securing Assad's survival, Russia burnished its prestige across the Middle East, a region where it had been making diplomatic inroads for more than a decade.[6] It also got to test weapons systems – ship- and submarine-launched cruise missiles – and showcase them to potential customers. The campaign testified to the achievements of military reform, ongoing since 2009, putting on display Moscow's capacity to mount expeditionary warfare far beyond the post-Soviet space. Most importantly, Syria gave Russia a major geopolitical boost. Putin emerged as a power broker in the Middle East and drew the US to the diplomatic table, with Foreign Minister Sergey Lavrov and State Secretary John Kerry negotiating a series of (stillborn) truces through 2016. A shadow of the superpower that the USSR once was, Russia was nevertheless engaging on a one-on-one basis with the Americans – and arguably gaining the upper hand.

More to the point, Putin took a gamble in Syria. By entering the war, he put on the line cooperative relations with Ankara, painstakingly built over the course of the 1990s and 2000s. In all likelihood though, he thought this was a risk worth taking. Erdoğan would have to deal with a *fait accompli*. Ties between the two countries reached their lowest point after a Turkish F-16 shot down a Russian ground-attack jet which had crossed into its airspace for seventeen seconds on 24 November 2015. The two pilots, who managed to eject, were then gunned down by Turkmen militiamen aligned with Turkey. The incident came in the wake of multiple violations of Turkish airspace by the Russians. Prime Minister Davutoğlu and Turkey's Ministry of Foreign Affairs had been complaining, to no avail.[7] And then someone up the chain of command, possibly President Erdoğan, gave the order to shoot.

Putin was livid. "A stab in the back by accomplices of terrorists," he raged at a press conference in Moscow.[8] Turkey, a country Russia considered a friend, was now the adversary. It was to pay a hefty price. The Russian Federation government then imposed economic sanctions: effectively banning tourist operators from selling package holidays in Turkey, stopping Turkish agricultural imports, introducing a visa regime and curbing Turkish construction companies operating in the domestic market. Deputy Prime Minister Mehmet Şimşek estimated the losses at about $10 billion, or over 1 per cent of Turkish GDP.[9] The Kremlin unleashed its disinformation machine as well, with stories implicating Erdoğan and members of his family in the oil trade with ISIS. In the meantime, Russian strikes cut off supply routes from Turkey to besieged eastern Aleppo and helped the YPG, or the Syrian Democratic Forces (SDF) of which the Kurdish militia formed the bedrock,[10] capture the strategic town of Tel Rifaat from Ahrar al-Sham in February 2016.

Turkey found itself in a tough spot. It was encircled, given the Russian presence in Crimea ("a true fortress" in Putin's words), in Syria as well as in the Southern Caucasus, with deployments at Gyumri, Armenia, a stone's throw from Turkey's border, beefed up.[11] Moscow controlled Syrian airspace, having deployed S-400 missiles at Hmeimim following the downing of its military jet. The Black Sea fleet was supplying the operation without interruption through the Turkish Straits, an international waterway governed by the 1936 Montreux Convention whose closure would have provoked even more vicious conflict.[12] Worryingly, NATO was of little relevance since Moscow's strategy was deliberately calibrated not to go over the bar set by Article 5 of the Atlantic Charter obliging the alliance to collectively defend a member coming under attack. Technically, Turkey was not at war with Russia and Syria was beyond the Atlantic Alliance's area of responsibility. Ankara's allies appeared wary of being dragged into a fight with the Russians. They had already declared their intentions or began pulling out their air defense systems deployed along the Turkish–Syrian border.[13] Secretary General Anders Fogh Rasmussen urged caution at an emergency meeting in Brussels right after the incident, while the US and France called on Moscow and Ankara to de-escalate.

At the time, international commentators raised alarm about an impending war. After all, the two former empires had fought at least a dozen wars between the sixteenth and the twentieth century, the reasoning went. Added to that was the threat of Russia and Turkey intervening on the opposing sides in Nagorno-Karabakh which, in April 2016, saw the deadliest fighting between Armenia and Azerbaijan since the early 1990s (soon to be eclipsed by the showdown in 2020). In reality, both Russia and Turkey acted with restraint and Putin succeeded in brokering a ceasefire. By that point, Erdoğan was already sending feelers to Moscow through the businessman Cavit Çağlar and Kazakhstan's President Nursultan Nazarbayev. In June, he even issued an apology to the Russians.[14] In other words, when Putin reached out to Erdoğan right after the coup attempt on 15 July 2016, he knew he was knocking on an open door. What he was also perfectly aware of was that the Turkish president had sufficient room for maneuver domestically, having taken charge of making foreign policy. He could easily rebrand Russia from an archfoe into a friend, and institutions as well as public opinion would happily tag along.

In the months and years after the two leaders restored ties, Turkey's pro-government media came up with good reasons to justify the U-turn. The officially sanctioned narrative contrasted Putin's support in the immediate aftermath of the coup with Western indifference or outright complicity.[15] After all, Russia had banned Gülen's movement in the mid-2000s, while the US, tellingly, failed to extradite the leader of "the Fethullahist Terrorist Organization," safe in his Pennsylvania compound.[16] Putin claimed to be a standard-bearer of the status quo, in contrast to Washington's meddling in other countries' internal affairs and undermining their duly elected leaders. As the insightful Turkish political analyst Soli Özel has observed, "[i]n contrast to the West's passivity as the coup unfolded, Russia stood by Ankara. Many Turks were deeply disappointed with the West's lack of solidarity at the time."[17] Thus, while there was a good chance Putin and Erdoğan would have eventually made up anyway, the putsch speeded up the rapprochement and provided a compelling story, to boot.

But, in the final analysis, the reason Erdoğan turned to Russia had a lot to do with Syria. For all intents and purposes, Russians were calling the shots now in a war critical to Turkey's national interest and, by extension, shaping the balance of power in the Middle East. In contrast to Obama's narrow focus on defeating ISIS which led him to befriend Kurdish nationalists, Putin could accommodate Ankara's objectives by letting it carve out a buffer zone south of the border and prevent the YPG/SDF from securing a land bridge from the Euphrates river to the Afrin enclave to the west. That is precisely what happened.

THE RUSSIA–TURKEY POWER COUPLE

Erdoğan's summit with "dear friend Putin" at the Constantine Palace near St Petersburg on 9 August 2016[18] made the reconciliation official. It also set the conditions for Turkish military intervention into Syria – and possibly other aspects of the Russo-Turkish quid pro quo, such as the agreement to purchase advanced weapons systems from Moscow. "Euphrates Shield" kicked off two weeks later, with the Turkish army and 10,000-strong FSA force taking the border city of Jarablus and subsequently besieging the ISIS stronghold of al-Bab. Russian jets pounded the jihadis from the air and one strike, on 9 February 2017, ended up killing several Turkish infantrymen. By that moment, however, such an incident counted as friendly fire. What mattered was that Turkish forces carved out a buffer zone in the north Aleppo province which stemmed the YPG's western march and, in due course, established an Ankara-run protectorate to shelter fighters as well as internally displaced persons (IDPs) from various parts of the country.[19] The safety zone Turkish authorities had been pitching to the US for years became a reality thanks to Russia. From a sore spot in relations, to be isolated from other economic and diplomatic dealings, Syria became the focus of Russian–Turkish cooperation.[20]

Russia benefited handsomely from the arrangement. Turkey withdrew support from the besieged rebels in eastern Aleppo, which was subjected to a fresh offensive by the regime, Iranian-backed militias and the Russians. In mid-December 2016, the Russian military and MİT (Turkey's National Intelligence Organization) mediated a deal to evacuate the civilians and opposition fighters.[21] Syria's largest city, partly held by the opposition since the summer of 2012, was in Assad's hands. Turkey was converted from an adversary to a partner on the ground. Even the murder of Russian ambassador Andrei Karlov, executed at point blank by a Turkish security guard in Istanbul resentful of Russia's ruthless air campaign, would not call into question the newly rekindled bonds. Aleppo's handover laid the foundations of Russian–Turkish–Iranian diplomatic talks launched in Astana, Kazakhstan's capital, in January 2017. Unlike the Geneva negotiations conducted under UN auspices, the Astana format excluded the US and bolstered Russia's role as a power broker in Syria. Turkey, a key NATO member, tilted towards Russia, a development underscored by the increased frequency of meetings and phone calls between Putin and Erdoğan.[22]

By teaming up with Russia and Iran, Turkey gave tacit endorsement for the reconquest of much of western Syria by the regime. In March 2017, the Astana negotiations yielded an agreement on setting up four de-escalation zones: around Idlib, in Rastan and Talbiseh north of Homs, in eastern Ghouta on the rural outskirts of Damascus, in Deraa and Quneitra along the border with Jordan. Hostilities were to be halted for an initial period of six months. Russia would continue to police the airspace while Turkey would vouch for the rebels. With arms silenced, negotiations between the opposition and the regime on a political settlement and a new constitution (that is, the draft Russia prepared) would go ahead.[23] Yet, soon enough, "de-escalation" proved little more than a fig leaf for the recapture of territory by the regime. By the summer of 2018, eastern Ghouta, rural Homs and Deraa/Quneitra were all in Assad's hands (or in many cases, indirect control) after Russia negotiated the rebels' surrender ("reconciliation")[24] and the transfer of rebels to Idlib or the Euphrates Shield area.

Yet one should not overlook the concessions Erdoğan squeezed out in his turn. First of all, he obtained Russia's go-ahead for Operation Olive Branch (January–March 2018), which dislodged the YPG from Afrin and established a second Turkish-controlled enclave in Syria.[25] Russian military observers embedded in the Kurdish forces which had acted as a deterrent against Turkey withdrew on 19 January, a day prior to the incursion. The Russian command had tried to persuade the Kurds to switch allegiance to Assad, using the Turkish threat as leverage. Failing to do that, they gave a *carte blanche* to Ankara and its Arab proxies, opening the airspace over Afrin too. The offensive exposed US unwillingness to stand by its Kurdish allies, as the Trump administration looked for ways to pull out troops from Syria. Turkey and Russia turfed out America, a win for Moscow's foreign policy in driving a wedge between two NATO allies. Capturing Afrin allowed Ankara to increase pressure on Manbij, on the western bank of the Euphrates, where US marines deployed alongside Kurdish militants. Erdoğan aimed at negotiating a phased American withdrawal and expanding the "Euphrates Shield" area.[26]

Next, Russia recognized Turkey's special role in the region around Idlib. Starting from October/November 2017, the Turkish military set up observation points in the area. By the summer of 2018, when Idlib became the last remaining rebel-held territory, their number rose to twelve. Meeting in Sochi on 17 September 2018, Putin and Erdoğan agreed to create a demilitarized zone separating regime forces and the opposition.[27] The Turkish side committed to disarm and disband Hayat Tahrir al-Sham, Jabhat al-Nusra's successor, which by that point had turned into the dominant faction on the ground. Idlib was home to more than 3 million people, including civilians and fighters resettled from other parts of the country; there was the threat of a massive wave of refugees into next-door Turkey if the regime seized the area. Moscow acquired powerful leverage over Erdoğan for whom the presence of more than 4 million Syrians in his country had long been a political headache. But, as we shall see, in due course Idlib exposed the limits of Russian–Turkish rapprochement and brought the two dangerously close to a showdown.

The partnership with Russia extended beyond Syria. Putin's first visit to Tukey following the "jet crisis" brought him to the World Energy Congress in Istanbul on 10 October 2016. There he signed the intergovernmental agreement on the TurkStream pipeline, a project conceived two years beforehand which would establish a transit route for Russian gas, bypassing Ukraine. Prior to that moment, the Turkish side had been driving a hard bargain concerning the commercial conditions around the venture. But the imperative to relaunch ties with Moscow softened their position and made them accept Russian terms.[28] Putin's visit also saw the finalization of a deal regarding the nuclear power plant at Akkuyu, on Turkey's Mediterranean coast. There again, the Turkish government offered tax breaks and other benefits to Rosatom it had previously refused to grant. Despite the economic reset in, the Russians were not in a hurry to lift trade restrictions imposed on Turkey during the crisis in relations – for example on agricultural imports.[29] Part of the story was that the Kremlin wanted to retain some political leverage over Ankara. But, equally, vested interests on the Russian side which had profited from the sanctions lobbied against the blanket opening of the market.

Though Turkey signed off on TurkStream, the tussle with Russia encouraged it to press ahead with the diversification of energy sources. During the crisis in 2015–16, BOTAŞ, the Turkish national gas company, signed a contract with Qatar for the purchase of liquefied natural gas (LNG). Turkey started investing heavily in LNG capacity – with two offshore terminals coming onstream between 2016 and 2018, one near Izmir and the other in Hatay province. The choice yielded dividends later on when prices went down and imports rose accordingly, including from US traders selling on the global spot markets, chipping away at Gazprom's market share. The Southern Gas Corridor, linking Turkey and its neighbors in Southeast Europe to the Caspian, similarly made headway. In the summer of 2019, the Trans-Anatolian Pipeline (TANAP) came online, offering BOTAŞ the opportunity to import 6 billion cubic meters, or about 12 per cent of the country's annual consumption, from Azerbaijan. In a nutshell, Turkey did not tether itself to Russia, despite the concessions it agreed to and the theatrics of Putin and Erdoğan who inaugurated TurkStream side by side in January 2020.[30]

However, the balancing act between Russia and the West proved hard to sustain. The US could tolerate Erdoğan's turn to Putin in Syria. Ditto for Ankara's dealings with Gazprom which went back decades. The import of strategic military kit, on the other hand, set a whole different ballgame in motion.

THE ART OF THE DEAL

On 2 August 2017, President Donald J. Trump signed into law the Countering America's Adversaries Through Sanctions Act (CAATSA). He was far from thrilled about this piece of legislation, a rare product of bipartisanship in a deeply polarized Congress. Going after Russian entities for meddling in US elections confirmed, in Trump's mind, the narrative of the Kremlin winning the presidency for him back in November 2016. "The Russia hoax," as he would tweet over and over, often at odd hours.

CAATSA spelled trouble for America's European allies, for example Germany, because of the Nordstream 2 pipeline,[31] but it came to haunt relations with Turkey too. At the very end of 2017, the Undersecretariat for Defense Industries (Savunma Sanayı Başkanlığı, SSB) announced that it had signed a deal and paid a deposit for two batteries of S-400 surface-to-air missiles from Russia, a purchase worth $2.5 billion financed by a Russian loan. In July 2019, Turkey received the first battery despite strong criticism from all quarters in Washington. Erdoğan stood defiant, along with 44 per cent of Turkish citizens who, according to a study by Kadir Has University, approved of the acquisition regardless of the West's objections.[32] Was America going to sanction its NATO ally for choosing a geopolitical rival to develop a vital piece of its defense infrastructure? In doing this, Turks jeopardized the Western alliance; the newly procured S-400s, experts asserted, could gather sensitive data from US-manufactured fighter jets which could end up – one way or the other – with the Russians. That included F-35, the next-generation stealth plane developed by America in partnership with close allies from across the globe.

The S-400 issue was a litmus test of just how bad relations between Ankara and Washington had turned by the late 2010s. The controversy regarding the Russian defense imports, billed by Erdoğan as a step towards boosting domestic industries through technology transfer, added to an ever longer list of issues where Turks and Americans found themselves at odds, which included the alliance between US Central Command (CENTCOM) and the YPG/SDF in Syria, and the fate of Fethullah Gülen. In Syria, the Trump administration abandoned all pretense of fighting the Assad regime by cancelling the Train and Equip program carried out by the CIA since 2013. Efforts to lobby the White House for Gülen's extradition crashed in February 2017 when General Michael Flynn, a prospective lobbyist, was forced to step down as national security advisor after less than a month on the job. The following month, FBI agents arrested in New York City Mehmet Hakan Attila, the deputy manager of Halkbank, Turkey's second biggest lender owned by the state. In May 2018, Attila was sentenced on charges of busting the sanctions against Iran, alongside businessman Reza Zarrab. The case was politically supercharged as it went back to the disclosures implicating Erdoğan and his inner circle from December 2013.[33] Lastly, Erdoğan's effort to engage America got off to a bad start. On 16 May 2017, during his visit to Washington, DC, a true battle broke out in front of the Turkish ambassador's residence on Sheridan Circle when the Turkish president's bodyguards attacked and beat up a group of Kurdish protestors. The incident led to arrest warrants and criminal charges by an US grand jury against members of Erdoğan's security detail.[34]

To be sure, relations between the US and Turkey had rarely been in a good shape since the golden decade in the 1950s. The Cyprus issue, the first Gulf War, the post-9/11 war on terror and the Iraq invasion all created friction. But it all went downhill in the 2010s with the 2016 coup attempt and the surge of anti-Americanism whipped up by the pro-Erdoğan media in a defining moment. Again, the Kadir Has University survey, quoted earlier, found that a full 81.3 per cent of respondents considered the United States as the greatest threat to Turkey (followed by Israel with 70.8 per cent). Equally, on the US side, Turkey became toxic. The Democrats disliked Erdoğan's strongman antics and his "bromance" with Trump, and held him responsible for human rights abuses at home. The right looked with suspicion at the president's Islamist roots, bemoaning his animosity against Israel and pre-Arab Spring flirtation with Iran. While in the old days Turkey could rely on many friends in the Pentagon, the State Department, in Congress and among pundits and media, it fell out of favor from the mid-2010s onwards. Erdoğan's embrace of Putin was the last straw.

Yet, for all the tensions, suspicions and recriminations, there has not been a complete breakdown. When the Trump administration finally imposed sanctions, in its last weeks in office (14 December 2020), SSB President İsmail Demir and three of his employees were singled out rather than Erdoğan's inner circle. A much more serious measure is Turkey's exclusion from the F-35 consortium in July 2019, which deprived it of a state-of-the-art fighter jet available to some of its competitors and cost the country's businesses billions in losses.[35] The Turkish president, in the meantime, probed all manner of salami tactics: for example proposing that the S-400s would be kept apart from the rest of the country's air defenses so as not to disrupt NATO infrastructure or even not to activate them. Erdoğan proposed a "reset" to Joe Biden, who won the US presidential elections in November 2020. He even played the Russian card, arguing that Turkey was the only NATO member willing to – and capable of – checking Moscow's expansionism. As we shall see, these claims, exaggerated though they are, contain a grain of truth. Eventually, the two presidents did meet, bumping fists rather than shaking hands (Covid-19 protocol) at the margins of the NATO summit in Brussels, in June 2021. Erdoğan tilted to the US, despite the recognition of the Armenian Genocide by Biden on 24 April.[36] Yet normalization in Ankara's ties with the US is bound to be incomplete. For all the positive momentum, the relationship has become largely transactional.[37] "Our so-called strategic partner," is how State Secretary Anthony Blinken described Turkey during his confirmation hearing in the Senate in January 2021.[38] The prospect of a second batch of S-400s brought up by Erdoğan in September 2021, months after his reconciliatory *tête-à-tête* with Biden, spells trouble.[39] Generally speaking, there has been a sea change, even in comparison to the 2000s and early 2010s when the US still viewed Turkey as a model country, while the AKP valued the connection with America – largely for instrumental reasons.

Transactionalism is one of the legacies of Trump's term at the White House. Back in January 2017, the arrival of a fellow populist at the White House was greeted as a blessing in Ankara. Here was an American president, a self-declared believer in pragmatism who had little time for abstractions such as democracy and human rights. Erdoğan could do business with him, unlike Obama, who had turned out to be such a disappointment. That is why Erdoğan avoided, for the most part, directing his rhetorical attacks at Trump personally. The object of his ire was either America as a whole or the administration. Whenever Trump threatened Turkey, as a rule through his Twitter account, Erdoğan would make the rejoinder that his colleague had been misinformed. Theatrics, such as the threat Trump made in October 2019 to "destroy" the Turkish economy through sanctions ("don't be a tough guy, don't be a fool") and the addressee's reaction – throwing the letter in the bin, proved just a smokescreen. The two got on just fine.[40] "Erdoğan plays Washington like a fiddle," wrote Steven Cook of the Council on Foreign Relations in September 2019.[41]

The proof was the US pull-out from the border areas in northeast Syria in October 2019, which enabled the Turkish armed forces and Turkey's Arab allies to take over a corridor between the towns of Ras al-Ayn (Sere Kanye in Kurdish) and Tal Abyad. Operation Peace Spring (*Barış Pınarı Harekâtı*) followed the withdrawal of the American marines embedded with the SDF agreed in a phone call between Erdoğan and Trump. The US president had pushed for an end of the Syrian deployment over a long time and had already made an announcement to that effect in December 2018, only to backtrack later. But now Erdoğan helped him out, by declaring victory against ISIS (the original reason marines entered Syria), and – not insignificantly – taking fuller control of foreign policy decision making. In December 2018, disagreements over Syria led to the resignation of US Defense Secretary James Mattis.[42] The rushed pull-out a year later, prompted in no small measure by the Turkish build-up and implicit threat that the US military could be caught in the cross-fire in case of an invasion, overruled the Pentagon and CENTCOM. They preferred a staged handover. It also rendered meaningless the so-called Manbij Roadmap of June 2018, envisioning the sharing of responsibilities between the US and Turkey in the key town. Erdoğan and Trump jointly outmaneuvered Congress, which was inflamed by the realization that the Kurdish allies in the fight against ISIS had been left high and dry. Senator Lindsey Graham, who proposed a sanctions bill in response to the Turkish incursion into northeast Syria, made a U-turn after Vice-President Mike Pence announced, on 17 October 2019, that he had concluded a ceasefire agreement in Ankara.[43]

The reshuffle in northeast Syria benefited Russia and the Assad regime. Kurdish militants allowed Moscow and Damascus (which kept footholds in Haseka and Qamishlo) to reoccupy parts of "Rojava" in order to check the advance of Turkey and its proxies. In a sense, Russia replaced the US as a guarantor of what remained of Kurdish autonomy in the wake of Peace Spring. America kept a 500-strong contingent ("we're keeping the oil," as Trump put it) in the Deir ez-Zor province, providing the YPG/PYD with a hedge. In the meantime, Turkey was able to declare another victory against the PKK affiliate, even if the enclave it carved out fell short of the map Erdoğan had waved at the UN General Assembly (24 September 2019) for a "safe zone" stretching more than 80 km south of the border. It was anyhow meant largely for domestic consumption: the Turkish public being told that 3 million Syrian refugees would be repatriated into the new Syrian enclave controlled by Ankara. Like Euphrates Shield and Olive Branch before it, Operation Peace Spring sent Erdoğan's popularity ratings sky-high. He shared in the spoils of US disengagement together with the Syrian regime and its Russian patron.

In the final analysis, Trump proved great news for Turkey. He delayed CAATSA sanctions as long as possible and enabled the takeover of yet another critical piece of real estate in Syria. But Erdoğan's success in dealing with Washington may come back to hurt him in the future. The Biden administration is sure to drive a much harder bargain, putting to the test the Turkish president and his deal-making skills.

In a TV interview aired on 21 November 2020, Erdoğan's advisor İbrahim Kalın berated the West for allowing Russia's expansion into Georgia (2008) and subsequently into Ukraine, Syria, and Libya.[44] Turkey alone was doing the job of containing Putin's designs – through contributing to NATO's presence in the Black Sea[45] and projecting force in Syria as well as regional conflicts such as Libya and Nagorno-Karabakh. The Biden administration had to cut Ankara some slack, in other words, forgo sanctions, and think about a reset. In reality, Turkey has not changed course with Trump's departure. It does its own thing, not fending for the West. The balancing act between Russia and the US has had one purpose: to sustain and broaden its influence, whether in the Middle East and North Africa, the Balkans or Africa.[46]

But Erdoğan's foreign ambitions go further. He has championed causes at the global level: from expanding the UN Security Council permanent members with a representative of the Islamic world (guess which country that would be?) to dispatching humanitarian aid to Somalia, to slamming Myanmar over the maltreatment of the Rohingya.[47] Interestingly though, he strikes a conciliatory tone vis-à-vis China with regard to Uyghurs and other Turkic groups in Xinjiang.[48] Raison d'état, as defined by Erdoğan of course, trumps any feelings of kinship and solidarity Turkish society, not least the MHP grassroots, may harbor.

The incursion into Syria in 2016 and its aftermath reinforced aspirations to, figuratively speaking, make Turkey great again. It also placed hard power at the center of Turkish foreign policy. Turkey's foray into Libya, deployments in the Gulf and the Horn of Africa, gunboat diplomacy in the Eastern Mediterranean and intervention in Nagorno-Karabakh all hark back to the summer of 2016. "New Turkey" seeks to secure its place in the regional and global pecking order through military strength first and foremost, not through diplomacy, trade and soft power as in the not-so-distant past.

The next chapter deep-dives into Turkish regional activism.

9
THE PURSUIT OF POWER

In the 2010s, Turkey staked out a vision for a regional order in the Middle East and North Africa under its leadership. Its political and socio-economic development set an example for local countries. Its Ottoman past endowed the country with cultural capital and connections to societies that the West, burdened by its colonial history and the bitter experience of US interventionism, did not possess. With the fall of Mohamed Morsi in Egypt and Assad's survival, however, Ankara's star shone less brightly. In essence, Saudi Arabia and Iran stepped in to thwart Erdoğan's grand plans. Yet the intervention in Syria in 2016 brought Turkey back into the game. Even if its ambitions for hegemony had floundered, it found and exploited new opportunities further away from its immediate neighborhood. In the years since 2016, Turkey gained fresh ground in the Gulf, in sub-Saharan Africa and eventually in Libya.

Turkish policy in the region reflects a plethora of factors. The US disengagement from the Middle East, a common thread running through the Obama and Trump administrations, opened space not only for regional powers, but also the likes of Russia and China, to fill the gap. Turkey wants its piece of the action, too. Then, there is the security imperative. Turkish policy makers see Syria, northern Iraq and the Eastern Mediterranean as key to the national interest. Next, the AKP's roots in political Islam put a special premium on the Middle East and North Africa but more recently also on Muslim-majority countries in the Global South. Last but not least, it is about personal ambition. Thanks to Erdoğan, Turkey has made foreign policy moves and taken gambles it would not have in previous eras.

THE ALLIANCE WITH QATAR

Erdoğan's partnership with Qatar, forged during the war in Syria, has been a key part of the story. Ankara has the military muscle and the diplomatic heft,

Doha the financial resources and regional networks. Both were actively backing the Muslim Brotherhood across the region in the glory days of the Arab Spring, but the alliance endured and solidified even as headwinds started to blow.[1] Turkey and Qatar have become a third bloc in the Middle East, in addition to the Iran-led one uniting the Assad regime, Hezbollah and various Shiʻa actors in Iraq, and the alliance uniting Saudi Arabia, al-Sisi's Egypt, the UAE plus Israel as an informal partner. Turkey has been pursuing a balancing act between these two rival poles, not unlike the policy it has adopted vis-à-vis the US and Russia.

The Turkish–Qatari pact showed its strength in 2017 when Saudi Arabia, along with its own partners, UAE, Bahrain and Egypt, severed diplomatic and trading ties with Doha and closed their airspace to its national carrier. Accusing Qatar of abetting terrorists (that is, the Muslim Brotherhood) and colluding with Iran, the Saudis cut off the emirate's land border too. Crown Prince Mohammed bin Salman (or MBS), the de facto ruler of Saudi Arabia, felt he had the backing of Donald Trump who had unprecedentedly chosen Riyadh for his first foreign trip in May 2017. As the Saudis ventured to take down their upstart sheikhdom a peg or two, Turkey rushed to the rescue. Erdoğan visited Doha not once but twice in the first months of the blockade. Turkey dispatched cargo ships and hundreds of planes with food supplies, teaming up with Iran and Iraq which kept their airspace open.[2] In addition, Ankara scaled up its military presence in Qatar, agreed back in 2014. The Turkish contingent at the Tariq bin Ziyad base (operational since April 2016) increased from 150 to over 3,000, enough to deter Riyadh.[3] Having sufficient breathing space, Emir Tamim bin Hamad al-Thani was in no rush to wave the white flag and accept the Saudis' terms for restoring ties, notably the expulsion of the Turkish troops. Thus, he rebuffed MBS's invitation to attend the Gulf Cooperation Council summit in Riyadh in December 2019. Turkey gained as a result. The deal Qatar and Saudi Arabia reached in January 2021, a truce more than a settlement, saw the Saudis backtracking from their demand for closure of the Turkish military base.[4]

Qatar repaid Erdoğan for his support. In August 2018, it okayed a $3 billion swap deal to help the Turkish central bank amidst a currency crisis tanking Turkey's economy. The Qataris also pledged $15 billion in direct investment, though only about a third materialized. Money from the hydrocarbon-rich Gulf state was likewise directed to Erdoğan's signature projects such as Canal Istanbul. Qatari organizations – for example the local chapter of the Red Crescent – became active in the areas in northern Syria controlled by Ankara too, such as the cities of al-Bab and Afrin. Last but not least, Qatargas started selling LNG to BOTAŞ, Turkey's national gas company. The initial Memorandum of Understanding (MoU) was signed in December 2015, at the first session of the Supreme Strategic Committee set up by the two countries, and a three-year supply contract followed in September 2017.[5]

As a result, Erdoğan's personal relationship with al-Thani, the only Middle East leader apart from Sudan's Omar al-Bashir to attend his inauguration in July 2018, grew stronger. At their summit in November that year, the emir said: "[B]e assured, Mr. President, that if Turkey needs anything in the future we will always stand with our friends and brothers."[6] Qatar promised another financial injection to the tune of $7 billion in December 2019.[7]

Qatar has provided Turkey with access to the Taliban in Afghanistan.[8] As the US announced its withdrawal in February 2020, following a deal with the Islamic militants signed in Doha, Ankara started exploring a future role as a guarantor of security at Kabul airport. The collapse of the pro-Western government in Afghanistan in mid-August 2021, days ahead of the American pullout, complicated those plans. Political ties to the Taliban but also to Pakistan may facilitate Turkey's role as a channel of humanitarian assistance, but the new authorities have been reluctant to agree on Turkish security presence at the capital's airport.

INTO AFRICA

Qatar has become Turkey's gateway to the Horn of Africa. Ankara and Doha partner in Somalia, for instance. In September 2017, a Turkish military base opened in Mogadishu, the largest such facility outside the country's borders. It followed in the footsteps of myriad humanitarian and development initiatives by state institutions such as TİKA[9] and the Diyanet as well as AKP-linked private bodies like İHH Humanitarian Relief Foundations or Deniz Feneri.[10] Sudan has also been involved. In 2017, Erdoğan and President Omar al-Bashir signed a 99-year lease for Suakin Island in the Red Sea. Qatar has likewise been nurturing economic and financial ties with the countries in question. Both

Somalia and Sudan refused to join Saudi Arabia, UAE and Egypt's boycott in 2017, despite their dependence on aid.[11] Somalia subsequently cut ties with the UAE for cosying up to breakaway Somaliland and accused the Gulf state of promoting separatism. In short, Ankara and Doha turfed out their competitors, co-opting the African country into their bloc. In the process, Turkey has developed its own "string of pearls" across the Mediterranean and the Red Sea, as the analyst Micha'el Tanchum has put it, drawing analogy with China's strategy in Asia.[12]

Somalia is but one chapter in Turkey's opening to sub-Saharan Africa. Economic and political relations with the region took off as early as the 2000s, with Gülenist schools and businesses planting the flag first. Then, the state moved in. By 2018, Turkey operated 41 embassies, up from just 12 back in 2003. Turkish Airlines flew to 52 destinations across 33 African countries, while trade expanded five-fold to $20 billion over the same timeframe.[13] Because of the struggle against Gülen, much of the Turkish state agenda, as in other corners of the world, consisted of combating the *cemaat*. Erdoğan took this upon himself in his frequent travels. As a result of his lobbying a number of countries, from Senegal to South Africa and from Madagascar to Niger and Angola, closed down schools affiliated with the movement.[14] Unlike in neighboring countries in the Middle East or the Balkans, Turkey enjoyed a warmer welcome across the continent, with which it shared little or no imperial history. Erdoğan exploited that fact, brandishing Turkey's non-Western identity. On a trip to Zambia, the Turkish president asserted his country was "not going to Africa to take their gold and natural resources as Westerners have done in the past" but in a pursuit of a "solid and sustainable partnership based on mutual benefits." His efforts enjoyed success. The leaders of Guinea-Bissau, Guinea, Equatorial Guinea, Zambia, Somalia, Sudan and Mauritania attended the Turkish president's inauguration in July 2018. Though for any of those countries, with the possible exception of Somalia, Turkey is hardly a top security and economic partner, they have responded positively to its entry into regional politics.

MURDER AT THE CONSULATE

Turkey's activism in the Gulf and beyond has been watched warily by Saudi Arabia and the UAE. The rivalry went back to the Arab Spring and the AKP's alignment with the Muslim Brotherhood. Riyadh took exception to Turkey's cooperation with its rival Iran. The brutal murder of Saudi journalist Jamal Khashoggi at the kingdom's consulate in Istanbul on 2 October 2018 brought the conflict into the open. The brazen act appeared to be a personal vendetta by Mohammed bin Salman, Saudi's de facto ruler. But Turkish authorities made sure that international audiences were spared no gruesome detail of the murder by a death squad dispatched by Riyadh, whose actions had been wire-tapped.[15] Erdoğan did not miss an opportunity to publicly shame the Saudis and thus gain leverage over US President Donald Trump, closely associated with MBS. "I cannot understand America's silence when such a horrific attack took place, and even after members of the CIA listened to the recordings we provided," he told public broadcaster TRT in February 2019.[16] But Saudis had leverage too. Investment from the Gulf monarchy remained a key priority for the Turkish government. As a tit for tat, Riyadh threatened to discourage the purchase of real estate in Turkey.[17]

Yet both sides kept political tensions under control – including through behind-the-scenes talks. In contrast to the UAE's policy in the Horn of Africa or in Libya, the Saudis did not challenge Erdoğan head-on. As with Russia or Iran, Turkey could not afford a collision with Saudi Arabia either. Indeed, the arrival of the Biden administration in the US, having no soft spot for MBS in contrast to Trump, led to a warming up in relations between Riyadh and Ankara. The thaw between the Saudis and Qatar smoothed the path to a rapprochement.[18] Foreign Minister Çavuşoğlu visited Riyadh in May 2021 while another delegation went to Cairo, relaunching dialogue with Sisi's Egypt, a Saudi ally. A cautious rapprochement ensued with the UAE as well, after a phone call between Erdoğan and Abu Dhabi Crown Prince Mohammed bin Zayed (MBZ) in late August 2021.[19]

Turkey's frictions with Saudi Arabia have not produced a tilt towards Iran, Riyadh's arch-rival in the Middle East. It is true that Ankara found a basis for cooperation with the Islamic Republic. Before the 2015 nuclear deal with the P5+1, Turkish banks were suspected of facilitating Iran's oil exports to India and other countries through elaborate schemes involving payment in gold.[20] These accusations resulted in the case brought against Halkbank in New York. From early 2017 onwards, Turkey and Iran engaged in Syria through the Astana Process, despite being on opposite sides of the conflict. They also joined forces in pressuring the KRG in northern Iraq to backtrack from the pursuit of independence following a referendum on 25 September 2017 (even though US intervention ultimately played a decisive role). Even after the Trump administration's withdrawal from the Iran nuclear deal (the JCPOA) in May 2018, Erdoğan pledged to preserve economic links to Tehran. "It is impossible for us to cancel relations with Iran with regard to oil and natural gas. We will continue to buy our natural gas from there," he declared in reaction to Washington's newly unveiled "maximum pressure" policy.[21] The Saudi blockade of Qatar made a difference too. In the words of Galip Dalay, Turkey "perceived a bigger threat from the regional aspirations of the anti-Iran camp than from those of Iran."[22]

Yet the rivalry between Ankara and Tehran went on. In December 2020, for instance, Javad Zarif upbraided Erdoğan for intervening in Azerbaijan's conflict with Armenia and accused him of promoting pan-Turkism and irredentism. Iranians watched with wariness Turkey's rising profile in the Southern Caucasus, through defense cooperation with Azerbaijan as well as with Georgia, and infrastructure projects such as the Baku–Kars railway.[23] Tensions in Syria did not abate either. Erdoğan preferred to coordinate bilaterally with Putin – rather than go through the Astana mechanism. Turkey and Iran remained at odds in a variety of other settings, from Lebanon to Iraq. Tehran was not oblivious of Turkey's role, on the side of Saudi Arabia, in the early stages of the Yemen war (2015–17). Erdoğan's overtures to Saudi Arabia came as a reminder that the rapprochement with the Iranians had been at best incomplete.[24]

In essence, Turkey maintains equidistance from Iran and Saudi Arabia, the protagonists in a Middle East power race, and seeks to assert its own agenda by cooperating and competing with both. In essence, Ankara cannot be a true friend to either the Iranians or the Saudis, but it cannot afford to be their adversary either (an observation which applies to Russian–Turkish relations too, of course).

THE EASTERN MEDITERRANEAN STAND-OFF

Turkey's bid to assert itself as a pivotal regional power plays out not just in the Gulf and in sub-Saharan Africa but in the Eastern Mediterranean, closer to home, too. Deposits of oil and natural gas discovered in the late 2000s have raised stakes in the region. All littoral countries, along with majors such as ExxonMobil, Total, Chevron and Shell have been keen to tap into offshore hydrocarbons, following the example of Israel, which started pumping gas from the Tamar field in 2013. Turkey, a large energy consumer, is no exception. Ideally, the finds should bolster neighborly cooperation in pursuit of shared gains. In practice, disputes over sovereignty have overshadowed the purely economic aspects of the issue.

Cyprus plays a special role, given the disagreements concerning its EEZ and the status and rights of the self-proclaimed Turkish Republic of Northern Cyprus. The dispute between Greece and Turkey over the extent of their territorial waters, national airspace, continental shelf and, inevitably, the EEZs, make matters even more complicated. In the 1980s and 1990s, these played out mostly in the Aegean Sea, but since 2017 they have spread to the Eastern Mediterranean as well. Specifically, Turkey disagrees that islands have a right to claim continental shelf and serve as a baseline for an EEZ. This not only applies to Cyprus, but also to Rhodes, Crete and, in slightly different sense, to Kastellorizo.[25]

So long as Turkey was pursuing membership in the EU in earnest, it had robust incentives to work with Greece and keep disagreements over Cyprus within limits. Ankara, along with the Cypriot Turks, maintained that Nicosia should not develop energy resources absent in a reunification deal and complained about any unilateral move in that direction. Even in the mid-2010s, when EU–Turkish relations had worsened, it appeared that a win-win solution was within reach. Oil and gas deposits motivated President Nicos Anastasiades and Mustafa Akıncı, leader of the breakaway Turkish Republic of Northern Cyprus (TRNC), recognized solely by Ankara, to relaunch reunification talks in May 2015. Cyprus had suffered a severe blow with a major banking and financial crisis two years prior. The prospect of shared profits from the offshore fields brought Cypriot Greeks and Turks together. Since the talks in Crans-Montana, Switzerland, ended in failure in July 2017, however, hydrocarbons became an apple of discord and drew in other states.

Turkey witnessed the consolidation of Greece and Cyprus's alliance with Israel which had developed through the 2010s in parallel with the deterioration in the Israelis' ties with Turkey. Greek and Israeli navies and air forces had started exercising together on a regular basis, with Israel using Greek airspace instead that of Turkey, as beforehand, for training. In August 2013, Israel,

Greece and Cyprus signed a three-way energy memorandum which, though focusing on electricity, set the scene for cooperation on natural gas too. Though an Israeli–Cypriot dispute regarding the delimitation of the Aphrodite offshore field has complicated matters, the so-called Energy Triangle has moved forward and even enlisted other countries.[26] In January 2020, Greece, Cyprus, Israel, Egypt – along with Italy, Jordan and the Palestinian Authority – launched the East Mediterranean Gas Forum (EMGF) in Cairo. Others are potentially also part of the arrangement: the US-based Noble Energy has been behind most of the findings in Aphrodite and holds 30 per cent of the shares. France has similarly taken Greece and Cyprus's side. With Israel already taking gas from the Levantine basin, Cyprus appears to be in a good position to follow suit in the 2020s, if market conditions are ripe.

Policy makers in Ankara interpreted such developments as a bid to encircle Turkey and deprive it of vital resources. Already in March 2017, Cyprus issued licenses to Exxon Mobil, ENI (Italy) and Total (France) for additional exploration blocks. The Turkish navy countered by stopping a vessel chartered by ENI in February 2018. TPAO issued licenses of its own in EEZs claimed by Greece as well as Cyprus. So did TRNC. *Barbaros Hayrettin Pasha*, an exploration vessel named after the famed seventeenth-century Ottoman admiral, began surveying the Cyprus shelf in April 2017. In spring 2019, Turkey dispatched drilling ships *Fatih* and *Yavuz*, the sobriquets of Mehmed II and Selim I respectively, two sultans whose conquests promoted the Ottoman Empire into a hegemonic power in the Eastern Mediterranean.[27] Owned by TPAO, the national oil company, the vessels were escorted by the Turkish navy, including frigates and submarines, signaling the militarization of the dispute. Hulusi Akar justified the build-up by saying that Greek ships were harassing *Barbaros*.[28] In February 2018, Turkey began to stage large-scale naval exercises in the area.[29]

Ankara's assertion of control put it at odds with the EU, which took Greece and Cyprus's side. It led to the decision by the Council (member states' foreign ministers) to impose travel bans and asset freezes on Turkish officials (November 2019).[30] Several weeks earlier, on a visit to Athens, the US Secretary of State Mike Pompeo declared drilling "illegal" and "unacceptable."[31] For his part, French President Emmanuel Macron lambasted Ankara's "imperial inclinations" and "deeply aggressive" attitude towards Greece and Cyprus.[32] Thus, the

Eastern Mediterranean became yet another arena – along with Syria – where Turkey and the West clashed.

Why did Erdoğan continue to press Turkey's claims, ignoring the push-back? First, because assertiveness gave him leverage in negotiations with Greece and the EU as a whole. On several occasions, he would withdraw exploration ships in order to dial down tensions and open room for diplomatic engagement. That is what happened in September 2020, for instance, in advance of exploratory talks with the Greeks arranged through mediation of Germany and the US.[33] In addition, Turkey did not issue licenses for waters west of the 28th meridian, in the zone covered by the delimitation deal with the GNA in Libya. Yet it did send out the *Oruç Reis*, one of the exploration ships, again the following month – to maintain pressure.

Second, the Eastern Mediterranean made a bridge between Erdoğan and nationalist factions advocating for Ankara to upgrade its naval power and assert its maritime sovereignty. Rear Admiral Cihat Yaycı, chief of staff of the navy between 2017 and 2020, who made his name by producing an algorithm to identify Gülenists within military ranks, would be one example. Another rear admiral, Cem Gürdeniz, the father of the *Mavi Vatan* (Blue Homeland) doctrine, urged Turkey to claim a vast portion of the Eastern Mediterranean as its EEZ.[34] Part of the *ulusalcı*/Eurasianist stream in Turkish politics just like Gürdeniz, Yaycı was imprisoned and subsequently acquitted in the so-called military espionage case. Yet Erdoğan has added a twist. He has repeatedly questioned the Lausanne Treaty concluded with Greece and the rest of the Entente Powers following the Kemalists' win in the Turkish War of Independence (1919–22), which, according to him gave up Turkish sovereignty over the Aegean islands. That is, Erdoğan attacked Mustafa Kemal's crowning achievement while bringing onboard nationalists from the Atatürkist camp.

Third, and perhaps most importantly, Turkey increased its naval capabilities and believed it was in a position to reap geopolitical benefits. Under the MİLGEM ("national ship") project, it manufactured four corvettes and a frigate (ordered by Pakistan).[35] Though the Turkish navy is stretched over the Black Sea (confronting a resurgent Russia), the Aegean and the Mediterranean, it is increasingly capable. In other words, Ankara is capable of defending its claims or, at the minimum, preventing other states from developing maritime projects deemed contrary to its interests.

That became apparent with the delimitation agreement Turkey concluded with the GNA based in Tripoli, Libya, in November–December 2020.[36] It came in response to a deal, three days earlier, by Greece, Cyprus and Israel for a 1,900-km undersea pipeline to ship gas to mainland Greece and ultimately Italy.[37] "Just as we taught a lesson to the terrorists in Syria, we will not cede ground to the bandits in the sea," Erdoğan boasted.[38] Essentially, he enlisted the GNA, the only ally remaining in the Eastern Mediterranean, to sign off on Turkey's claim for an EEZ stretching well south of the Turkish shore and past the Greek island of Crete. Though the legality, or indeed the practical application, of the deal was questionable ("null and void" declared Greece, Cyprus and Egypt – joined later by France, the UAE[39] as well as the Libyan parliament in Tobruk) it provided some leverage to Ankara. The Tripoli-based GNA was not in control of areas of the coast which served as a baseline for the Libyan EEZ agreed with the Turks. The GNA also failed to ratify it. Its successor, the Government of National Unity, installed in February 2021, is unlikely to do so either. At the same time, the EastMed pipeline, advanced by Greece, Cyprus and Israel, is shrouded in uncertainty too, because of Turkey's opposition and also doubts whether it is economically viable. In effect, Ankara and its rivals are deadlocked.[40]

In parallel, the situation in Northern Cyprus has shifted for the worse. The presidential elections TRNC held in October 2020 saw the incumbent Mustafa Akıncı defeated by Ersin Tatar, a hardliner who had previously served as a prime minister. Tatar openly campaigned on a two-state solution, dismissing the UN-led reunification talks. Visiting the north in late July 2021, on the 47th anniversary of the 1974 Turkish intervention, Erdoğan aired a similar call. Previously, Akıncı had supported the Crans-Montana talks. He had had an interlocutor in Anastasiades, a backer of the Annan Plan at the ill-fated 2004 referendum. But with a more nationalistic leader in charge, plus a combative Erdoğan governing in tandem with the MHP in Ankara, the prospects for a detente in Cyprus look grim. Raising the stakes, in the summer of 2021 the Northern Cypriot authorities and Turkey reopened Varosha/Maraş, a beachfront quarter of Famagusta abandoned back in 1974. The future of the neighborhood and the return of its Greek residents, possibly under a UN administration, had been one of the issues long discussed in the reunification talks, including a round that took place in April 2021.[41] Now the Turkish side created a *fait accompli*.

THE MILITARIZATION OF TURKISH FOREIGN POLICY

Turkey's hamfisted tactics in the Eastern Mediterranean reflect an apparent lesson Ankara decision makers took from Syria: military power works. Back in the "zero-problems" era, Turkey relied on trade, investment, people-to-people contacts and the like to project influence. Commerce and soft power are still relevant for Turkish policy in Africa and the Balkans.[42] But from the Euphrates Shield operation in Syria onwards hard power has become Ankara's external tool of choice. In the space of 2020 alone, Turkey intervened in three hotspots – Libya, Idlib and Nagorno-Karabakh – to emerge victorious in all three.

Libya

The decision to send troops in Libya, in the throes of a civil war since 2014, did not come out of thin air. Though Turkey stood aloof during the NATO campaign which toppled Gaddafi in 2011, it became involved in the politics of the country subsequently. Together with the Qataris, Ankara backed the local chapter of the Muslim Brotherhood as well as militias based in the town of Misrata, initially part of the so-called Libya Dawn Coalition. After December 2015, they threw their weight behind the GNA, which was backed by both Islamist and secular factions, including the local branch of the Ikhwan.[43] On the other side of the barricade were President al-Sisi of Egypt, the UAE and Russia, siding with Khalifa Haftar's Libyan National Army (LNA) acting on behalf of the House of Representatives based in Libya's east.

As the conflict deepened, Turkey scaled up its assistance to Tripoli. In June 2019, Erdoğan acknowledged that his government had provided the GNA, led by Prime Minister Fayez al-Sarraj, with equipment (drones, heavy weapons, armored vehicles), intelligence and military advisors. Haftar did not appreciate that. He had opposed Turkey's participation in a peace conference convened in Palermo, Italy, under UN auspices (November 2018).[44] Then, in June 2019, the Libyan warlord closed all Turkish businesses in eastern Libya and detained six sailors. "Haftar is nothing but a pirate," Erdoğan responded.[45]

However, despite being implicated in Libya's internal politics, Turkey was under no pressure to mount a military intervention. What appears to have changed Erdoğan's mind is, first, the geopolitical gains he could make; second, that he could recoup some of the investment lost as a result of the 2011

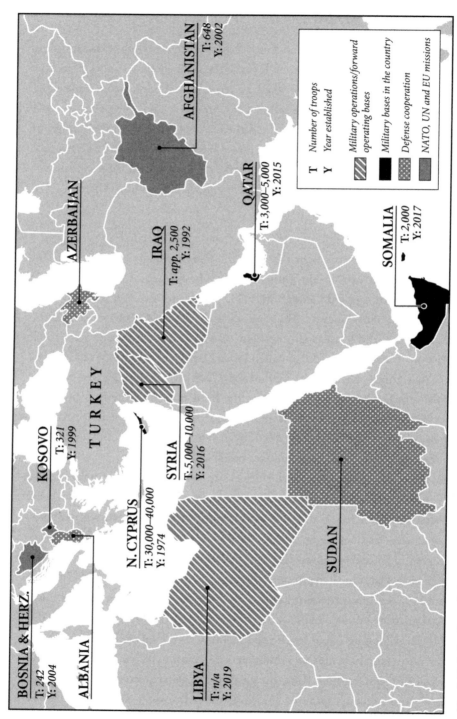

Map 3. Turkey's military deployments

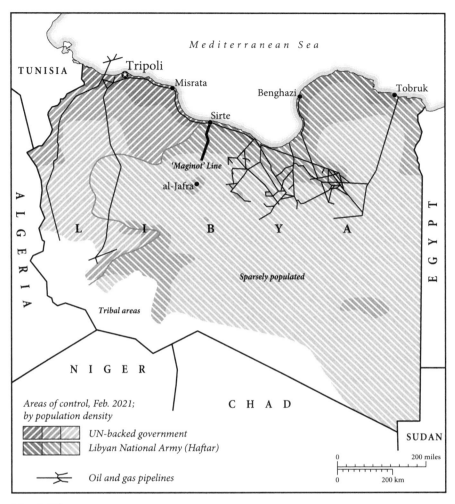

Map 4. Libya

intervention, estimated at $19 billion; and third, as demonstrated by the EEZ delimitation deal from November 2019, in order to advance claims in the Eastern Mediterranean.

Erdoğan borrowed from the Russian playbook in Syria. First, he took onboard international law by asserting that a UN-recognized administration invited the intervention. Second, the campaign itself was kept within limits, similar to Russia's assistance to Assad. Rather than put "boots on the ground," Turkey relied on air power and proxy fighters. By January 2020, a reported

2,000 Syrians from the Ankara-supported and trained Syrian National Army[46] were deployed on the frontlines around Tripoli.[47] They were said to have been offered a monthly salary of $2,000 for the job, in addition to prospective Turkish citizenship. Private military contractors, such as the SADAT company, founded by retired Brigadier General Adnan Tanrıverdi, were also in the field, just like their opposite numbers from Russia, the Wagner company, fighting for Haftar.[48] In both cases, money from the Gulf – Qatar and the UAE respectively – paid for the mercenaries. In addition, Turkey's navy appeared close to Libya's shores.[49] In late March 2020, the BBC released images of cargo ships bringing in heavy weaponry – in violation of the UN-imposed embargo – to the government in Tripoli.[50]

Yet nothing seems to have made a greater difference than Bayraktar TB2, Turkey's Unmanned Aerial Vehicle (UAV). "You have to understand the Libyan geography. Libya is a vast country with open spaces and semi-desert areas even in coastal areas where no one basically can hide troop movements," said Salah Bakkoush, a political analyst and former advisor to the High Council of the Libyan state.[51] Drones took a toll on Haftar's forces, expanded GNA intelligence gathering capacity and ended the LNA's air superiority.[52] By early June 2020, the so-called Battle of Tripoli was won with the capture of the al-Watiya airport next to the capital and the town of Tarhouna, a Haftar stronghold in the area. The GNA moved the frontline to Sirte, the gateway to the eastern oilfields, and the Jufrah airbase, the LNA's operational hub in central Libya.[53] Foreign Minister Çavuşoğlu went on a victory lap in late June 2020, together with Berat Albayrak and Hakan Fidan.[54] Setting up a base in al-Watiya and possibly a naval facility in Misrata was part of the agenda, as under the Qaddafi-era energy and infrastructure agreements.[55] "It's Turkey's Libya now," observed analyst Tarek Megerisi.[56] Ankara became the patron of the GNA, investing heavily in the reform of the armed forces and the interior ministry.

Libya added a new dimension to relations with Russia, a top ally of Haftar. Putin and Erdoğan appealed for ceasefire in January 2020 ahead of an international conference in Berlin. Defeating the LNA's offensive, Ankara entertained the idea of an Astana-like forum with Moscow and called for Haftar's withdrawal from Sirte. However, Russia beefed up the LNA's defenses – for example, sending in military jets operated by mercenaries to the Jufrah airbase and helping build fortifications. In response to the UN-led peace process, Turks insisted they would withdraw their forces only after Russians did so. Despite the formation of a unity government in February 2021 with strong connections to Turkey and the lowering of tensions between Turkey and the UAE,[57] a new proxy conflict was not to be ruled out. Still, Ankara secured its position as a top power broker in the North African country, in much the same way as Russia had in Syria.

Idlib

In February 2020, Turkish ground forces and UAVs prevented Assad from taking over Idlib, the last remaining rebel-held enclave in northwest Syria. A regime offensive, which gathered momentum in late 2019, threatened to push hundreds of thousands of new refugees, many already displaced from other parts of Syria, across the Turkish border. The Russians, whom Ankara saw as a moderating influence on the regime, went along with the onslaught, delivering air strikes on both military and civilian targets. Their reasoning was that Turkey had failed to deliver on its commitment to defuse the Hayat Tahrir al-Sham.[58] Deploying Turkish troops in Idlib, ostensibly to reinforce the observation points agreed with Russia, Erdoğan was in a position to inflict substantial losses on the Syrian regime. But Turkey absorbed casualties too. On 27 February 2020, 34 servicemen were killed in an air raid, which the Turkish authorities attributed to Assad but likely was carried out by Russia.[59] Having come dangerously close to the brink, both Russia and Turkey sought – yet again – accommodation. Importantly, the Russians did not close Syrian airspace during the showdown and guaranteed the safety of Turkish observation points surrounded by the regime. Meeting in Moscow on 5 March, Putin and Erdoğan unveiled a ceasefire as well as an agreement to open the M4 highway connecting Latakia and Aleppo – to be policed jointly by Russians and Turks. In effect, Turkey transformed parts of Idlib into its fourth protectorate in Syria, alongside Afrin, northern Aleppo and the Peace Spring zone in the northeast. As in Libya, the use of military force gave it additional political leverage and helped to recommit Russia to its goals. Even if the deal was far from foolproof, Turkey's foothold in Idlib appeared secure thanks to the presence of at least 7,000 troops on the ground, along with heavy equipment and air support.[60] Erdoğan continued to rely on personal diplomacy with Putin to maintain the status quo in the enclave. At a bilateral summit in Sochi, 29 September 2021, he reportedly pressured the Russian president to halt the air strikes against the Turkish-backed Syrian National Army.[61]

Nagorno-Karabakh

In Nagorno-Karabakh, which saw an all-out war between Armenia and Azerbaijan in September–November 2020, Russia and Turkey faced off once more. Ankara aided Azerbaijan by dispatching Syrian fighters, military instructors, UAVs and reportedly its own air force.[62] The war wrongfooted Russia as it exposed its waning influence in its own backyard, its inability to restrain Armenia and Azerbaijan as well as the irrelevance of the defensive alliance with Yerevan. Ceasefires brokered by the Kremlin did not hold. Turkey scored points at Russia's expense as the Azeris recovered territory Armenians had controlled since the early 1990s, including Shusha/Shushi, Karabakh's historic center. In effect, Erdoğan inserted Turkey into Moscow's claimed privileged sphere of influence, much as Putin did in 2015 with Syria.[63] A Kremlin-mediated deal (9 November 2020) led to the deployment of Russian peacekeepers, something Baku had previously rebuffed. Though Moscow seemingly gained the upper hand, Erdoğan declared victory too. The agreement foresaw the opening of a transport corridor between Azerbaijan proper and Turkey through the Nakhichevan exclave. Ankara also set up a military observation point, claiming a stake in the Russian-led peacekeeping operation.[64]

Though the outcome fell short of Turkish ambitions to establish a 2+2 mechanism for managing Karabakh,[65] where Moscow and Ankara would feature as equal powerbrokers, it still had huge symbolic impact. The war set off a wave of nationalist fervor across Turkey. On 29 September 2020, cars adorned with Azerbaijan flags staged an impromptu procession in front of the Armenian patriarchate in the Istanbul quarter of Kumkapı. The Armenians had been taught a lesson. Erdoğan rode the wave too. His portraits, along with those of President Ilham Aliyev, were all over reconquered towns, along with the Turkish national flag. In December 2020, Erdoğan attended a victory parade in Baku. Not that long ago, Turkish foreign policy was all about finding a diplomatic solution to Nagorno-Karabakh. The Armenian Opening of 2009 was winning praise as a crowning achievement of the "zero-problems" approach to the neighborhood. Now, Turkey's military force and newly developed capabilities set the tone. Turkic brotherhood stood vindicated: music to the ears of Erdoğan's coalition partners from the Nationalist Action Party.

Northern Iraq

Turkey has stepped up its military operations in northern Iraq too. Starting in May 2019, army and gendarmerie units launched Operation Claw (*Pençe Hareketi*), seizing villages and strategic heights in the Hakurk, Metina and Zap regions from the PKK and establishing new military outposts. By the summer of 2020, the air force, as well as UAVs, were carrying out massive airstrikes on targets in the Sinjar mountains, a region populated by the Yazidi religious community that had previously been victimized by ISIS. That was in addition to raids on PKK bases in Qandil. Such operations are aimed at applying "maximum pressure" on Kurdish militants already squeezed in northeast Syria.[66] Overall, they have brought Turkey deeper into KRG-run northern Iraq. But this also raises tensions with Iran and the authorities in Baghdad. Tehran backs powerful militias present on the ground, such as the Popular Mobilization Forces (PMF) which share the control of Sinjar with the PKK.[67]

Syria, Libya and Nagorno-Karabakh, along with the Eastern Mediterranean and Africa, are testament to Turkey's unbridled geopolitical ambitions. What drives its trigger-happy policy, however: Erdoğan or the external challenges which demand a muscular response? Is it the new sultan's imperial designs or power competition in the Middle East and beyond in an era when the US, the former hegemon, is reluctant to police regional order?

The answer is, obviously, both. It is nigh on impossible to imagine another Turkish leader, especially in the past, authorizing an intervention in Libya, setting up bases in the Gulf, or confronting Russia. Ankara's reluctance to step in during the Nagorno-Karabakh conflict in the 1990s provides an instructive contrast with the present. Also, it is notable that the opposition in the Grand National Assembly voted "no" to the Libyan deployment in 2019. Erdoğan's iron grip over the state machine, unrivaled access to power resources (money or military capabilities), the absence of institutional checks and his control over the media narrative explains his ability to take geopolitical gambles with little or no domestic pushback. Add to the mix his suspicion of the West, his desire to be the top dog in the Middle East and beyond, and informal ties to foreign leaders like Putin, Trump or the Qatari ruling family and you get a better picture of what New Turkey's foreign policy is all about.

Yet Turkey's actions are also shaped by the environment the country finds itself in. The implosion of Syria and the Hobbesian rivalry it set in motion is exhibit number 1 here. The recourse to brute force to clamp down on Kurds and build buffer zones to guard Turkish territory proper from new refugee waves carry a strong whiff of *Realpolitik*. And this has enjoyed broad support from across the political spectrum as a result, with the exception of the pro-Kurdish HDP of course. The turn to Russia is similarly attributable to the quest for security and Turkey's assessment that its priorities clash with those of the US. Likewise, the sovereignty disputes in the Eastern Mediterranean are just another chapter in a conflict with Greece and Greek Cypriots dating back to times long before the AKP appeared on the scene.

Then, there is the timeless appeal of Turkish nationalism. While talking up "New Turkey's" aspirations to lead Muslims or be a pillar in a multipolar global order, Erdoğan is simultaneously tapping deeply felt resentment and suspicions towards the outside world. The West has been rebranded from a normative ideal to the ultimate "Other." The US is at best a partner of convenience, at worst, an existential threat. Neighbors are not to be trusted but approached from a position of strength. Russia is a friend today but who knows about tomorrow, and so on. And not to forget, nationalism shapes Turkey's attitude to Syria and the Kurdish issue in the region, a throwback to the 1990s. This lone wolf mentality is not of Erdoğan's making, but it is nonetheless as central to his political repertoire as the themes of Muslim solidarity or Ottoman nostalgia. This is not surprising: in the final analysis, nationalism holds the key to the Turkish president's political survival at home.

However, the self-image in question does not correspond to reality. As the following chapter argues, Turkey remains, for better or worse, economically and even socially anchored in Europe. Turkey's bonds with the EU, its constituent countries and satellites, have been much more resilient than those with America.

10

EUROPE: FROM PARTNERSHIP TO RIVALRY?

"Heeeey, European Union, come to your senses," Erdoğan inveighed while addressing a group of AKP provincial leaders. "If you try to label this operation an invasion, our job is simple. We will open the gates and send 3.6 million refugees your way."[1] The previous day, 9 October 2019, Turkish armed forces and their Syrian allies had launched Operation Peace Spring in northeast Syria. EU members were threatening arms embargoes in response. Many made good on their words – and in short order.[2] Once an accession hopeful exposed to the EU's vaunted transformative power, here was Turkey challenging the foundational principles of European integration. Ankara's foreign policy had swapped diplomacy, the pursuit of cross-border cooperation and win-win commercial ties for a knee-jerk reliance on military force and arm twisting. Rather than an open political system based on the rule of law, minority rights and democratic accountability, a one-man regime with a demagogue at the helm. The European dream of the 1990s and 2000s had turned into a nightmare. Not least for the asylum seekers facing tear gas and rubber bullets at the Pazarkule crossing with Greece.

Add to that corrosive rhetoric painting Europeans as dishonest and lacking respect. In the run-up to the 2017 constitutional referendum, Erdoğan took on Germany and the Netherlands for preventing his ministers from campaigning among the Turkish diaspora. In October 2019, it was Emmanuel Macron's turn to provoke Erdoğan's ire. He lashed out at the French president's remark about NATO being "braindead" for allowing Ankara's "crazy" invasion of Syria, calling it "sick and shallow criticism." The feud continued. "What problem does this person called Macron have with Muslims and Islam? Macron needs treatment on a mental level," Erdoğan told the AKP cadres in Kayseri, central Anatolia, a year later, in October 2020.[3] What the *reis* had in mind was the French president's legislative proposal on curbing "Islamic separatism," a prime example of Islamophobia as far as the Turkish government is concerned.

Yet remarkably enough, neither fiery verbiage coming from Ankara nor Europe's pushback produced an unbridgeable political rift. In late September 2018, Erdoğan went on an official visit to Germany, opening a gigantic new mosque in Cologne. Several days later, Dutch Foreign Minister Stef Blok took the stage as a keynote speaker at the annual forum of TRT, the Turkish public broadcaster, in Istanbul. The Netherlands sent an ambassador to Ankara, ending a seven-month hiatus. Similarly, the spat over Syria and the Eastern Mediterranean in 2019–20 gave way to a détente of sorts. As 2021 set in, the Turkish government was touting a "positive agenda" while Erdoğan called for a new Turkey–EU summit to relaunch ties. Probing for oil and gas around Cyprus was halted to allow for talks with Greece. Turkish officials all the way to the president stressed that Turkey and the EU were "in the same boat" in the ongoing Covid-19 pandemic, and that membership in the EU remained a long-term objective.[4] All that does not really add up to a fully fledged reset. "The relationship has been fraught with cynicism, double talk, deceit, from both sides and from the beginning," as Marc Pierini, former head of the EU delegation put it, referring to the immediate run-up to the membership talks in 2004–5.[5] Still, it speaks volumes about the durability of ties.

Erdoğan knows that the EU needs Turkey. European decision makers have been all too happy to pass on the burden of looking after Syrian refugees. Turkey is a buffer absorbing migrants from more far-flung places such as Iraq, Afghanistan or even sub-Saharan Africa, too. Fearful of the surging far right, European politicians have forged a pact with Turkey and are prepared to pay for its services. But as this chapter shows, Turkey needs Europe just as well. The country's faltering economy highlights the value of the EU, still the leading trading and investment partner. Once Turkey prided itself on its economic success while commentators and government officials pointed with *Schadenfreude* to the eurozone's malaise.[6] But those days are long gone. No wonder the levels of approval for membership in the EU have grown, jumping from 55.1 per cent to 61.1 per cent between 2018 and 2019.[7] For better or worse, the EU and Turkey remain entangled and interdependent. Though the Turkish leadership is fixated on the Middle East, the country has not quite severed the umbilical cord with Europe. Finally, there is NATO. Turkey's pursuit of "strategic autonomy," to borrow a phrase from Macron, does not exclude relying on the Atlantic

Alliance as a hedge against Russia. Turkey remains "part of the larger European space," to quote the respected foreign policy analyst Soli Özel.[8]

All things considered, mutual dependence has given rise to a partnership of convenience. Not the lofty vision of Turkey Europeanizing and conforming with the EU's normative prescriptions but not a bona fide antagonistic relationship either. Still, conflicts are common and will remain so, as long as Erdoğan calls the shots.

EUROPE'S GATEKEEPER

There is no better illustration of the transactional turn in EU–Turkish relations than the refugee deal reached in March 2016. Signed by then Prime Minister Ahmet Davutoğlu, it seemed to tip the power balance in Ankara's favor. But it also put on display how overlapping interests kept Turkey in Europe's orbit.

Back in the mid-2010s, Europe was facing a quandary. In 2015 alone, 1 million asylum seekers, primarily Syrians, Iraqis and Afghans, had crossed the Mediterranean. According to the UN High Commissioner for Refugees, 4,000 of them had drowned – the tragic fate that befell Aylan Kurdi, a 3-year-old boy from Kobani in northwest Syria whose lifeless body was washed up on Bodrum's shore in September 2015. Up to three-quarters of all entries had happened via Greece, with islands like Lesvos, Chios or Kos mere miles away from the Turkish coast. On 27 August 2015, Chancellor Angela Merkel took a radical step, promising Syrian refugees safe haven in Germany. That led to a spike of crossings, with asylum seekers – of different national backgrounds – scrambling to make it from the islands to Thessaloniki and from there, via the Western Balkans, into Austria and Germany. The images of hundreds of thousands trekking across Southeast and Central Europe, a humanitarian crisis of massive proportions, sparked a backlash by the far right. The Alternative for Germany (AfD) party reached double-digit percentages in regional polls over the spring of 2016. By October–November 2015, countries like Hungary, Austria, Serbia and Macedonia were tightening border controls. Even Germany, formally adhering to the open-door policy, reinstated border checks with Austria in a bid to stem the tide.

For Merkel, striking a bargain with Ankara therefore became the only viable alternative to an intra-EU implosion. Central Europeans were angry at

Germany for exposing them to the migratory surge through a unilateral decision. Greece and Italy bore a long-standing grudge towards the rest of the EU for their reluctance to share the burden – for example resisting a system of national quotas for resettling refugees the EU had adopted. The so-called Dublin Regulation allocating responsibilities between member states for handling asylum applications lay in tatters. So long as Turkey could keep would-be asylum seekers, the EU would be spared from internecine squabbling, could keep internal borders open and prevent populists from gaining additional ground.

The Turkish leadership took advantage of the situation and pressed for concessions: funding for the millions of Syrians already in the country, visa liberalization with the EU or even a restart of the accession negotiations that had virtually ground to a halt after the clampdown on the Gezi protests in 2013. Once in the prime minister's office, Ahmet Davutoğlu reinvented himself – from the architect of Turkey's foray into the Middle East he became the chief proponent of the European agenda. He sought to build on the progress already made, such as a roadmap listing technical conditions for lifting of visas dating back to December 2013, similar to ones successfully implemented by the Western Balkan countries. Having François Hollande in the Elysée, rather than Turko-skeptic Nicolas Sarkozy, helped as well. The refugee crisis handed Davutoğlu an opportunity to shine and, to a degree, emancipate himself from Erdoğan, his hitherto patron.

The EU meant business, too. As with other neighboring countries in North Africa, Eastern Europe or the Balkans, it assigned Turkey the role of a territorial buffer with the visa roadmap. It was packaged together with a readmission treaty by which Ankara undertook to take back any third-country national entering from its territory if their asylum application in the EU was rejected. Yet the Turkish government deferred implementation of the agreement in question linking it to the removal of visas. Absent that, the EU had to beef up its offer. Lo and behold, by the end of 2015, as the refugee crisis peaked, the EU was mulling an assistance package to the tune of €3 billion in exchange for a Turkish promise to stem illegal border crossings and take asylum seekers back from Greece.

Davutoğlu grabbed this opportunity with both hands. He talked up the merits of a migration arrangement to a skeptical Erdoğan. A deal with Europe put wind into Davutoğlu's sails. It could revive moribund ties with the EU and involve Europeans more deeply in the Syrian issue, albeit on the humanitarian side. A grand bargain would also empower the prime minister's faction against rivals within Erdoğan's entourage.[9]

The deal reached on 18 March 2016[10] was therefore the prime minister's crowning achievement. So much so, that it sparked fears in the Saray and precipitated Davutoğlu's downfall not long after. The attainment of visa-free travel with the EU boosting the prime minister's profile was an unnerving prospect from Erdoğan's perspective. The somber predictions that the agreement itself would not outlast Davutoğlu, or that it would collapse because of the post-July 2016 wave of repression, proved ill-conceived. Despite all the bad blood with Erdoğan, Brussels lived up to its commitment, disbursing €3 billion in 2016–17 alone and earmarking the same sum for 2018–19. The number of crossings from Turkey went down, though not as dramatically as hoped. By the end of the decade, 144,000 had crossed the Aegean since the start of the agreement, fewer than in the first three months of 2016.[11] Where the deal faltered was with Turkey's obligation to take back "all migrants not in need of international protection" as well as those intercepted in Turkish territorial waters, and the EU's agreement to take a Syrian refugee for every returnee.[12] By December 2019, however, only 2,000 people had been returned to Turkey from the Greek islands and fewer than 25,000 Syrians resettled in the EU.[13] In essence, the EU–Turkey agreement boiled down to funding for refugees in order for them to stay on Turkish soil.

The bargain prompted an uproar from various quarters. Critics of Erdoğan alleged that Europe was giving him a free pass. That was true only in part, for the Turkish government had to make concessions itself too, such as giving up on visa liberalization. The post-coup crackdown and the state of emergency removed the restart of membership talks from the agenda, too. Also, the deal gave the European Commission a large say over the disbursement of the money. Rather than pay a lump sum to be spent at Ankara's discretion, Brussels directed tranches to specific government agencies tasked with preparing detailed plans and reports. The deal sustained cooperation at the technical/bureaucratic level at a time when Turkey and Europe had drifted apart. In the meantime, Erdoğan's repeated bluffs that he could open the gates again came to nothing. Still, Germany and other EU member states did their best not to burn bridges with the Turkish president, aware of the high stakes.

Another set of criticisms had to do with the humanitarian ramifications of the deal. Europe denied the right of asylum to destitute Syrians, Iraqis or Afghans fleeing from war and persecution. Turkey hardly qualified as a safe third country either, human rights NGOs contended. Non-Europeans were not eligible for refugee status because of a geographic exception Ankara had applied to the 1950 Geneva Convention. But the EU raised humanitarian arguments, too. Gerald Knaus, credited as the agreement's intellectual father, portrayed it as a first step towards a more humane regime. The ultimate goal, he opined, was to "spare [asylum seekers] a risky sea crossing and a perilous trek through the Balkans."[14] "Turkey and the EU [. . .] agreed to step up efforts against migrant smugglers," read the joint statement from March 2016. The problem was that the EU did a stellar job in keeping its end of the bargain. Reception centers on Greek islands remained overcrowded, for instance, and conditions appalling. Greece was left on its own to deal with processing asylum applications, too. In other words, the EU's main goal appeared to be deterring would-be migrants rather than improving the system.

Greece was able to capitalize on European support only in the spring of 2020, when Erdoğan finally decided to play hardball. On 29 February, he had declared the border to be open and as a result thousands of people turned up at the banks of the Evros/Meriç attempting to wade through, as well as at the land crossing at Pazarkule/Kastanies.[15] Afghans and Syrians were gathered by the authorities from various parts of Istanbul, told that the border was open, then bussed to Pazarkule escorted by special police and TV crews.[16] Pandemonium ensued, as the asylum seekers tried to tear down the border fence. Police on the Greek side showered the entrants with rubber bullets in order to push them back. Athens accused Erdoğan of piling pressure on the EU in order to bring the latter onto his side regarding the Idlib crisis in Syria.[17] This argument resonated with others. Austrian Chancellor Sebastian Kurz called out the Turkish authorities for using migrants as pawns. The European Commission's Ursula von der Leyen, who visited the region along with the head of the EU Council Charles Michel and David Sassoli, the speaker of the European Parliament, heaped praise on Greece as "Europe's Shield" and promised an extra €700 million.[18] Frontex, the EU's border agency, dispatched 100 additional personnel to assist the Greeks. Neighboring Bulgaria opened dams on its territory to flood the Evros/Meriç river downstream. Erdoğan overplayed his hand and, sadly, asylum seekers bore the brunt.

EUROPE: FROM PARTNERSHIP TO RIVALRY?

This episode notwithstanding, there is a good chance that the EU and Turkey will renew the 2016 agreement for another five-year period beyond 2021. At the time of writing, Erdoğan is lobbying Germany and the EU Council's Portuguese presidency for a summit to address the matter. Though interests on both sides are aligned, the Turkish government will, yet again, seek to shape the deal according to its wishes. Ankara would want to have fuller control over the money coming from Brussels, with fewer conditions and strings attached. That will allow it, among other things, to spend the funds in northern Syria, with the Europeans bankrolling and legitimating the Turkish-run buffer zones hosting large numbers of IDPs.[19] Erdoğan has been adamant that the arrangements will not cover refugees from Afghanistan following the Taliban takeover in August 2021. "Turkey will not act as EU warehouse," he told Charles Michel, the EU Council president.[20] Almost certainly, the EU side will hold the line too and insist on setting its own rules, modalities and timetables.

The refugee deal underscores Turkey's self-image of an independent power rather than a supplicant or eternal candidate for EU membership. The view in Ankara is that Europe, whether represented by influential states or the Brussels-based institutions, could be a partner or an obstacle in this quest depending on the issue. Erdoğan does not shy away from fanning conflict if it suits his domestic and foreign policy goals.

"WE KNOW THE DUTCH FROM SREBRENICA"

Turkey's recurrent squabbles with core European countries such as Germany, France and the Netherlands put on full display Erdoğan's methods. The 2017 referendum and the presidential/parliamentary elections the following year were particularly tense. In the run-up to the constitutional plebiscite, the German and the Dutch governments banned Turkish politicians from campaigning in their respective countries. The Netherlands expelled Family Affairs Minister Fatma Betül Sayan Kaya while Foreign Minister Mevlüt Çavuşoğlu was prevented from landing. That came as a snub to AKP outreach to the diaspora, with at least 1.5 million holding Turkish citizenship in Germany alone. In response, Erdoğan denounced Berlin's "Nazi practices."[21] Turkey blocked the Dutch ambassador from re-entering the country and threatened to cancel the refugee agreement.

"We know the Dutch from Srebrenica," Erdoğan raged, referring to the failure of UN peacekeepers from the Netherlands to prevent the slaughter of 8,000 Bosniak men and boys in the summer of 1995. The Turkish president's fans took to the streets. In March 2017, a demonstration in Rotterdam, where the Turkish family affairs minister was supposed to appear, escalated into a riot.[22] In the end Erdoğan got what he wanted. In the constitutional referendum, 65 per cent of Turks in Germany, 72 per cent in Austria and 73 per cent in the Netherlands voted for the constitutional changes, compared to 51.4 per cent in the nationwide count.

History repeated itself with the twin elections in 2018. It was then Germany and Austria that prohibited rallies. "Our view is clear," declared Foreign Minister Heiko Maas: "In the three-month period before elections in a foreign country, no election campaigning will take place in Germany."[23] Erdoğan snapped back. His visit to Germany in September, after the elections were done and dusted, came as an opportunity to change tack. Yet the Turkish president took on his hosts, during the official dinner at that, calling them out for harboring terrorists: pro-Kurdish organizations, members of the Gülen movement as well as liberals finding refuge in the Federal Republic.

Beyond Erdoğan's rhetorical outbursts, meant largely for domestic consumption, European governments are on the alert with regard to the Turkish state's penetration of diaspora communities, whether through imams appointed by the Diyanet or MİT operatives.[24] Austria took a hard line – moving to close down seven mosques and expel dozens of clerics in 2018. The conservative government of Sebastian Kurz, backed by the far-right Austrian Freedom Party (FPÖ), enacted a law from 2015 aimed to counter the spread of radical Islam.[25] Though neither Germany nor the Netherlands have gone that far, distrust between them and Turkey is pervasive.

Relations with France have been equally troublesome. Legislation on fighting "Islamic separatism," pushed by President Macron in the wake of the assassination of a high school teacher, triggered a mini-crisis in late 2020. On that occasion, Erdoğan called for a boycott of French goods (it's debatable whether many Turks complied). Unlike Germany, however, France has responded in kind. Macron defines Turkey as a strategic competitor rather than a difficult partner. Paris and Ankara are at odds across regional flash-points, including Libya and the Eastern Mediterranean. In Macron's vision, the essence of the EU's own quest for strategic autonomy – a key concept in

French political discourse – is the ability to balance against and set the terms of engagement with the Turks. In January 2021, France finalized a deal with Greece for the supply of 18 Dassault Rafale fighters. The previous September, the *Charles de Gaulle*, a nuclear-powered aircraft carrier, was deployed in the Eastern Mediterranean alongside the Greek navy in a clear message to Turkey.[26] Paris has stepped up defense cooperation with both Athens and Nicosia, with Macron visiting Cyprus in January 2019. Importantly, French company Total holds an offshore exploration license granted by the Cypriot government.[27]

In contrast to the French, the German leadership believes in diplomacy and the power of economic integration, a view shared by Merkel and by her successor as leader of the Christian Democrats, Armin Laschet. What is at play is the intimate connection at the societal level, thanks to the numerous Germans of Turkish descent. Uğur Sahin and Özlem Türeci, the brains behind the BioNTech-Pfizer anti-Covid vaccine, film director Fatih Akin (Akın) and footballer Mesut Özil, an ardent Erdoğan supporter, all illustrate the strong bonds running between the two countries. Germany's pacific political culture and aversion to military power, another difference from France, shapes its position on Turkey (as well as Russia) too.

THE GREEK–TURKISH CONFLICT REDUX

Nowhere is the divergence between France and Germany, as well as within the EU as a whole, as striking as in the case of the Eastern Mediterranean. In 2019–20, Turkey's clash with Greece and Cyprus (or "the Greek [*Rum*] Administration of the South," as Ankara calls it) put on the table the issue of EU sanctions. But member states have been at odds as to how far-reaching they should be. In February 2020, foreign ministers zeroed in on two executives in the state-owned Turkish Petroleum Corporation, Vice-President Mehmet Ferruh Akalın and Deputy Director of the Exploration Department Ali Coşkun Namoğlu.[28] Greece hoped the EU would go after high-value targets such as Berat Albayrak, Erdoğan's son-in-law, who, as an energy minister, oversaw the launch of the seismic survey vessel *Oruç Reis* in April 2017. Erdoğan and his inner circle were not included. In December 2020, Angela Merkel and Bulgarian Prime Minister Boyko Borisov – backed by Spain, Italy, Hungary and Malta – blocked tougher measures, such as tariffs or an arms embargo – yet again.[29] Greece, Cyprus, Austria and France were overruled.

In typical EU fashion, the response to Turkey is based on the lowest common denominator. Yes, sanctions and punishments are needed. But why slam the door in Erdoğan's face when so much is at stake? In December 2020, the EU tasked High Representative for Foreign and Security Policy Josep Borrell to draft a list of individuals to be sanctioned, yet as of the time of writing, the actual decision is still pending. There is an agreement in principle on cutting pre-accession aid but the sums are relatively limited: €145 million for 2020.[30] Since 2016, the Council of the EU has ignored several (non-binding) resolutions by the European Parliament to freeze accession negotiations, still ongoing on paper, because of human rights abuses in Turkey.[31]

With the EU internally divided, Greece has been balancing against Turkey through a coalition of the willing. Beyond France, it relies on Italy and Egypt, as well as the United Arab Emirates, Ankara's adversary in Libya as well as in the Horn of Africa (see Chapter 9). The Greek government reached a maritime delimitation deal with Italy in June 2020, that had been pending for decades.[32] In August that year, Cairo and Athens signed an agreement to designate their EEZs, too. "It is the absolute opposite of the illegal, void and legally unfounded MoU that was signed between Turkey and Tripoli," commented Foreign Minister Nikos Dendias, referring to the deal between Erdoğan and Libya's Government of National Accord. "Following the signing of this agreement, the nonexistent Turkish–Libyan memorandum has ended up where it belonged from the beginning: in the trash can."[33] Of course, Turkey has not been idle, courting support from Germany, Italy, Malta and Spain, in addition to Tunisia, Algeria and Lebanon.[34]

Tensions in the Eastern Mediterranean need not be a prelude to a military showdown. Both Greece and its allies and Turkey share an interest in negotiating. However, each of the parties would rather talk from a position of strength. In January 2021, Athens and Ankara launched a round of exploratory negotiations, after a five-year break. In response, the EU started talking of engagement with Turkey yet again, with the Head of the Commission Ursula von der Leyen and the European Council President Charles Michel heading to Ankara in April 2021.[35] The European Council in June 2021 welcomed the "de-escalation in the Eastern Mediterranean," highlighting negotiations on the update of the Customs Union and the renewal of the 2016 refugee deal.[36] What is missing is a third party to act as honest broker, the role fulfilled by the United States at the peak of disputes in the Aegean during the mid-1990s. The Trump administration took the side of Greece, with relations between Washington and Athens blooming thanks to a raft of defense and energy deals. Biden is yet to come up with a policy of his own.

THE SCRAMBLE FOR THE BALKANS

The Western Balkans, the EU's backyard or, even better, inner courtyard, has been another bone of contention. Turkey's influence became apparent during Erdoğan's inauguration as an executive president in July 2018. Virtually all Balkan leaders, including Serbian President Aleksandar Vučić, turned up.[37] There were no EU dignitaries in attendance, however, with the exception of Hungarian Prime Minister Viktor Orbán and President Rumen Radev of Bulgaria. While the West lamented the demise of democracy, Balkan neighbors along with Orbán, hardly a paragon of liberalism and the rule of law either, embraced Erdoğan's Turkey as a political and economic partner. At least one of the countries in question had played a role in the pre-election campaign. Bosnia and Herzegovina had hosted a mass rally back in May. Barred from campaigning in Germany, Austria and the Netherlands, Erdoğan had summoned his supporters from across Europe to Sarajevo's Zetra Olympic Centre. From the Bosnian capital, he had spoken out against "certain European countries" working to divide Turkish citizens along ethnic and sectarian lines.[38] There was the New Turkey posing as the leader of not only all Muslims in the Balkans but also Europe. That was nothing new of course. Under Turgut Özal in the early 1990s Turkey aspired to such a role. Yet back then, it portrayed itself as a bridge between the West and the Ottoman Empire's former possessions. This time around Erdoğan was telling his admirers he stood against Europe.

Turkey's go-it-alone policy and anti-Western rhetoric has added to fears, locally as well as in the EU, that the Balkans is turning into the epicenter of a geopolitical contest. Russia, at loggerheads with the West since the annexation of Crimea, has been pushing against NATO and EU expansion. China has expanded its economic footprint through billions in soft loans paying for new highways, bridges, energy generation facilities and so on across the region.

Turkey, linked to Balkan countries by its history and geography, is enacting its own neighborhood policy too. Its arsenal includes trade, investment, popular culture (widely watched TV soaps for instance), connections to local elites and money funneled through the Diyanet and TİKA.[39] In Bosnia alone, Turkey has implemented some 900 projects between 1995 and 2020, among them the restoration of the historic Careva Džamija (*Hünkâr Camii*) mosque dating back to the 1450s, and the creation of a haematology ward at Sarajevo's clinical center. Accordingly, Turkey enjoys a popularity among Bosniaks only matched by the affection Bosnian Serbs have towards Russia. Ethnic Turks, many Albanians as well as other Muslims in North Macedonia, Kosovo and Serbia share similar sentiments. Turkish security services throw their weight around too. MİT caused a stir in Kosovo when it captured and transferred six prominent Gülenists in March 2018.[40] A diplomat was expelled from Bulgaria for interfering in domestic politics.[41] The Turkish presence in the Balkans is not all about Ottoman nostalgia and developmental assistance but has a harder edge too.

What sets Turkey apart from the EU is the focus on the strong leader as well as on religious identity. In the words of Erdoan Shipoli, an academic at Georgetown University, "[Turkish outreach's] main goal right now is not to increase Turkey's influence – it's to increase Erdoğan's [. . .] popularity. We know that [the Turkish state] sets up these rallies and takes a couple of people in Prizen, Skopje or Novi Pazar and gives them pictures of Erdoğan to show that he has sympathizers everywhere."[42] While the EU encourages democratic consolidation and the rule of law, Turkey's main political export appears to be the cult of the strong leader.[43]

Turkey puts strong emphasis on Islam as well as on the Ottoman legacy. The Diyanet has been in the Balkans since the 1990s, when it was combating Salafist influences from the Gulf. For the past decade, however, the Turkish government's top goal is also to stamp out the Gülenists, dismantle their infrastructure and transfer their assets to the Maarif Foundation.[44] Once a vanguard of Turkish influence, the *cemaat* has turned into a liability. Yet getting rid of Gülen is not feasible without the cooperation of Balkan leaders and governments, which in turn underscores the importance of personal connections between Erdoğan and the likes of Albanian Prime Minister Edi Rama, the Bosniak leader Bakir Izetbegović, or Boyko Borisov in Bulgaria. But even though he is dependent on the locals, the Turkish president faces no competition as to his claim to be the voice of Islam in the region.

To be sure, the EU is far from faultless. The vaunted membership perspective offered to the region has been deferred. After Croatia joined in 2013, the EU set its sights on Montenegro and Serbia but negotiations moved at a slow pace. North Macedonia, renamed after a deal with Greece resolving the so-called issue, had to wait several years, along with Albania, to be given the green light for starting talks in spring 2020. Having fulfilled all technical conditions, Kosovo, much like Turkey, is still denied visa-free travel for fear of an influx of migrants. For EU leaders like Emmanuel Macron internal consolidation, especially at the level of the eurozone, comes before further expansion. That attitude breeds frustration in the region. "European solidarity turned out to be a fairy tale," murmured Serbian President Aleksandar Vučić at the outset of the Covid-19 pandemic, praising China for offering a helping hand. Needless to say, Turkey has profited from the limbo too. In October 2017, Erdoğan was a welcome guest of Vučić's in the Muslim-majority Sandžak region of Serbia. A large crowd cheered the two strongmen. Watching a Turkish leader in the company of Slobodan Milošević's one-time minister of information was a bizarre sight. But it did shine a light on the fact that the times had changed.

Despite all that, Turkey does not quite fit the bill as an EU adversary. Thanks to the Customs Union, it remains part of the European economic space. The same is true of the Western Balkans which are all benefiting from free trade arrangements with the EU and are aligning their legal systems with the *acquis communautaire*. Turkey's leading trading partners in Southeast Europe are not Muslim-populated countries like Bosnia, Albania or Kosovo but Romania, Bulgaria and Greece. Not only do they import from Turkey but they also export strongly back. Turkey is among the top five export markets for all those three countries. Serbia comes next.[45] The size of one's economy and depth of integration into the EU is a better predictor for the intensity of economic exchange with Turkey than culture or history. No wonder that a common complaint heard in Sarajevo is that Turkish dignitaries talk of brotherhood with Bosniaks but Turkish investment mainly lands in neighboring Serbia.

On the security side, Turkey remains part of NATO and, as such, supports its expansion to the Balkans. The Grand National Assembly ratified Montenegro and North Macedonia's accession treaties without delay in 2017 and in 2019 respectively. That stands in stark contrast to Russia's vigorous opposition to the Atlantic Alliance's expansion. There is also no opposition, rhetorical or substantive, from Ankara vis-à-vis EU enlargement, which benefits Turkey too because of the trade opportunities it opens. On paper, if not in reality, Turkey remains a candidate country and therefore in the same basket as the Western Balkans. More than 150 Turkish servicemen and women take part in the EU peacekeeping mission in Bosnia (EUFOR), to which Turkey is the second-largest contributor after Austria. In the Western Balkans, Turkey has no alternative offer to the region to woo it away from Euro-Atlantic institutions, as Russia has thanks to the Eurasian Economic Union or the Collective Security Treaty Organization, a sort of a Moscow-led replica of NATO.

The last point to take into account is that Turkish presence does not necessarily imply direct influence over policies and decisions on the ground. Foreign Minister Ahmet Davutoğlu's shuttle diplomacy between Serbia and Bosnia and Herzegovina in 2010–11 looked impressive on paper.[46] Yet, beyond some initial concessions the main achievement of that era turned out to be the opening with Serbia, which burgeoned under Erdoğan and Vučić. Turkey plays no central role in Kosovo, arguably the most significant issue in the region. The EU leads on "normalization talks" between Belgrade and Pristina, with the US, and occasionally Russia, coming into the picture. All in all, Turkish ambitions have been scaled down. The Serbia–Bosnia–Turkey trilateral summits are now focused on more immediate issues such as the highway connecting Belgrade and Sarajevo.[47]

THE ENERGY NEXUS

Energy is another area where the EU's and Turkey's interests remain aligned, putting aside the Eastern Mediterranean. Both Turkey and the European countries are consumers and therefore historically dependent on imports of oil and natural gas. About a third of the crude oil feeding the Turkish energy system comes from Iraq. In the 2000s, Russia became the most important source of gas. Faced with dependency on external suppliers, both the EU and Ankara have a shared interest to diversify sources in order to be able to guarantee stability of supply and secure lower prices.

That is particularly pertinent for gas, a commodity traded under long-term contracts signed by national companies and therefore susceptible to the ebbs and flows of political relations between supplier and consumer states. Turkey's ambition is to turn from a recipient of natural gas into a full-fledged player on transnational markets, capable of sourcing shipments from hydrocarbon-rich neighbors and reselling it to downstream customers west of its border. The EU too, especially since the 2006 and 2009 cut-offs of deliveries through Ukraine, has put forward strategies for reducing dependence on Russia. That is done primarily through encouraging integration of national grids and passing legislation to boost competition internally.

The Southern Gas Corridor linking Europe to the Caspian, via Turkey, has been a top priority as well. It became reality in November 2020 when the Trans-Adriatic Pipeline (TAP) came online connecting Turkey to Italy via Greece and Albania. TAP is an extension of the Trans-Anatolian Pipeline (TANAP), which has been in operation since 2018. Thanks to TANAP/TAP, Turkey is able to transit 10 billion cubic meters (bcm) annually. A fifth of that volume will be consumed by neighbors such as Greece and Bulgaria. As a result, Gazprom – the dominant supplier in Southeast Europe – is bound to lose market share to the Shah Deniz consortium, in which Azerbaijan's national company SOCAR is one of the key players. Shah Deniz is committed to double TAP's capacity in the 2020s in order to supply both the Western Balkans and the EU.

Turkey's firm commitment to the Southern Gas Corridor stands in contrast to its thriving cooperation with Russia. Indeed, in January 2020, Vladimir Putin and Tayyip Erdoğan inaugurated in Istanbul the TurkStream natural gas pipeline connecting the two countries through the Black Sea. Aimed to divert up to 31.5 bcm of gas away from the Ukraine route, TurkStream, along with the nuclear power station at Akkuyu, has come to symbolize the ever closer political and commercial ties between Moscow and Ankara. Its restart was one of the main deliverables in the rapprochement between Putin and Ankara in August 2016, following the near breakdown of relations over the downed Russian fighter jet. With the new connection, Gazprom expected to consolidate its foothold on the Turkish market against competitors such as Iran, Azerbaijan or Qatar.

But reality has proven more complex. The global glut of gas and oil, and falling prices, incentivized Turkish importers, state-owned utility BOTAŞ first and foremost, to reduce purchases of Russian gas. The latter's share plunged from 52 per cent (28.69 bcm) in 2017 to 47 per cent in 2018 (23.64 bcm), to just 33 per cent (15.9 bcm) in 2019. Turkey started turning to LNG from Algeria, Nigeria, Qatar and even the US. Traded at record-low prices, it covered 29 per cent of consumption in the country for 2019. What also favored the boom was the heavy investment into LNG terminals and storage capacity during the 2010s.

The surge of LNG imports puts Turkey in an advantageous position vis-à-vis Russia as long-term supply contracts come up for renegotiation. BOTAŞ and four private companies importing through the so-called Western route, currently served by the TurkStream pipeline, are up for renewal at the close of 2021. BOTAŞ's contract for 16 bcm a year, shipped through the Blue Stream pipeline running under the Black Sea since 2005, expires at the end of 2025 too. Ankara will no doubt try to extract better terms from the Russians, such as a discount on price or lowering the take-or-pay quota, which is currently at 80 per cent of the contracted annual offtakes and so on. "The availability of cheap spot LNG and falling gas demand is a signal to our existing pipeline suppliers that they need to be flexible," Deputy Energy Minister Alparslan Bayraktar said in February 2020.[48]

The concessions Turkey may squeeze out from suppliers sets a precedent for EU importers too. Clearly this is also the case for Greece, which is similarly turning to LNG, as well as Bulgaria and Romania, Athens' partners in a terminal (floating storage and regasification unit) to be installed off the north-eastern Greek port of Alexandroupolis. From the perspective of natural gas, Turkey remains part of the larger European marketplace. Small wonder then that Gazprom Export, the Russian firm's external trading arm, still classifies Turkey as "Western Europe."

IT'S THE ECONOMY

The energy connection points to an undeniable fact: Turkey remains an integral part of the European marketplace. The EU remains the country's principal trading partner as well as by far the top source of investment. The figures and data tell a story which puts the bellicose rhetoric coming from Erdoğan in perspective. Turkey is the EU's fifth leading trading partner, after the US, UK, China and Switzerland. It is a more important destination for European exports than Russia and it sells more goods back to the EU than Japan (though Russia and Japan are ahead on imports and exports respectively).[49] In the 2010s, the EU-27 went from 46 per cent of Turkey's total exports to 50 per cent. The EU accounts for a third of Turkey's imports, compared to China with 10 per cent, Russia with 7 per cent and the US with 5 per cent. And, whatever the weather, the EU accounts for about two-thirds of the FDI in the country.

The Customs Union – a more advanced form of integration than post-Brexit UK's trade agreement – keeps the two economies joined at the hip. The rapid growth on the AKP's watch in the 2000s would have not been possible without seamless access to a 500-million-strong market (EU-27 plus UK). In the period between 1996 and 2016, exports jumped five times. Turkey was turning into a "trading state."[50] Though the country diversified its export portfolio over these years, the EU retained its lead. And the Customs Union did not hamper Turkey, as liberalization of trade with the rest of the world proceeded at a constant pace.[51] Importantly, tariff-free access to the European market, as well as the removal of certain non-tariff barriers (e.g. rules of origin), have been a boon for investment.

The automotive sector provides an illuminating case study. Car makers such as Fiat, Renault, Hyundai or Toyota and their suppliers and subcontractors set up shop in Turkey because of the tariff-free access to the EU secured through the Customs Union. Over 80 per cent of the automotive exports, worth $20 billion, go to Europe each year. That corresponds to a tenth of Turkish sales abroad. That's not just vehicles but also components then re-exported to the EU. Indeed, Turkey has become key to pan-European production chains in manufacturing."[52]

To be sure, the Customs Union has been plagued with problems from the outset. First, because it binds Turkey to the terms of agreements the EU concludes with third countries – including large economies such as South Korea (2011), Canada (2017) and Japan (2019). Ankara needs to sign a separate deal with each of those countries in order to be able to access their markets – or achieve "geographical alignment" in Euro-speak.[53] Typically, that has not been a problem with states on the European periphery entering into free trade agreements with the EU. Turkey has been successful in negotiating treaties with the countries of the Western Balkans and the bulk of the countries in North Africa and the Middle East covered by the so-called Euro-Med initiative. But dealing with bigger players wielding political and economic leverage is more challenging. There is a difference between bargaining with Bosnia and Herzegovina, and bargaining with Japan. Without a say in EU institutions, the Turkish government is in no position to take advantage of the collective weight of the EU-27 in order to secure maximum benefits. There is no mechanism for Ankara to influence Brussels' negotiations with third parties either. At the same time, Turkey has been successful in negotiating an agreement with the UK, in December 2020, which parallels the one Britain concluded with the EU. This is not trivial as Britain is Ankara's second biggest trading partner after Germany.

The second sticking point is that the EU–Turkey Customs Union is limited to industrial goods and excludes services. Services are one item on the Turkey's export list that is going upwards – $58.6 billion in 2018 and $63.6 billion in 2019.[54] Transportation and tourism lead the way. Unlike trade in industrial goods, the trade in services registered a surplus of $31 billion for Turkey in 2019.[55] That is nearly equal to Turkey's trade deficit over the same year.[56] Bringing services into the trading arrangement would be highly beneficial – advancing the alignment of Turkish legislation and regulatory frameworks with the EU's, attracting FDI, prompting innovation and the kind of structural reforms needed for Turkey to overcome what economists label "the middle-income trap." Studies project a 430 per cent surge in the export of services and 95 per cent of agricultural sales should the Customs Union be extended. Turkish GDP would rise by 1.84 per cent.[57] The EU, for its part, will gain by accessing public procurement and service markets.[58]

Turkey and the EU accepted the need to update the Customs Union back in the 2000s, carrying out talks on services. More recently, in May 2015, Cecilia Maelstrom and Economy Minister Nihat Zeybekçi unveiled plans to "modernize" the arrangement.[59] The European Commission produced a blueprint, putting forward two options: an Enhanced Commercial Framework and a Ukraine-style Deep and Comprehensive Free Trade Area. In either scenario, the updated Customs Union would cover services along with public procurement, rules on establishment, non-tariff barriers and so on.[60] Coupled with visa liberalization, this would amount to nothing less than a privileged partnership of the kind European conservatives rooted for in the mid-2000s. Turkey's official position is that the prospective Customs Union talks are parallel to the accession negotiations and therefore do not cancel the latter. But in reality, the update of the trading arrangement stands as a clear alternative to the stalled EU talks.

Yet, as ever, politics stands at odds with economic rationality. Turkey's democratic decline from the 2016 onwards and the conflicts with the EU it spawned have precluded the deepening of integration. In August 2017, German Chancellor Angela Merkel called for the freezing of Customs Union talks.[61] Tensions with other member states – the Netherlands, Greece, Cyprus and more recently France – have not helped either. On 26 June 2018, the General Affairs Council formally decided that "further work on the modernization of the Customs Union" would not go ahead, singling out (1) democratization and improving rule of law, and (2) alignment with the EU's foreign policy, as preconditions.[62] Ditto for bad blood between Ankara and the European Parliament, though it has no formal role in the initial stages of Customs Union negotiations. The European Commission's mandate request submitted to the Council in December 2016 became stuck. It was unblocked only in March 2021, as a reward for Turkey dialing down pressure on Greece and Cyprus in the Eastern Mediterranean.[63] Though the EU softened its democratic conditionality, the process of updating the Customs Union is far from irreversible.

Economic volatility in Turkey makes the upgrade of economic ties with the EU all the more necessary. Growth rates plunged even before the Covid-19 pandemic, hitting 2.9 per cent of GDP in 2018 and just 0.9 per cent of GDP the following year. This compares to an average annual growth of about 7 per cent in the good years between 2000 and 2007, and a whopping 11 per cent in 2011, as Turkey emerged from the global financial crisis. Low growth has exposed structural vulnerabilities made worse by the consumption and real estate/construction spree funded by debt denominated in foreign currency, the cornerstone of the AKP-era economic model.[64] Between 2008 and 2018, private sector credit to GDP ratio rose from 27 per cent to 70 per cent. The Turkish lira headed downhill. In September 2017, $1 traded for 3.4 Turkish lira but a year later the rate reached $1 to 6.3 lira. Despite the recovery in 2019, the lira crossed the psychological threshold of 8 lira to $1 in October 2020, losing more than a fifth of its value over the year.[65] It reached 12–13 lira to $1 in November 2021. The sharp depreciation has had a damaging effect on living standards and has been a thorn in Erdoğan's side.

Regrettably, Erdoğan resists any policy adjustment in response. He has been insistent on keeping interest rates low to maintain growth, sparing no criticism of the "interest rate lobby," and firing central bankers for daring to voice dissent. The construction industry, aligned with the AKP, has been thriving on easy credit, but other businesses have been hurt by runaway inflation. To keep afloat, Turkey has burned through its foreign currency reserves, down from $80 billion in December 2019 to just $48.9 billion in May 2020. It has rebuffed any idea of soliciting help from the IMF, with all strings attached, and instead solicited aid from Qatar via a currency swap agreement. Cosmetic changes have not made a huge difference. For instance, the sudden resignation of Erdoğan's son-in-law, Berat Albayrak, as financial minister and the appointment of a technocrat, Naci Ağbal, as a central bank governor favoring rate hikes (December 2020) helped the lira recover value. In addition, in March 2021, Erdoğan announced the launch of human rights reforms – a move seeking to reassure the West, no doubt. But soon thereafter the government reversed course. The pro-Kurdish HDP faced closure, while Erdoğan replaced Ağbal[66] with a loyalist parroting the party line about the evil of interest rates. The Turkish lira headed precipitously south as a result, a classic example of Erdoğanomics.

This episode brings out a lesson as to the limits of rapprochement with the EU. While Turkey has an interest in expanding its access to the European market, there are serious impediments precluding such a move. Beyond the issue of democracy and human rights or the disputes with EU member states, they have to do with the politico-economic model built on Erdoğan's watch. The *yerli ve millî* campaign, subsidies to crony businesses, the state's involvement in key enterprises such as Turkcell, Türk Telekom and Turkish Airways, the liquidity pumped into state-owned banks and pressure on private lenders to keep credit going, or even duties imposed on imports amidst the Covid-19 pandemic all demonstrate the trend towards economic nationalism.[67] As *The Economist* has noted, "Turkey is trying to emulate China's growth strategy (featuring state-backed credit for property and infrastructure investment) without the benefit of its docile depositors and trapped savings."[68] That is why volatility is bound to persist. In the meantime, Turkey will continue to engage with the EU but, when possible, do so on its own terms.

EPILOGUE
What Next?

Erdoğan rose to power two decades ago. Love him or hate him, he has left his mark on both Turkey and its neighbors, including the EU. Under Erdoğan's watch, Turkey has grown richer and more influential but has also become less free, more confrontational and trigger-happy in its foreign policy and, eventually, economically stagnant. But what will Turkey look like in another twenty years? Where is it heading after the roller-coaster ride of the 2010s?

Speculating about Turkey's future is an inherently dicey enterprise. Even well-informed suppositions run the risk of being swept aside and rendered useless by events. Still, some trends are easy to spot.

First off, Turkey in twenty years will still be Erdoğan's Turkey. All things being equal, he will in all likelihood still be in charge. Erdoğan won't surrender power. His iron grip on the country's politics won't change, whatever the cost. Yes, the opposition could capture a majority in the Grand National Assembly. But in such a cohabitation scenario, Erdoğan will still have the upper hand thanks to the presidential constitution. His control over the judicial branch, including the Constitutional Court, a plethora of regulatory and administrative bodies, and security agencies will tip the scales. Not to mention the informal role he would wield within the economy. Erdoğan's opponents could even pose a challenge for the presidency in 2023, with his popularity ratings now at an all-time low and the popular mayors of Istanbul and Ankara breathing down his neck.[1] Indeed, Ekrem İmamoğlu and Mansur Yavaş might have a fair shot at the presidential race in 2023, capitalizing on economic discontent and the backlash against refugees from Syria and now Afghanistan. Yet what matters is who counts the votes as much as how many ballots each candidate gets.[2] At worst, the regime could resort to repression in order to secure its survival.[3] It will also instrumentalize nationalism and reignite old-school culture wars to drive a wedge in the opposition, which currently spans the entire political spectrum, from religious conservatives to hardline secularists and from nationalists to the pro-Kurdish HDP.[4]

The big question is whether an aging Erdoğan would still be up to the job a decade or two from now. Health and age concerns will no doubt give urgency to finding a successor who could take the reins in due course, a question which is already hanging in the air as a Damocles' sword. And as we know from other authoritarian regimes, a transition of power puts the system under tremendous strain. It increases uncertainty, raises fears among incumbent elites about their place within the hierarchy and the assets they have accumulated and exacerbates rifts between rival factions within the government and its clientele. Erdoğan's heir – whatever his name (chances are it won't be a "her") – may struggle to preserve stability in the face of discord, economic volatility and external challenges. Bereft of Erdoğan's charisma, appeal to grassroots and informal authority over the elite, the next leader will face an uphill battle. In such circumstances, bargaining and entering into compromises with the opposition, or even sharing power, could be the only viable strategy to ensure political survival. This could entail a switch back to a parliamentary system, scrapping presidentialism altogether or at least recasting the constitutional balance of power. In other words, the Turkey of the future may follow a trajectory familiar from the so-called "third wave" democratization in Southern Europe and Latin America in the 1970s and 1980s. It would see the post-Erdoğan AKP losing its hegemonic status but continuing to play a cornerstone role in the political system.

But Erdoğan's Turkey does not imply he would be running the show. Even without him, Erdoğanism will live on. Think of Peronism, Gaullism and any number of -isms in countries far and near. The narratives of political and economic empowerment, of putting Islam again at the center of public life and of turning Turkey into a great power in the Middle East and beyond will resonate with the conservative electorate. Erdoğan will be a father figure and his historical legacy will live on for generations to come. But it would be as divisive as ever. What the AKP faithful will be celebrating as Turkey's golden age the other half of the country will remember as a dark era of repression and unfreedom. Brace for the coming memory wars, reminiscent of the present-day battles over Atatürk or Abdülhamid II.

At the same time, an essential chunk of Erdoğan's political agenda is likely to remain unfulfilled. AKP rule might reshape the ways Turkey's citizens think about history and collective identity, placing Islam at the center. Yet there is no indication that it is producing a uniformly pious society. As conservative a country as Turkey is, secularism appears to be gaining, not losing ground. A 2018 survey by pollster Konda found, for instance, that the percentage of those identifying as "religious conservatives" had dropped from 32 to 25 per cent in the space of a decade.[5] The share of citizens fasting during the holy month of Ramadan went from 77 to 65 per cent. The AKP's dominance does not translate into a wholesale identity shift. There is a good chance it is actually yielding the opposite effect as it erodes the appeal of Islamist politics. All things being equal, the fault lines in Turkey's society and politics will continue as before. They will have a profound impact on the future political trajectory, though admittedly only a split in the AKP-voting, religious conservative camp could overturn the balance.[6] The Kurdish issue will not go way either, particularly as HDP (or its successors) solidify their position of kingmaker in politics, as happened during the mayoral elections in Istanbul back in 2019.

What also is not changing is Turkey's love–hate relationship with the West. At the time of writing, Erdoğan is going through a reset with both the US and the EU. His tête-à-tête with President Joe Biden on the margins of the NATO Summit in June 2021 struck a positive tone. The EU is content with the de-escalation of tensions in the Eastern Mediterranean, and it is discussing a renewal of the 2016 refugee deal with Ankara, and possibly the updating of the Customs Union. There is, furthermore, a parallel conversation about how Turkey fits in the so-called European Green Deal.[7] The takeaway is that complete separation from the West is not likely, despite the abrasive rhetoric coming from Erdoğan and his supporters. Clear majorities within the country support continued membership in NATO. Economic hardship has broadened the appeal of the EU as well. According to Kadir Has University's annual poll on foreign policy, close to 60 per cent supported accession in 2021.[8]

Two decades from now, Turkey will still be a major regional power. Ankara might well choose to scale back its military and diplomatic footprint across the Middle East, North and sub-Saharan Africa, but it will stay in Syria and northern Iraq for the long haul. Exiting and surrendering control over the enclaves across the Syrian border will be difficult and Turkey will continue to provide security, governance and economic development in those areas. Turkish foreign policy might still be driven by the ambition for regional leadership but a more realistic appraisal of the country's capabilities, as well as the interests of other key actors in the Middle East, is essential to success. The same is true of other regions such as the Balkans, where Turkey is in no position to substitute the EU, or the South Caucasus where Russia will continue to wield leverage. Most of all, in order to project influence in the neighborhood, Turkey needs to put its house in order first: it needs to revert to high levels of economic growth, strengthen institutions and, not least, restart its democratization. Only then will it be able to tap its soft power potential to the full.

NOTES

INTRODUCTION: THE STRONGMAN'S PLAYBOOK

1. Quoted in Bahattin Gönültaş, "Turkey Fighting for Global Energy Security: Erdoğan," Anadolu Agency, 10 October 2016.
2. The feeling was mutual. Obama described Erdoğan to Jeffrey Goldberg as "a failure and an authoritarian, one who refuses to use his enormous army to bring stability to Syria." "The Obama Doctrine," *The Atlantic*, April 2016. Needless to say, the remark did not go down well with the Turkish president.
3. "Why the European Union Needs Turkey", St John's College, Oxford, 28 May 2004. Reported in Marinela Raouna, "No Cold Turkey," *Cherwell*, 4 June 2004. Full text of the speech: *Insight Turkey* 6(3), July–September 2004, pp. 7–15.
4. *C.P. Cavafy: Collected Poems*, trans. Edmund Keeley (Princeton, NJ: Princeton University Press, 1975).
5. There is a vast literature on the impact of societal cleavages on Turkish politics, going all the way back to Şerif Mardin, "Center-Periphery Relations: A Key to Turkish Politics?" *Daedalus* 102(1), 1973, pp. 169–90.
6. Of course, the *mağduriyet* (victimhood) mythology is open to criticism. Prior to the 1990s, the military accommodated Islam to a degree, with the so-called Turkish-Islamic synthesis playing a prominent role in the aftermath of the 1980 coup.
7. *Reis* (The Chief), a biographical film telling Erdoğan's story from childhood through to his imprisonment in 1998, was aired on the eve of the constitutional referendum in 2017.
8. *Arabesk* (Arabesque) is a popular musical genre drawing on Middle Eastern influences and associated with Turkey's cultural and historic connections with southern neighbors.
9. "Başkan Erdoğan Türkiye Gençlik Zirvesi'nde konuştu," *Takvim*, 3 November 2018.
10. Unless specified otherwise, all dollar figures quoted in this book refer to US dollars. As the Harvard economist Dani Rodrik has pointed out, the real increase – at constant prices adjusting for inflation – over that period of rapid growth was 64 per cent for GDP and 43 per cent for GDP per capita. Still impressive, yet far from the three-fold expansion touted by Turkish authorities. "How Well Did the Turkish Economy Do Over the Last Decade?" Dani Rodrik's Blog, 20 June 2013, https://rodrik.typepad.com/dani_rodriks_weblog/2013/06/how-well-did-the-turkish-economy-do-over-the-last-decade.html
11. Karabekir Akkoyunlu and Kerem Öktem, "Existential Insecurity and the Making of a Weak Authoritarian Regime in Turkey," *Journal of Southeast European and Black Sea Studies* 16(4), 2016, pp. 505–27.
12. Murat Somer, "Understanding Turkey's Democratic Breakdown: Old vs. New and Indigenous vs. Global Authoritarianism," *Journal of Southeast European and Black Sea Studies* 16(4), 2016, pp. 484–6. Hakan Övünç Ongur "*Plus Ça Change*: Re-articulating Authoritarianism in the New Turkey," *Critical Sociology* 44(1), 2018, pp. 45–59.
13. In reality, Islam has always been part of Turkey's national self-definition, whether implicitly or openly. Secularist elites regarded non-Muslim-minority communities (Greeks, Armenians,

Jews) as the "Other." Despite formal commitment to equality under the law, such groups suffered discrimination (e.g. the so-called Wealth Tax imposed in 1942). By contrast, predominantly Muslim-ethnic communities such as the Kurds and others became subject of assimilation into the Turkish national mainstream. The AKP made the linkage between Islam and Turkishness more explicit, in keeping with the Millî Görüş tradition. For the different articulations of Turkish nationalism, both secular and religious conservative, see Jenny White, *Muslim Nationalism and the New Turks* (Princeton, NJ: Princeton University Press, 2014).

14. Soner Çağaptay, *The New Sultan: Erdoğan and the Crisis of Modern Turkey* (London: I.B. Tauris, 2017).
15. Mustafa Kemal is always referred to as "Gazi (pious warrior) Mustafa Kemal." I'm thankful to Lisel Hintz for drawing my attention to this detail.
16. On the parallel between the Hamidian regime and Turkey under Erdoğan, see Ethem Eldem, "Sultan Abdülhamid II: Founding Father of the Turkish State? (Keynote Address)," *Journal of the Association of Ottoman and Turkish Studies* 5(2), Fall 2018, pp. 25–46.
17. Along with experience with constitutionalism which dates back to the late Ottoman era.
18. Galip Dalay, "Turkey and the West Need a New Framework," in Galip Dalay, Ian Lesser, Valeria Talbot and Kadri Taştan, *Turkey and the West: Keep the Flame Burning*, Policy Paper 6, German Marshall Fund, Brussels, June 2020, pp. 5–7.
19. "Türkiye Kamuoyunda Avrupa Birliği Desteği ve Avrupa Algısı Araştırması 2019," *İktisadi Kalkınma Vakfı*, October 2019, p. 7.
20. Caroline Feehan and Lisel Hintz, "Burden or Boon? Turkey's Tactical Treatment of the Syrian Refugee Crisis," Middle East Institute, 10 January 2017.
21. Remark at a session on Turkey's Presidential Constitution, Southeast European Studies at Oxford (SEESOX), 3 March 2021.
22. Alexander Cooley and Daniel H. Nexon, "The Illiberal Tide," *Foreign Affairs*, 26 March 2021.
23. Malik Mufti, *Daring and Caution in Turkish Strategic Culture: Republic at Sea* (Basingstoke: Palgrave, 2009), p. 3.
24. See the address by a departing Turkish ambassador to the US to local Muslims. "Farewell Message from Ambassador Serdar Kılıç to Muslim American Community," Turkish Embassy in Washington, DC, 2 March 2021, http://washington.emb.mfa.gov.tr/Mission/ShowAnnouncement/382098. The AKP speaks of *kutlu yolculuk/yürüyüş* (holy march) or *dava* (mission) in uniting (Sunni) Muslims. Kemal Kirişci, *Turkey and the West: Fault Lines in a Troubled Alliance* (Washington, DC: Brookings Institution, 2017), p. 17.
25. For instance: Ömer Taşpınar, "Turkey's Middle East Policies: Between Neo-Ottomanism and Kemalism," Carnegie Endowmen, 7 October 2008; Lisel Hintz, taking issue with "Neo-Ottomanism" as a term, speaks of an Ottoman Islamist "identity proposal," contrasting it with Republican nationalism, pan-Turkic nationalism and Western liberalism. *Identity Politics Inside Out: National Identity Contestation and Foreign Policy in Turkey* (Oxford: Oxford University Press, 2018), pp. 36, 49–57. Also M. Hakan Yavuz, *Nostalgia for Empire: The Politics of Neo-Ottomanism* (Oxford: Oxford University Press, 2020).
26. "The imperial paradigm views Turkey's external environment as capable of yielding great rewards if only one is open to engaging with and trying to reshape it." Mufti traces its origins to the rule of Adnan Menderes' Democrat Party in the 1950s. Mufti, *Daring and Caution*, pp. 4, 29–36.
27. Turkey received a $15 billion swap line from Qatar too. Talks with the European Central Bank and the Federal Reserve in the US led to a dead end.
28. Hugh Pope and Nigar Göksel, "Turkey Does Its Own Thing," Chatham House, 1 December 2020. See also Lisel Hintz, "No One Lost Turkey: Turkey's Foreign Policy Quest for Agency with Russia and Beyond," *Texas National Security Review* 2(4), August 2019, pp. 143–50.

1. THE PAST ISN'T ANOTHER COUNTRY

1. For a general overview of the 1990s, see Erik-Jan Zürcher, *Turkey: A Modern History* (London: I.B. Tauris, 2017, 4th revised edn), ch. 16: "Years of Crisis, 1994–2002"; Kerem Öktem, *Angry Nation: Turkey Since 1989* (London: Zed Books, 2011), chs 7, 8 and 9.
2. For an in-depth discussion of the political impact of urbanization, including the role of municipalities and social networks connected to political parties in the provision of welfare, see Yeşim Arat and Şevket Pamuk, *Turkey Between Democracy and Authoritarianism* (Cambridge: Cambridge University Press, 2019), ch. 2: "A Long Wave of Urbanization."
3. Arat and Pamuk make a similar point about the 1990s as a formative period, looking at trends such as rapid urbanization and transformation, the failure of the incumbent elites to respond to societal demands, cultural struggles, etc. See Arat and Pamuk, *Turkey Between Democracy and Authoritarianism*.
4. Speech at dinner given by Turkish prime minister, 7 April 1988. Transcript available at: www.margaretthatcher.org/document/107211. Thatcher first professed her admiration of "Özalism" during the Turkish prime minister's visit to Britain in February 1986. See: www.margaretthatcher.org/document/106331
5. Some of those reforms had been put on the drawing board by Süleyman Demirel's government, which was toppled by the coup in September 1980. They started being implemented while the military was in charge.
6. The Customs Union came into force in 1996, after Özal's death, but is still part of his legacy.
7. Still, the average growth rates stayed below those in the 1960s and 1970s when Turkey saw a period of rapid industrialization. See Sumru Altug, Alpay Filiztekin and Şevket Pamuk, "Sources of Long-term Economic Growth for Turkey, 1880–2005," *European Review of Economic History* 12(3), February 2008, pp. 393–430.
8. Tosun Arıcanlı and Dani Rodrik (eds.) *The Political Economy of Turkey: Debt, Adjustment and Sustainability* (Basingstoke: Palgrave Macmillan, 1990). Dani Rodrik, "Premature Liberalization, Incomplete Stabilization: The Özal Decade in Turkey," in Michael Bruno, Stanley Fischer, Elhanan Helpman, Nissan Liviatan and Leora Meridor (eds.) *Lessons of Economic Stabilization and Its Aftermath* (Cambridge, MA: MIT Press, 1991).
9. On Özal and his era, see İhsan Sezal and İhsan Dağı (eds.) *Kim Bu Özal? Siyaset, İktisat, Zihniyet* (Istanbul: Boyut Yayıncılık, 2001). Also his memoirs, Turgut Özal, *Turgut Özal'ın Anıları*, compiled by Mehmet Barlas (Istanbul: Sabah Yayınları, 1994).
10. Balkan Talu and İrfan Bozan, *İmam Hatip Liseleri Efsaneler Ve Gerçekler* (Istanbul: Turkish Foundation for Economic and Social Studies [TESEV], 2004), p. 67.
11. Cengiz Çandar, *Turkey's Mission Impossible: War and Peace with the Kurds* (Lanham, MD: Lexington Books, 2020), ch. 5: "Özal, Talabani, Öcalan." Çandar advised Özal on the Kurdish issue and acted as an intermediary with the PKK leadership. See also his memoir, *Mesopotamia Ekspresi: Bir Tarih Yolculuğu* (Istanbul: İletişim, 2014).
12. Ziya Öniş, "Turgut Özal and His Economic Legacy: Turkish Neo-liberalism in Critical Perspective," *Middle Eastern Studies* 40(4), July 2004, pp. 113–34.
13. The referendum brought back Necmettin Erbakan, Refah's leader, who had been banned from politics following the 1980 coup.
14. Altug, Filiztekin and Pamuk, "Sources of Long-term Economic Growth."
15. Fatih Kaya and Selihan Yılar, "Fiscal Transformation in Turkey over the Last Two Decades," *OECD Journal of Budgeting* 1, 2011 pp. 59–74.
16. The information about the crash might have been leaked to the media by the National Intelligence Organization (MİT) seeking to undermine the Refah–Yol coalition. Zürcher, *Turkey: A Modern History*, p. 335.
17. In 2021, mafia boss Sedat Peker, a prominent underworld figure in the 1990s, alleged that the assassination of Mumcu had been ordered by Interior Minister Ağar.
18. The term has since gained currency to the point of becoming commonplace in the political discourse of the US under Donald Trump.

19. Raşit Kaya and Barış Çakmur, "Politics and Mass Media in Turkey," *Turkish Studies* 11(4), 2010, pp. 521–37.
20. Henri Barkey and Graham Fuller, *Turkey's Kurdish Issue* (Lanham, MD: Rowman and Littlefield, 1997).
21. M. Hakan Yavuz, "Five Stages of the Construction of Kurdish Nationalism in Turkey," *Nationalism and Ethnic Politics* 7(3), 2001, pp. 1–24.
22. Figures from the Turkish defense ministry, the military and police, quoted in Ezgi Başaran, *Frontline Turkey: The Conflict at the Heart of the Middle East* (London: I.B. Tauris, 2017), p. 31.
23. On the GAP project, see Joost Jongerden, "Dams and Politics in Turkey: Utilizing Water, Developing Conflict," *Middle East Policy* 17(1), Spring 2010, 137–43.
24. Over 378,000 were forcefully evacuated under the state of emergency between 1987 and 2002. Some authors set the figure of internally displaced and exiled persons from the region at 4.5 million. Başaran, *Frontline Turkey*, p. 31.
25. Christopher de Bellaigue, "The Battle for Turkey: Can Selahattin Demirtaş Pull the Country Back from the Brink of Civil War?" *Guardian*, 29 October 2015.
26. Yılmaz conveyed the same message during a pre-election rally in the city in 2002. "Yılmaz: Avrupa'ya Diyarbakırsız gidilmez," *Radikal*, 12 October 2002.
27. Çandar, *Turkey's Mission Impossible*, pp. 111–64.
28. Öktem, *Angry Nation*, ch. 8: "Fighting Terror: The Guardian State in Western Turkey."
29. The MHP was established in 1965 by Colonel Alparslan Türkeş, a prominent figure in the 1960 military coup. Its youth wing, the Grey Wolves (*Bozkurtlar*), was at the forefront of the undeclared civil war with the left which raged through the 1970s. Banned after the 1980 coup, the party was re-established in 1983 and eventually reclaimed its old name in the early 1990s.
30. Ziya Öniş and Barry Rubin (eds.) *The Turkish Economy in Crisis* (London: Frank Cass, 2003).
31. Guzin Gulsun Akin, Ahmet Faruk Aysan and Levent Yildiran, "Transformation of the Turkish Financial Sector in the Aftermath of the 2001 Crisis," in Ziya Öniş and Fikret Şenses (eds.) *Turkey and the Global Economy: Neo-liberal Restructuring and Integration in the Post-Crisis Era* (Abingdon: Routledge, 2009), pp. 73–101.

2. TURKEY IN THE POST-COLD WAR WORLD

1. At the time, Bülent Ecevit, leader of Cem's Democratic Left Party (DSP), was speaking of a "region-centric foreign policy" (*bölge-merkezli dış politika*). On the continuity with the pre-AKP period, see Kirişci, *Turkey and the West*, p. 153.
2. *OECD Observer*, issue 140, May 1986, pp. 4–8. Available at: www.oecd-ilibrary.org/docserver/observer-v1986-3-en.pdf
3. Sam Cohen, "Turkey Takes a Tentative Step towards the Soviet Union by Signing a Trade Agreement," *Christian Science Monitor*, 27 December 1984.
4. William Hale, *Turkish Foreign Policy 1774–2000* (London: Frank Cass, 2000), pp. 177–8.
5. İhsan Dağı, "Human Rights, Democratization and the European Community in Turkish Politics: The Özal Years, 1983–87," *Middle East Studies* 37(1), January 2001, pp. 17–40.
6. Quoted in Meltem Müftüler-Baç, "Turkish Economic Liberalization and European Integration," *Middle East Studies* 31(1), January 1995, p. 85.
7. The European Commission quoted the "substantial developmental gap between Turkey and the Community" along with the conflict with Greece. Commission of the European Communities, Commission opinion on Turkey's request for accession to the Community, SEC (89) 2290 final, Brussels, 20 December 1989.
8. Öniş, "Turgut Özal and His Economic Legacy."
9. See Chapter 9.
10. Alexis Heraclides, *The Greek–Turkish Conflict in the Aegean* (London: Palgrave Macmillan, 2010), p. 124.
11. Hale, *Turkish Foreign Policy*, pp. 167–9.

12. Philip Robins, *Suits and Uniforms: Turkish Foreign Policy since the Cold War* (London: Hurst, 2003), pp. 275–83.
13. Kemalist Turkey was first cast as a model for the reforms carried out by Amanullah Han in Afghanistan starting in 1928. In the 1930s, it inspired Reza Shah's modernization initiatives in Iran and in the 1950s those in Tunisia led by Habib Bourguiba.
14. Özal interviewed by Bruce Kuniholm and Ole Holsti for the Living History Program at Duke University, 26 March 1991. Transcript and video available at: http://livinghistory. sanford.duke.edu/interviews/turgut-ozal/
15. Güven Sak, "From the Adriatic Sea to the Great Wall of China," *Hürriyet Daily News*, 12 August 2017, www.hurriyetdailynews.com/opinion/guven-sak/from-the-adriatic-sea-to-the-great-wall-of-china-116644
16. Graham Fuller and Ian Lesser, *Turkey's New Geopolitics: From the Balkans to Western China* (New York: Routledge, 1993), ch. 3: "Bridge or Barrier? Turkey and the West after the Cold War."
17. Hale, *Turkish Foreign Policy*, p. 205; Robins, *Suits and Uniforms*, pp. 69–70. Admittedly, the veteran leader, known for the memorable adage "yesterday is yesterday, today is today" (*dün dündür, bugün bugündür*), adapted to his new role with ease.
18. The conflict over Nagorno-Karabakh, an autonomous region within Azerbaijan populated largely by Armenians, started in 1988 with intercommunal violence but escalated into a full-blown war in the winter of 1991–92.
19. Hale, *Turkish Foreign Policy*, pp. 271–5.
20. Robins, *Suits and Uniforms*, pp. 343–73.
21. In March 1997, the leaders of Christian Democratic parties, including Germany's Helmut Kohl, issued a declaration stating that "the EU [was] a civilization project and within this civilization project Turkey [had] no place." Hale, *Turkish Foreign Policy*, p. 239.
22. Mufti, *Daring and Caution in Turkish Strategic Culture*, pp. 17–29.
23. Halis Akder, "Turkey's Export Expansion in the Middle East, 1980–1985," *Middle East Journal* 41(4), autumn 1987, p. 553.
24. The month before, in August 1990, Turkey also closed off the Kirkuk–Ceyhan oil pipeline. It reopened only in 2000.
25. Foreign Minister Ali Bozer and Defense Minister Safa Giray had tendered their resignations as well. Bozer complained about Özal's overreach and the risks involved in Turkey sending troops to northern Iraq. See his interview "Beyaz Saray'da beni görüşmeye almadılar," *Hürriyet*, 10 January 2000. William Hale, "Turkey, the Middle East and the Gulf Crisis," *International Affairs* 68(4), October 1992, pp. 679–92.
26. Özal's ability to stretch his powers to the point of acting as a de facto executive president also mattered, from Erdoğan's perspective.
27. However, the Defense and Economic Cooperation Agreement was renewed in 1992 only for a year and 8 out of 12 US bases on Turkish soil were closed by mid-1994. Washington discontinued military aid to Turkey in 1999. Turkey faced criticism in Congress over its human rights record, even if it could count on support in the Pentagon and the State Department.
28. Mufti, *Daring and Caution*, pp. 87–109; Robins, *Suits and Uniforms*, p. 163 ff.
29. In 1995, Syria and Greece signed a deal allowing Greek fighter jets to land in Syrian bases.
30. Mahmut Bali Aykan, "The Turkish–Syrian Crisis of October 1998: A Turkish View," *Middle East Policy* 6(4), June 1999, pp. 174–91.
31. Robins, *Suits and Uniforms*, pp. 260–5.
32. Erbakan famously called for an Islamic Union, having opposed Turkey's ambitions to join the EC and later the EU, since the 1970s. Concurring with European conservatives, he described the EU as a "Christian club." For an early analysis of his politics, see Binnaz Toprak, "Politicisation of Islam in a Secular State: The National Salvation Party in Turkey," in Said Amir Arjomand (ed.) *From Nationalism to Revolutionary Islam* (Basingstoke: Palgrave Macmillan, 1984), pp. 119–33.

33. For a history and concise overview of the disputes: Alexis Heraclides, "The Unresolved Aegean Dispute: Problems and Prospects," in Alexis Heraclides and Gizem Alioğlu Çakmak (eds.) *Greece and Turkey in Conflict and Cooperation: From Europeanization to De-Europeanization* (Abingdon: Routledge, 2019).

34. Bill Clinton, *My Life* (New York: Random House, 2010), p. 697.

35. Dimitar Bechev, *Rival Power: Russia in Southeast Europe* (New Haven, CT: Yale University Press, 2017), p. 125.

36. Stephen Kinzer, "Turkey, Rejected, Will Freeze Ties with the European Union," *New York Times*, 15 December 1997.

37. Turkey's frictions with the EU (as well as the Western European Union [WEU], a defense cooperation body of which it was an associate member) lingered on through the 1990s. Policy makers in Ankara were concerned that turning the WEU into a security pillar within the EU risked undermining NATO while drawing on its military assets. In essence, Turkey would be obliged to defend Europe without a reciprocal commitment on the EU's part. Hale, *Turkish Foreign Policy*, pp. 229–33.

38. Hasan Özertem, Habibe Özdal, Turgut Demirtepe and Kerim Has, *Türkiye-Rusya İlişkileri: Rekabetten Çok Yönlü İşbirliğine* (Ankara: USAK, 2013), p. 21. Ecevit drew fire at home, including for allegedly promising the Russian ambassador in Ankara not to insist that his three-day visit include a trip to Chechnya. "Ecevit'in Çeçen Sıkıntısı," *Yeni Şafak*, 22 October 1999.

39. Oktay Tanrısever, "Turkey and Russia in Eurasia," in Lenore Martin and Dimitris Keridis (eds.) *The Future of Turkish Foreign Policy* (Cambridge, MA: MIT Press, 2004). Also Gençer Özcan, Evren Balta and Burç Beşgül (eds.) *Kuşku ile Komşuluk. Türkiye ve Rusya İlişkilerinde Değişen Dinamikler* (Istanbul: İletişim, 2017).

40. Point 12, Helsinki European Council, Presidency Conclusions, 10 and 11 December 1999. Available at: www.europarl.europa.eu/summits/hel1_en.htm. Turkey lifted its veto on the EU Rapid Reaction Force, enabling the conclusion of the so-called Berlin Plus agreement between NATO and the EU (2002) and the deployment of peacekeeping missions in Macedonia and Bosnia after 2003.

41. A detailed account in James Ker-Lindsay, *Crisis and Conciliation: A Year of Rapprochement between Greece and Turkey* (London: I.B. Tauris, 2007).

42. Meltem Müftüler-Baç, "Turkey's Political Reforms and the Impact of the European Union," *South European Society & Politics* 10(1), March 2005, pp. 16–30.

43. Philip Robins, "The 2005 BRISMES Lecture: A Double Gravity State – Turkish Foreign Policy Reconsidered," *British Journal of Middle Eastern Studies* 33(2), 2006, pp. 199–211.

3. GOLDEN YEARS

1. Anadolu Agency, 3 October 2005, www.ab.gov.tr/p.php?e=37622

2. Established in 1969, Millî Görüş (National View) was a movement associated with Necmettin Erbakan and the political forces he led: the National Order Party (1970–1), the National Salvation Party (1972–81), Welfare (Refah) Party (1983–98) and the Virtue (Fazilet) Party (1998–2001). Its ideology mixed political Islam and Turkish nationalism. After the Constitutional Court closed down Fazilet in 2001, Erbakan established the Felicity (Saadet) Party, while the faction around Erdoğan and Gül split into the AKP.

3. On "White Turks" and "Black Turks," see Simon A. Waldman and Emre Çalışkan, *The New Turkey and Its Discontents* (Oxford: Oxford University Press, 2017), pp. 12–14. Also Michael Ferguson's reflections on the political uses of racialized language. "White Turks, Black Turks and Negroes: The Politics of Polarization," *Jadaliyya*, 29 June 2013, www.jadaliyya.com/Details/28868

4. European Stability Initiative (ESI), *Islamic Calvinists: Change and Conservatism in Central Anatolia*, 19 September 2005, www.esiweb.org/publications/islamic-calvinists-change-and-conservatism-central-anatolia

5. Sultan Tepe, "Turkey's AKP: A Model 'Muslim Democratic Party'?" *Journal of Democracy* 16(3), 2005, pp. 69–82. For a skeptical view: William Hale, "Christian Democracy and AKP: Parallels and Contrasts," *Turkish Studies* 6(2), 2005, pp. 293–310.

6. Ruşen Çakır and Fehmi Çalmuk, *Recep Tayyip Erdoğan, Bir Dönüşüm Öyküsü* (Istanbul: Metis Yayınları, 2001), p. 144.
7. Yalçın Akdoğan, *AK Parti ve Muhafazakar Demokrasi* (Istanbul: Alfa Yayınları, 2005).
8. There were influential individuals such as businessman Cüneyd Zapsu, a founding member of the AKP, who likewise helped establish contacts across the Atlantic.
9. See Nora Onar, "Kemalists, Islamists, and Liberals: Shifting Patterns of Confrontation and Consensus, 2002–06," *Turkish Studies* 8(2), 2007, pp. 273–88.
10. The AKP had also strong backing from MÜSİAD (Independent Industrialists and Businessmen Association, Müstakil Sanayici ve İşadamları Derneği), a group established in 1990 with a conservative/pious Muslim orientation.
11. "Diplomatlar şoke oldu," *Milliyet*, 26 May 2005.
12. Ahead of the 2011 elections, 167 out of 340 sitting MPs were excluded from the electoral lists. "Many AKP and CHP MPs Are Left Off the Election Candidate Lists," Economist Intelligence Unit, 3 May 2011. The purge was in part driven by the simmering conflict with the Gülenists. Selim Koru, *The Institutional Structure of "New Turkey,"* Black Sea Strategy Paper, Foreign Policy Research Institute, February 2021, p. 35. However, there were liberals who were removed too, such as Zeynep Dağı, a university professor, and Suat Knıklıoğlu, the former head of the Foreign Policy Committee.
13. Ergun Özbudun, "AKP at a Crossroads: Erdoğan's Majoritarian Drift," *South European Society and Politics* 19(2), 2014, pp. 155–67.
14. The Annan Plan was a blueprint for a reunification of Cyprus developed by the UN Secretary General Kofi Annan on a Security Council mandate. It went through five revisions between 1999 and 2003 but was finally defeated at a referendum held simultaneously in both parts of Cyprus on 24 April 2004. While Turkish Cypriots backed the plan by a large margin, two-thirds of the Greeks voted "no."
15. Murat Yetkin, "E-muhtıra erken seçimi gündeme taşıdı," *Radikal*, 29 April 2007.
16. Nazlı Ilıcak, "27 Nisan ve CHP," *Sabah*, 18 April 2012.
17. The Court ruled, on 1 May 2007, that the vote was null and void because of the lack of quorum. "YSK: Abdullah Gül'ün hatırlattığı Anayasa Mahkemesi'nin 2007'deki '367 Kararı' neydi?" BBC Turkish, 7 May 2019.
18. The CHP attempted to block the passage of amendments in parliament, as well as through appeals to the Constitutional Court. For a detailed account, see Carol Migdalovitz, "Turkey's 2007 Elections: Crisis of Identity and Power," Congressional Research Service, US Congress, 11 July 2007. Available at: https://fas.org/sgp/crs/mideast/RL34039.pdf
19. For an analysis of the vote, see Ali Çarkoğlu, "Ideology or Economic Pragmatism: Profiling Turkish Voters in 2007," *Turkish Studies* 9(2), 2008, pp. 317–44.
20. The AKP overcame the quorum requirement thanks to the Nationalist Action Party (MHP) and the Democratic Left Party (DSP), which took part in the vote having fielded alternative candidates. The DSP broke ranks with CHP, its coalition partner in the elections.
21. For a snapshot of the Turkish economy in the 2000s: Öniş and Şenses (eds.) *Turkey and the Global Economy.*
22. Health care and public housing through TOKİ (Toplu Konut İdaresi, Mass Housing Administration) enjoyed great popularity though, as Arat and Pamuk observe quoting a range of studies, the actual record in both policy areas was mixed. Arat and Pamuk, *Turkey Between Democracy and Authoritarianism*, pp. 100–1.
23. Shaun Walker, "This Is the Golden Age: Eastern Europe's Extraordinary 30-year Revival," *Guardian*, 26 October 2019. Marcin Piatkowski, *Europe's Growth Champion: Insights from the Economic Rise of Poland* (Oxford: Oxford University Press, 2019).
24. Zürcher, *Turkey: A Modern History*, p. 367.
25. The Treaty Establishing a Constitution for Europe was signed by the member states in October 2004 but was defeated by referendums in France and the Netherlands the following year. Its institutional provisions, such as the establishment of the position of a President of the European Council, then made it through in the Treaty of Lisbon (2009).

26. Presidency Conclusions, Copenhagen European Council, 12 and 13 December 2002, para. 18, www.consilium.europa.eu/media/20906/73842.pdf
27. Çigdem Nas and Yonca Özer, *Turkey and EU Integration: Achievements and Obstacles* (Abingdon: Routledge, 2017), p. 59.
28. "Turkey Signals U-turn on Adultery," *BBC News*, 14 September 2004. On the impact on EU conditionality on women's rights: Arat and Pamuk, *Turkey Between Democracy and Authoritarianism*, pp. 237–40.
29. Waldman and Çalışkan, *The New Turkey and Its Discontents*, pp. 22–4.
30. Ibid., pp. 19–31.
31. In June 2008, the Constitutional Court struck down constitutional amendments making possible for women wearing headscarf, some two-thirds of Turkey's female population, to enter university. Justices found the changes to the basic law violated the principle of secularism. Three years before, the European Court of Human Rights upheld, in the *Leyla Şahin v. Turkey* case, the ban on headscarves in higher education establishments.
32. Meltem Müftüler-Baç, "Turkey's Political Reforms and the Impact of the European Union," *South European Society & Politics* 10(1), March 2005, pp. 16–30. See also Ergun Özbudun and Ömer Faruk Gençkaya, *Democratization and the Politics of Constitution-making in Turkey* (Budapest: Central European University Press, 2009).
33. The OHAL region was gradually shrunk following the 1999 arrest of Öcalan.
34. See Başaran, *Frontline Turkey*.
35. The full ban on Kurdish instituted in 1983 was technically lifted in 1991.
36. In the case of both the AKP and the DTP, closure proceedings were initiated by Abdurrahman Yalçınkaya, the prosecutor general.
37. Gareth Jenkins, "Terrorism, Counter-insurgency and Societal Relations," in Alp Özerdem and Matthew Whiting (eds.) *The Routledge Handbook of Turkish Politics* (Abingdon: Routledge, 2019), pp. 266–74.
38. See Emre Taner's interview with Gonca Şenay, "Sır istihbaratçı anlattı," *Al Jazeera*, 10 November 2016.
39. Cengiz Çandar, "The Perennial Kurdish Question and Failed Peace Processes," in Özerdem and Whiting (eds.) *The Routledge Handbook of Turkish Politics*, pp. 253–63. Amed Dicle, *Türkiye-PKK Görüşmeleri (2005–2015)* (Diyarbakır: Mezopotamya, 2017).
40. Terörle Mücadele Kanunu (3713, 12 April 1991), T.C. Çumhurbaşkanlığı Mevzuat Bilgi Sistemi, www.mevzuat.gov.tr/MevzuatMetin/1.5.3713.pdf
41. Oxford Analytica, "TURKEY: Neutralising PKK Requires KRG Engagement," 14 November 2007.
42. Howard Eissenstat, *Erdoğan as Autocrat: A Very Turkish Tragedy*, Project on Middle East Democracy (POMED) report, 12 April 2007, https://pomed.org/pomed-report-Erdoğan-as-autocrat-a-very-turkish-tragedy/
43. Katherine Baldwin and Selçuk Gökölük, "Blair Promotes Turkish EU Membership," Reuters, 20 January 2007. Blair's views were shared by other British Europhiles. "The question to ask is not what Europe will do for Turkey, but what Turkey has done for Europe," wrote Timothy Garton Ash in his *Guardian* column back in October 2005. "How the Dreaded Superstate Became a Commonwealth," *Guardian*, 6 October 2005. Other member states which supported Turkey included Spain, Portugal, Italy, Finland, Sweden and the new entrants from Central and Eastern Europe.
44. Article 2, Negotiating Framework. Luxembourg, 3 October 2005, https://ec.europa.eu/neighbourhood-enlargement/sites/near/files/pdf/turkey/st20002_05_tr_framedoc_en.pdf
45. The declaration by the Turkish Ministry of Foreign Affairs ahead of Cyprus's accession reads as follows: "The Greek Cypriots, who will join the EU on 1 May 2004, have no authority to represent the whole of Cyprus or the Turkish Cypriots. They cannot claim authority, jurisdiction or sovereignty over the Turkish Cypriots, who have equal status, or over the entire Island of Cyprus. They cannot impose the 'Republic of Cyprus' on the Turkish Cypriots. Thus, the Greek Cypriots who organized themselves under their own constitutional order

and within their boundaries cannot be the legitimate government representing the whole of Cyprus and the Turkish Cypriots." Ministry of Foreign Affairs of Turkey, Press Release Regarding the EU Enlargement, 1 May 2004, reproduced in UN Document CD/1738, 18 August 2004, Annex 3.

46. Turkey's legal position is that the state of Cyprus, as established in 1960, ceased to exist in 1963 when intercommunal violence made Cypriot Turks leave common institutions. In November 1983, Ankara recognized the "Turkish Republic of Northern Cyprus" as a sovereign state. See James Ker-Lindsay, *The Cyprus Problem: What Everyone Needs to Know* (Oxford: Oxford University Press, 2011).

47. This was a follow-up from the institutional battles concerning NATO's, and consequently Turkey's role, in the EU's foreign and security pillar. See Chapter 2.

48. It was also decided to make it a condition for closure of talks on all 35 negotiation chapters.

49. Estelle Shirbon, "France's Sarkozy Secures Constitutional Reform," Reuters, 21 July 2008.

50. In the *Leyla Şahin v. Turkey* ruling from 2004, the ECtHR upheld the Turkish law prohibiting female students wearing headscarves from attending lectures, seminars and tutorials at universities. Though the EU had nothing to do with the judgment, it dented the reputation of "Europe," in the eyes of AKP supporters, as a protector of religious freedom and ally in the fight against the secularist establishment.

51. The full text of the Regensburg Lecture (12 September 2006) is available at: www.vatican. va/content/benedict-xvi/en/speeches/2006/september/documents/hf_ben-xvi_ spe_20060912_university-regensburg.html. However, in a conciliatory move Benedict XVI visited Turkey a month later and even held prayers together with Mustafa Cağrıcı, the head of the Diyanet. The second papal visit to Istanbul in nearly two thousand years also included a joint declaration with the Ecumenical Patriarch Bartholomew referring to Turkey's Christian roots. Predictably, this stirred controversy too. Ian Fisher, "Pope Benedict XVI Prays at Blue Mosque in Turkey," *New York Times,* 30 October 2006.

4. "ZERO PROBLEMS WITH NEIGHBORS"

1. Davutoğlu in conversation with Marc Grossman, hosted by the Council of Foreign Relations, 14 April 2010. Transcript available at: www.cfr.org/event/conversation-ahmet-Davutoğlu-0

2. Ahmet Davutoğlu, "Turkish Foreign Policy and the EU," *Turkish Policy Quarterly* 8(3), Fall 2009, p. 12. See also his *Stratejik Derinlik: Türkiye'nin Uluslararası Konumu* (Istanbul: Kure Yayınları, 2001).

3. For a snapshot of Turkish foreign policy towards neighbors of the era: Ronald H. Linden et al., *Turkey and Its Neighbors: Foreign Relations in Transition* (Boulder, CO: Lynne Rienner, 2011); Mehmet Karlı, Ayşe Kadıoğlu and Kerem Öktem (eds.) *Another Empire: A Decade of Turkey's Foreign Policy under the Justice and Development Party* (Istanbul: Bilgi University Press, 2012).

4. Kemal Kirişci calculates that trade with neighbors expanded seventeen-fold between 1991 and 2010 and seven-fold with the EU. Either way, the trend towards diversification was clear. Kemal Kirişci, "Turkey's Engagement with Its Neighborhood: A 'Synthetic' and Multidimensional Look at Turkey's Foreign Policy Transformation," *Turkish Studies* 13(3), September 2012, pp. 319–41.

5. According to data from the Turkish Statistical Institute (TÜİK), the UAE accounted for 6 per cent of exports, or $8 billion, as compared to 6.2 per cent/$8.2 billion for the UK and 9.8 per cent/$13 billion for Germany. See www.tuik.gov.tr

6. Iran was an exception.

7. Data available through www.tcmb.gov.tr/

8. Kirişci, "Turkey's Engagement with Its Neighborhood," p. 320. Still, in 2009, the country was visited by 12 million people from the EU (minus Bulgaria, Romania and Greece). See Ahmet Evin et al., *Getting to Zero: Turkey, Its Neighbors and the West* (Washington, DC: The Transatlantic Academic, 2010), p. 10, www.bosch-stiftung.de/sites/default/files/publications/pdf_import/Report_TA_GettingtoZeroFINAL.pdf

9. On 28 March 2011, as Syria was descending into a political crisis, the Turkish central bank hosted an international conference entitled "Enhancing ShamGen Banking," with the governors of the central banks from Syria, Jordan and Lebanon attending.
10. "Başbakan'dan üçüncü balkon konuşması," *Hürriyet*, 12 June 2011.
11. İbrahim Kalın, "Soft Power and Public Diplomacy in Turkey," *Perceptions* 16(3), autumn 2011, p. 10.
12. Examples of societal and economic actors involved in projecting Turkey's influence abroad were aplenty: from the Turkish Economic and Social Studies Foundation (TESEV), a liberal think-tank supported by the EU, to conservative charitable organizations like the İHH Humanitarian Relief Foundation, to diaspora organizations such as KAFDER (North Caucasus) and BalGöç and RUMDER (the Balkans). Business associations such as the conservative MÜSİAD, TÜSİAD, DEİK (Dış Ekonomik İlişkiler Kurulu, Foreign Economic Relations Council), the Turkish Exporters' Assembly (TİM), the Union of Chambers and Stock Exchanges of Turkey (TOBB) and TUSKON associated with the Gülen movement all played a role, too.
13. Philip Robins, "Turkey's 'Double Gravity' Predicament: The Foreign Policy of a Newly Activist Power," *International Affairs* 89(2), March 2013, p. 381.
14. Davutoğlu drew on two intellectual traditions: first, on Islamic theology, stressing categories such as *Tawahid* (the oneness of God) and *Tanzih* (the purity of God), and second, on classical geopolitics developed by authors such as Halford Mackinder (1861–1947) and Friedrich Ratzel (1844–1904), the intellectual father of the concept of "Lebensraum." Aaron Stein, *Turkey's New Foreign Policy: Davutoğlu, the AKP and the Pursuit of Regional Order* (London: RUSI, 2014), pp. 6–9. See also Behlül Özkan, "Turkey, Davutoğlu and the Idea of Pan-Islamism," *Survival* 56(4), August–September 2014, pp. 119–40. On "Grand Restoration," see Davutoğlu's speech at Diyarbakır's Dicle University on 15 March 2013, www.mfa.gov.tr/disisleri-bakani-ahmet-davutoglu_nun-diyarbakir-dicle-universitesinde-verdigi-_buyuk-restorasyon_-kadim_den-kuresellesmeye-yeni.tr.mfa
15. Full transcript published by the *Guardian*, 29 June 2004.
16. "The US–Turkish Partnership, Remarks to the American Turkish Society" (Meet the Ambassadors Series), The Knickerbocker Club, New York, 10 February 2005, https://2001-2009.state.gov/p/us/rm/42115.htm
17. Out of 550 MPs in total, 264 voted for, 250 were against, 19 abstained and 17 were not present. Technically there was a majority in the Grand National Assembly but the resolution failed to clear the required threshold. Ertan Efegil, "Why Did the Turkish Government Reject the Memorandum on 1 March?" *Insight Turkey* 6(1), January–March 2004, pp. 105–12. See also William Hale, *Turkey, the US and Iraq* (London: Saqi, 2007), p. 106 ff.
18. "Turkey: Why the Vote Went South," 3ANKARA1350_a, 3 March 2003. Available at: https://wikileaks.org/plusd/cables/03ANKARA1350_a.html
19. "Ex-minister Reveals Why Turkish Parliament Voted 'No' to Participation in Iraq War," *Daily Sabah*, 15 February 2016.
20. "Turkey: Why the Vote Went South." Despite Pearson's assertions, Gül was leaning more towards Arınç than to Erdoğan. Exchange with a former associate of Gül's, March 2021.
21. "Turkey: Former President Demirel Tells Ambassador Turkey Must Mend Fences with US," 03ANKARA2596, 22 April 2003. Available at: https://wikileaks.org/plusd/cables/03ANKARA2596_a.html
22. Soner Çağaptay, "Turkey after the July 2007 Elections: Domestic Politics and International Relations," testimony before the US Commission on Security and Cooperation in Europe on 26 July 2007, Washington, DC.
23. "Turkey: Troubled Terrain for Pope Benedict," Pew Research Center, 27 November 2006, www.pewresearch.org/global/2006/11/27/turkey-troubled-terrain-for-pope-benedict/
24. "Turkey Defies the US with a Syria Visit," *BBC News*, 13 April 2005.
25. "Türkiye, Rusya ve İran'la ittifak arayışında olmalı," *Sabah*, 8 March 2002.
26. A US cable from 2003 identified three, mutually opposed, groups in the general staff – Atlanticists – e.g. Chief of General Staff Hilmi Özkök, Nationalists (*ulusalcı*) and Eurasianists.

Insofar as the latter two shared suspicions towards the EU and US, the boundary was fuzzy. "The Turkish General Staff: A Fractious and Sullen Political Coalition," 03ANKARA2521, 18 April 2003, https://wikileaks.org/plusd/cables/03ANKARA2521_a.html

27. İhsan Dağı, "A Pro-Russian Turkish General?" İhsan Dağı's Blog, 8 June 2007, http://ihsandagi.blogspot.com/2007/06/pro-russian-turkish-general.html

28. Popular in the 1960s and 1970s, Maoism cast a long shadow over Turkish political life, with a number of liberal activists, and the PKK's founder Abdullah Öcalan, tracing their political roots to its doctrines.

29. Perinçek's daily *Aydınlık* had connections to the military. According to the US embassy, "Second Army Commander Gen. Fevzi Turkeri has long used the nationalist socialist weekly 'Aydinlik' to leak scurrilous, anti-American stories (e.g. accusations that the US materially supports PKK/KADEK)." "The Turkish General Staff."

30. Suat Kınıklıoğlu and Valeriy Morkva, "An Anatomy of Turkish–Russian Relations," *Journal of Southeast European and Black Sea Studies* 7(4), December 2007, pp. 533–53.

31. Interviews with Turkish diplomats, Ankara, June 2015.

32. F. Stephen Larabee, "Turkey Rediscovers the Middle East," *Foreign Affairs,* July/August 2007.

33. And the only one, until Egypt signed the Camp David Accords in 1979.

34. "Some 10 Palestinians to Go to Turkey in Captive Swap," Reuters, 18 October 2011.

35. Omri Efraim, "Peres Lauds Erdoğan efforts on Shalit," *Ynetnews,* 10 December 2011.

36. Peter Walker, "Syria and Israel Officially Confirm Peace Talks," *Guardian,* 21 May 2008.

37. For more on the deepening ties between Turkey and Syria after 1998, see Chapter 5. See also Raymond Hinnebusch and Özlem Tur (eds.) *Turkey–Syria Relations: Between Amity and Enmity* (Abingdon: Routledge, 2013).

38. Erdoğan spent time on the phone with Assad working out some details, www.brookings.edu/wp-content/uploads/2016/06/USTurkeyIsrael-TriangleFINAL.pdf

39. "We were calling them but they kept us in the dark." Conversation with a senior Turkish policy maker, Ankara, November 2010.

40. The so-called Gaza Freedom Flotilla was organized by the İHH Humanitarian Relief Foundation to deliver supplies to Gaza, under Israeli-Egyptian blockade. Israeli forces hijacked the *Mavi Marmara*, one of the ships, in international waters on the night of 30–31 May 2010. Nine activists, resisting the commandoes, were killed and a tenth died later from the injuries sustained. Dozens more were wounded.

41. Kirişci, *Turkey and the West,* p. 158–9.

42. In March 2013, Netanyahu offered an apology for the *Mavi Marmara* in a telephone call with Erdoğan, agreeing to compensate the families of the victims, a precondition set by Turkey.

43. Mehmet Karlı, "Discourse vs. Figures: A Reality Check for Turkey's Economic Depth," in Karlı, Kadıoğlu and Öktem (eds.) *Another Empire*, p. 154.

44. Dmitry Zhdannikov, "Exclusive: How Kurdistan Bypassed Baghdad and Sold Oil on Global Markets," Reuters, 17 November 2015. Gönül Tol, *Untangling the Turkey–KRG Energy Partnership: Looking Beyond Economic Drivers*, Global Turkey in Europe, Policy Brief 14, March 2014.

45. See Bill Park, "Turkey, US and KRG: Moving Parts and the Geopolitical Realities," *Insight Turkey* 14(3), 2012, pp. 109–25.

46. Elin Kinander, "The Turkish–Iranian Gas Relationship: Politically Successful, Commercially Problematic," Oxford Institute for Energy Studies, January 2010, www.oxfordenergy.org/wpcms/wp-content/uploads/2010/11/NG38-TheTurkishIranianGasRelationship-ElinKinnander-2010.pdf

47. See: http://turkishpolicy.com/article/940/turkey-iran-energy-economy-and-politics-in-the-face-of-sanctions

48. On Iran's attitude to Kurdish nationalism, see Walter Posch, "Fellow Arians and Muslim Brothers: Iranian Narratives on the Kurds," in Gareth Stansfield and Mohammed Shareef (eds.) *The Kurdish Question Revisited* (London: Hurst, 2017).

49. Güney Yıldız, "PKK Kurdish Deal with Turkey May Worry Iran and Syria," *BBC News,* 10 May 2013.

50. Interviews in Istanbul and Ankara, November 2010.

51. In April 2010, US President Obama sent a letter to Erdoğan and Brazilian President Luiz Ignacio "Lula" da Silva in which he set conditions for a deal on the Iranian nuclear program, notably shipping 1200 kg of nuclear material to a third country. That paved the way to a preliminary deal announced in Tehran by Turkey and Brazil, non-permanent member of the UN Security Council on 17 May 2010, together with Iran. That was a major diplomatic coup for Ankara. However, the day after the Obama administration unveiled new sanctions coordinated with the P5+1 group against the Islamic Republic, torpedoing the Turkish-Brazilian initiative. That development undermined trust between the AKP leadership and Washington. See Sinan Ülgen, "A Place in the Sun or Fifteen Minutes of Fame? Understanding Turkey's New Foreign Policy," *Carnegie Papers*, Carnegie Europe, December 2010, p. 3.
52. "Caspian Makan: I Cannot Believe It Yet. I Still Think I Will See Neda Again," *Observer*, 15 November 2009.
53. Quoted in Baskın Oran, "Proactive Policy with Many Hunches on the Back," in Karlı, Kadıoğlu and Öktem (eds.) *Another Empire*, p. xv. Wexler was speaking to *Cumhuriyet* (Republic), the former flagship of the one-party state and beacon of secularism. But unlike Erbakan's overtures to Iran in 1996, this time around there was wider acceptance in Turkey of cooperation with Tehran.
54. Pelin Turgut, "Obama in Turkey: Winning Hearts, Healing Rifts," *Time*, 7 April 2009.
55. "Sezer asker gönderilmesine karşı," *CNN Türk*, 25 August 2006.
56. "Golubaia mechta stala potokom," *Rossiyskaya gazeta*, 18 November 2005.
57. The discovery of natural gas in the Eastern Mediterranean in 2009 ended such plans.
58. Fiona Hill and Ömer Taşpınar, "Turkey and Russia: Axis of the Excluded?" *Survival* 48(1), 2006, pp. 81–92.
59. Ahu Özyurt, "The Russia House," *Hürriyet Daily News*, 23 October 2015.
60. Boris Yeltsin came twice to Istanbul, in 1992 and 1998. Yet both visits were for multilateral summits, the Black Sea Economic Cooperation and Organization for Security and Co-operation in Europe.
61. BP had to temporarily close another pipeline running from Baku to the Georgian port of Supsa.
62. Cheney had been in Ankara earlier that year, in March.
63. An Armenian expert quoted in Fiona Hill, Kemal Kirişci and Andrew Moffatt, "Armenia and Turkey: From Normalization to Reconciliation," *Turkish Policy Quarterly* 13(4), winter 2015, p. 135.
64. In 2015, the centennial of the genocide, Turkish leaders, who previously had acknowledged the trauma and the suffering of the Armenians but stopped short of using the "g-word," took a combative tone. Kirişci, *Turkey and the West*, pp. 134–6.
65. Address by H.E. Ahmet Davutoğlu, Minister of Foreign Affairs of the Republic of Turkey, at the Opening Session of the Alliance of Civilizations' First South East Europe Ministerial Conference, 14 December 2009, Sarajevo, www.mfa.gov.tr/address-by-h_e_-ahmet-Davutoğlu_-minister-of-foreign-affairs-of-republic-of-turkey-at-the-opening-session-of-the-alliance-of-civilizations_-first-south-east-europe-ministerial-conference_-14-december-2009_-sarajevo.en.mfa
66. Darko Tanasković, *Neoosmanizam: Povratak Turske na Balkan* (Belgrade: Službeni glasnik, 2010).
67. In 2015, NBG sold Finansbank to a company from Qatar.
68. Jahja Muhasilović, "Turkey's Faith-based Diplomacy in the Balkans," *Rising Powers Quarterly* 3(3), December 2018, pp. 63–85. Ahmet Erdi Öztürk and İştar Gözaydın, "A Frame for Turkish Foreign Policy via the Diyanet in the Balkans," *Journal of Muslims in Europe* 7(3), October 2018, pp. 331–50.
69. Both Russia and Turkey are members of the Peace Implementation Council (PIC) overseeing the Dayton Peace Agreement and the Office of the High Representative, the internationally appointed administrator of Bosnia and Herzegovina.
70. Nemanja Čabrić, Maja Nedelkovska, Donjeta Demoli and Amina Hamzić, "Turks Bewitch the Balkans with Their Addictive Soaps," *Balkan Insight*, 1 May 2013, https://balkaninsight.com/2013/05/01/turks-bewitch-the-balkans-with-their-addictive-soaps/

71. Dimitar Bechev, "Turkey in the Balkans: Taking a Broader View," *Insight Turkey* 14(1), 2012, pp. 131–46. For a general study of Turkish policy in the region: Ahmet Erdi Öztürk, *Religion, Identity and Power: Turkey and the Balkans in the Twenty-first Century* (Edinburgh: Edinburgh University Press, 2020).

5. A RUDE AWAKENING

1. David Kirkpatrick, "Premier of Turkey Takes on Regional Role," *New York Times*, 13 September 2011.
2. Cihan Tuğal, *The Fall of the Turkish Model: How the Arab Uprisings Brought Down Islamic Liberalism* (London: Verso, 2016), p. 4.
3. Ibid.
4. See Marc Lynch, *Arab Spring: The Unfinished Revolutions of the New Middle East* (New York: Public Affairs, 2013).
5. Ahmet Davutoğlu, "Zero Problems in a New Era: Realpolitik Is No Answer," *Foreign Policy*, 21 March 2013.
6. Stein, *Turkey's New Foreign Policy*, p. 36.
7. "Gül'ün Tunus izlenimleri," *Al Jazeera*, 12 March 2012.
8. Turkey reportedly advised the Brotherhood to resist the call for early elections and to continue to occupy Rabia Square in August 2013. Exchange with a former Turkish policy maker, March 2021. Support for the demonstrations ran strong in Turkish society too. Istanbul Mayor Kadir Topbaş proposed renaming one of the city's squares after Rabia. "Four-finger Salutes as Turks Back Egypt Protestors," Reuters, 19 August 2013.
9. "İşte Erdoğan'ın yaptığı Rabia'nın anlamı – Rabia ne demek, İzle," *Türkiye Gazetesi*, 21 January 2018. Tuğal, *The Fall of the Turkish Model*, p. 2 (the cover of Tuğal's book features Erdoğan making the Rabia sign).
10. In March 2021, in a bid to relaunch relations with Egypt, Turkey demanded pro-Brotherhood channels tone down criticism of the Al-Sisi regime. "Turkey Asks Egyptian Opposition to Tone Down Criticism: TV Channel Owner," Reuters, 19 March 2021. On Ikhwan members exiled in Turkey, see the conversation with the scholar Mustafa Menshawy (Doha Institute for Graduate Studies) for the Turkey Book Talk podcast, 8 December 2020, https://turkeybooktalk.podbean.com/e/mustafa-menshawy-on-muslim-brotherhood-members-in-exile-in-turkey/
11. Ümit Çetin, "NATO'nun Libya'da ne işi var," *Hürriyet*, 1 March 2011.
12. Seumas Milne, "Turkey Offers to Broker Libya Ceasefire as Rebels Advance on Sirte," *Guardian*, 27 March 2011.
13. "Turkey Says Offered Gaddafi Guarantee to Quit Libya," Reuters, 10 June 2011.
14. Ian Traynor, "Libya: NATO to Control No-fly Zone after France Gives Way to Turkey," *Guardian*, 24 March 2011.
15. Jeffrey Goldberg, "The Obama Doctrine," *The Atlantic*, April 2016.
16. Which, of course, informed the tough stance Russia took on Syria.
17. See Chapter 9.
18. Though, to be sure, Turkey chose to ignore the uprising in Bahrain in February–March 2011 where the majority Shi'a came out in protest against the Sunni monarchy, inspired by the changes in Tunisia and Egypt.
19. The phrase had been in circulation before. See Talip Küçükcan, "Ortadoğu'nun İlham Kaynağı Türkiye," SETA, 23 October 2010, www.setav.org/ortadogunun-ilham-kaynagi-turkiye/. Kemal Kirişci has proposed an alternative term, *demonstrative effect*. "Turkey's Demonstrative Effect," *Insight Turkey* 13(2), 2011, pp. 33–55.
20. Mensur Akgün, Gökçe Perçinoğlu and Sabiha Senyücel Gündoğar, *The Perception of Turkey in the Middle East* (Istanbul: TESEV Publications, 2009), www.files.ethz.ch/isn/118599/ArabPerspectivesRapWeb.pdf
21. Osman Bahadır Dinçer and Mustafa Kutlay, "Turkey's Power Capacity in the Middle East," USAK Report 12-04, Toronto, June 2012.

22. Christopher Phillips, "Into the Quagmire: Turkey's Frustrated Syria Policy," Middle East and North Africa Programme Briefing Paper, MENAPBP04/12, Chatham House, p. 4. See also his *The Battle for Syria: International Rivalry in the Middle East* (New Haven, CT: Yale University Press, 2016, 2nd edn, 2020) for a comprehensive account of the conflict.

23. In 2008 Ankara committed $6.3 million to 42 cooperative projects as part of the new Syrian–Turkish Inter-Regional Cooperation. Christopher Phillips, "Turkey's Global Strategy: Turkey and Syria," SR007, LSE IDEAS, London School of Economics and Political Science, 2011, p. 37.

24. Bilal Y. Saab, "Syria and Turkey Deepen Relations," Brookings Institution, 6 May 2009, www.brookings.edu/articles/syria-and-turkey-deepen-bilateral-relations/

25. Waltina Scheumann, and Omar Shamaly, "The Turkish–Syrian Friendship Dam on the Orontes River: Benefits for All?" in Aysegül Kibaroglu and Ronald Jaubert (eds.) *Water Resources Management in the Lower Asi-Orontes River Basin: Issues and Opportunities* (Geneva, Graduate Institute of International and Development Studies; Istanbul: MEF University, 2016), pp. 125–37.

26. Hassan Hassan, "The Gulf States: United against Iran, Divided over Islamists," in Julian Barnes-Dacey and Daniel Levy (eds.) *The Regional Struggle for Syria* (London: European Council on Foreign Relations, 2013), pp. 17–24. Similar to Turkey, the Gulf monarchies, including the resurgent Qatar, had profited from a period of rapprochement with Damascus which peaked in 2009–10.

27. Sam Dagher, *Assad or We Will Burn the Country: How One Family's Lust for Power Destroyed Syria* (London: Little Brown, 2019).

28. *Today's Zaman*, 1 August 2011.

29. Philips, "Into the Quagmire," p. 6.

30. Loğoğlu has consistently called for normalization of relations with Damascus.

31. The scandal was ongoing from 2014. "İşte Erdoğan'ın yok dediği silahlar," *Cumhuriyet*, 29 May 2015. The videos circulated by the prominent mafioso Sedat Peker in May–June 2021 also made allegations of weapon transfers to radical groups in Syria. See Fehim Taştekin, "Turkish Mobster's Revelations Extend to Arms Shipments to Syria," *Al-Monitor*, 2 June 2021.

32. Weapons paid for by Gulf donors were reportedly delivered to Ankara's Esenboğa airport and then onwards to the border.

33. Regan Doherty and Amena Bakr, "Secret Turkish Nerve Center Leads Aid to Syria Rebels," Reuters, 27 July 2012.

34. Mustafa al-Sabbagh, secretary-general of the Syrian National Coalition, and the prime minister it appointed, Ghassan Hitto, an ethnic Kurd, had Qatar's backing. Hitto resigned in September 2013, six months into his term, signaling a victory by Saudi Arabia over Qatar.

35. Hassan, "The Gulf States," p. 22.

36. Yezid Sayigh, "Endgame for the Syrian National Coalition," Carnegie Middle East Center, 17 May 2013. Brotherhood-linked militias funded by Qatar were influential in Syria's north: e.g. Liwaa al-Tawhid in Aleppo and Ahfad al-Rasoul in Idlib.

37. Turkey hosted a round of talks between P5+1 in Istanbul, 2011.

38. Exchange with a former Turkish policy maker, March 2021.

39. Exchange with the author, November 2013.

40. Anthony Cordesman, "Syria's Uncertain Air Defense Capabilities," Commentary, Center for Strategic and International Studies, Washington, DC, 6 May 2013.

41. Turkey shot down a Syrian plane over Hatay (23 March 2014) and an Mi-17 helicopter (September 2015).

42. Ian Traynor, "UK Forces EU to Lift Embargo on Syria Rebel Arms," *Guardian*, 28 May 2013.

43. Phillips, *The Battle for Syria*.

44. Marc Lynch, "What's Really at Stake in the Syria Debate," *War on the Rocks*, 20 October 2016, https://warontherocks.com/2016/10/whats-really-at-stake-in-the-syria-debate/

45. "The Ephemeral Alevi Opening," *The Economist*, 11 August 2012.

46. Nuh Yılmaz, "Turkey: Goodbye to Zero Problems with Neighbors," in Barnes-Dacey and Levy (eds.) *The Regional Struggle for Syria*, p. 71.

47. ISIS and al-Nusra initially mulled a merger, as they shared the same organizational and ideological roots, but eventually turned against each other in 2014. Charles Lister, *The Syrian Jihad, Al Qaeda, the Islamic State and the Evolution of an Insurgency* (London: Hurst, 2015), pp. 119–20.
48. "Dışişleri: Irak'ta 80 Türk Rehin," *Hürriyet*, 11 June 2014.
49. That was the bloodiest terrorist attack on Turkish soil, overshadowing the devastating explosion in the border town of Reyhanlı on 11 May 2013. Though the authorities pinned the attack on the Assad regime, Jabhat al-Nusra could have been a plausible perpetrator as well.
50. Interviews with Turkish diplomats, Ankara, June 2014.
51. The US Air Force carried out its first strike against ISIS in July and on 7 August Obama authorized further military action. A month later, "Operation Inherent Resolve" was in full swing. France, UK, Australia, Canada, the Netherlands as well as Jordan, Saudi Arabia, UAE, Bahrain and Qatar started carrying out air strikes too. The KRG pushed ISIS away from Erbil and the Sinjar mountain siege was broken. Daesh started to lose ground in central Iraq due to a counter offensive of Iran-backed militias.
52. Constanze Lesch, "Turkey Denies New Deal Reached to Open Airbases to US in Fight against ISIS," *Guardian*, 13 October 2014.
53. The PYD goes back to 2003. Its armed wing, the YPG (People's Protections Units, Yekîneyên Parastina Gel) was established at the beginning of the Syrian war. The PYD as well as the PKK is part of the so-called Kurdistan Communities Union (Koma Civakên Kurdistan, KCK), an umbrella organization uniting Kurdish actors from across the Middle East who accept Abdullah Öcalan's program for "democratic confederalism." See further in Zeynep Kaya and Robert Lowe, "The Curious Question of the PYD–PKK Relationship," in Stansfield and Shareef (eds.) *The Kurdish Question Revisited*, pp. 275–87.
54. Kurdish militias occasionally clashed with the regime as well, e.g. in Aleppo.
55. Aydoğan was commenting on Barzani's visit to Diyarbakır in November 2013 in support of the peace process initiated by the PKK and the Turkish government. Umut Uraş, "Kurdish Leader Makes Historic Turkey Visit," *Al Jazeera*, 20 November 2013.
56. The KNC put forward ideas for a Syrian federation, involving dropping "Arab" from the state's official name, Syrian Arab Republic. However, the Arab-dominated Syrian National Coalition, but also the more radical Salafist factions, opposed such changes.
57. "Salih Muslim's Ankara Visit Marks a Major Policy Change," *Rudaw*, 29 July 2013.
58. See Michael Knapp, Anja Flach and Ercan Ayboğa, *Revolution in Rojava: Democratic Autonomy and Women's Liberation in Syrian Kurdistan* (London: Pluto Press, 2016, originally published in German in 2015).
59. Constanze Letsch, "Turkey Denies New Deal Reached to Open Airbases to US in Fight against ISIS." *Guardian,* 13 October 2014.
60. Cale Salih, "Is Tal Abyad a Turning Point for Syria's Kurds?" *BBC News*, 16 June 2015.
61. Half of those resided in 17 camps spread over 8 Turkish provinces. Another 155,000 were in towns along the border with Syria. Oxford Analytica, "Domestic Fallout Hampers Turkey's Syria Policy," OA Daily Brief, 3 July 2013.
62. International Crisis Group, *Turkey's Syrian Refugees: Defusing Metropolitan Tensions*, Report 248, Europe and Central Asia, 29 January 2018, www.crisisgroup.org/europe-central-asia/western-europemediterranean/turkey/248-turkeys-syrian-refugees-defusing-metropolitan-tensions
63. Suat Kınıklıoğlu, "Syrian Refugees in Turkey: Changing Attitudes and Fortunes," SWP Comment 05, Stiftung Wissenschaft und Politik (SWP), Berlin, 5 February 2020.
64. Philips, "Into the Syrian Quagmire," p. 15.

6. ERDOĞAN WINS

1. Erdoğan, quoted in Sabrina Tavernise, "Turkish Court Blocks Islamic Candidate," *New York Times*, 2 May 2007.

2. On the peculiarities of *laiklik*, Turkey's version of secularism, see Chapter 1.
3. Sabrina Tavernise, "Turkey's High Court Overturns Headscarf Rule," *New York Times*, 6 June 2008.
4. The Constitutional Court upheld the headscarf prohibition.
5. Abdüllatif Şener, a former deputy prime minister who had left the AKP in 2007, was waiting in the wings, having started a political platform of his own, the Yeni Oluşum Hareketi (New Formation Movement), later renamed the Turkey Party.
6. The Peace and Democracy Party (Barış ve Demokrasi Partisi, BDP) had already been registered in 2008, as Kurdish activists anticipated that the DTP was at a risk of closure like its predecessors, HADEP and DEHAP.
7. "Turkey Needs More Reform, European Union Says after Vote," CNN, 13 September 2010.
8. "Youtube'a erişim yasağı," *Hürriyet*, 6 March 2007.
9. Pre-trial detention has been used and abused in Turkey, both historically and under Erdoğan. See, for instance, the European Court of Human Rights' judgment in *Şık v. Turkey* (No. 2), Application No. 36493/17, 24 November 2020. Also, *Kavala v. Turkey*, Application No. 28749/18, 10 December 2019.
10. Evren (1917–2015) was eventually tried and sentenced to life imprisonment in June 2014. He died while appealing the sentence. The other surviving coup leader, General Ali Tahsin Şahinkaya (1925–2015), was similarly sentenced to life but died while under house arrest.
11. *Hürriyet*, 1 August 2010. Şakir Dinçşahin, "A Symptomatic Analysis of the Justice and Development Party's Populism in Turkey, 2007–2010," *Government and Opposition* 47(4), 2012, pp. 618–40.
12. Ersin Kalaycıoğlu, "*Kulturkampf* in Turkey: The Constitutional Referendum of 12 September 2010," *South European Politics and Society* 17(1), 2012, pp. 1–22.
13. The CHP endorsed 20 of the 23 constitutional amendments.
14. "Fethullah Gülen'in referandum yorumu," *Habertürk*, 1 August 2010. In his victory speech after the plebiscite, Erdoğan himself thanked the "brothers from across the ocean."
15. "Turkish Reform Vote Gets Western Backing," *BBC News*, 13 September 2010.
16. "The European Union Welcomes Turkey's Constitutional Reform Victory," *Deutsche Welle*, 13 September 2010.
17. Some courts stood their ground even after the hardening of the regime in the aftermath of the 2016 coup attempt. In February 2020, a judge acquitted philanthropist Osman Kavala, who was tried on trumped-up charges in connection to the Gezi protests.
18. Presentation at Southeast European Studies at Oxford (SEESOX), 3 March 2021. In July 2019, the Constitutional Court cleared the so-called Academics for Peace charged with supporting terrorism. Likewise, the Court found in January 2018 that the writer Mehmet Altan's rights to fair trial were breached. However, the Court ruled in the opposite direction in December 2020, in Osman Kavala's case, ignoring the previous judgment by the European Court of Human Rights.
19. Ninety-three per cent of the individual applications to the Constitutional Court have been decided in favor of the plaintiff.
20. Perinçek was sentenced to life in August 2013 but his sentence was later overturned
21. Waldman and Çalışkan, *The New Turkey and Its Discontents*, pp. 31–8.
22. All discussed in Chapter 1.
23. The debate around the deep state, which peaked in the 2000s, has recently made a comeback with the revelations of fugitive mafia kingpin Sedat Peker about his links to the Turkish government and security services. The YouTube videos Peker started releasing in early May 2021 have gone viral. See Patrick Keddie and Umut Uras, "Sedat Peker's Case: Videos Grip Turkey, Rattle Government," *Al Jazeera*, 31 May 2021.
24. "Evet milletin savcısıyım," *Yeni Şafak*, 16 August 2008.
25. Öktem, *Angry Nation*, ch. 14: "The Guardian State Exposed," pp. 159–63.
26. Şık and Şener were set free in March 2012. Yet in 2015, Şık was put on trial again, for publishing a book on the AKP's alliance with the Gülenists, now declared an enemy.

Accused of belonging to a terrorist organization, he was kept in solitary confinement without a sentence for over a year between December 2016 and March 2018. The legal saga is still ongoing.

27. The sentence was commuted to 20 years.
28. There was a third case, in addition to the Ergenekon and Balyoz cases, the Military Espionage case, which again targeted the top brass.
29. Having served as commander of the gendarmerie, Özel had not gone through the hoops in his career progression. Under the normal practice, the head of the First Army and then of the land forces would become the chief of the general staff. Hilmi Özkok, Yaşar Büyükanıt and İlker Başbuğ had all been in charge of the First Army.
30. Halil Karaveli, "A Growing Convergence of Perceptions: The Turkish Military and the AKP," *Turkey Analyst* 2(17), 18 September 2009.
31. Robert Tait, "Turkey Appoints Anti-Islamist Army Chief," *Guardian*, 5 August 2008.
32. The AKP's share of the vote rose to 49.83 per cent, the highest it ever scored in parliamentary elections.
33. Pınar Doğan and Dani Rodrik, *Balyoz: Bir Darbe Kurgusunun Belgeleri ve Gerçekler* (Istanbul: Destek Yayınları, 2017)
34. "They walked the halls swinging their arms around, like they owned the place," a bureaucrat described Gülenist officials in various departments of the state in the wake of the 2010 referendum. Quoted in Koru, *The Institutional Structure of "New Turkey,"* p. 34.
35. For instance, the so-called Deniz Feneri case involving embezzlement of millions by a Turkish German charity close to the AKP.
36. "We will not leave this country to the hegemony of capital. You were able to play with governments as if you were playing with cats and dogs in the past, but you cannot do it with this government." Mark Champion and Joe Parkinson, "Turkish Prime Minister, Business Lobby Face Off," *Wall Street Journal*, 19 August 2010.
37. Kerem Öktem, "Why Turkey's Mainstream Media Chose to Show Penguins Rather than Protests," *Guardian*, 9 June 2013.
38. The change of ownership prompted an exodus of journalists, notably Murat Yetkin, *Hürriyet's* editor-in-chief.
39. On the pro-AKP media: Waldman and Çalışkan, *New Turkey and Its Discontents*, pp. 125–30.
40. See Erkan Saka, *Social Media and Politics in Turkey: A Journey through Citizen Journalism, Political Trolling, and Fake News* (Washington, DC: Lexington Books, 2019).
41. On the KCK, see Seevan Saeed, *Kurdish Politics in Turkey: From PKK to KCK* (Abingdon: Routledge, 2017), pp. 76–134.
42. Dilek Kurban and Serkan Yolaçan, *Kürt Sorunun Çözümüne Dair Bir Yol Haritası: Bölgeden Hükümete Öneriler*, TESEV report, December 2008, www.tesev.org.tr/wp-content/uploads/rapor_Kurt_Sorununun_Cozumune_Dair_Bir_Yol_Haritasi_Bolgeden_Hukumete_Oneriler.pdf
43. Commission of the European Communities, *Turkey 2009 Progress Report*, COM (2009) 533, Brussels, 14 October 2009, p. 30.
44. Alexander Christie-Miller, "The PKK and the Closure of Turkey's Kurdish Opening," Middle East Research and Information Project, 4 April 2010, https://merip.org/2010/08/the-pkk-and-the-closure-of-turkeys-kurdish-opening/
45. Çandar, *Turkey's Mission Impossible*, ch. 8: "Oslo, Talking on Security."
46. The prime minister sought to embarrass the CHP's leader Kılıçdaroğlu, a native of Dersim, too. "Turkey's PM Erdoğan Apologises for 1930s Kurdish Killings," *BBC News*, 23 November 2011.
47. There were spoilers along the way, such the assassination of PKK co-founder Sakine Cansız and two other activists in Paris on 9 January 2013.
48. "Öcalan's Statement: Key Excerpts," *BBC News*, 21 March 2013.
49. Çandar, *Turkey's Mission Impossible*, ch. 9.
50. Osman Baydemir, "The 'We Know Best' Democracy," in Dimitar Bechev (ed.) *What Does Turkey Think?* (London: European Council on Foreign Relations, 2011), pp. 43–9. See also Waldman and Çalışkan, *The New Turkey and Its Discontents*, pp. 184–9.

51. Setting up a "Wise Men's Commission" (Akil Adam Komisyonu) did not make the situation any better. Thankfully, it was soon renamed "Wise Persons Commission" (Akil İnsanlar Komisyonu). Still, women accounted for less than a fifth of the 63 members of the group. For a gender perspective on the Kurdish issue, see Nadje Al-Ali and Latif Tas, " 'War Is Like a Blanket': Feminist Convergences in the Kurdish and Turkish Women's Rights Activism for Peace," *Journal of Middle East Women's Studies* 13(3), 2017, pp. 354–75.

52. To get a sense of the diversity of the protest, only around 41 per cent of the participants had voted for the CHP in the 2011 elections. Waldman and Çalışkan, *The New Turkey and Its Discontents*, pp. 103–4.

53. "Cumhurbaşkanı Gül'den Gezi Parkı açıklaması," *Hürriyet*, 3 June 2013.

54. "Gezi Parkı, işgal alanı değildir," *Cumhuriyet*, 11 June 2013.

55. Conversation with the author, Istanbul, June 2013.

56. Joshua D. Hendrick, *Gülen: The Ambiguous Politics of Market Islam in Turkey* (New York: New York University Press, 2013).

57. "Profile: Gülen's Hizmet Movement," *BBC News*, 18 December 2013. In the words of a bureaucrat: "[The Gülenists] had bright people with fancy degrees applying for key public institutions. It was government policy to hire them. It came straight from the minister." Koru, *The Institutional Structure of "New Turkey,"* p. 34. Gülen himself reportedly counts Antonio Gramsci as a favorite author, on account of the Marxist's ideas about cultural hegemony. Conversation with a Turkish expert, November 2012.

58. "Arrest Warrant Issued for Former Turkish Intelligence Chief," CNN, 10 February 2012.

59. "Islamic Scholar Criticizes Turkish Government Response to Gezi Protests," *Hürriyet Daily News*, 20 March 2014.

60. Aslı Aydıntaşbaş, "The Good, the Bad and the Gülenists," European Council on Foreign Relations, 23 September 2016.

61. Constanze Letsch, "Leaked Tapes Prompt Calls for Turkish PM to Resign," *Guardian*, 25 February 2014.

62. Later on, Gül took it upon himself to deny any involvement with the *cemaat*. "Former President Gül Denies Any Link to Gülen Group," *Hürriyet Daily News*, 5 January 2017.

63. Anecdotally, AKP voters shrugged off the corruption revelation with the ubiquitous adage "*çalıyor ama çalışıyor*" ("yes, they steal [like any politician does] but they also work/deliver").

7. THE NEW TURKEY

1. Peter Kenyon, "Turkey's President and his 1,100-room 'White Palace'," National Public Radio, 24 December 2014.

2. Putin was there on 1 December 2014, the second international leader after Pope Francis to visit the presidential palace.

3. Çağaptay, *The New Sultan*.

4. Turkey's Strategic Vision 2023. Available at: www.tsv2023.org/index.php/en/proje.html

5. New Turkey (*Yeni Türkiye*) was first used in the AKP's manifesto for the June 2015 general elections. I am thankful to Ayşe Kadıoğlu for the reminder.

6. Bahar Başer and Ahmet Erdi Öztürk (eds.) *Authoritarian Politics in Turkey: Elections, Resistance and the AKP* (London: I.B. Tauris, 2017); Berk Esen and Şebnem Gümüçü, "Rising Competitive Authoritarianism in Turkey," *Third World Quarterly* 37(9), 2016, pp. 1581–606.

7. Freedom House, *Freedom in the World 2020: A Leaderless Struggle for Democracy*, February 2020, p. 14, https://freedomhouse.org/sites/default/files/2020-02/FIW_2020_REPORT_BOOKLET_Final.pdf. Turkey has registered sharp decline in other indices measuring democracy, including those published by the Varieties of Democracy (V-Dem) Institute and the Economist Intelligence Unit.

8. Jason Brownlee, "Why Turkey's Democratic Decline Shakes Up Democratic Theory," Monkey Cage Blog, *Washington Post*, 23 March 2016, www.washingtonpost.com/news/monkey-cage/wp/2016/03/23/why-turkeys-authoritarian-descent-shakes-up-democratic-theory/

9. "Turkey's Erdoğan is Inaugurated as President," *BBC News*, 28 August 2014.
10. Nick Tattarsall and Tulay Karadeniz, "Erdoğan Chairs Turkish Cabinet, Pushing Presidential Powers," Reuters, 19 January 2015.
11. And between 2014 and 2018, of the prime minister.
12. On the Pelican group, see Hannah Lucinda Smith, *Erdoğan Rising: The Battle for the Soul of Turkey* (London: William Collins, 2019), ch. 4: "Erdoğan and Friends."
13. In early 2016, Gül's name was removed from the list of the AKP's founders.
14. In parallel, the parliamentary elections in 2015 marked the departure of many former AKP deputies thanks to the three-terms rule in the party statutes.
15. Albayrak served as minister of energy (2015–18), moving to the Ministry of Finance (2018–20).
16. Soylu originally came from the True Path Party (DYP), and in a sense brought with him the baggage of Tansu Çiller and Interior Minister Mehmet Ağar's scorched earth campaign waged against the PKK in the mid-1990s. Soylu joined the AKP in 2012, having previously been the leader of the DYP's successor, the Democrat Party. Like Erdoğan, he comes from the Black Sea region.
17. For the full cast of characters, see Nicholas Danforth, "The Outlook for Turkish Democracy: 2023 and Beyond," Policy Notes, Washington Institute, 2020, pp. 3–7, www.washington-institute.org/media/632?disposition=inline
18. On Turkey's crony capitalist model, Ayşe Buğra and Osman Savaşkan, *New Capitalism in Turkey: The Relationship Between Politics, Religion and Business* (Cheltenham: Edward Elgar, 2014).
19. As Berk Esen and Şebnem Gümüşçü argue, clientelism also accounts for the AKP's authoritarian tilt. See their "Why did Turkish Democracy Collapse?"
20. Özge Kemahlıoğlu, "Winds of Change? The June 2015 Parliamentary Election in Turkey," *South European Society and Politics* 20(4), December 2015, pp. 445–64.
21. Burcu Özçelik, "What the HDP Success Means for Turkey," Comment, Carnegie Endowment, 11 June 2015, https://carnegieendowment.org/sada/60370
22. The CHP lost a little over 1 per cent of its vote compared to 2011, but its caucus expanded by seven members.
23. Sabri Sayarı, "Back to a Predominant Party System: The November 2015 Snap Election in Turkey," *South European Society and Politics* 21(2), 2016, p. 267.
24. "Seni başkan yaptırmayacağız," *Cumhuriyet*, 17 March 2015. Note the use of the informal "you" ("sen" rather than "siz"). As Selim Koru cleverly points out: "a leftist and the leader of an ethnic and linguistic minority, spoke to Erdoğan, the leader of the religious and cultural majority, as an equal." *The Institutional Structure of "New Turkey,"* p. 15.
25. Osman Baydemir (HDP) later claimed that the party proposed to Erdoğan support for an AKP minority cabinet or an AKP–CHP coalition. Koru, *The Institutional Structure of "New Turkey,"* p. 17.
26. Opinion polls supported his intuition. Sayarı, "Back to a Predominant Party System," p. 268.
27. In the meantime, the AKP exploited the opposition's disunity to elect İsmet Yılmaz as parliamentary speaker (1 July 2015) after four rounds of votes.
28. Max Hoffman and Michael Werz, "Turkey's Right Rises Again," Center for American Progress, Washington, DC, 3 November 2015.
29. Kerem Öktem and Karabekir Akkoyunlu, "Exit from Democracy: Illiberal Governance in Turkey and Beyond," *Journal of Southeast European and Black Sea Studies* 16(4), November 2016, pp. 469–80.
30. Çandar, "The Perennial Kurdish Question," in Özerdem and Whiting (eds.) *The Routledge Handbook on Turkish Politics*, p. 262.
31. Ioannis Grigoriadis, "The Peoples' Democratic Party (HDP) and the 2015 Elections," *Turkish Studies* 17(1), 2016, pp. 39–46.
32. Çandar, "The Perennial Kurdish Question."
33. "Başbakan Davutoğlu: Silahın dili sona erecek," NTV, 28 February 2015. Davutoğlu showed a penchant for symbolic gestures. During a visit to Diyarbakır in January, he referred

to Öcalan as *serok* (leader in Kurdish), a bold move by any account, given the PKK's image in the minds of most Turks.

34. Önder visited Qandil five days before the meetings and had talked to Öcalan the previous day.
35. "Erdoğan: Silah bırakma lafla olmaz," *Al Jazeera Türk*, 11 March 2015.
36. For the various parties' calculations, see Burak Bilgehan Özpetek, *The Peace Process between Turkey and the Kurds: Anatomy of a Failure* (Abingdon: Routledge, 2017), ch. 3: "Why Did the Peace Process Fail?"
37. Başaran, *Frontline Turkey*, pp. 124–49.
38. "Ağrı'da gerçekte ne yaşandı?," *BBC Türkish*, 13 April 2015.
39. "AKP beyannameye süreci ekledi," *Al Jazeera Turk*, 21 April 2015.
40. International Crisis Group, "A Sisyphean Task? Resuming Turkey–PKK Peace Talks," Briefing 77, Europe and Central Asia, 17 December 2015.
41. *Sınırdaki Düşman: Türkiye'nin DAİŞ İle Mücadelesi* (Ankara: SETA Foundation, 2016), p. 36.
42. William Armstrong's interview with Deniz Cifci, *Turkey Book Talk* podcast, 24 September 2019, https://armstrongwilliam.wordpress.com/2019/09/24/deniz-cifci-on-the-fissures-within-kurdish-politics-in-turkey/
43. Videos of Turkish trucks circulated on Kurdish nationalist websites from 2014 onwards.
44. Speech in the aftermath of a bombing attack in Gaziantep, 21 August 2016. Available at: www.hdp.org.tr/en/our-co-chair-mr-selahattin-demirtas-speech-on-the-massacre-in-gaziantep/8782/
45. On Kurdish demands, see Başaran, *Frontline Turkey*, pp. 157–8.
46. The decision to break the ceasefire, taken by the KCK, a Kurdish umbrella organization dominated by the Qandil command, seemed to undercut Öcalan too.
47. The YDG-H had come to prominence in January 2015 when its members clashed with supporters of the conservative Islamist Free Cause Party (Hür Dava Partisi or Hüda Par) in Cizre.
48. "KCK: 'Kürdistan halkı için özyönetimden başka bir seçenek kalmamıştır'," *T24*, 12 August 2015.
49. Of course, that claim had to be taken with a pinch of salt. The takeover of HDP-run municipalities by government-appointed officials in the autumn of 2015, for instance, was accompanied by the removal of multi-lingual signs on public buildings. In February 2016, IMC, a liberal pro-Kurdish TV channel established in 2011, was taken down from Türksat – to be banned in October that year.
50. Demirtaş's trip to Moscow in November 2015, amidst tensions between Turkey and Russia, was not a wise decision.
51. Abdullah Öcalan called on party supporters to stay neutral and not take part.
52. "İşte CHP'nin darbe raporuna muhalefet şerhi," *Sözcu*, 12 June 2017.
53. The most senior participant in the coup, General Akın Öztürk, had served as a commander of the Turkish Air Force between 2013 and 2015. A third of the 220 brigadier generals were associated with the coup, but only 14 per cent of the major generals.
54. The abortive coup attempts by Colonel Talât Aydemir took place in February 1962 and May 1963. But the 1960–3 interventions, attempted or successful, involved junior officers, a difference with 2016. See Berk Esen, "A Praetorian Army in Action: A Critical Assessment of Civil–Military Relations in Turkey," *Armed Forces and Society* 47(1), 2020, pp. 201–22.
55. Yaprak Gürsoy, "The 15 July 2016 Failed Coup and the Security Sector," in Özerdem and Whiting (eds.) *The Routledge Handbook on Turkish Politics*, p. 286.
56. Işık Koşaner, former chief of general staff, argued that was the case. "Işık Koşaner neden istifa ettiğini açıkladı," *Hürriyet*, 26 October 2016. See also Dexter Filkins, "Turkey's Thirty-year Coup, Did an Exiled Cleric Try to Overthrow Erdoğan's Government?" *The New Yorker*, 17 October 2016.
57. Notably, cadets from the war academies in Ankara and Istanbul played a key part in the coup on 27 May 1960.

58. Kadri Gürsel, "Turkey's Failed Coup Reveals 'Army within an Army,'" *Al Monitor*, 22 July 2016.
59. Metin Gürcan, "Never Again! But How? State and Military after the 15 July Coup," Istanbul Policy Center, April 2017; "Bir Darbe Girişimi Anatomisi," *T24*, 18 July 2016. Gürcan called it a WhatsApp coup, after the smartphone application used by the putschists to communicate with one another.
60. Gönül Tol, Matt Mainzer and Zeynep Ekmekci, "Unpacking Turkey's Failed Coup: Causes and Consequences," Middle East Institute, 17 August 2016. Also Berk Esen and Şebnem Gümüşçü, "Turkey: How the Coup Failed," *Journal of Democracy* 28(1), January 2017, pp. 59–73.
61. The count included 63 policemen and 3 pro-government soldiers. Prime Minister Yıldırım's office counted 36 killed and 49 wounded among the putschists. Gürsoy, "The 15 July 2016 Failed Coup."
62. The lifting of the state of emergency coincided with the passage of anti-terror legislation (Law 7145 from 25 July 2018) empowering the authorities to detain individuals without pressing charges for up to 4 days, as well as to impose lockdowns at the local level over 15 days. Criticized for extending the state of emergency beyond its expiry date, the provisions of this law also allow for the dismissal of military personnel and public servants. "Turkey Parliament Approves New Anti-Terror Law," *Al Jazeera*, 25 July 2018. See also İnsan Hakları Derneği (Human Rights Association), "Sürekli OHAL'i Düzenleyen 7145 Sayılı Kanun Hakkında," Press Statement, 1 August 2018, www.ihd.org.tr/surekli-ohali-duzenleyen-7145-sayili-kanun-hakkinda/
63. Gürsoy, "The 15 July 2016 Failed Coup," p. 290.
64. Kavala was acquitted February 2020 but then re-arrested and new charges laid against him in connection to the coup.
65. Kararname KHK 668. *Resmi Gazete*, 25 July 2016. The same decree removed hundreds of military officers from their roles.
66. Businesses and economic assets connected to the *cemaat* were taken over by the state too.
67. Constanze Letsch, "Turkey Shuts 15 Media Outlets and Arrests Opposition Editor," *Guardian*, 30 October 2016.
68. Şık was set free in 2018 but then sentenced to 10 months in prison in 2019.
69. Quoted in "The Legacy of an Attempted Coup in Turkey," *The Economist*, 15 April 2017.
70. "A&G'nin araştırma sonucu: Terörün arkasında ABD var," *Aydınlık*, 8 January 2017.
71. In a similar vein, the US faced accusations of being behind the 1980 coup too.
72. "İşte Türkiye'nin yerli ve milli silahları!," *CNN Türk*, 16 October 2019.
73. "Yerli ve milli SUV ve sedan bir arada! Kırmızı beyaz," *Habertürk*, 27 December 2019.
74. "Erdoğan: Siz milli de yerli de olamazsınız," *BBC Turkish*, 29 September 2015.
75. "Turkey's President Erdoğan is Grabbing Yet More Power," *The Economist*, 21 January 2017. What certainly helped Bahçeli to change tack was the support he received from the government in defeating a challenge by Meral Akşener and Sinan Oğan for the leadership of the MHP in the summer and autumn of 2016. Koru, *The Institutional Structure of "New Turkey,"* p. 20.
76. This was foreseen from the outset. Sinan Ülgen, "Get Ready for a More Aggressive Turkey," *Foreign Policy*, 2 July 2018.
77. Opposed to this amendment, the dissidents within the MHP, including Meral Akşener, joined the "No" campaign.
78. For an outline of the amendments, see Sinan Ekim and Kemal Kirişci, "The Turkish Constitutional Referendum Explained," Order from Chaos Blog, Brookings Institution, 13 April 2017, https://www.brookings.edu/blog/order-from-chaos/2017/04/13/the-turkish-constitutional-referendum-explained/. Also Koru, *The Institutional Structure of "New Turkey,"* pp. 4–6.
79. "Yeni Anayasa anketinden çok konuşulacak sonuçlar," *Sözcu*, 28 December 2016.
80. Serap Yazıcı, "Constitutional Amendments of 2017: Transition to Presidentialism in Turkey," GlobaLex, NYU School of Law, September 2017, www.nyulawglobal.org/globalex/2017_Turkey_Constitution_Amendments.html
81. Steven Levitsky and Lucan A. Way, "The Rise of Competitive Authoritarianism," *Journal of Democracy* 13(2), 2002, pp. 52–3. See also Esen and Gümüşçü, "Rising Competitive Authoritarianism."

82. "Observer Says up to 2.5 Million Turkish Referendum Votes Could Have Been Manipulated," *Reuters*, 18 April 2017.

83. See Orçun Selçuk, Dilara Hekimci and Onur Erpil, "The Erdoğanization of Turkish Politics and the Role of the Opposition," *Journal of Southeast European and Black Sea Studies* 19(4), 2019, pp. 541–64.

84. The dysfunctionality of the executive presidential system was at play too: 24 out of total of 55 presidential decrees adopted between 2018 and 2020 had to be corrected ex post to fix legal errors. Routine decisions are taken to the highest level rather than delegated. Transaction costs have increased as a result. Presentation by Ersin Kalaycıoğlu, panel on Turkey's New Constitution, Southeast European Studies at Oxford (SESOX), 3 March 2021. Recording available at: www.youtube.com/watch?v=k0H9T8. Also Gareth Jenkins, "Turkey's Dysfunctional Presidential System," *Turkey Analyst*, 5 May 2020.

85. During the campaign, for instance, İnce made a pledge to open the world's largest Islamic university in the southeastern city of Şanlıurfa. "Dünyanın en büyük islami Bilimler Üniversitesi'ni Şanlıurfaya kuracağım," *Yurt Gazetesi*, 6 June 2018.

86. F. Michael Wuthrich and Melvyn Ingleby, "A Pushback against Populism: Running on 'Radical Love' in Turkey," *Journal of Democracy* 31(2), April 2020, pp. 24–40.

87. "Seçim sonuçları: Ekrem İmamoğlu 800 binden fazla oy farkla İstanbul Büyükşehir Belediye Başkanı seçildi," *BBC Turkish*, 24 June 2019.

88. Melih Gökçek's term in Ankara lasted from 1994 (the same election in which Erdoğan won Istanbul's mayoralty) till 2017, when he lost his job in an intra-AKP purge.

89. MHP has retained influence over policy making, not least because of Erdoğan's aversion to taking decisions which might prove unpopular with the Turkish public. As a result, relations with the AKP, its partner in the "Citizen Alliance", have been marred by discord. The parties could separate lists in the next parliamentary elections, with the AKP opting for an alliance with smaller conservative and center-right factions as well as, possibly, a Kurdish party. Mehveş Evin, "What Does Lowering Election Threshold to 7% Mean for Turkish Politics?" *Duvar English*, 3 September 2021.

90. Turkey's GDP expanded by 1.8 per cent in 2020, impressive in comparison to other large economies, but still insufficient to reverse the low-growth trend.

91. Alev Coşkun, "128 milyar dolar nerede? Kime, hangi isimlere satıldı?" *Cumhuriyet*, 25 April 2021. Dorian Jones, "Questions over Missing Billions Pose Challenge to Erdoğan," *VOA*, 26 April 2021.

92. Koray Çalışkan, "From Competitive toward Full Authoritarianism," *New Perspectives on Turkey* 58, May 2018, pp. 5–33.

8. "OUR SO-CALLED STRATEGIC PARTNER"

1. Remarks by Vice-President Biden and President Erdoğan of Turkey in Pool Spray, Presidential Palace, Ankara, 25 August 2016, https://obamawhitehouse.archives.gov/the-press-office/2016/08/25/remarks-vice-president-biden-and-president-Erdo%C4%9Fan-turkey-pool-spray

2. Gülnur Aybet, "Joe Biden's Visit to Ankara and Solving Pressing Issues," *Al Jazeera*, 24 August 2016.

3. Evren Balta, remarks at a briefing session hosted by the Heinrich Boell Foundation, 10 December 2010. See also Evren Balta and Mitat Çelikpala, "Turkey and Russia: Historical Patterns and Contemporary Trends in Bilateral Relations," in Güneş Murat Tezcür (ed.) *The Oxford Handbook of Turkish Politics* (Oxford: Oxford University Press, forthcoming).

4. Anton Lavrov, *The Russian Air Campaign in Syria: A Preliminary Analysis*, CNA Occasional Paper, June 2018, www.cna.org/CNA_files/PDF/COP-2018-U-017903-Final.pdf

5. Major General Qasem Soleimani, commander of the Quds Force, visited Moscow in July 2015 in the run-up to the military intervention. Laila Bassam and Tom Perry, "How an Iranian General Plotted Out Syrian Assault by Moscow," *Reuters*, 6 October 2015.

6. Dimitar Bechev, Stanislav Secrieru and Nicu Popescu (eds.) *Russia Rising: Putin's Foreign Policy in the Middle East and North Africa* (London: I.B. Tauris, 2021).

7. Emre Erşen, "Evaluating the Fighter Jet Crisis in Turkish–Russian Relations," *Insight Turkey* 19(4), 2017, pp. 85–104.
8. "Turkey's Downing of Russia Jet 'Stab in the Back' – Putin," *BBC News*, 24 November 2015.
9. "Mehmet Şimşek'ten Rusya itirafı: '9 milyar dolar'," *Cumhuriyet*, 7 December 2015.
10. The SDF was formed in October 2015 by the YPG along with various Arab, Assyrian and other forces. It was backed by the US Central Command (CENTCOM). See Suleiman al-Khalidi and Tom Perry, "New Syrian Rebel Alliance Formed, Says Weapons on the Way," Reuters, 12 October 2015.
11. International Crisis Group, *Russia and Turkey in the Black Sea and the South Caucasus*, Europe and Central Asia Report no. 250, Brussels, 28 June 2018.
12. Bechev, *Rival Power*, pp. 139–76.
13. Burak Ege Bekdil, "US Begins Removing Patriot Missiles from Turkey," *Defense News*, 11 October 2015.
14. Right after the plane was shot down, Turkish authorities delivered the bodies of the two dead pilots to Russia, in a goodwill gesture.
15. In a call on 17 July, Putin expressed condolences for the coup's victims and urged a return to order and stability. Obama called two days later, even though he had rejected the putsch on 15 July.
16. AKP members also blamed the downing of the Russian jet in November 2015 on Gülenists in the air force. "Rus Savaş Uçağının Fetö Tarafıdan Düşürüldüğü İddiası," *Milliyet*, 7 October 2017.
17. Soli Özel, "Whither Turkey–Russia Relations?" Robert Bosch Academy, 2020, www.robert-boschacademy.de/de/perspectives/whither-turkey-russia-relations. Şener Aktürk, "Relations between Russia and Turkey before, during, and after the Failed Coup of 2016," *Insight Turkey* 21(4), Fall 2016, pp. 97–113.
18. The site carried special symbolism. The palace goes back to Catherine the Great's grandson Grand Duke Konstantin Pavlovich. Himself named after the Roman emperor Constantine the Great, the grand duke was a central figure in Catherine's so-called Greek Plan (*Grecheskii Proekt*) developed in the 1780s. It foresaw the restoration of the Byzantine state under Russian suzerainty and with Konstantin Pavlovich on the throne.
19. Turkey has since largely incorporated the areas in question into its jurisdiction: turning the lira into official tender, connecting the local electricity grid to its national network, investing in infrastructure and providing public services. See Aslı Aydıntaşbaş, *A New Gaza: Turkey's Border Policy in Northern Syria*, Policy Brief, European Council on Foreign Relations, May 2020.
20. Dimitar Bechev, "Russia and Turkey: The Promise and Limits of Partnership," in Bechev, Secrieru and Popescu (eds.) *Russia Rising*.
21. Kareem Shaheen, "Aleppo: Russia–Turkey Ceasefire Deal Offers Hope of Survival of Residents," *Guardian*, 13 December 2016.
22. Selim Koru, *The Resiliency of Turkey–Russia Relations*, Black Sea Strategy Paper, Foreign Policy Research Institute, November 2018, p. 15, www.fpri.org/wp-content/uploads/2018/11/bssp2-koru.pdf
23. The initial Russian draft from 23 January 2017 was rejected by Turkey because it foresaw autonomy for the Kurdish region. See Pavel K. Baev and Kemal Kirişci, *An Ambiguous Partnership: The Serpentine Trajectory of Turkish–Russian Relations in the Era of Erdoğan and Putin*, Turkey Project Policy Paper, Brookings Institution, September 2017, p. 11. From 2018 onwards, Russia started hosting the so-called Syrian Constitution Committee with representatives of the government and various opposition factions.
24. As a rule, "reconciled" forces remained in control of their townships and regions. Fadi Adleh and Agnes Favier, *"Local Reconciliation Agreements for Syria": A Non-starter for Peacebuilding*, Research project report, Middle East Directions, Robert Schumann Center for Advanced Studies, European University Institute, 2017.

25. After the takeover, many Kurds left Afrin and were replaced by Arab settlers from the suburbs of Damascus. Jamie Dettmer, "Kurds Say Turkey Plans to Reshape Demographics in Northern Syria," *VOA*, 29 January 2018.
26. Aaron Stein, "Roadmap to Nowhere: Manbij, Turkey and America's Dilemma in Syria," *War on the Rocks*, 29 June 2018.
27. Maria Tsvetkova, "Russia and Turkey Agree to Create Buffer Zone in Syria's Idlib," Reuters, 17 September 2018.
28. For instance, BOTAŞ dropped its demand for a price cut on Gazprom deliveries under the long-term contract signed, following protracted bargaining, in 2011.
29. Russian authorities kept the so-called "tomato ban" until May 2018. See Baev and Kirişci, *An Ambiguous Partnership*, p. 7.
30. Dimitar Bechev, "TurkStream: Geopolitical Implications and Future Prospects," Al Sharq Center, 28 May 2020.
31. Nordstream 2 involves a partnership between Gazprom and Western companies like Royal Dutch Shell, E.ON and Wintershall.
32. Cihan Dizdaroğlu, Mustafa Aydın and Sinem Akgül Açıkmeşe, *Turkish Foreign Policy: Research on Public Perceptions*, Kadir Has University survey, July 2019, www.khas.edu.tr/en/haberler/research-public-perceptions-turkish-foreign-policy-2019-0
33. See Chapter 6.
34. But Erdoğan offered no excuses, even asserting that Trump had offered his apologies for the unseemly episode.
35. The losses have been estimated at around $9 billion. The list of companies affected includes Roketsan, Havelsan, Alp Aviation, Ayesas, Kale Aerospace, Tübitak–SAGE, the Turkish Aerospace Industries (TAI) and the Turkish subsidiary of the Dutch Fokker Elmo. See Ece Toksabay and Tuvan Gümrükçü, "Turkish Defense Firms Set to Lose Billions after F-35 Removal," Reuters, 18 July 2019.
36. Obama promised to recognize the genocide during his 2008 campaign but never did so while in office.
37. Soli Özel and Serhat Güvenç, "US–Turkey Relations since World War II: From Alliance to Transactionalism," in Tezcür (ed.) *The Oxford Handbook of Turkish Politics*.
38. "U.S. Secretary of State Nominee Calls NATO Ally Turkey a 'So-called Strategic Partner'," Reuters, 19 January 2021.
39. Hümeyra Pamuk, "Erdoğan SAys Turkey Plans to Buy More Russian Defense Systems," Reuters, 27 September 2021.
40. In October 2018, Turkey released Andrew Brunson, a Protestant minister originally from North Carolina who had been in detention over alleged links to the 2016 coup plotters. His case, at the center of a diplomatic rift between Washington and Ankara, resonated with Trump's conservative base. Therefore, the release, ahead of the US mid-term elections in November, was a gift of sorts from the Saray to the White House. Trump met Brunson at the Oval Office. "Andrew Brunson: Trump Meets US Pastor Freed by Turkey," *BBC News*, 18 October 2018. In the meantime, the sanctions imposed by Trump, through tweets, such as doubling steel and aluminium tariffs, helped Erdoğan rally Turkish public opinion behind the flag. It was a win-win. Lisel Hintz, "No One Lost Turkey: Turkey's Foreign Policy Quest for Agency with Russia and Beyond," *Texas National Security Review* 2(4), August 2019, pp. 149–50.
41. Steven A. Cook, "Erdoğan Plays Washington Like a Fiddle," Council for Foreign Relations, 3 September 2019.
42. Julian Borger, "Mattis' Resignation Triggered by Phone Call between Trump and Erdoğan," *Guardian*, 21 December 2018.
43. Jake Sherman, "Pence Announces Ceasefire Deal with Turkey," *Politico*, 17 October 2019.
44. İbrahim Kalın interviewed by NTV, "Cumhurbaşkanlığı Sözcüsü İbrahim Kalın NTV'de'," 21 November 2020.
45. The ostentatious camaraderie with Russia aside, Turkey has contributed to NATO's "tailored forward presence" in the Black Sea that was the response to the annexation of Crimea. The policy includes frequent exercises, rotation of naval ships from allies outside the Black Sea,

including the US, and a multinational framework brigade stationed near Constanţa, Romania. Turkey's role in the alliance's containment strategy vis-à-vis Moscow is a major reason why Bucharest has been arguing for engagement with Ankara and against sanctions in EU deliberations. See "Boosting NATO's Presence in the East and Southeast," www.nato.int/cps/en/natohq/topics_136388.htm

46. See Çağaptay, *Erdoğan's Empire*, pp. 231–65.
47. "Turkey's Erdoğan Presses World Leaders to Help Myanmar's Rohingya," Reuters, 4 September 2017.
48. In 2009, Erdoğan characterized the Chinese actions in the province as "genocide" but ten years later said people in Xinjiang lived happily. Ankara's shift is based on both commercial and strategic rationale. Kuzzat Altay, "Why Erdoğan Has Abandoned the Uyghurs," *Foreign Policy*, 2 March 2021.

9. THE PURSUIT OF POWER

1. Birol Başkan, *Turkey and Qatar in the Tangled Geopolitics of the Middle East* (New York: Palgrave Pivot, 2016).
2. The Qatar crisis led to a rift between Saudi Arabia, on the one hand, and Turkey and Qatar, on the other, in Yemen. In March 2015, Turkey and Qatar approved Operation Decisive Storm, launched by Ryadh against the Iran-backed Houthis. The 2017 crisis, however, led to the expulsion of the Al-Islah party, supported by Doha and Ankara and connected to the Muslim Brotherhood, from the Saudi-led military coalition. Ali Bakeer and Giorgio Cafiero, "Turkey's Influence in Yemen," *TRT World*, 1 May 2018.
3. "Turkish Parliament Approves Troop Deployment to Qatar," *Al Jazeera*, 7 June 2017. A second base is under construction too. Hande Fırat, "A New Military Base in Qatar to Inaugurate in Autumn," *Hürriyet Daily News*, 14 August 2019.
4. Güney Yıldız, "GCC/Qatar Reconciliation: Good or Bad News for Turkey?" Point of View, Stiftung Wissenschaft und Politk (SWP), Berlin, 18 January 2021.
5. "Qatargas, BOTAŞ Sign New Three Year LNG Agreement," Anadolu Agency, 20 September 2017.
6. *Qatar Tribune*, 27 November 2018.
7. Fehim Taştekin, "Turkey Sees Greater Partnership with Qatar than Is Apparent," *Al Monitor*, 4 December 2019. "Another 7 Billion of Qatari Investment to Flow into Turkey," *Daily Sabah*, 3 December 2019.
8. Tom Bateman, "Afghanistan: Qatar and Turkey Become Taliban's Lifeline to the Outside World," *BBC News*, 2 September 2021.
9. Magdalene Mukami and Mohammed Dhaysane, "Somalia Thrives with a Helping Hand from TİKA," Anadolu Agency, 16 October 2019, www.aa.com.tr/en/africa/somalia-thrives-with-helping-hand-from-tika/1615224
10. Mehmet Özkan, "The Turkish Way of Doing Development Aid? An Analysis from a Somali Laboratory," in Isaline Bergamasch, Phoebe Moore and Arlene B. Tickner (eds.) *South–South Cooperation Beyond the Myths: Rising Donors, New Aid Practices?* (Basingstoke: Palgrave Macmillan, 2017), pp. 59–79.
11. "Qatar to Build New Port at Somalia's Hobyo," *Al Jazeera*, 8 August 2019.
12. Micha'el Tanchum, "Turkey's String of Pearls: Turkey's Overseas Naval Installations Reconfigure the Security Architecture of Mediterranean–Red Sea Corridor," Fokus 4/2019, Austrian Institute for European and Security Policy (AIES), 2019.
13. Asya Akça, "Neo-Ottomanism: Turkey's Foreign Policy Approach to Africa," *New Perspectives in Foreign Policy*, 17 April 2019, Center for Strategic and International Studies, Washington, DC; Andres Schipani and Laura Pitel, "Erdoğan's Great Game: Turkey Pushes into Africa with Aid, Trade and Soaps," *Financial Times*, 18 January 2021.
14. Akça, "Neo-Ottomanism."
15. The Turkish government shared with Western governments secret tapes recorded at the Saudi Consulate. Ezgi Erkoyun, "Turkey Gave Khashoggi Tapes to European Nations, Erdoğan Says," Reuters, 10 November 2018.

16. "Erdoğan Slams US 'Silence' over Khashoggi, Demands Saudi Answers," *Al Jazeera*, 4 February 2019.
17. Abas Al Awati and Çağan Koç, "Saudis Let Wallets Do the Talking to Punish Turkey for Khashoggi," Bloomberg, 22 November 2018; Amberin Zaman, "Turkey Groans under Economic Pressure from Saudis," *Al Monitor*, May 2019.
18. Andrew Wilks, "Turkey, Saudi Arabia Eye Improved Ties after Gulf Crisis Ends," *Al Jazeera*, 25 January 2021.
19. "Turkey-UAE: Erdoğan and MBZ Discuss Bilateral Ties During Phone Call," *Middle East Eye*, 30 August 2021.
20. Jonathan Schanzer, "How Iran Benefits from an Illicit Gold Trade with Turkey," *The Atlantic*, 17 May 2013.
21. Dorian Jones, "Erdoğan Defies Trump over Iran Sanctions," *VOA*, 27 September 2019.
22. Galip Dalay, "Turkish–Iranian Relations Are Set to Become More Turbulent," German Marshall Fund, 9 February 2021.
23. The Baku–Tbilisi–Kars railway was originally agreed in 2005 by the presidents of Turkey, Azerbaijan and Georgia. It became a reality, after multiple delays, in October 2017.
24. Dalay, "Turkish–Iranian Relations"; see also Çağaptay, *Erdoğan's Empire*, ch. 9: "Competing Persians," pp. 155–69.
25. For an overview of the disputes, see Nikos Tsafos, "Getting East Med Energy Right," Commentary, Center for Strategic and International Studies, Washington, DC, 26 October 2020.
26. Cyprus has signed EEZ delimitation agreements with Egypt (2003) and Lebanon (2007).
27. Meliha Benli Altunışık, "Turkey's Eastern Mediterranean Quagmire," Middle East Institute, 18 February 2020.
28. Ece Toksabay and Michele Kambas, "Turkey Won't Allow Greek Interference in East Med Activities – Minister," Reuters, 24 October 2018.
29. Bülent Usta, "Turkey Conducts Largest Naval Exercise," Reuters, 28 February 2019.
30. The EU response to Turkish moves in the Eastern Mediterranean is discussed further in Chapter 10.
31. David Brunnstrom and Renee Maltezou, "US Warns Turkey over Offshore Drilling Near Cyprus," Reuters, 5 October 2019.
32. "Macron Criticises Turkey's Imperial Inclinations as Row Between Countries Escalates," *Guardian*, 1 November 2020.
33. Nektaria Stamouli, "Ship's Return Home Raises Hopes of Greece–Turkey Tensions Cooling," *Politico.eu*, 15 September 2020.
34. On *Mavi Vatan*, see Ryan Gingeras, "Blue Homeland: The Heated Politics behind Turkey's New Maritime Strategy," *War on the Rocks*, 2 June 2020.
35. TCG *Anadolu*, an amphibious assault ship/light aircraft carrier equipped with a landing helicopter dock, is in the works too. H.I. Sutton, "Turkey's New Assault Carrier Will Transform Navy," *Forbes*, 13 May 2020.
36. On 28 November 2019, the Turkish government signed two MoUs with the GNA: one foreseeing direct deployment of Turkish troops and one on maritime matters. A legal agreement delimiting EEZs followed on 1 December.
37. The EastMed gas pipeline's estimated cost is €6–7 billion and is planned to take seven years to complete. Its annual capacity is 10 billion cubic meters (bcm).
38. Amberin Zaman, "Eastern Mediterranean Crisis Balloons as Turkish Drill Ships Multiply," *Al Monitor,* July 2019.
39. On Turkey's competition with the UAE, see Aslı Aydıntaşbaş and Cinzia Bianco, *Useful Enemies: How Turkey–UAE Rivalry Is Remaking the Middle East*, Policy Brief, European Council on Foreign Relations, 15 March 2021.
40. At the time of writing, Turkey and Greece are talking to each other yet again, with the two foreign ministers exchanging visits in April–May 2021.
41. Menelaos Hadjicostis, "A 'Homecoming' to a Ghost Town Sparks Greek Anguish", Associated Press, 10 September 2010.

42. Çağaptay, *Erdoğan's Empire*.
43. Omar Ashour, *Between ISIS and a Failed State: The Saga of Libyan Islamists*, Working Paper, Project on US Relations with the Islamic World, Brookings Institution, August 2015.
44. Giovana De Maio, "The Palermo Conference on Libya: A Diplomatic Test for Italy's New Government," Order from Chaos Blog, Brookings Institution, 19 November 2018, https://www.brookings.edu/blog/order-from-chaos/2018/11/19/the-palermo-conference-on-libya-a-diplomatic-test-for-italys-new-government/.
45. "Libya: Haftar Bans Flights, Boats from Turkey," *Al Jazeera*, 29 June 2019.
46. The SNA was formed in December 2017 in the Turkish-run enclave in the northern Aleppo province. It incorporated factions of the Free Syrian Army.
47. Bethan McKernan and Hussein Akoush, "Exclusive: 200 Syrian Troops Deployed to Libya to Support Government," *Guardian*, 15 January 2020.
48. Dicle Eşiyok, "Turkish Military Contractor SADAT Has Always Been in Libya," *Ahval*, 4 January 2020.
49. Vasilis Nedos, "Turkish Frigates Sailing between Crete and Libya," *Kathimerini*, 30 May 2020.
50. "Turkey Sends Secret Arms Shipments to Libya," *BBC News*, 26 March 2020.
51. Murat Sofuoğlu, "How Turkish Drones Are Changing the Course of the Libyan Civil War," *TRT World*, 22 May 2020.
52. Ben Fishman and Conor Hiney, "What Turned the Battle for Tripoli," Brief Analysis, Policy Watch 3314, Washington Institute, 6 May 2020.
53. Jalel Harchaoui, "The Pendulum: How Russia Sways Its Way in Libya," *War on the Rocks*, 7 January 2021. Still, in a gesture to Russia, Turkish armed forces allowed Wagner mercenaries to withdraw from the Tripoli area.
54. "Turkey Says Lasting Ceasefire Discussed with Libyan PM," *TRT World*, 17 June 2020.
55. Orhan Coşkun and Tuvan Gümrükçü, "Turkey Eyes Libya Bases for Lasting Military Foothold: Source," Reuters, 15 June 2020.
56. Tarek Megerisi, "It's Turkey's Libya Now," European Council on Foreign Relations, 20 May 2020.
57. Discussions with Libyan expert, February 2021. Enes Canlı and Mucahit Aydemir, "Libya to Keep 'Distinguished Ties' with Turkey: Interim Premier," Anadolu Agency, 25 February 2021.
58. See Chapter 8.
59. The Russian military rejected a Turkish request to open Syrian airspace for helicopters to evacuate the wounded to medical facilities across the border, literally minutes away by air. Transport overland increased the number of casualties. Conversation with an international expert with sources within the Turkish military, February 2021.
60. Ali Bakeer, "The Fight for Syria's Skies: Turkey Challenges Russia with New Drone Doctrine," Middle East Institute, 26 March 2020.
61. "Putin Hails Compromises with Erdoğan at Sochi Talks," RFE/RL, 29 September 2021.
62. Ragıp Soylu, "Turkish F-16s Kept in Azerbaijan 'as Deterrent against Armenian Attacks'," *Middle East Eye*, 8 October 2020; Ed Butler, "Syrian Mercenaries Used as Cannon Fodder in Nagorno-Karabakh," *BBC News*, 10 December 2020
63. Another example in that respect is the thriving links between Turkey and Ukraine, which also focus on defense cooperation. See International Crisis Group, *Russia and Turkey in the Black Sea*. In October 2020, presidents Zelensky and Erdoğan signed a cooperation agreement covering the defense industrial sector. "Erdoğan Hails Deepening Cooperation with Ukraine," *TRT World*, 16 October 2020.
64. The Grand National Assembly authorized the deployment on 17 November 2020.
65. Nagorno-Karabakh falls in the purview of the so-called Minsk Group within the Organization for Security and Co-operation in Europe chaired by Russia, France and the United States.
66. Turkey's actions are reportedly more effective than the cross-border operations in the 1990s and 2000s, thanks to the technological advances the armed forces have made. They have the potential to disrupt the PKK's infrastructure in the area, including tunnels and cave

hideouts. Can Kasapoğlu, "Maximum Pressure: Turkey's Anti-PKK Counter-terrorism Campaigns in Northern Iraq," *Terrorism Monitor* 19(9), 7 May 2021.
67. Oxford Analytica, "Iraq's Disputed Sinjar Will Be a Long-term Flashpoint," 12 March 2021.

10. EUROPE: FROM PARTNERSHIP TO RIVALRY

1. "Cumhurbaşkanı Erdoğan: 'Ey Avrupa Birliği kendinize gelin'," *Haberler.com*, 10 October 2019.
2. Zia Weise and Jacopo Barigazi, "EU Countries Agree to Suspend Arms Exports to Turkey," *Politico.eu*, 14 October 2019.
3. "Turkey's Erdoğan and French President Macron Butt Heads – Again," *Al Jazeera*, 26 October 2020.
4. President Erdoğan's Message on Europe Day, Presidency of the Republic of Turkey, 9 May 2020. Available at: www.tccb.gov.tr/en
5. Email exchange with the author, February 2021.
6. Interviews in Ankara, March 2011.
7. Dizdaroğlu, Aydın and Açıkmeşe, *Turkish Foreign Policy*.
8. Remark at a Roundtable on "Turkey, Russia and the West in the Middle East," hosted by Stiftung Wissenschaft und Politik, Berlin, 23 June 2020.
9. Mehul Srivastava and Alex Barker, "Davutoğlu's Future Hangs on Success of EU–Turkey Visa Deal," *Financial Times*, 2 May 2016.
10. Concluded through a common statement by the European Council (the 28 heads of state and government of the EU) and Turkey. Full text available at: www.consilium.europa.eu/en/press/press-releases/2016/03/18/eu-turkey-statement/
11. "The Aegean Tragedy – Key Facts and Key Steps," ESI, 24 January 2020, www.esiweb.org/publications/aegean-tragedy-key-facts-and-key-stepsm
12. Asylum applications were to be assessed in Turkey prior to resettlement in member states. The total number of refugees to be taken was capped at 54,000.
13. "Aegean Plan 2.0 – Preventing a Disaster in the Times of Corona," *ESI Newsletter*, 3/2020, 20 March 2020.
14. "EU–Turkey Statement 2.0," ESI, 16 March 2021,www.esiweb.org/proposals/eu-turkey-statement-20
15. Pazarkule lies in a Turkish enclave the right bank of the Evros/Meriç, unlike the bulk of the Greek–Turkish border in Thrace which follows the river. That is why the Pazarkule/Karaağaç area, adjacent to the city of Edirne, has been a preferred route for illegal border crossings.
16. "İnsanlığın sınırı: Polis eskortlu mülteci otobüsleri, Yunanistan otoritelerince darp edildikten sonra geri itilen insanlar," Amnesty International Turkey, 10 March 2019. Exchange with former European Commission official, February 2021.
17. See Chapter 9.
18. "EU Chief Says Greece Is Europe's Shield in Migrant Crisis," *BBC News*, 3 March 2020.
19. Interview with former high-ranking European Commission official, February 2021.
20. Ayla Jean Yackley, "Turkey Will Not Act as Europe's 'Warehouse' for Afghan Regufees, Says Erdoğan." *Financial Times,* 26 August 2021.
21. Philip Oltermann, "Erdoğan Accuses Germany of 'Nazi Practices' over Blocked Political Rallies," *Guardian*, 5 March 2017.
22. "Dutch Riot Police Break Up Pro-Erdoğan Demonstration in Rotterdam," Reuters, 12 March 2017.
23. "Turkey President Recep Tayyip Erdoğan Plans Election Rally in Europe," *Deutsche Welle*, 24 April 2018.
24. In 2017, the Bundestag intelligence committee demanded probes into spying following publications in *Die Welt*. Ian Johnson, "Report: Turkey's MIT Agency Menacing 'German Turks'," *Deutsche Welle*, 21 August 2016; "Report: German Politicians under Surveillance by Turkish Intelligence," *Deutsche Welle*, 28 June 2017.

25. "Austria to Shut Down Mosques, Expel Foreign-funded Imams," Reuters, 8 June 2018.
26. France sent a frigate and Rafale fighters to the island of Crete in a show of solidarity with Greece. "Amid Tensions with Turkey, Greece in Joint Manoeuvres with France," Reuters, 13 August 2020.
27. Salim Kahraman, "French Naval Presence in Eastern Mediterranean Not Just About Energy," *Ahval*, 17 July 2019.
28. "EU Sanctions Top Turkish Petroleum Executives for East Mediterranean Drilling," *Duvar*, 28 February 2021.
29. Sarantis Michalopoulos, "Merkel and Borissov Blocked EU Sanctions against Turkey at Summit: Sources," *Euractiv*, 11 December 2020.
30. Yet, since 2017, Turkey has lost about a third of its funding. The EU transferred €3.5 billion in 2014–20 (on top of the €6 billion allocated for the Syrian refugees). That is €1.8 billion less than was originally budgeted. Answer given by Vice-President Mogherini on behalf of the European Commission. Question reference: E-002279/2019 (Marco Zanni), European Parliament, 24 September 2019.
31. When MEPs voted 307 in favor, 109 against and 143 abstentions in March 2019, Ömer Çelik, AKP spokesman, characterized the act as "worthless, invalid, and disreputable." Gilbert Reilhac, "EU Parliament Calls for Freeze on Turkey's Membership Talks," Reuters, 13 March 2019.
32. "Greece, Italy Sign Deal Delimiting Maritime Zones," *Al Jazeera*, 9 June 2020.
33. "Egypt and Greece Sign Agreement on Exclusive Economic Zone," Reuters, 6 August 2020.
34. "7 Countries to Join Turkish Naval Exercise in East Mediterranean," *Daily Sabah*, 27 April 2020.
35. A visit tainted by the so-called "sofa incident," when von der Leyen was not offered a seat next to Erdoğan unlike her male colleague, Charles Michel.
36. European Council Conclusions, 25 June 2021, www.consilium.europa.eu/en/press-releases/2021/06/25/european-council-conclusions-on-external-relations-24-june-2021/
37. "Balkan Leaders Flock to Erdoğan Inauguration," *Balkan Insight*, 9 July 2018.
38. "Erdoğan Bosna Hersek'te: Avrupa'nın Bize Karşı Tavrının Sebebi Oradaki Türklerin Dağınıklığıdır," *BBC Turkish*, 20 May 2018.
39. For an informed and insightful discussion of Turkish outreach to the region, drawing on a wealth of interviews with local Turks and Muslim elites, see Öztürk, *Religion, Identity and Power*.
40. Fatos Bytyci, "Kosovo Investigates Seizure of Turkish Nationals," Reuters, 31 March 2018.
41. "Bulgaria Expels Turkish Diplomat for Conducting Islamist Activity," *Euractiv*, 22 February 2016.
42. Darko Janjević, "Erdoğan Wants Balkans as 'Leverage' on Europe: Expert," *Deutsche Welle*, 18 March 2017.
43. Öztürk, *Religion, Identity and Power*, p. 50.
44. "Maarif Foundation: Turkey's International Education Juggernaut," *Daily Sabah*, 16 June 2020. However, as Erdi Öztürk observes, the *cemaat* has roots in the region and the AKP's dominance is not complete. "Power balances can change in an incomprehensible manner at unexpected times." Öztürk, *Religion, Identity and Power*, p. 218.
45. Data from the Turkish Statistical Institute, www. turkstat.gov.tr. Dimitar Bechev, "Turkey's Policy in the Balkans – Continuity and Change in the Erdoğan Era," *Südosteuropa Mitteilungen* 59(5–6), 2019, pp. 34–45.
46. See Chapter 5.
47. Bechev, "Turkey's Policy in the Balkans."
48. In addition to Russia, Turkey is driving a hard bargain vis-à-vis Azerbaijan (6.6 bcm contract expiring in April 2021) and Nigeria (LNG deal ending in December). A three-year contract with Qatar (LNG) will be up for renewal at the end of the year, but the diplomatic and security alliance between Ankara and Doha will likely help smooth talks.
49. In 2019, Turkey imported goods worth €70 billion from the EU, while exports stood at €68 billion. Data from TurkStat.

50. Kemal Kirişci, "The Transformation of Turkish Foreign Policy: The Rise of the Trading State," *New Perspectives on Turkey* 40, Spring 2009, pp. 29–56.
51. Sinan Ülgen and Yiannis Zahariadis, "The Future of Turkish–EU Trade Relations: Deepening vs Widening," *Turkish Policy Quarterly* 3(4), 2004, pp. 17–59.
52. Gabriel Felbermayr, Rahel Aichele and Erdal Yalçın, "EU–Turkish Customs Union: How to Proceed," *VOX*, 23 July 2016, https://voxeu.org/article/eu-turkish-customs-union-how-proceed
53. The only case where Turkey has an agreement in place, but not the EU, is Malaysia. In this case, Turkey also entered into free trade negotiations after the EU, but Turkey's negotiations proceeded faster than the EU's. As a result, by implementing its free trade agreement with Malaysia on 1 August 2015, Turkey is violating key provisions of the Customs Union, in particular the principle of alignment to the EU customs tariff.
54. The international trade in services (both import and exports) corresponded to 8 per cent of Turkey's GDP in 2005 to 12.2 per cent in 2019. Meanwhile, the same ratio for the global economy as a whole grew from 11 per cent to 13.5 per cent over the same period of time. Ahmet Adnan Aken and Didem Yazıcı, "Structure of Turkey's Export of Services," Turkish Central Bank Blog, 19 April 2021, https://tcmbblog.org/wps/wcm/connect/blog/en/main+menu/analyses/structure+of+turkeys+exports+of+services
55. Gökhan Ergöcun, "Turkey: Services Exports Hit Historic High in 2019," Anadolu Agency, 14 February 2020.
56. "Turkish Trade Deficit Narrows to $31.13 bln in 2019 – Trade Ministry," Reuters, 3 January 2020.
57. Felbermayr, Aichele and Yalçın, "EU–Turkish Customs Union: How to Proceed."
58. Kemal Kirişci and Onur Bülbül, "The EU and Turkey Need Each Other. Could Upgrading the Customs Union Be the Key?" Order from Chaos Blog, Brookings Institution, 29 August 2017, https://www.brookings.edu/blog/order-from-chaos/2017/08/29/the-eu-and-turkey-need-each-other-could-upgrading-the-customs-union-be-the-key/
59. "EU, Turkey Announce Modernization of Custom Union," *Hürriyet Daily News*, 12 May 2015.
60. European Commission, Directorate-General for Trade, *Study of the EU–Turkey Bilateral Preferential Trade Framework, Including the Customs Union, and an Assessment of Its Possible Enhancement*, Final Report, 26 October 2016, https://trade.ec.europa.eu/doclib/docs/2017/january/tradoc_155240.pdf
61. Celal Özcan, "Merkel Conveys Germany's Veto on Customs Union Update with Turkey to Juncker," *Hürriyet Daily News*, 31 August 2017.
62. General Affairs Council, Council Conclusions on Enlargement and the Stabilization and Association Process, 26 June 2018, Point 35, www.consilium.europa.eu/media/35863/st10555-en18.pdf
63. Statement of the Members of the European Council, 25 March 2021, Point 11, www.consilium.europa.eu/media/48976/250321-vtc-euco-statement-en.pdf
64. Marc Pierini, "Options for the EU–Turkey Relationship," Carnegie Europe, 3 May 2019.
65. Marc Jones, "Turkish Lira – Fair Value or Fair Game?" Reuters, 20 August 2020.
66. Ağbal became the third central bank governor to be sacked in two years.
67. "Turkey's Illiberal Economic Model Will Extend Further," Oxford Analytica Daily Brief, 3 August 2020.
68. "Unanchored in Ankara," *The Economist*, 25 March 2021.

EPILOGUE

1. "MetroPoLL anketi yayımlandı: Yavaş ve İmamoğlu Erdoğan'ı geride bıraktı", *Cumhuriyet*, 18 September 2021.
2. It is notable that the AKP and the MHP have recently agreed to lower the 10 per cent electoral threshold to 7 per cent. The goal is to make sure that the ultranationalists make it into the next Grand National Assembly. See Nergis Demirkaya, "With Lower Election Threshold, AKP and MHP May Enter Separately," *Duvar English*, 10 September 2021.

3. Similarly, Soner Çağaptay contends Erdoğan will cling to power till the biiter end. See *A Sultan in Autumn: Erdoğan Faces Turkey's Uncontrolable Force*s (London: Bloomsbury, 2021).

4. Prominent examples of such divisive tactics aim at polarizing society and boosting the AKP include the bid to ban HDP, the change of status of Hagia Sophia, originally a Byzantine cathedral built by Emperor Justinian, from a museum to a mosque (July 2020) and the renunciation of the so-called Istanbul Convention, a legal treaty on combating violence against women Turkey signed up to as part of the Council of Europe.

5. "10 Yılda Ne Değişti?" KONDA Araştırma ve Danışmanlık, survey based on fieldwork in March–April 2018, https://interaktif.konda.com.tr/en/HayatTarzlari2018/#firstPage

6. In recent years, the AKP has been consistently losing support. Erdoğan is, on the whole, more popular than the party, and many vote for the AKP "for the *reis*" despite the party itself, while others are defecting to splinter groups such as Gelecek and Deva. I am thankful to Karabekir Akkoyunlu for bringing up this point.

7. On 6 October 2021, Turkey ratified the Paris climate agreement, the last G20 member to do so.

8. Mustafa Aydın et al., *Public Perceptions on Turkish Foreign Policy*, Survey, Kadir Has University, 15 June 2021, https://khas.edu.tr/en/arastirma/khasta-arastirma/khas-arastirma-lari/turk-dis-politikasi-kamuoyu-algilari-arastirmasi-2021

CONTEMPORARY TURKEY: A SELECT BIBLIOGRAPHY

General surveys

Kerslake, Celia, Kerem Öktem and Philip Robins (eds.) *Turkey's Engagement with Modernity: Conflict and Change in the Twentieth Century* (Palgrave, 2010).

Özerdem, Alparslan and Matthew Whitting (eds.) *The Routledge Handbook of Turkish Politics* (Routledge, 2019).

Tezcür, Güneş Murat (ed.) *The Oxford Handbook of Turkish Politics* (Oxford University Press, 2021).

Zürcher, Erik-Jan, *Turkey: A Modern History* (4th revised edn, I.B. Tauris, 2017).

Domestic politics under AKP

Arat, Yeşim and Şevket Pamuk, *Turkey Between Democracy and Authoritarianism* (Cambridge University Press, 2019).

Başer, Bahar and Ahmet Erdi Öztürk (eds.) *Authoritarian Politics in Turkey: Elections, Resistance and the AKP* (I.B. Tauris, 2017).

Baykan, Toygar Sinan, *The Justice and Development Party in Turkey: Populism, Personalism, Organization* (Cambridge University Press, 2020).

Bosco, Anna, Senem Aydın-Düzgit and Susannah Verney (eds.) *The AKP Since Gezi Park: Moving to Regime Change in Turkey* (Routledge, 2020).

Çağaptay, Soner, *The New Sultan: Erdoğan and the Crisis of Modern Turkey* (I.B. Tauris, 2014).

Çarkoğlu, Ali and Barnet Rubin (eds.) *Religion and Politics in Turkey* (Routledge, 2013).

Cook, Stephen, *False Dawn: Protest, Democracy, and Violence in the New Middle East* (Oxford University Press, 2017).

Esen, Berk and Şebnem Gümüşçu, "Rising Competitive Authoritarianism in Turkey," *Third World Quarterly* 37(9), 2016, pp. 1581–606.

Gençkaya, Ömer Faruk and Ergun Özbudun, *Democratization and the Politics of Constitution-making in Turkey* (Central European University Press, 2009).

Grigoriadis, Ioannis, *Trials of Europeanization: Turkish Political Culture and the European Union* (Palgrave, 2009).

Karaveli, Halil, *Why Turkey Is Authoritarian: From Atatürk to Erdoğan* (Pluto Press, 2018).

Kuru, Ahmet and Alfred Stepan (eds.) *Democracy, Islam and Secularism in Turkey* (Columbia University Press, 2012).

Lord, Ceren, *Religious Politics in Turkey: From the Birth of the Republic to the AKP* (Cambridge University Press, 2018).

Öktem, Kerem, *Angry Nation: Turkey Since 1989* (Zed Books, 2009).

Öktem, Kerem and Karabekir Akkoyunlu (eds.) *Exit from Democracy: Illiberal Governance in Turkey and Beyond* (Routledge, 2019).

Özkırımlı, Umut (ed.) *The Making of a Protest Movement in Turkey: #occupygezi* (Palgrave, 2014).

Saka, Erkan, *Social Media in Turkey: A Journey through Citizen Journalism, Political Trolling and Fake News* (Lexington Books, 2020).

Smith, Hannah Lucinda, *Erdoğan Rising* (William Collins, 2020).

Waldman, Simon and Emre Çalışkan, *The New Turkey and Its Discontents* (Oxford University Press, 2017).

Yavuz, M. Hakan and Bayram Balcı, *Turkey's July 15th Coup: What Happened and Why.* (University of Utah Press, 2018).

Nationalism, identity and the Kurdish issue

Başaran, Ezgi, *Frontline Turkey: The Conflict at the Heart of the Middle East* (I.B. Tauris, 2017).

Çandar, Cengiz, *Turkey's Mission Impossible: War and Peace with the Kurds* (Lexington Books, 2020).

Çifçi, Deniz, *The Kurds and the Politics of Turkey: Agency, Territory and Religion* (I.B. Tauris, 2021).

Kadıoğlu, Ayşe and Fuat Keyman, *Symbiotic Antagonisms: Competing Nationalisms in Turkey* (University of Utah Press, 2011).

Taşpınar, Ömer, *Kurdish Nationalism and Political Islam in Turkey: Kemalist Identity in Transition* (Routledge, 2005).

Türkmen, Gülay, *Under the Banner of Islam: Turks, Kurds, and the Limits of Religious Unity* (Oxford University Press, 2021).

White, Jenny, *Muslim Nationalism and the New Turks* (Princeton University Press, 2014).

Political economy

Buğra, Ayşe and Osman Savaşkan, *New Capitalism in Turkey: The Relationship between Politics, Religion and Business* (Edward Elgar, 2014).

Öniş, Ziya and Fikret Şenses (eds.) *Turkey and the Global Economy: Neo-liberal Restructuring and Integration in the Post-crisis Era* (Routledge, 2010).

Pamuk, Şevket, *Uneven Centuries: Economic Development of Turkey since 1820* (Princeton University Press, 2018).

Society and culture

Göle, Nilüfer, *The Forbidden Modern: Civilization and Veiling* (University of Michigan Press, 1997).

Muedini, Fait, *LGBTI Rights in Turkey: Sexuality and the State in the Middle East* (Cambridge University Press, 2018).

Saktanber, Ayşe and Deniz Kandiyoti, *Fragments of Culture: The Everyday of Modern Turkey* (Bloomsbury, 2001).

Stokes, Martin, *Republic of Love: Cultural Intimacy in Turkish Popular Music* (University of Chicago Press, 2010).

Temelkuran, Ece, *Turkey: The Insane and the Melancholy* (Zed Books, 2016).

Özyürek, Esra, *Nostalgia for the Modern: State Secularism and Everyday Politics in Turkey* (Duke University Press, 2006).

White, Jenny, *Turkish Kaleidoscope: Fractured Lives in a Time of Violence* (Princeton University Press, 2021).

Foreign policy

Başkan, Birol and Ömer Taşpınar, *The Nation of the Ummah: Islamism and Turkish Foreign Policy* (SUNY Press, 2021).

Çağaptay, Soner, *Erdoğan's Empire: Turkey and the Politics of the Middle East* (I.B. Tauris, 2019)

Hale, William, *Turkish Foreign Policy since 1774* (3rd edn, Routledge, 2013).

Hintz, Lisel, *Identity Politics Inside Out: National Identity Contestation and Foreign Policy in Turkey* (Oxford University Press, 2018).

Keyman, Fuat and Şebnem Gümüşçu, *Democracy, Identity and Foreign Policy in Turkey* (Palgrave, 2014).

Kirişçi, Kemal, *Turkey and the West: Fault Lines in a Troubled Alliance* (Brookings Institution, 2017).

Mufti, Malik, *Daring and Caution in Turkish Foreign Policy* (Palgrave, 2009).

Öktem, Kerem, Ayşe Kadıoğlu and Mehmet Karlı, *Another Empire? A Decade of Turkey's Foreign Policy under the Justice and Development Party* (Bilgi University Press, 2012).

Phillips, Christopher, *The Battle for Syria: International Rivalry in the New Middle East* (2nd edn, Yale University Press, 2020)

Robins, Philip, *Suits and Uniforms: Turkish Foreign Policy since the Cold War* (Hurst, 2003).

Robins, Philip, "Turkey's 'Double Gravity' Predicament: The Foreign Policy of a Newly Activist Power," *International Affairs* 89(2), March 2013, pp. 381–97.

Stein, Aaron, *Turkey's New Foreign Policy: Davutoğlu, the AKP and the Pursuit of Regional Order* (RUSI, 2014).

Tuğal, Cihan, *The Fall of the Turkish Model: How the Arab Uprisings Brought Down Islamic Liberalism* (Verso, 2016).

Yavuz, M. Hakan, *Nostalgia for the Empire: The Politics of Neo-Ottomanism* (Oxford University Press, 2020).

INDEX

INDEX

INDEX

INDEX

INDEX

INDEX